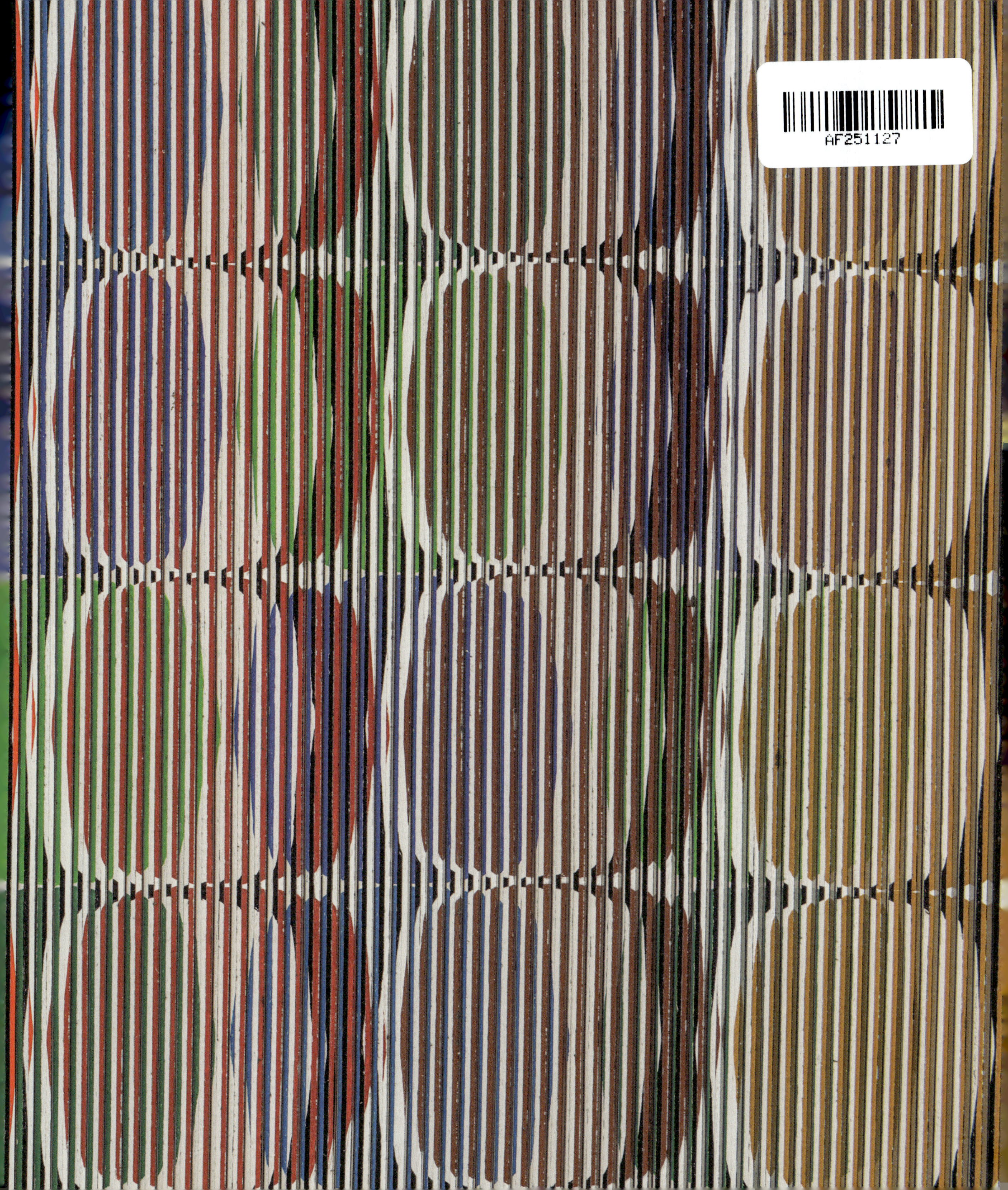
AF251127

KINESTHESIA

LATIN AMERICAN KINETIC ART

1954-1969

KINESTHESIA

LATIN AMERICAN KINETIC ART

1954-1969

Dan Cameron

with essays by
Jesús Fuenmayor
María José Herrera
Frederico Morais
Héctor Olea
Cristina Rossi
Isabel Plante

Palm Springs Art Museum

DelMonico Books•Prestel Munich, London, New York

PUBLISHED WITH THE ASSISTANCE OF THE GETTY FOUNDATION

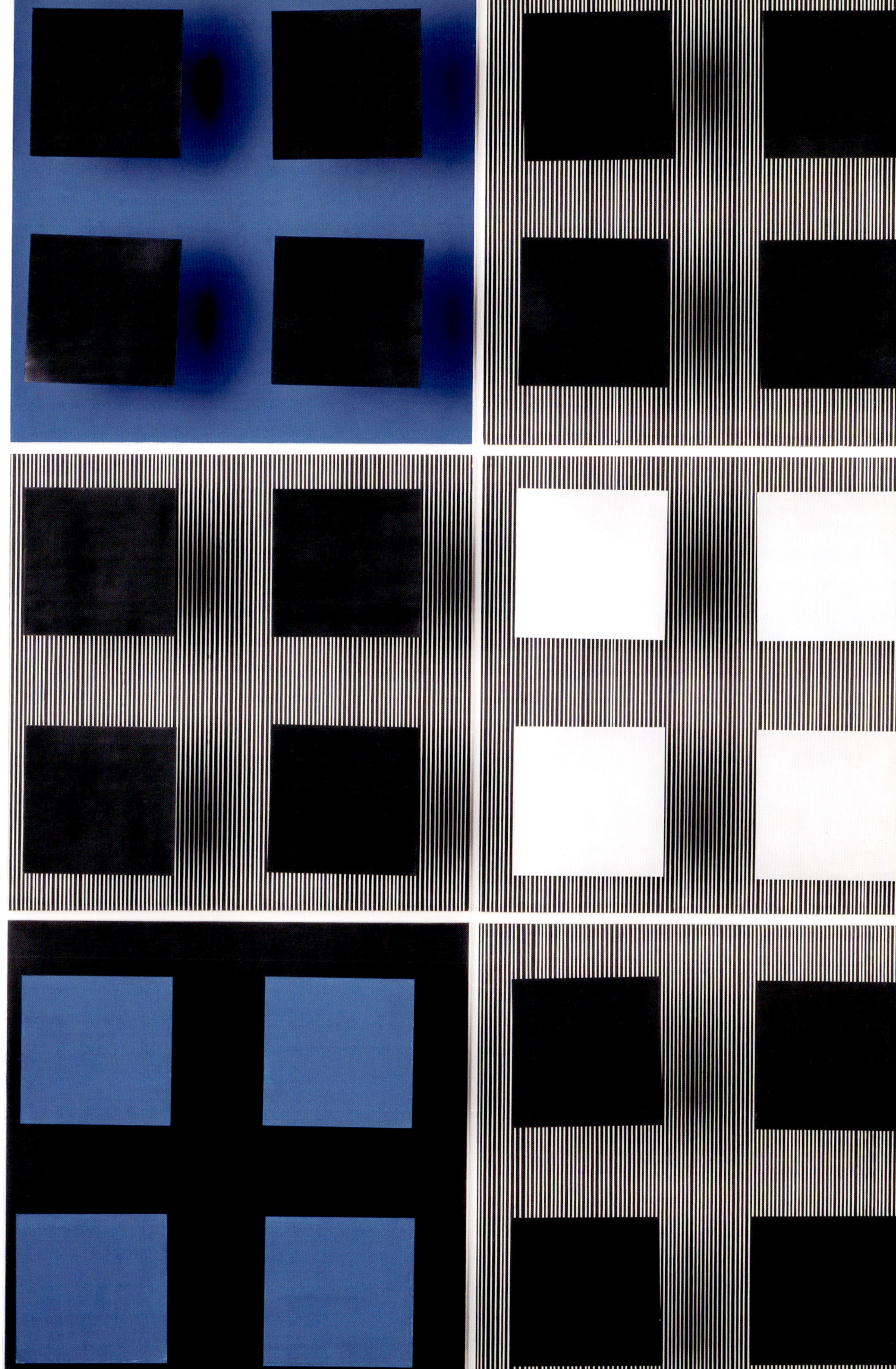

CONTENTS

FOREWORD

Elizabeth Armstrong

THIS PUBLICATION AND THE EXHIBITION it accompanies unite two overlapping subjects that are unfamiliar to most Americans: South American abstract art of the mid-twentieth century and the movement known as Kinetic Art. By exploring the position of Latin American artists at the forefront of an innovative international art movement, *Kinesthesia: Latin American Kinetic Art 1954–1969* seeks to bring new perspectives to artworks of fifty or sixty years ago, demonstrating that they communicate today with an intensity that makes them seem as if they were created just now.

In the late 1950s through the 1960s, Paris was the epicenter of Kinetic Art, a dynamic movement that seemed to herald an era of potential intersection between art and technology. Attracting artists from disparate corners of Europe, South America, and the Middle East, Kinetic Art seemed at first to follow from movements such as Surrealism, which rapidly evolved from its scandalous pre-war origins in Parisian salons and studios and dramatically changed ideas about art across the globe. Kinetic Art's eventual impact, in the U.S. in particular, was more muted, so much so that, until recently, its major innovators remained mostly unknown to the museum-going public.

When I first learned of the prospect of this exhibition from the Getty Foundation, one of the many reasons I was intrigued was that much of the architectural and artistic legacy of Palm Springs belongs to the same midcentury period as the works included in this project. Another reason was that the Light and Space movement, which originated in Southern California, shares with Kinetic Art an interest in the perception of light and color beyond the limits of the object. The partnership between Palm Springs Art Museum and the Getty Foundation would both break important new ground in the understanding of Latin American art and provide a dynamic, relevant, and participatory experience for our visitors. Knowing that independent curator Dan Cameron has

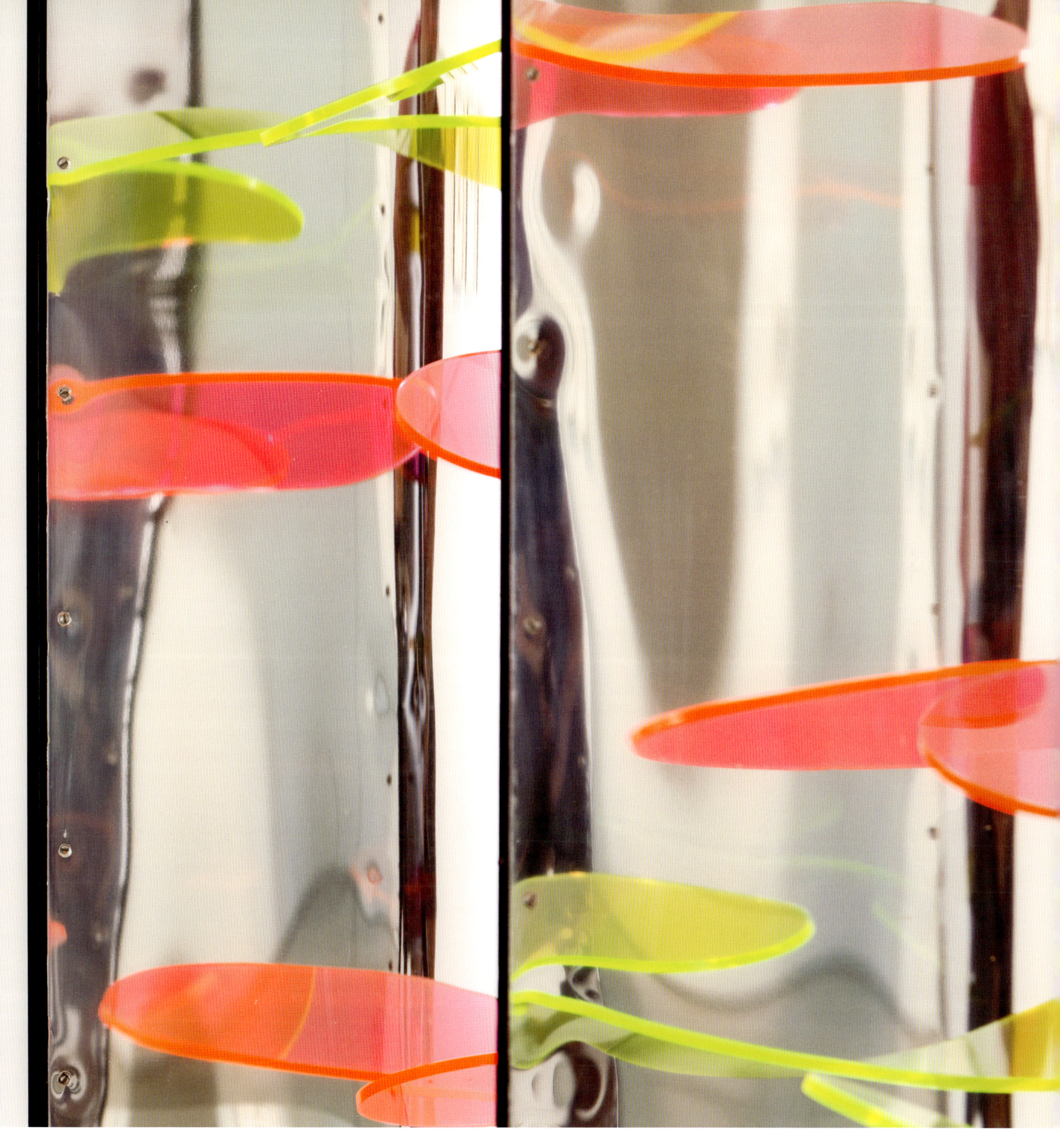

Martha Boto, *Déplacements optico-hydrauliques*, 1970 (detail)

extensive knowledge of Latin American art was yet another compelling reason. Dan had begun this project when he was at Orange County Museum of Art, and we thank them for the gestation of this project. Having worked with Dan in the past, I also knew that he is an adventurous curator, and that Latin American art has been of particular interest to him for more than twenty-five years. After seeing examples of the remarkable works Dan uncovered during the two-year research phase of the exhibition, we decided that it was perfect for Palm Springs Art Museum, and we were glad that Dan agreed.

This exhibition and the accompanying publication would have been impossible without the generosity and foresight of the Getty Foundation. In developing the parameters for Pacific Standard Time: LA/LA, and for funding both the research and implementation phases of this ambitious exhibition, they have made a tremendous gift to the people of Southern California. A substantial grant from the Warhol Foundation for the Visual Arts supplemented this crucial support, and made the project fully achievable.

Dan's efforts in coordinating the contributions by the many scholarly collaborators in this project were ably assisted by the members of the Palm Springs Art Museum staff, in particular Chief Curator Katherine Hough and our Director of Collections and Exhibitions Management, Alicia Thomas, who brought together and organized the myriad requirements of a project of this scope. The Palm Springs Art Museum Board of Trustees, faced with the challenges of exhibiting analog media from a half-century ago, have given their full support for *Kinesthesia*, and for this they have my deep gratitude. Each of the catalogue's authors has produced an insightful essay about the artists and their works, and two authors who were also members of the Curatorial Advisory Committee, Jesús Fuenmayor and María José Herrera, have given crucial logistical support along the way.

I am especially appreciative of the institutions, galleries, and individuals who have lent their support by entrusting to us their valuable and fragile treasures for the period of this exhibition. The families of the nine artists represented in this exhibition — three of them are alive and continue to work — have been fully supportive of this project, and my deepest thanks go to them for offering the world an artistic vision that, once experienced, is impossible to forget.

Elizabeth Armstrong
The JoAnn McGrath Executive Director
Palm Springs Art Museum

Dan Cameron

MUSEUM EXHIBITIONS ARE OF NECESSITY complex undertakings involving the coordinated efforts of dozens of skilled individuals, sometimes across geographical and cultural boundaries. When this complexity is compounded by the challenge of presenting multidisciplinary objects, often motorized, produced fifty or more years ago in cities thousands of miles away, good teamwork is required at every stage of the process.

The proposal for *Kinesthesia: Latin American Kinetic Art 1954–1969* grew out of conversations held in fall 2012 with Dennis Szakacs, then Executive Director of Orange County Museum of Art (OCMA), who decided to make it the museum's research proposal to the Getty Foundation for Pacific Standard Time: LA/LA, and its implementation came about through conversations with Liz Armstrong, Executive Director of Palm Springs Art Museum. Since Liz, Dennis, and I had collaborated together successfully in 2008 on the Peter Saul retrospective at OCMA, it seems fitting that an indirect three-way conversation among us is how this exhibition came to be.

During 2013–14 at OCMA, Albert Lopez, Fatima Manalili, and Alyssa Cordova were all instrumental in laying the groundwork for my curatorial investigations and assisting with research travel, a responsibility later taken up by Fatima Manalili and Johnny Sampson on an independent basis. In Palm Springs, the resourceful teamwork of Katherine Hough and Alicia Thomas has been key to pulling all of the moving parts together.

The Curatorial Advisory Committee for *Kinesthesia* played a crucial role in terms of understanding the technical and philosophical challenges presented by Kinetic Art in different art centers at different times, and the perspective offered by expatriate Latin American artists living in Paris during the 1950s and 1960s. Among the members of this committee, Ramon Castillo, Daniel Garza, Isabel Plante, Mari Carmen Ramírez, and Alma Ruiz provided ongoing expertise

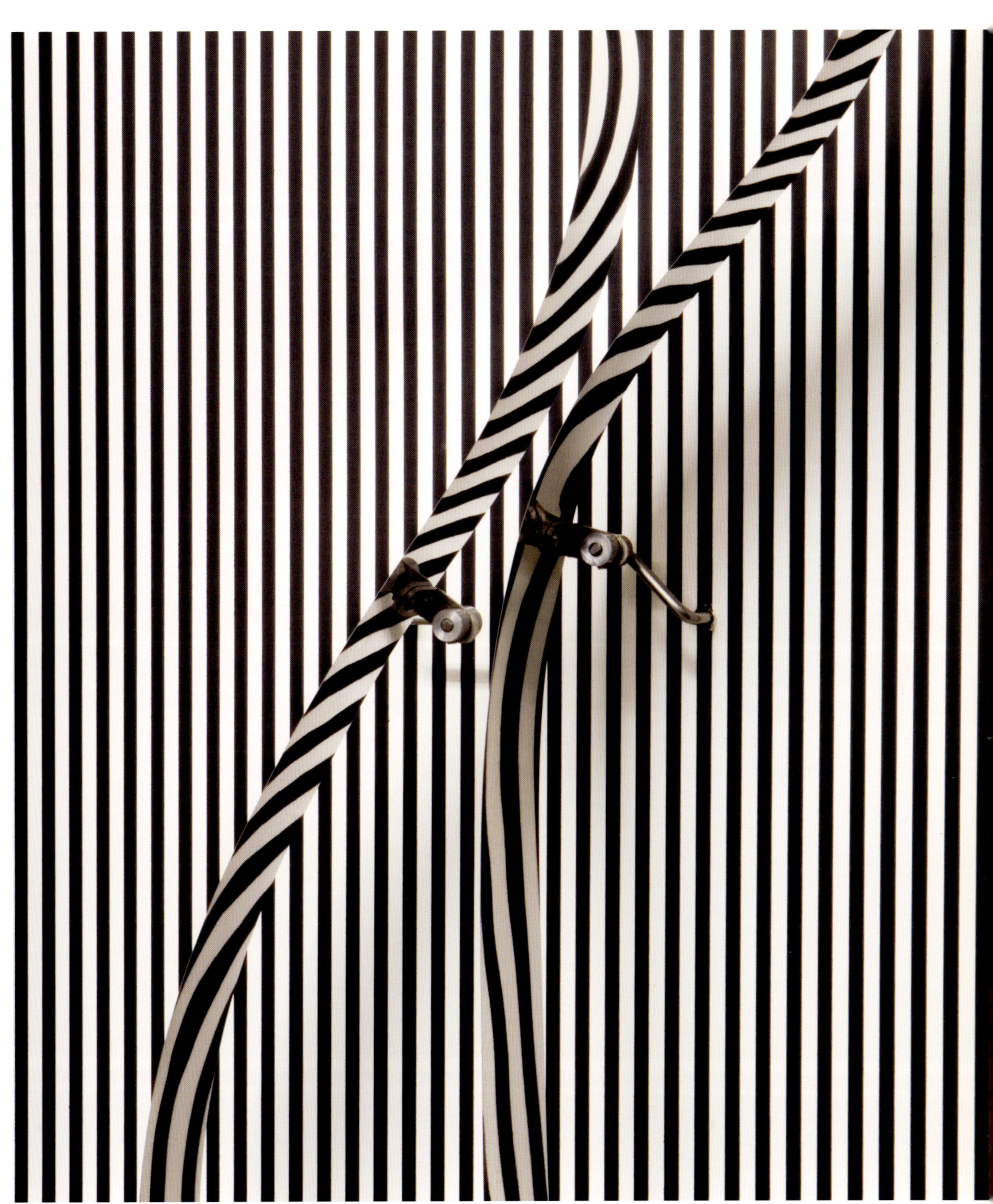

Julio Le Parc, *Formes en contorsion sur trame*, 1966 (detail)

and counsel about my impending choices, and Jesús Fuenmayor has been an insightful collaborator both on Venezuelan Kinetic Art in general and on the fabrication of architectural maquettes for Alejandro Otero's monumental kinetic sculptures.

This exhibition would have been inconceivable without the efforts of one colleague in particular, María José Herrera, who led the way with her groundbreaking 2012 Museo Nacional de Bellas Artes exhibition, *Real/Virtual: Arte cinético argentino en los años sesenta*. Maria José's openness to critical and historical discussion and generosity with her time and knowledge have been indispensable for my own work, and the graciousness of her staff at Museo de Arte Tigre was much appreciated by the attendees of the first Curatorial Advisory Committee. During the research phase in Argentina, the efforts of Paola Montenegro were much appreciated, as was the generosity of the patrons who shared their private collections with me: Julio Crivelli, Anibal Yazbeck Jozami, Guillermo Katz, Gustavo Teller, and Gabriel Vazquez. Foundation Espigas provided important historical research materials, and the respective curatorial staffs at Museo Sívori, Museo de Arte Moderno in Buenos Aires, Museo de Arte Latinoamericano in Buenos Aires, Museo de Arte Contemporáneo Latinoamericano in La Plata, and Museo Caraffa y Centro de Arte Contemporáneo in Córdoba were very generous with their time and attention in sharing the examples of Kinetic Art in those collections with me. Eduardo Rodríguez and Perla Benveniste allowed me to see their works from the Kinetic Art period; and Alejandro Vidal and Cristian Mac Entyre both patiently hosted me for a personal inspection of their late fathers' oeuvres. Finally, the late Gyula Kosice and his family were extremely gracious in welcoming me to the studio and permitting me to have an extended visit with the master.

In Venezuela, insights into Villanueva's synthesis of the arts provided by Rafael Pereira were deeply inspiring, and the Colección Mercantil provided an in-depth look at the stylistic changes in Venezuelan art from the late 1940s forward. Representatives from the Foundation Galeria de Arte Nacional provided a directory of all the modern artworks in the country's nationally consolidated collections, and several private collectors were kind enough to invite us into their homes — all coordinated by Jesús Fuenmayor, who also served as a personal chaperone in Caracas. Over the course of my visits to Rio de Janeiro, Beny Palatnik was very generous with his time and with arrangements for meeting with his father, and both Daniel Roesler and Lydia de Santis at Galeria Nara Roesler were helpful with logistics and loans.

Paris was the center of Kinetic Art, and my research there was greatly assisted by arrangements for meetings with such renowned specialists as Arnauld Pierre and Matthieu Poirier, as well as Denis Kilian of Galerie Denise René. Valerie Demarco, Yamil Le Parc, and Barbara Rossi shared details about their respective father's artistic careers, and the studios of Carlos Cruz-Diez and Julio Le Parc provided unstinting support for my investigations. I am also indebted to the collections staff of the Musée National d'Art Moderne at the Centre Pompidou, who provided important bibliographical details and made firsthand observation possible. Additional logistical support was provided by Galerie Perrotin.

Here in the U.S., numerous individuals have provided generous assistance with this exhibition and publication. Of these, special thanks go to Ella Fontanals-Cisneros at Cisneros Fontanals Art Foundation in Miami; Gabriel Pérez-Barreiro of Colección Patricia Phelps de Cisneros; and Maria Ines Sicardi and Allison Ayers of Sicardi Gallery in Houston. The lending institutions, especially the Museum of Modern Art, New York; Museum of Fine Arts, Houston; the Blanton Museum in Austin; the University of Arizona Museum of Art, Tucson; and the Organization of American States Art Museum of the Americas in Washington, D.C., have been extremely generous with their loans, as have Diane and Bruce Halle of Phoenix.

Dan Cameron
New York, 2017

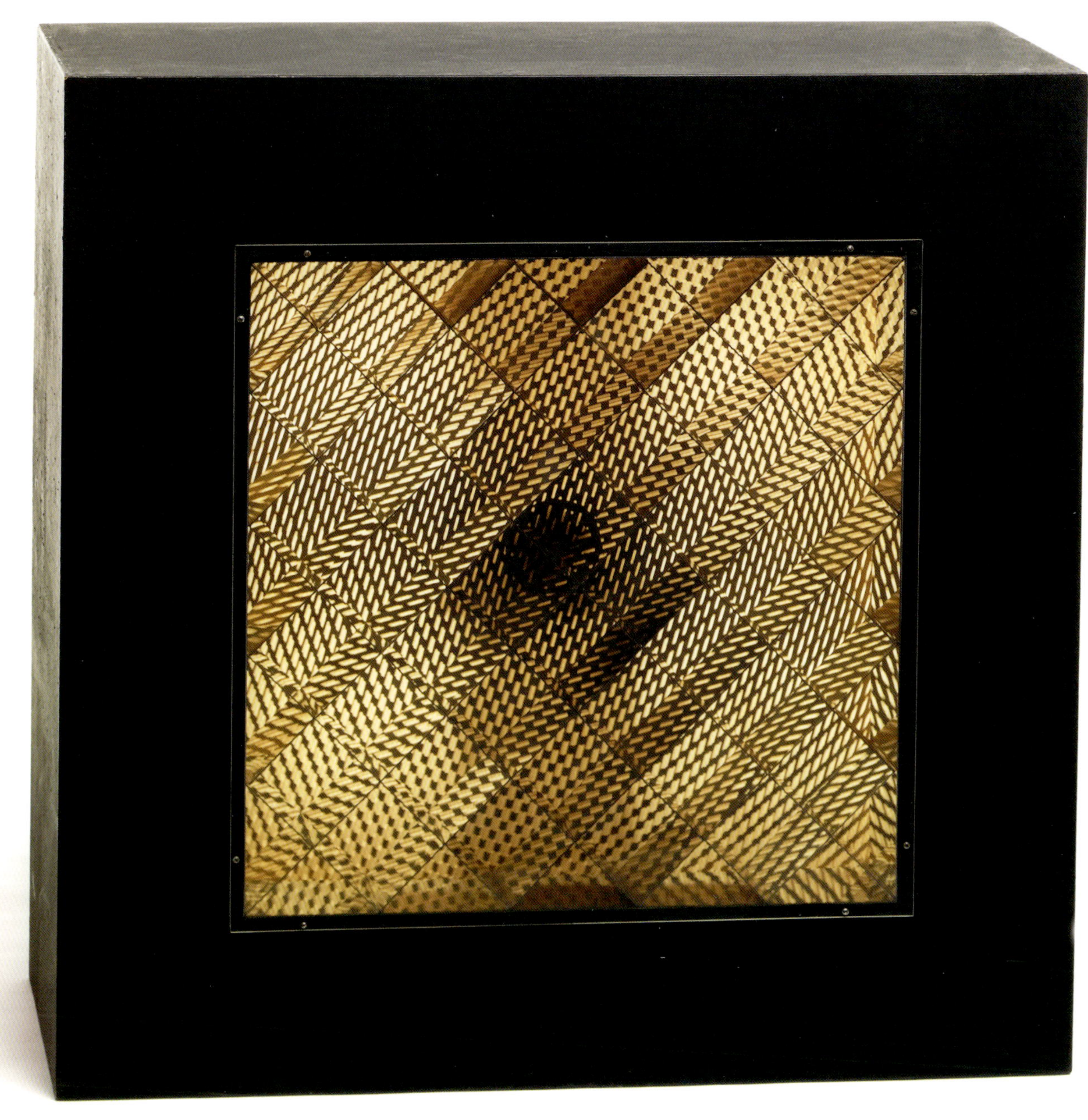

MARTHA BOTO   *Labyrinthe diagonal*, ca. 1965
Plywood, Plexiglas, light bulbs, aluminum, duralumin, and motor, 27 ½ × 27 ½ × 13 in. (69.9 × 69.9 × 33 cm)
Collection of Leslie and Brad Bucher, Houston. Courtesy of Sicardi Gallery, Houston

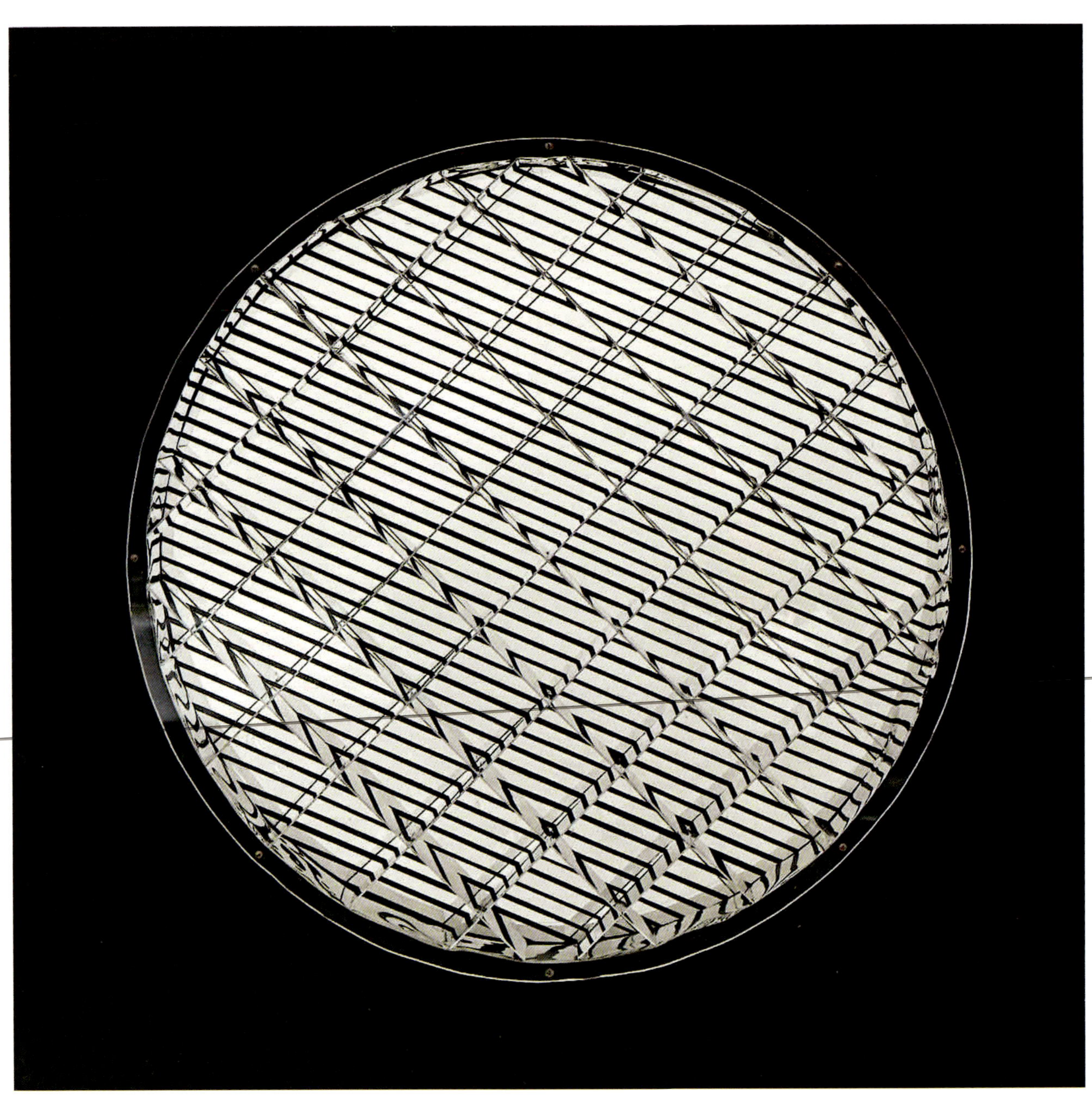

MARTHA BOTO *Graphisme kaleidoscopique*, 1965
Painted mirrors and Plexiglas in wood box with electric switch, 26 ½ × 26 ½ × 5 ½ in. (67.3 × 67.3 × 14 cm)
The Ella Fontanals-Cisneros Collection, Miami

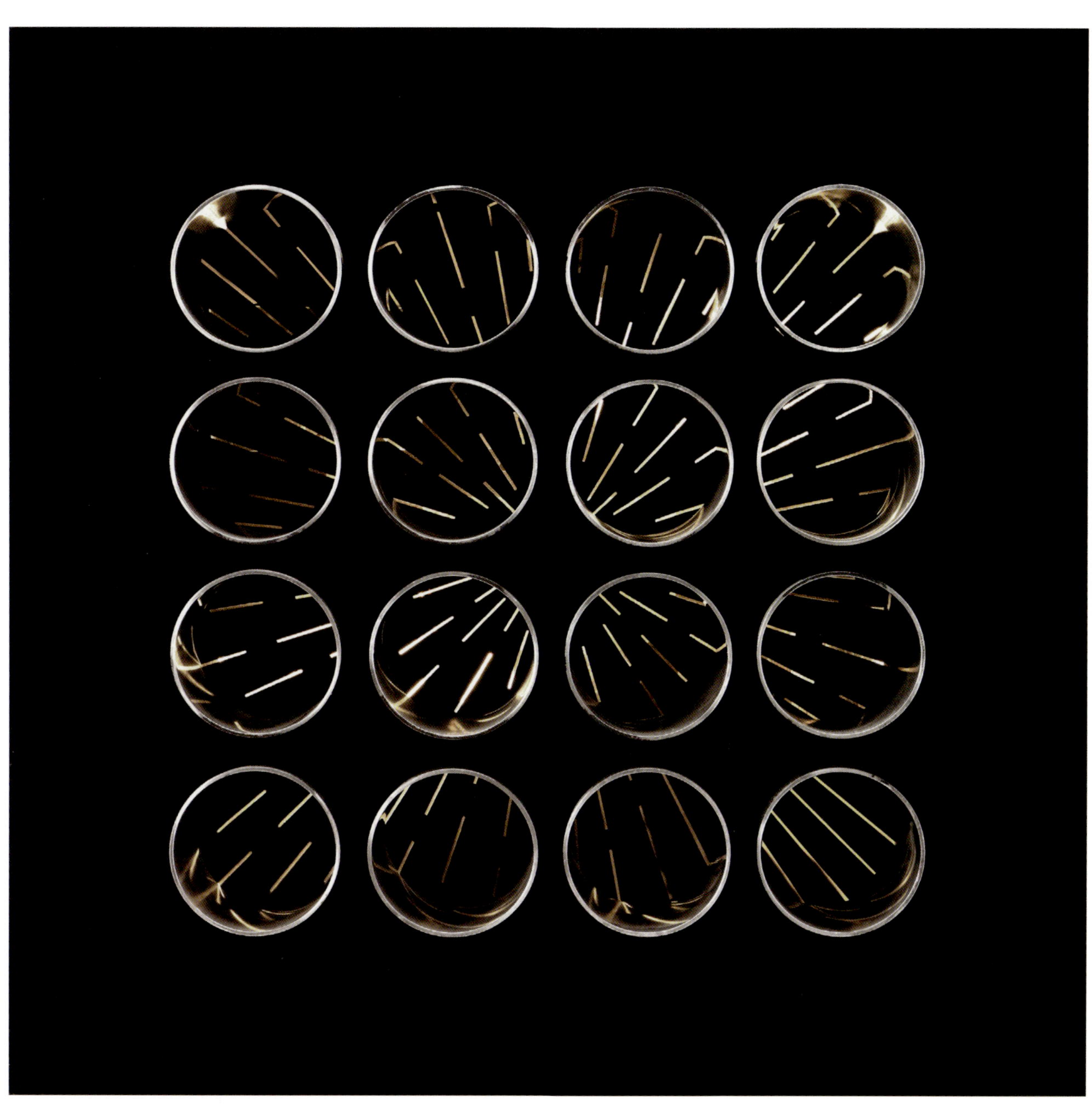

MARTHA BOTO *Optique electronique*, 1965
Painted wood, light, aluminum, and electric motor, 25 ½ × 25 ½ × 13 ½ in. (64.8 × 64.8 × 34.3 cm)
The Museum of Fine Arts, Houston. Gift of Benbow and Jean Bullock, 2004.1617

MARTHA BOTO *Optique hélicoidal (Mouvement)*, 1967
Plexiglas, aluminum, plywood, and motor, 79 ½ × 23 ¼ x 15 ⅜ in. (201.3 x 64 x 39 cm)
Collection of Gérard and Maria Rose Guilbert, Paris. Courtesy of Sicardi Gallery, Houston

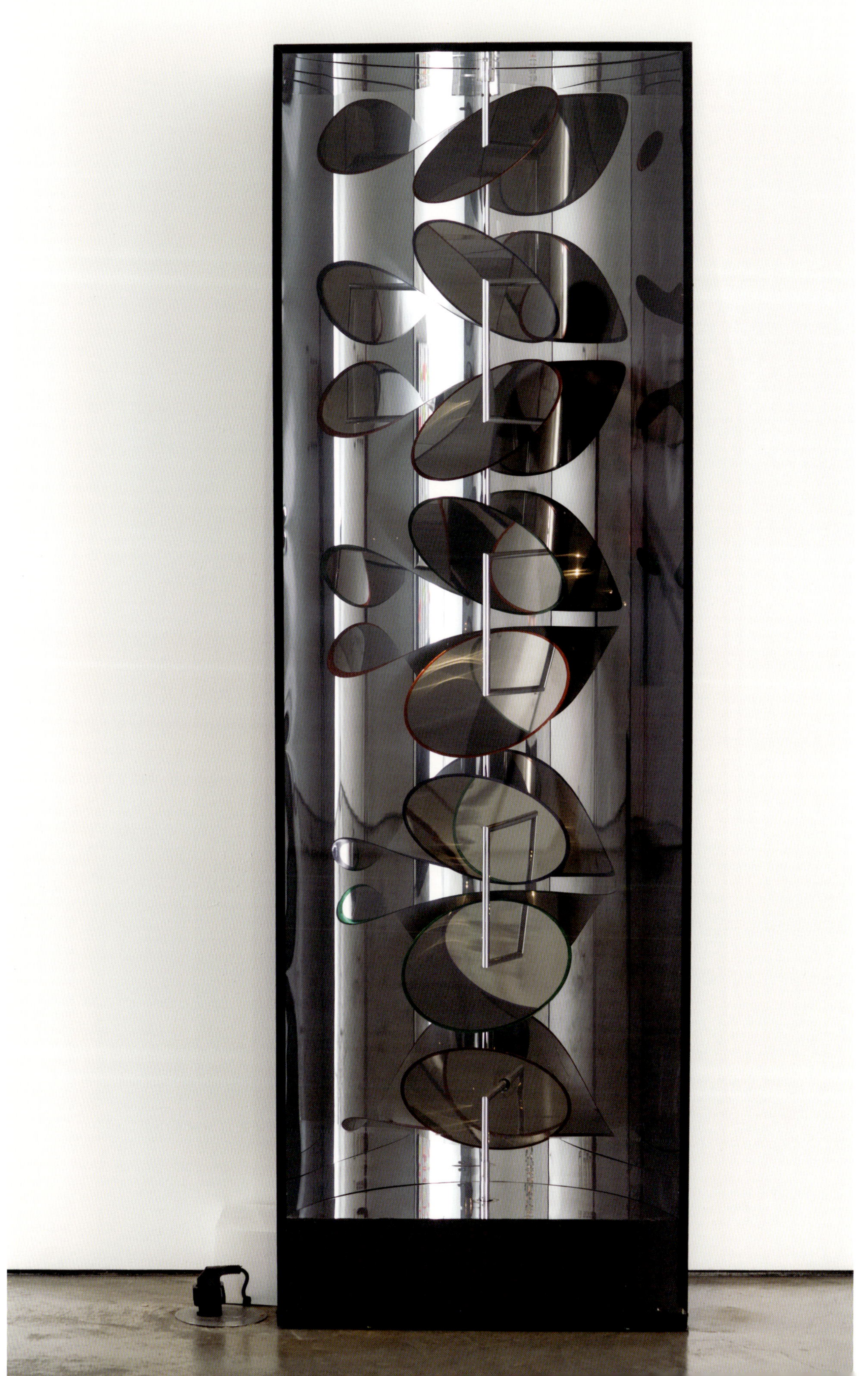

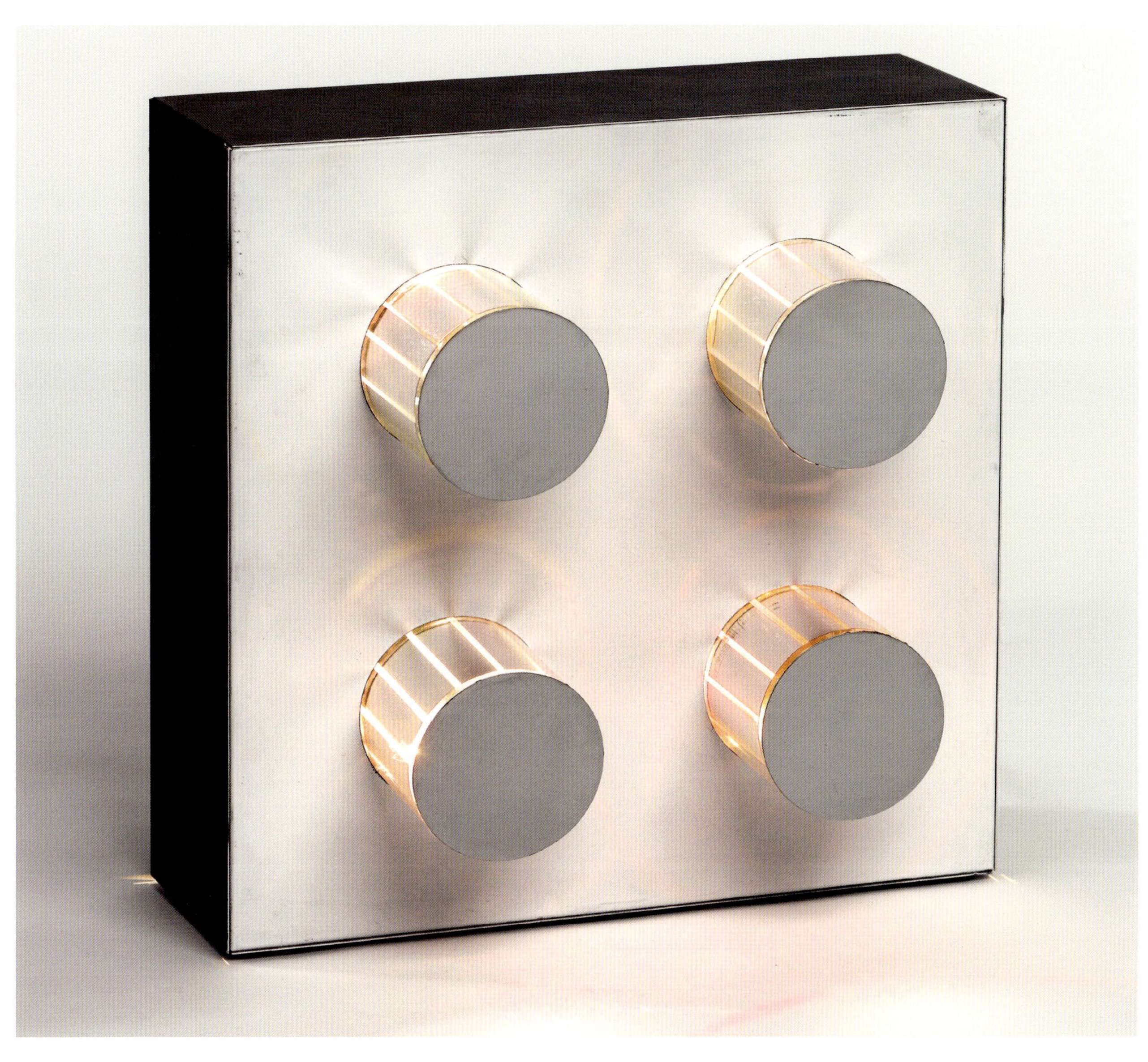

MARTHA BOTO *Dynamo*, 1969
Metal, plastic, and electric motor, 17 ½ × 16 ½ × 9 in. (44.5 × 41.9 × 22.9 cm)
Courtesy of Sicardi Gallery, Houston

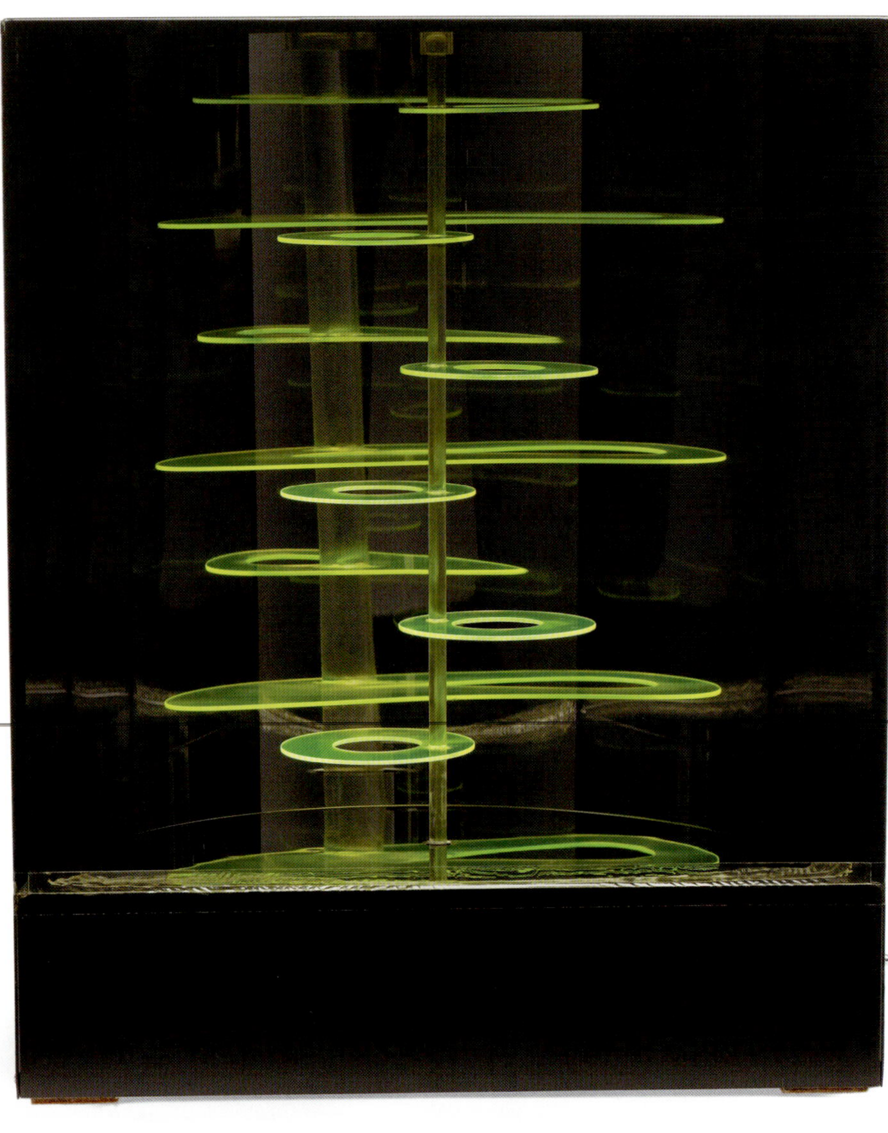

MARTHA BOTO *Déplacements optiques*, 1968
Plexiglas, metal, wood, and motor, 18 ¾ × 15 × 8 ⅝ in. (47 × 38.2 × 22 cm)
Collection of Gérard and Maria Rose Guilbert, Paris. Courtesy of Sicardi Gallery, Houston

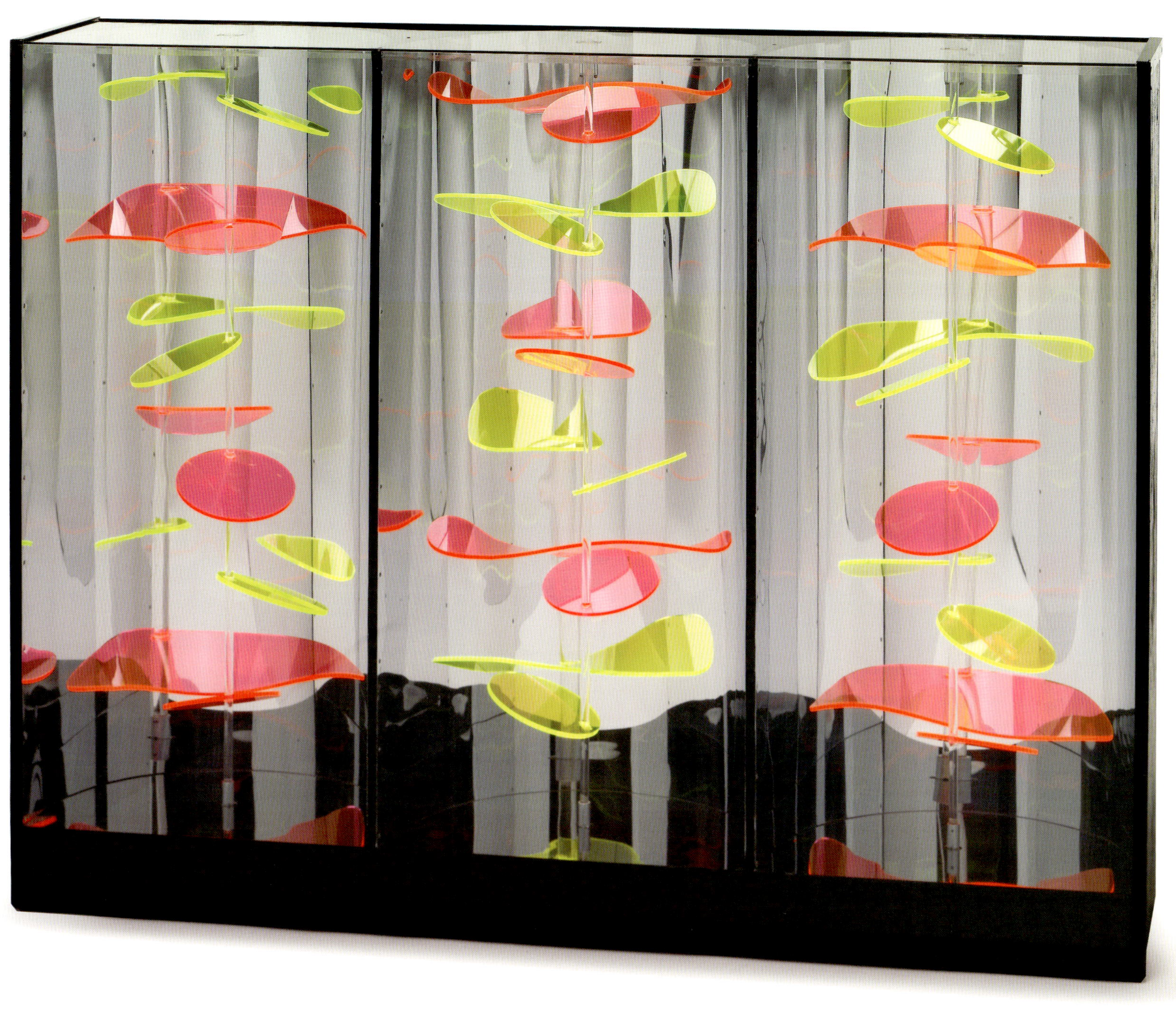

MARTHA BOTO *Déplacements optico-hydrauliques*, 1970
Plexiglas, aluminum, plywood, and motor, 39 ⅞ x 51 ⅜ x 11 ⅞ in. (101.3 x 130.6 x 29 cm)
Collection of Gérard and Maria Rose Guilbert, Paris. Courtesy of Sicardi Gallery, Houston

ELECTRIC SHADOWS

Dan Cameron

 2000 exhibition *Force Fields: Phases of the Kinetic* in Barcelona,[1] Kinetic Art has been enjoying a surge of interest in the twenty-first century, so much so that high-minded ideals expressed by its founders half a century ago seem almost prophetic today. While Kinetic Art's comeback might at first be mistaken for the symptom of a general nostalgia for all things midcentury — with the works themselves serving as emissaries from a society that was once peacefully resolved in its attitudes about new technologies and their role in our daily lives — such a reading is undercut by our awareness that there is little or no evidence such a society ever existed. Our feelings about new technologies have always been divided between wariness and amazement, no less so now than in the 1950s and 1960s, and our current feelings about Kinetic Art reflect that inherent discord. But if we judge by the enthusiastic crowds that flocked to the Grand Palais in Paris in 2013 to see the exhibition *Dynamo*,[2] it seems more plausible to suggest that the pioneers and key innovators of Kinetic Art were decades ahead of their time, and perhaps even that the public of the twenty-first century is in a better position to understand and appreciate an earlier generation's experiments in movement and light than a viewership that was far more attuned to the nuances of traditional easel painting.

This exhibition and the accompanying volume rest on two fundamental premises. The first is that Kinetic Art is one of the most perplexingly underrated developments of twentieth-century art, and the second is that Latin American artists were both pioneers in Kinetic Art's development and among its most profound exponents. It is important to cite these premises in tandem, if only because they appear to be causally connected — at least insofar as an audience within the United States is assumed. The first premise would be invalid if this exhibition were taking place in France, where Kinetic Art was long a popular style; while the second would make a different kind of sense in Argentina or Venezuela, where some of the most celebrated artists of the last century were active in the kinetic mode. For reasons that will be explored in greater detail, Kinetic Art never proved especially popular in the U.S., but then even a cursory overview of the subject indicates that most important developments within vanguard Latin American art over

1. At the Museu d'Art Contemporani, Barcelona.

2. The curators of the exhibition were Serge Lemoine and Matthieu Poirier. As indicated by its subtitle, *Dynamo: A Century of Light and Movement in Art 1913–2013* was based on the premise that Kinetic Art provides a continuum for understanding recent art history, with several works by younger artists included alongside historical examples.

the last half-century have experienced a long delay in reaching a North American public. In the face of differences of cultural heritage and historical understanding, it has been left to the present occasion to make the argument in this country that these artists' accomplishments are more than worthy of attention today. Based on how little we do know about them as a result of the genre's exclusion from conventional histories of mid-twentieth-century art, it's even possible that these enigmatic, blinking analog machines and objects from the 1950s and 1960s, which in many ways foretell the screens and devices of our own digital age, have the capacity to communicate something meaningful to our present time and place about perceptual frontiers and the ever-shifting boundaries between technology, the public, and new art.

If the most relevant corollary to the argument that Kinetic Art was ahead of its time is that the visual languages of movement and mutation employed by the artists of that generation — blinking, filtering, fading, rotating, shimmering — have been fully internalized by the habitués of the world of Snapchat and Vine, another key factor is that the Kinetic Art of fifty years ago uncannily resembles much art being made today. Artistic investigations into how the properties of light could be harnessed as a medium go back centuries, but there is little question that digital technologies have made accessible an endless array of artists' tools, enabling the user to achieve in a series of clicks and drags what might have required hours or days of manual labor in the past. With these tools now in wider use, a range of visual connections have also started to emerge with respect to other examples of twentieth-century art that might not have seemed meaningful to an earlier generation of art historians or curators. Developments like Kinetic Art can, for instance, be linked with the emergence a few years later of a generation of artists in Southern California who were primarily interested in isolating and framing the effects of natural light on visual perception. The relationship is not one of cause and effect, but an inference based on the principle that interrelated breakthroughs can and do occur in certain highly specialized fields dispersed around the globe, and that the points of confluence between these distinct breakthroughs are not always based on conventional historical models of who traveled where, or who was directly influenced by the work of whom.

The occasion for *Kinesthesia* presented itself in the wake of a meticulously selected and installed survey of Argentine Kinetic Art from the 1960s, organized in 2012 by the curator María José Herrera for the Museo Nacional de Bellas Artes in Buenos Aires. Most of the twenty artists in that exhibition are still largely unknown outside of highly specialized circles, and a preliminary inquiry revealed a hidden paradox within the exhibition's subject matter. Until quite recently, it would have been extremely challenging, if not impossible, to develop an overview of Argentine Kinetic Art, precisely because so many of its most important practitioners had left the country and moved to Paris some fifty or even sixty years before, and most were already deceased. Despite the dynamic visual interplay among the works within the exhibition, the chronological and geographic framework of these artists' career biographies was cleanly bifurcated: those who left, and those who stayed, with only infrequent professional or pedagogical territory in common. Until 2012 the Argentine public had been deprived of a composite picture of expats and non-expats together, but it is unlikely they would have found solace prior to that in the European understanding of the topic, which tended to minimize the significance of a specifically Argentine history that contributed to the formation of many of these artists, and more or less eliminated the later Buenos Aires chapter altogether. This problem pointed to another challenge: how to determine the degree to which this intercontinental bifurcation affected the way the history of Kinetic Art was eventually written across Latin America. Underlying these concerns was a fundamental question of taxonomy: if artists from Latin America had played a pioneering role in the development of Kinetic Art, as appeared increasingly certain, why didn't a historical category labeled Latin American Kinetic Art already exist? Or, to take the Argentine situation as a starting point, under what conditions might a cultural phenomenon that occurred on both sides of the Atlantic Ocean be referred to today as a single, shared artistic history?

With these conditions in mind, in order to organize the present exhibition and undertake the research it entailed, a species of art-historical fiction had to be developed, in which a new category was coined to collectively identify a group of artists who in their heyday may have viewed, and been viewed by, peers and contemporaries through dramatically different lenses. For example, inside Argentina, where artistic tides have changed just as rapidly as in Paris, if not more so, artists who had enjoyed limited success through their association with Kinetic Art were more or less sidelined by the mid-1970s — first, as a natural outcome of shifting tastes, and later because of growing political instability within the country, as a result of which intellectuals,

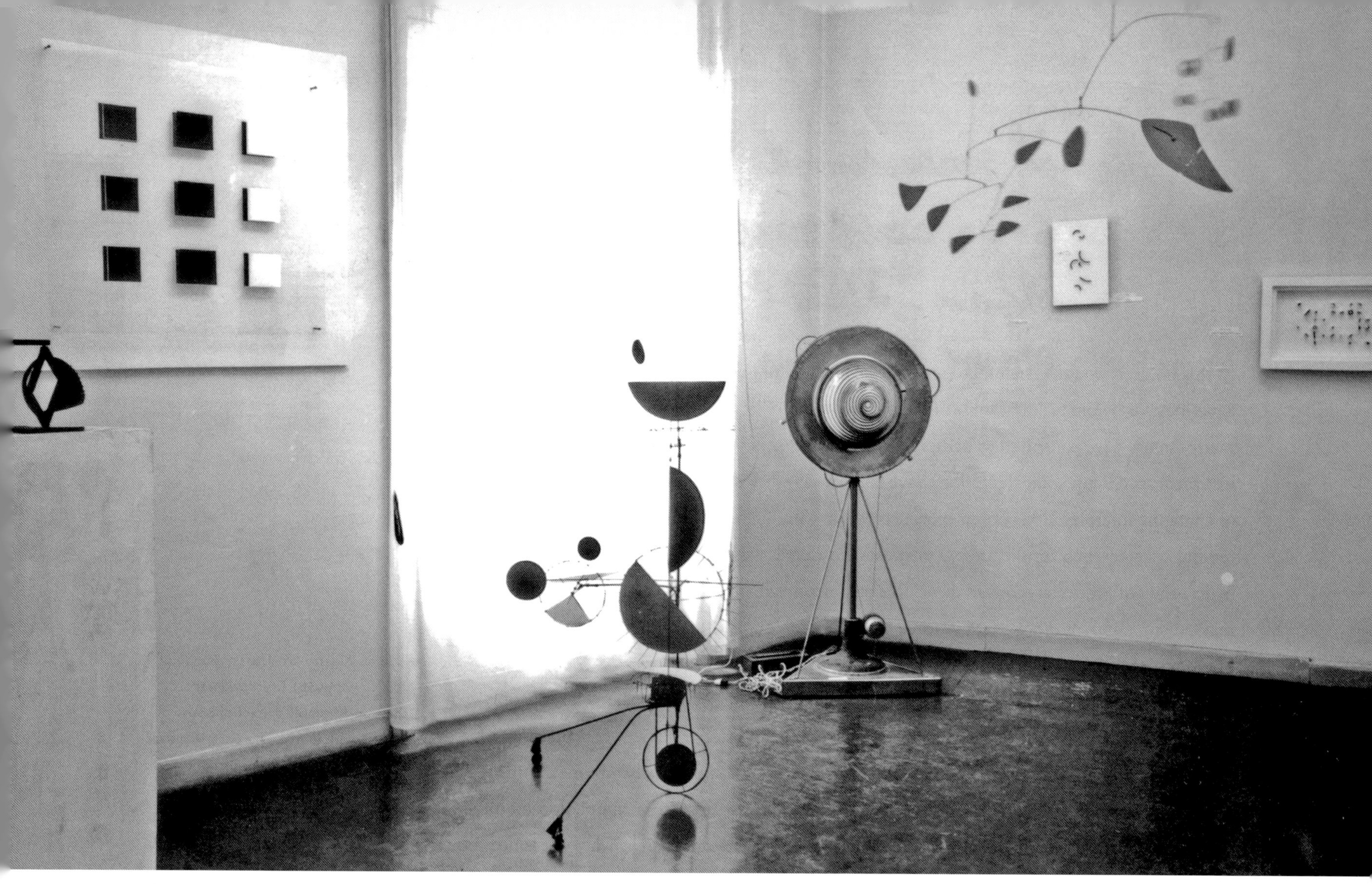

Installation view of the exhibition *Le Mouvement*, Galerie Denise René, Paris, April 1955. Works by Duchamp, Soto, Calder, Tinguely, and Agam

activists, artists, students, and cultural workers associated with the political left were potentially subjected to state-sponsored terrorism. In the Paris of the 1950s and 1960s, by contrast, not much weight was attached to where a person came from, since the mere fact of having landed in the City of Light was what truly mattered in the thick postwar ambience of cosmopolitan fraternity and fervent political debate. Paris was where one escaped the confines of one's upbringing, and artists from Argentina and Venezuela in particular found themselves pushed to challenge their own limits in light of the artistic experiments being carried out all around them. Paris was where the studios of Max Bill, Fernand Léger, and Georges Vantongerloo — artistic giants whose equal could not be found in Argentina or Venezuela — were a train ride away. Most crucially, for the international impact of Kinetic Art to become so extensive, Denise René's groundbreaking 1955 exhibition *Le Mouvement* could have taken place only at a gallery in Paris, where so many of its practitioners also lived. By the end of the turbulent 1960s, it can even be said that Kinetic Art was embraced as the official state style, and the Musée National d'Art Moderne at the Centre Pompidou, which opened in 1977, has continued to bestow prominence upon various members of the Kinetic Art generation, through to the present day.

At this point, it would be helpful to try to develop a working definition of precisely what
Kinetic Art is before tackling some of the historical and critical questions it poses. Although
many factors have conspired to hamper a clear public understanding of the movement's
historical specificity, some definitions have fallen away since its heyday, either through disuse
or changing interpretations of certain artists' work, with the result that only two definitions
require consideration for the present purposes. So-called "active" Kinetic Art is recognizable
by its inherent propensity toward detectable movement, whether by force of wind, electricity,
magnetism, water, or other energy source. The viewer might interact with the artwork directly,
but motion is generated by the object with or without an actual spectator. So-called "passive"
Kinetic Art appears only to the viewer's perception to be moving, and it appears that way only
so long as the viewer is the one doing the moving, seeming to stop if the viewer remains
absolutely still. For some years, Kinetic Art's pioneering critic Guy Brett championed a third
definition, which might be retroactively labeled "interactive," or art whose completion requires
that it be activated through the physical intervention of a spectator.[3] While such work is no
longer considered part of Kinetic Art, the best-known examples are the artworks of Brazilian
Neoconstructivists Lygia Clark and Hélio Oiticica, which prodded the viewer toward a state
of play and free association in which the artworks have a dynamic function as performance
garments or therapeutically manipulated objects. A more relevant exponent of this third offshoot
is Uruguayan Cubist Juaquín Torres-García, whose varied artistic production included simple
wooden toys intended to be manipulated by the user, and whose example was reflected a few
years later in works of Madí, thereby proving highly influential for a group of young Argentine
and Uruguayan abstract artists who would later cite Torres-García's whimsical, intimate objects
as direct precursors of their own experiments.

A close relative of Kinetic Art, from which some differentiation is invariably required, is
Op Art, so named for its propensity to deploy illusionistic representations of geometric lines,
patterns, and shapes in order to fool the viewer into perceiving either deep space or a warped
and/or fractured relief space. Because its visual impact depends on maintaining a perfectly flat
picture plane, Op Art tends to be excessively linear, its surface scored by straight or curved lines
rendered in close proximity to one another. There has always been a relatively porous boundary
between Kinetic Art and Op Art, in part because the works of certain artists have at different
times been associated with each camp. Victor Vasarely, who played a key role in the genesis of

3. In his *Kinetic Art: The Language of
Movement* (1968), Brett underscores
the transformable aspect of both
artists' work to make his case, while also
singling out the non-kinetic light works
of Dan Flavin and François Morellet as
extending the boundaries still further.

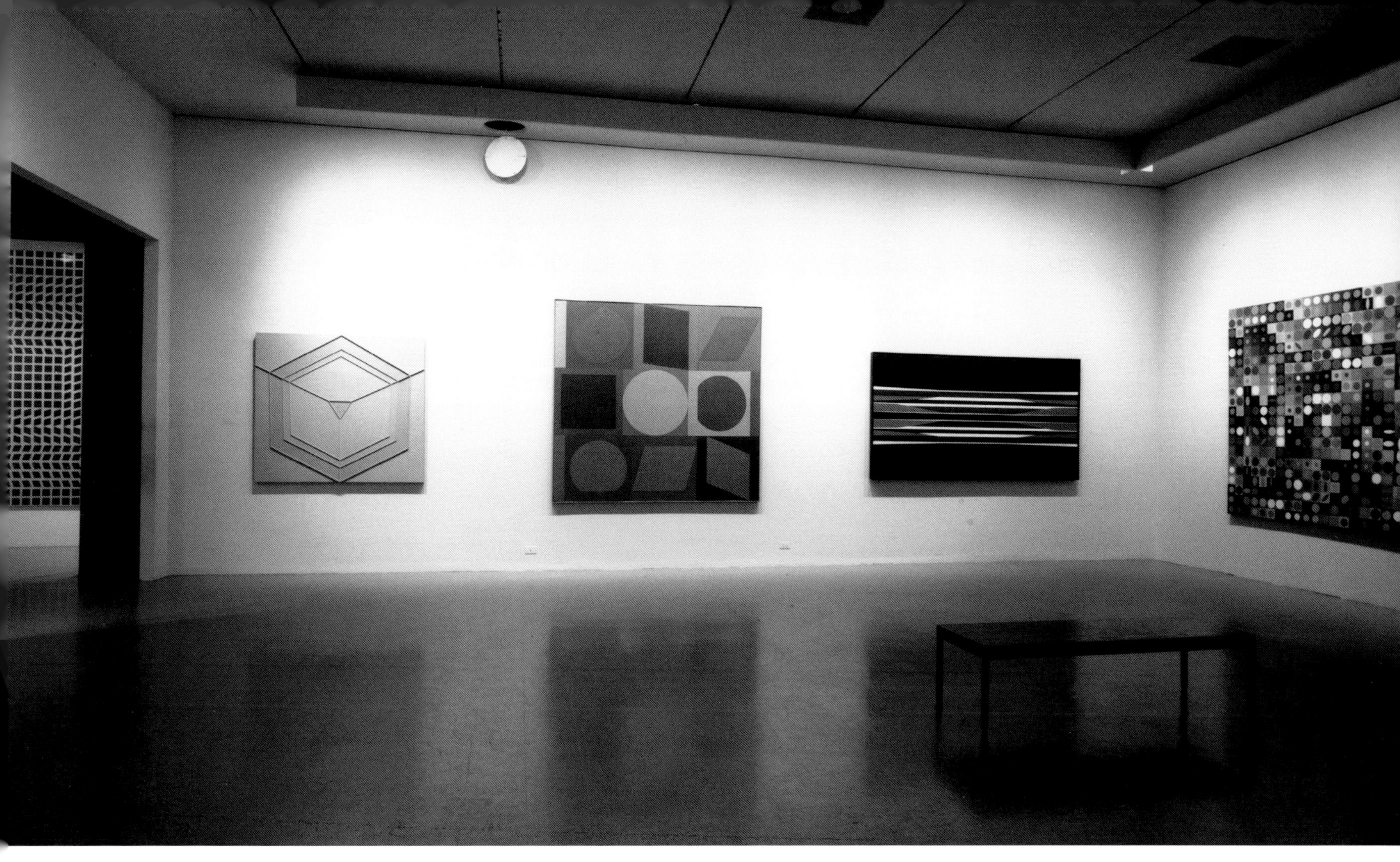

Installation view of the exhibition *The Responsive Eye*, February 25 through April 25, 1965. The Museum of Modern Art, New York, Photographic Archive. The Museum of Modern Art Archives, New York

Kinetic Art, is also Op's most immediate direct forebear in painting. Op Art's roots, like those of Kinetic Art, extend to Dutch and Russian Constructivist painting and sculpture of the 1910s and 1920s, but the phenomenon did not attain international visibility until the 1965 exhibition *The Responsive Eye* at the Museum of Modern Art, which succeeded in introducing the work of Vasarely and Bridget Riley — not to mention Carlos Cruz-Diez, Julio Le Parc, and Horacio García-Rossi — to a wider public, while somewhat muddying its premise by including such non-Op geometric abstract painters as Robert Irwin, John McLaughlin, Kenneth Noland, and Frank Stella. As a direct result of MoMA's efforts, Op Art became something of a household word in the U.S., but almost invariably employed in the pejorative as an example of an art movement that wasn't really a movement at all but merely an eccentric symptom of a befuddled era.

Much of the critical reception of *The Responsive Eye* was openly hostile, but despite the departure of curator William Seitz from MoMA's staff shortly after the exhibition — generally seen as a sign of the Board of Trustees' disapproval — the exhibition was an unprecedented public and media success, drawing record numbers of visitors willing to endure long waits to experience the spectacle for themselves. In fact, although it might have seemed for a moment that Op might become the abstract counterpart to Pop, the absence of a major American artist pursuing Op (or Kinetic Art, for that matter) with the formal rigor of a Riley made it an especially tough sell, especially since by 1965 the names of Roy Lichtenstein, Claes Oldenburg, James Rosenquist, and Andy Warhol were on their way to being consecrated within the local art lexicon. Critic Thomas B. Hess handed *The Responsive Eye* the quintessentially New York–snub with an *Art News* review, dismissing Op as "'Out-of-Town Art' . . . pursued as fanatically in South Dakota as in the South of France."[4] The notion that for Hess, a region of France and South Dakota existed at comparable levels of provincialism illustrates how determined many opinion makers were to transform a movement with the imprimatur of official French culture into an object of disdain. It was anathema to this new mindset that an international art movement originating in Paris — where all the movements from Impressionism to Surrealism had been born — could be imported to New York, and that American artists would eagerly jump on board.

At the time of *The Responsive Eye*, and a decade after *Le Mouvement*, Kinetic Art's foothold in the U.S. was quite tenuous. The cultural tug-of-war then playing out between Paris and New York, and a membership roster heavily weighted with artists from South America, appear to be among the underlying reasons Americans know so little about the movement today. In the late 1940s, with the U.S. flexing its postwar geopolitical muscle, the recognition of Abstract Expressionism as a homegrown style — albeit one with plainly evident international roots — signaled a major shift in American politics and culture, with Paris as the capital of advanced art being systematically supplanted by New York, where many European artists and thinkers had migrated in the late 1930s and early 1940s. As historian Serge Guilbaut has persuasively argued, a protectionist spirit regarding art and music became prominent in the U.S. in the early 1950s, its goal to persuade reluctant Europeans that Americans were capable of producing objects of beauty as sublime and accomplished as those of their counterparts across the Atlantic, and that the critical standards applied to the paintings of Picasso and Duchamp could also be used to judge the works of Pollock and De Kooning. The political subtext to this campaign was the Cold War, and the U.S.'s efforts to win over European sensibilities were tailored to provide an appearance of overall benevolence, while its policies in Southeast Asia and Cuba were increasingly coming under rhetorical fire from the European cultural intelligentsia. The campaign reached a climax of sorts in 1964 at the Venice Biennial, when for the first time an American artist — Robert Rauschenberg — won the Golden Lion for painting, resulting in

4. Hess's review, "You can hang it in the hall," ran in the April 1965 issue of *Art News*, which republished it in 2015 on the occasion of *The Illusive Eye*, held at El Museo del Barrio in New York.

scandalized accusations that the U.S. was "colonizing" European culture. Two years later, despite rampant rumors that the Pop artist Roy Lichtenstein would be the Golden Lion winner, the surprise decision by the international jury to award the prize to the little-known Argentine artist Julio Le Parc, who had been living in Paris for more than a decade, was interpreted as a potent signal that European cosmopolitanism was reasserting itself — by way of a Latin American artist.

In early 2016, El Museo del Barrio in New York observed the fiftieth anniversary of *The Responsive Eye* by presenting a succinct overview of Kinetic and Op Art under the title *The Illusive Eye*. Exhibition curator and then-director Jorge Daniel Veneciano explained the title's reference to its predecessor as a means of addressing the exclusion of Latin American artists from previous considerations of the subject, while looking beyond European theories of perception for the work's context to Egyptian and Eastern mysticism. Among the more than fifty artists in the Museo del Barrio project, one can find nearly every artist in the present exhibition: Martha Boto, Carlos Cruz-Diez, Horacio García-Rossi, Gyula Kosice, Julio Le Parc, Alejandro Otero, Abraham Palatnik, Jesús Rafael Soto, and Gregorio Vardánega. Also represented were Argentine painters Eduardo Mac Entyre and Miguel Ángel Vidal, who in 1959 launched a proto-Op movement of their own, Pintura Generativa (Generative Painting). Without over-indulging in historicist fantasy, *The Illusive Eye* offered, a half-century after the fact, the first-ever glimpse in the U.S. of the accomplishments of these (and an array of other) artists at the height of their careers. Before there was Kinetic Art, a range of developments in modernism directly incorporated physical motion, and prior to this, a broad historical lineage of art openly explored the qualities of movement. In his landmark study *Origins and Development of Kinetic Art* (1968), historian Frank Popper highlighted tendencies that appear in the work of certain French Impressionists, particularly Degas and Monet, linking them to Eadweard Muybridge's concurrent photographic experiments in rendering animal and human locomotion one frame at a time. Tracing movement in Post-Impressionism, from Seurat's use of pictorial vibrancy to Van Gogh's *Starry Night* and Gauguin's Tahitian "world of rhythm," Popper's narrative effectively fuses the development of Kinetic Art with the core achievements of the modernist canon: Picasso's and Léger's proto-Cubist figures; the Futurists Balla, Severini, and Boccioni; Kandinsky's early abstractions. Marcel Duchamp was arguably the first major artist to tie his artistic practice to an ongoing engagement with the kinetic realm. From his 1912 *Nude Descending a Staircase* to his *Bicycle Wheel* readymade a year later, Duchamp kept returning to the problem of movement through the early 1920s, eventually building the *Rotorelief* series of motorized spinning discs to generate cinematic optical illusions. Notwithstanding Duchamp's consistent efforts to develop movement as a sculptural element, the first artists to apply the term "kinetic" to visual art were the Russian siblings Naum Gabo and Antoine Pevsner in 1920, and it was Gabo who first exhibited a single steel strip set in motion by an electric motor that same year, giving it the title *Kinetic Construction*. Although thirty-five more years would pass before the first major exhibition of Kinetic Art took place, the wheels, so to speak, were set in motion.

A number of Paris-based artists, in particular the American sculptor Alexander Calder, persistently investigated movement through the late 1920s and early 1930s, although little concerted effort to formalize these efforts within European art could be seen until well into the 1950s. After Calder moved to Paris from New York in 1926, his works evolved from the renowned *Cirque Calder* (1926–31), made up of small wire figures he referred to as "drawing in space," to suspended multi-form structures with discrete moving parts — dubbed "mobiles" by Duchamp himself — in the early 1930s. The term was eventually applied to all of Calder's moving sculptures, long after the initial exhibition of those that were essentially passive, their motion caused by wind and other forces. Calder returned to the U.S. in 1933, but his impact on the Paris art scene persisted, so much so that when the Venezuelan architect Carlos Raúl Villanueva began applying his ideas about a "synthesis of the arts" to his master plan for the Ciudad Universitaria in Caracas, Calder was one of the artists whose participation was deemed essential to the undertaking. The Ciudad Universitaria, which occupied a full twenty-five years of Villanueva's life and incorporates forty buildings spread over two square kilometers, was the first project to bring many of Kinetic Art's historical antecedents together with younger practitioners. Commissions from the formative generation included Jean Arp, Laurens, Léger, and Pevsner. Representing the current generation of Venezuelan artists were Alejandro Otero, whose long Paris sojourn (1945–52) had made him the de facto agent of artistic change in Venezuela; and Soto, who in 1950 had also moved to Paris, where he would spend the rest of his life. But the two artists whose work represented an intergenerational bridge between those two groups were

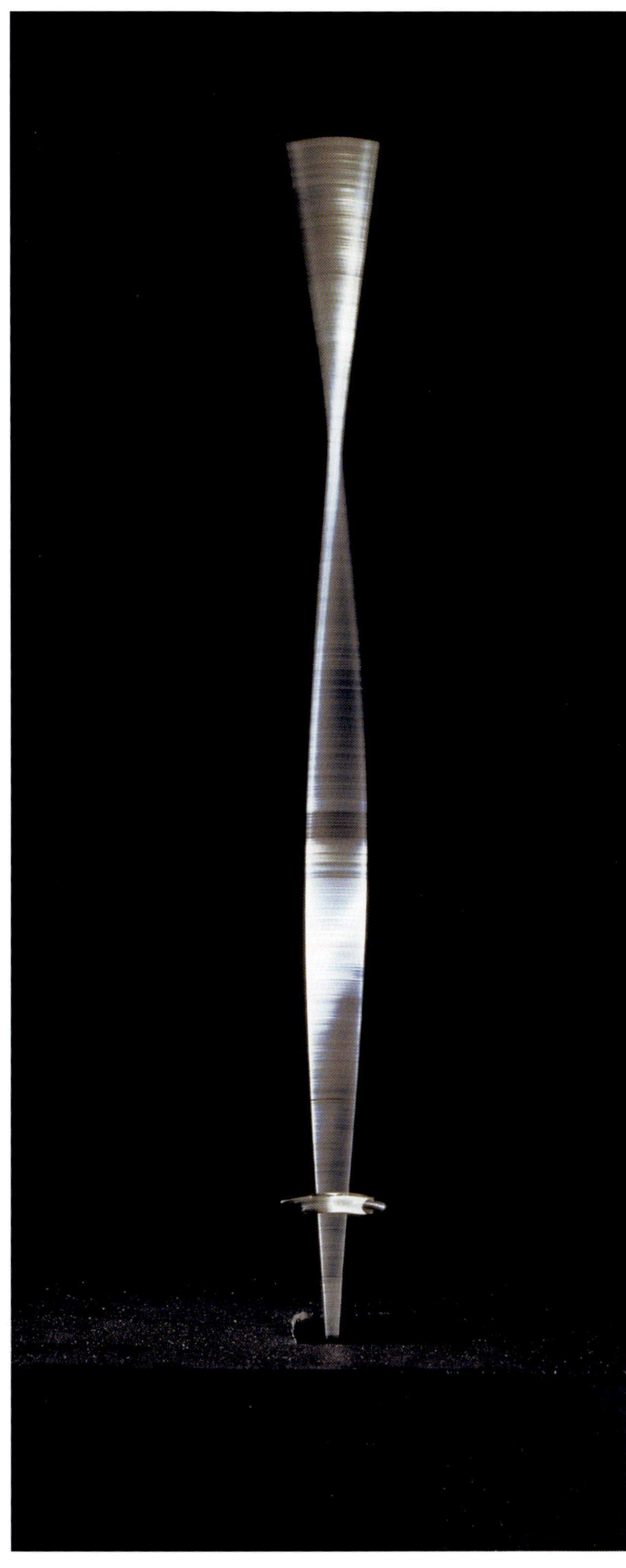

Calder, whose *Clouds* installation of acoustic panels in the Magna Aula is considered by many to be his greatest artistic achievement, and Vasarely, who personally created three new site-specific works on the campus, and acted as Villanueva's agent for the works produced in Paris at the Susse Frères Foundry by Arp, Léger, and Pevsner.

Vasarely's foundational role in the birth of both Kinetic Art and Op Art as separate international movements on two continents would be difficult to overstate. Born in Pécs, Hungary, Vasarely moved to Budapest in 1925 to study Bauhaus principles, and to Paris in 1930, where he soon painted *Zebra*, the first example of what later became known as Op Art. Despite his precocious accomplishment, Vasarely's employment as a graphic artist, his pedagogical aspirations, and his tangential chapter painting in an expressionistic style sidetracked his artistic development for years, so that the geometric optical style for which he was later renowned came to fruition only in the late 1940s. By the end of 1939, however, Vasarely met aspiring art dealer Denise René (1913–2012) at the Café Flor,[5] and the couple's names would soon be closely linked as the team behind Kinetic Art's successes. Waiting out the invasion and occupation of Paris, René opened her gallery in 1944 with an exhibition of Vasarely's works, and soon the pair was fiercely devoted to promoting the visual language of geometric abstraction, which eventually included cultivating a protracted interchange between France and South America that defined the early years of the Kinetic Art movement. Exhibitions of Vasarely's work at the Fine Arts Museums of Buenos Aires (1958) and Caracas (1959) followed. Although he was never a practitioner of Kinetic Art as such, Vasarely's sculpture *Plus/Minus* in Villanueva's Ciudad Universitaria, in which tile patterns in the floor trace the shadow of the sun as it moves across the patio, is a rare example of his more inventive engagements with actual, as opposed to retinal, movement. While disagreement might linger over how decisive a role Vasarely played in the wildly successful *Le Mouvement*, the inclusion of new works by the young Soto alongside better-known figures such as Calder, Duchamp, and Vasarely himself represents an instantaneous change in the way Latin American artists had been incorporated into the narrative history of modern art. Rather than serving as secondhand followers of major movements in European art, for the first time Latin Americans were considered Kinetic Art's co-authors.

Among expatriate South Americans in Paris, Alejandro Otero was another catalytic figure. Returning to Caracas in the midst of his Paris sojourn, Otero set off a minor scandal in 1949 simply by showing his series *Las Cafeteras* (The Coffeepots) at the Museo de Bellas Artes. Employing broad, open brushstrokes within a loosely Cubist composition on a large scale, the *Cafeteras* were dramatically unlike anything a Venezuelan artist had attempted before, and even if by Parisian standards they did not quite represent the cutting edge, to a new generation

5. *The Daily Telegraph*, "Denise René [Obituary]," September 27, 2012.

6. Letter from Alejandro Otero, from *Alfredo Boulton and His Contemporaries* (New York: Museum of Modern Art, 2008), 187–88.

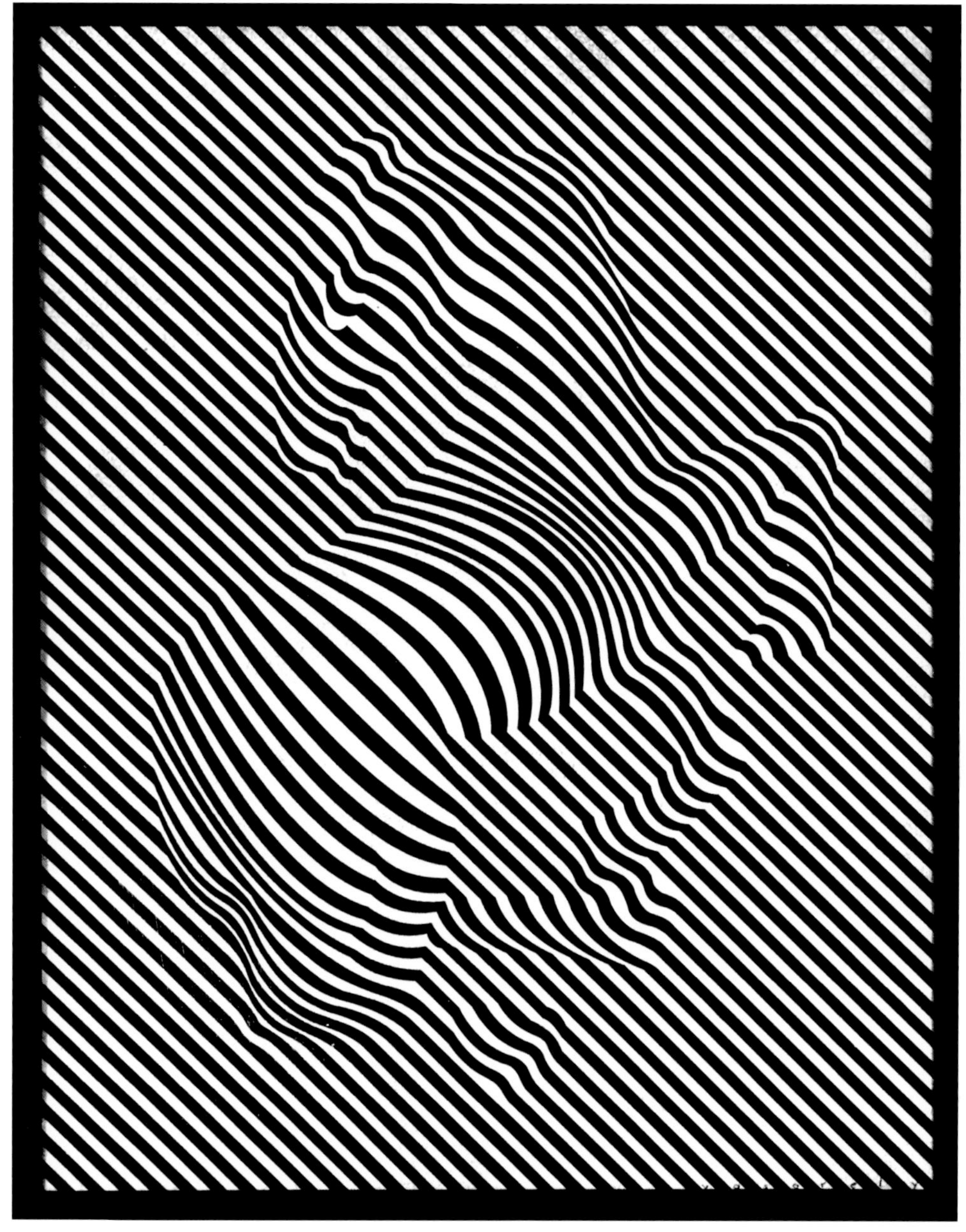

Victor Vasarely, *Zebra*, 1944. Courtesy Michèle Vasarely

of artists in Caracas the exhibition signaled an era of dynamic engagement with abstraction. While still in Venezuela, Otero began his *Coloritmo* series, an integral step in the articulation of Kinetic Art in South America, although just as eventful was his formation, on returning to Europe in 1959, of the group Los Disidentes, composed primarily of other Venezuelan expats working in abstraction. A tireless agitator for modernism his entire life, Otero was one of the artists closest to Villanueva, and his engagement with the Ciudad Universitaria project from its earliest iterations is evident in letters exchanged between them and with their mutual friend, the architect Alfredo Boulton. Otero envisioned an outdoor sculpture exhibition throughout Caracas, with participation by the current Young Turks of Paris modernism.[6]

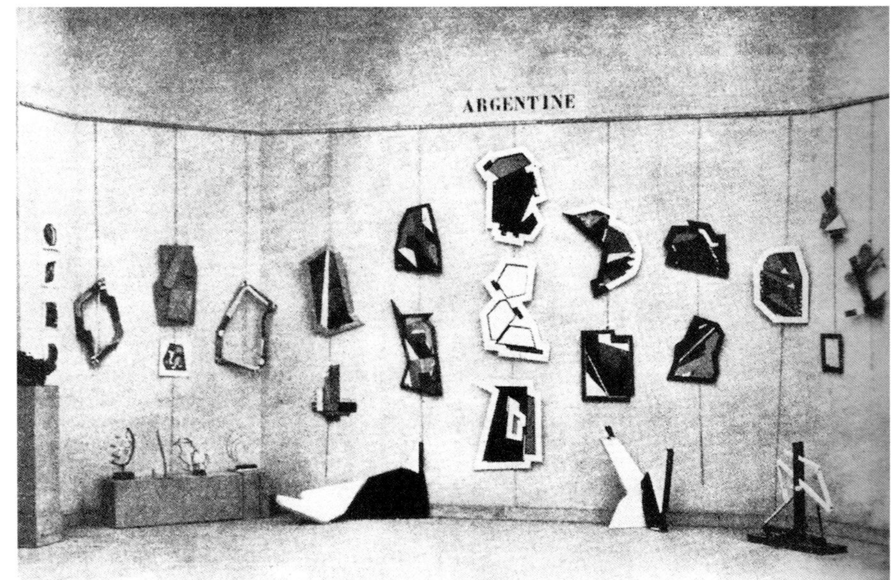

Argentine Room, Salon des Réalités Nouvelles, Paris, 1948. Works by Gyula Kosice, Ánibal J. Biedma, María Bresler, Juan Delmonte, Jacqueline Lorin-Kaldor, Ricardo Pereyra, Rhod Rothfuss, Rodolofo Uricchio, Diyi Laañ, and Raymundo Rasas Pet (Kosice's pseudonym)

Although born in provincial Ciudad Bolívar, Jesús Rafael Soto studied art in Caracas, and ran the Escuela de Artes Plásticas in Maracaibo from 1947 to 1950. He received a travel grant to go to Paris for six months, where he quickly fell in with the group of artists connected with René's gallery and the Salon des Réalités Nouvelles, which included Yaacov Agam, Jean Tinguely, and Vasarely. During his first years in Paris, while developing optical reliefs that incorporate sheets of Plexiglas painted with layers and rows of dots whose arrangement triggers an effect like *moiré* as the viewer moved in relation to it, Soto made his living playing his guitar at cafes and restaurants. By 1954 he had arrived at the first of a series of works, *Metamorphosis*, that would qualify him for inclusion in *Le Mouvement*, and he rapidly became one of the burgeoning movement's leading representatives. Because Soto's 1954 *Desplazamiento de un elemento luminoso* inspired other artists who made use of the inherent curvature of its plastic surfaces to magnify the optical impact of the viewer's location, it is also the earliest artwork included in this exhibition. The work demonstrates Soto's singular ability to transform the flat two-dimensionality of Vasarely's optical compositions into an immersive sculptural experience in which the visual experience was literally projected outward, away from the surface of the wall. This made him a formidable counterpart to the Israeli-born Agam, who moved to Paris from Zurich a year after Soto arrived from Caracas and followed a similar career path. The two shared the honor of being the two artists in *Le Mouvement* whose work was considered a genuine discovery, even by seasoned Parisian audiences.

The third Venezuelan artist included in this discussion, who made his maiden visit to Paris just as *Le Mouvement* was ending, was Carlos Cruz-Diez, who had only begun working in abstraction the year before, although his interest in color originated with earlier research, while he was still a student, into Impressionism. Like Otero and Soto, Cruz-Diez had studied at the Escuela de Artes Plásticas y Aplicadas in Caracas, and participated in discussions with both men, but by 1957 his first encounter with Kinetic Art at the René gallery had pushed him toward the possibility of using colored light as a medium. Two years later, Cruz-Diez had become a kinetic artist himself through the invention of the *Physichromie*, which explores the physical properties of light through the incorporation of innumerable narrow vertical ridges covering the painting's surface, whose gradations change to the extent that each surface of each ridge shows a different fragment of the whole image at different "moments." When viewed from a position directly in front of the painting, these ridges distribute the different colorations equally, but a shift to the left or right activates one position in favor of the other. The effect on the painting's surface is as dramatic as it had been in Soto's works, with the main difference between the two being Cruz-Diez's exploration of a full palette of colors, while much of Soto's art through the 1960s verges on the monochromatic. Cruz-Diez's most ambitious early works, the *Chromosaturation* series first developed in 1965, propel the viewer through a sequence of four rooms, each saturated with a different color. As a direct precursor to the earliest room-size installations of Robert Irwin and James Turrell, Cruz-Diez's *Chromosaturation* was one of the twentieth century's most complete expressions of pure color, experienced separately from its application to a given surface.

Much as Alejandro Otero's late-1940s sojourn in Paris paved the way for Soto's later successes in that city, Gregorio Vardánega's early career seems to have provided a blueprint for Le Parc, his junior by five years. By 1946, Vardánega was an active participant in the various manifesto-driven factions operating in Buenos Aires from the late 1940s through the 1950s, producing partly transparent relief works using shaped Plexiglas perforated with tightly wound string, and multi-panel painted abstractions attached to vertical sheets of glass. Although Tomás Maldonado has the distinction of being the first Argentine artist of his generation to have traveled abroad in search of direct interaction with the titans of French modernism, in 1948 Vardánega made an extended visit to Paris with Uruguayan artist Carmelo Arden Quin. There they met Denise René, Vantongerloo, Pevsner, and Max Bill, among many others, and Vardánega exhibited in prominent Parisian salons, including the Salón de l'Amérique Latine. When he returned to Argentina in 1949, Vardánega was certain that France offered a more promising future for his generation, and it was partly as a result of his enthusiasm that Le Parc applied for the grant from the French government that would bring him to France in 1958. Vardánega and his wife, Martha Boto, followed a year later, but by then Vardánega's approach had fully evolved, his works incorporating arrangements of colored lights timed in sequential patterns. Almost from the moment of their arrival, Boto and Vardánega focused their artistic energies on what was to become their long-standing shared interest: harnessing motor-driven movement of light for sculptural and pictorial purposes. Their boxlike vignettes tend to function best in contained spaces, while Le Parc's more open-frame works using projected animated light soon filled much larger rooms. The frequently complex sequences and variations within Vardánega's programs edged closer to the problem-solving sequential tasks that computer software would soon make universal, whereas the visual impact of Martha Boto's work is best conveyed through the slow, repetitive movement of multiple identical parts, producing a continuous illuminated flow.

Boto's embrace of movement came a few years later than Vardánega's, but she had become a fully committed participant in the earliest abstract art movements in Buenos Aires while still in her teens. She and Vardánega, in fact, co-founded one of those movements, Artistas No Figurativos, in 1956. In Boto's abstract paintings from the early 1950s, a few small-scale shapes tend to be carefully composed over monochromatic (often white) fields, while sharp disruptions in internal scale are used to suggest empty spaces. She even began experimenting with suspended Plexiglas mobiles, including some that incorporated colored water, while still in Buenos Aires, but Boto's kinetic work did not begin in earnest until after she moved to Paris and participated in the 1960 Paris Biennial. Unlike most of her peers, Boto seemed most interested in considering light, motion, and color as a single, fused entity, and emphasizing as much as possible the inherent perceptual qualities of the materials she worked with, such as aluminum and stainless steel, rather than basing her experiments on notions of sequence (like Vardánega) or scale (like Le Parc).

The meteoric development of Julio Le Parc's artwork after his arrival in Paris is central to this discussion. He played an unusually active role in the artistic trajectories of many of those artists who surrounded him, and was also among the first artists in any medium to set the physical and conceptual limits of what would become known as installation art. During his studies at the Escuela Nacional de Bellas Artes in Buenos Aires, along with Hugo Demarco, Horacio García-Rossi, and Francisco Sobrino, Le Parc was a well-known student activist whose leadership qualities were legendary. The three aforementioned artists moved to Paris at the same time as Le Parc, and two of them co-founded the collective Groupe de Recherche d'Art Visuel (GRAV), which generally eschewed object-making in favor of social action. A year prior to winning the Golden Lion prize in Venice in 1966, Le Parc had returned to the convention of signing his works as the production of a solitary artist, but his ability to connect a lifelong set of political convictions with

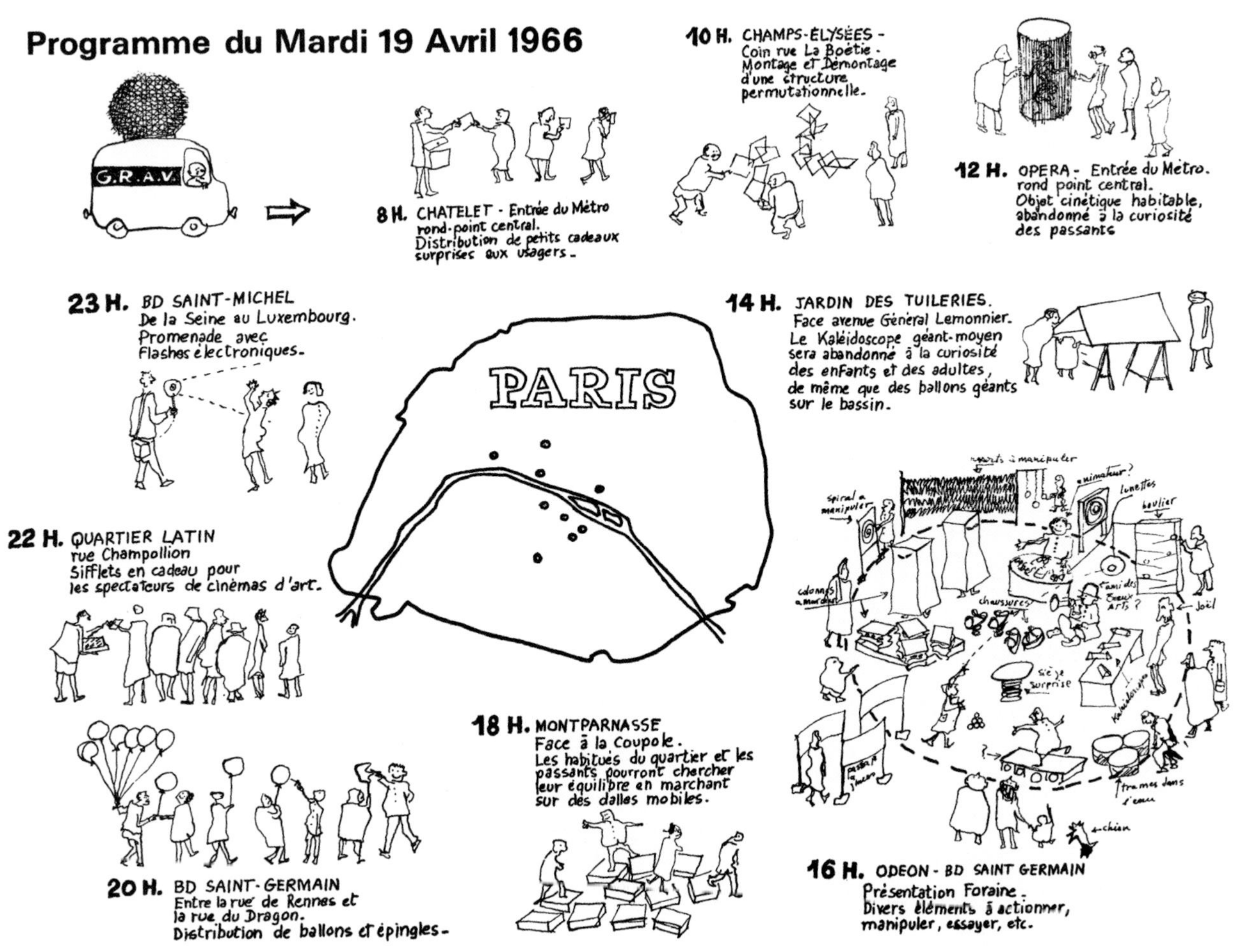

Groupe de Recherche d'Art Visuel (GRAV), *Une journée dans la rue*, April 1966, pamphlet. Julio Le Parc Archive, Paris

the broad range of ideological paths available in postwar Paris was reinforced by GRAV, which relentlessly pushed art toward a level of social interaction that declared the public to be a co-author and primary collaborator. Le Parc has always been deeply committed to the principle that his art be fully accessible to a public that possesses no formal background in art, which at the time constituted a marked departure from the increasingly elitist direction of the artistic avant-garde operating in the rest of the world. In purely sculptural terms, Le Parc was also the first artist to fully flesh out the spatial possibilities of the electrically illuminated, or *lumière,* option that had been hinted at as far back as the early 1950s, and that would in turn be elaborated on by an entire generation of Le Parc's fellow Argentines, both Paris- and Buenos Aires–based: Perla Benveniste, Boto, Hugo Demarco, Armando Durante, García-Rossi, Eduardo Rodríguez, and Vardánega.

Accordingly, the contribution of Horacio García-Rossi to the genesis and flourishing of Kinetic Art is entwined with his close adolescent friendship with Le Parc. Before migrating to Paris and becoming a co-founder of GRAV — along with François Morellet, Joël Stein, Jean-Pierre Yvaral (Vasarely's son), among others — García-Rossi was producing kinetic-inspired gouaches in the late 1950s,[7] and by 1963 he built his first machine-based box, although it required the viewer to turn its handle. His earliest light boxes, including one from 1965–66 framing his name in luminous block letters, demonstrate a degree of conceptual self-reflexivity, largely because they were made in the wake of Le Parc's, Vardánega's, and Boto's forays into the same stylistic niche. And yet García-Rossi's contribution to Kinetic Art remains distinct, insofar as he successfully employed screens, mirrors, filters, and lenses to consistently distort the source of the illumination and blur the patterns, which would in turn trigger subtle shifts in color, shape, and boundary. Hewing as closely as possible to the iconic shapes of circle, line, and point, García-Rossi developed an internally complex vocabulary of shifting hues and intensities that seem to come from deep within the work's core.

7. It is generally acknowledged that this stylistic shift occurred in response to Vasarely's 1958 exhibition at the Museo Nacional de Bellas Artes.

THE PRECEDING HISTORICAL NARRATIVE closely follows the contours of Popper's own description of the rise of Kinetic Art, published in 1968, and it is hardly surprising that his version strongly supports the implicit premise that in spite of the sheer productivity of kinetic artists working in Germany and Italy, Paris was the movement's incontestable point of origin, just as it had been for all prior stylistic developments during the modern era. Even Kinetic Art's validation as a historical movement has always been implicitly understood as inseparable from its core location in Paris. While there is little point today in debating the accuracy of this reading, contesting it suggests an overview of Kinetic Art that rests on the principle that the achievements of some Latin American artists most identified with the movement might be irrelevant to its articulation as a European phenomenon. It has been taken for granted that Kinetic Art became an international movement only because those artists who played the most significant roles during its years of maximum impact left their various home countries and traveled to Paris, to gather with artistic rebels and visionaries of all nations, forging new ideas and movements together as part of a universal fraternal order of like-minded poets, painters, and intellectuals. Since that scenario did turn out to be more or less true for many of the artists in this exhibition, there is an understandable tendency to make it true for all, when in fact Kinetic Art developed more or less simultaneously in both Europe and South America. Even so, the unique trajectory of each artist's stylistic growth is considerably more nuanced than such an open-ended explanation permits, especially when considered in relation to the variety of events that differentiate how Kinetic Art as a movement played out in the two continents. Most conspicuously, Popper's formulation does not fully consider the case of the iconoclastic Brazilian artist Abraham Palatnik, who in 1951 produced an installation-scaled, illuminated, machine-driven *Kinechromatic Device* for the inaugural São Paulo Biennial, and in so doing paved the way for nearly every light-based kinetic artist who followed, whether in South America or Europe. Nor does Popper's account fully explain the case of Alejandro Otero, who drew his deepest knowledge of artistic practice from many years living in Paris, but realized the scope of those ambitions only on his return to Venezuela, where his reach was smaller but his public was in many ways larger.

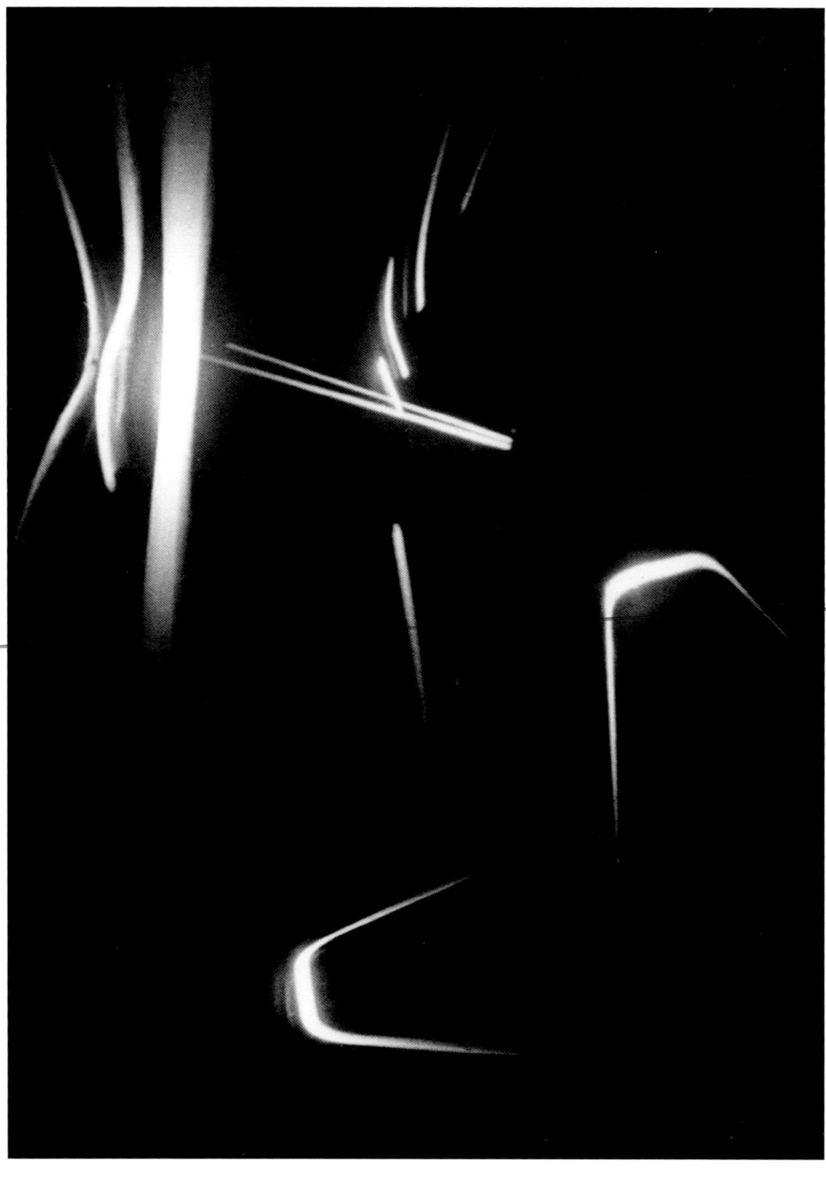

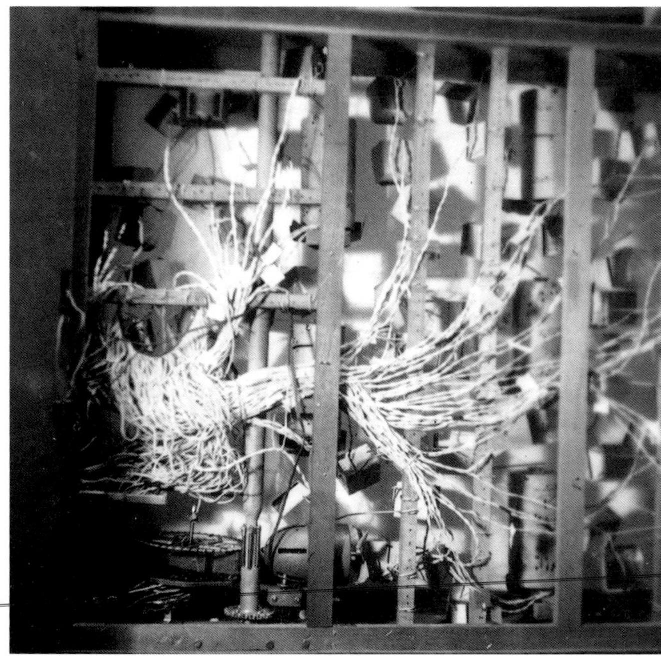

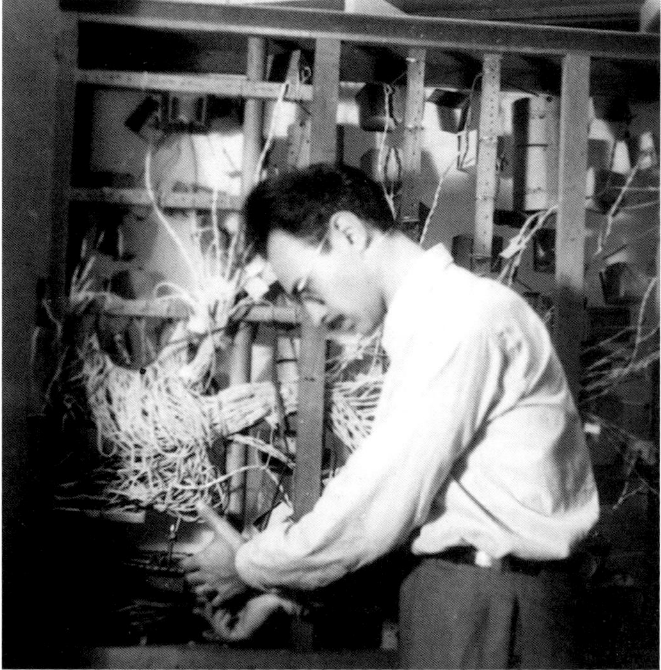

Works by Abraham Palatnik, 1949–50, on view at
the first São Paulo Biennial, above and above right:
Cinecromático; back of *Cinecromático*

Right: Abraham Palatnik with *Cinecromático*

Until now, the Europe–South America artistic interchange has been described almost exclusively as a Paris-Venezuela and Paris-Argentina phenomenon, when in fact the confluence of ideas, events, and artistic advances in Argentina and Venezuela from the mid-1940s onward were increasingly synchronous with developments unfolding in other parts of the world, and in the case of Villanueva's Ciudad Universitaria, a step or two ahead of most. Argentine and Uruguayan abstract painting, particularly examples from Madí and its offshoots, was shown and discussed with some regularity in Paris through the late 1940s and early 1950s, to the extent that Madí-originated ideas about shaped paintings, for example, were soon absorbed into a generalized European discourse about abstraction's more suggestive possibilities. Even though the patronage structures of Argentina and Venezuela could not adequately support the sustained generational transformation that artists from both countries were realizing through their works, that did not make them any less Latin American for persevering with their vision thousands of miles away from their homelands.

To take another step in contesting the conventionally Euro-normative view of Kinetic Art, one need look no further than the vanguard painting and poetry magazine *Arturo*, which in 1944 brought to the foreground one of Argentina's most influential twentieth-century artists, Gyula Kosice (1924–2016). Kosice, who was born near the Czech–Hungarian border and brought to Argentina by his parents at age four, was orphaned at eleven and raised by a bibliophile relative who exposed him at a early age to the art and writings of Leonardo da Vinci. An autodidact not just in art but also in poetry — at which he particularly excelled — Kosice was perpetually attuned to the possibilities of merging artistic and scientific ideals, and his greatest ongoing project, *La ciudad hidroespacial* (The Hydrospatial City) was his consummate expression of a fusion of Da Vinci's own philosophies. Yet, although he was co-founder of *Arturo* as well as an active member of both the Arte Concreto-Invención group and Madí — the latter continued to flourish despite Kosice's rancorous falling out with founder Carmelo Arden Quin a few years later — Kosice's influence on Kinetic Art has never been properly evaluated.

There are various reasons that the name Gyula Kosice might be largely unfamiliar to most visitors to an exhibition of Latin American Kinetic Art in the U.S. Despite extended visits to Paris in 1957–58 and 1962, and a year-long sojourn, by himself, in New York in 1965, Kosice remained very much a lifelong resident of Buenos Aires. With a growing family and a relatively secure national reputation, Kosice, despite ambitions to be recognized at the international level, stayed very much part of a local scene, where his work remained relatively obscure. Unfortunately, Kosice's absence from most histories of Kinetic Art published after Popper's is explicable less as an oversight than as an intentional relegation to the margins of inconvenient information. Granted, Kosice's deep interest in hydraulics, his insistence on spending decades in pursuit of a single theme, and his irascible temperament — combined with the gradual shift in art-world fashion away from Kinetic Art in the 1970s and the political isolation of Argentina during the 1976–81 military dictatorship — helped shrink Kosice's stature from an acknowledged pioneer of Latin American Kinetic Art to someone whose achievements are recalled mostly by specialists in the field. Setting Kosice's role aside further obscured the deep points of connection between his achievements and those of Le Parc or Vardánega, and between Kosice and other Latin American artists such as Abraham Palatnik, the Romanian-born Cuban artist Sandu Darié, or even the Chilean kinetic artist Matilde Pérez, who worked in a studio alongside Le Parc's for an extended period in the early 1960s, and then returned to Santiago to develop her own brand of Kinetic Art in relative isolation for the next fifty years.

The careers of these artists, considered in isolation, seem to be the exception to the rule, but taken as a whole they are as vital to the history of Kinetic Art as the stories of those artists whose names are incontestably associated with the movement's greatest achievements, such as Cruz-Diez, Le Parc, and Soto. The case of Palatnik, in this regard, is revelatory. His participation in the São Paulo Biennial was confirmed only at the last minute, arranged by his friend Mario Pedrosa, the curator, following the cancellation of a group of Japanese artists. Palatnik was further undercut because biennial officials, convinced that his contribution was neither painting nor sculpture,

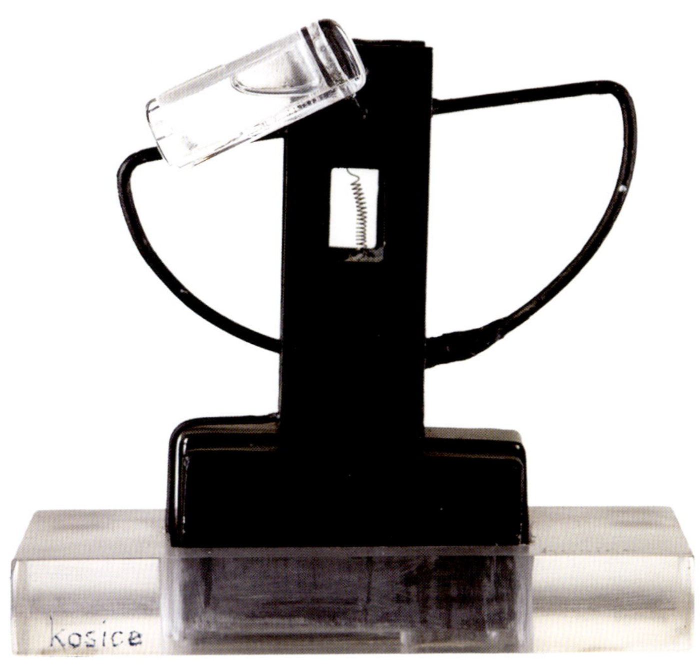

Gyula Kosice, *Una gota de agua acunada a toda velocidad*, 1946.
Plexiglas, water, and movement, 4 ¾ x 3 ⅞ x 2 ¼ in. (12 x 10 x 6 cm).
Centre Pompidou Collection

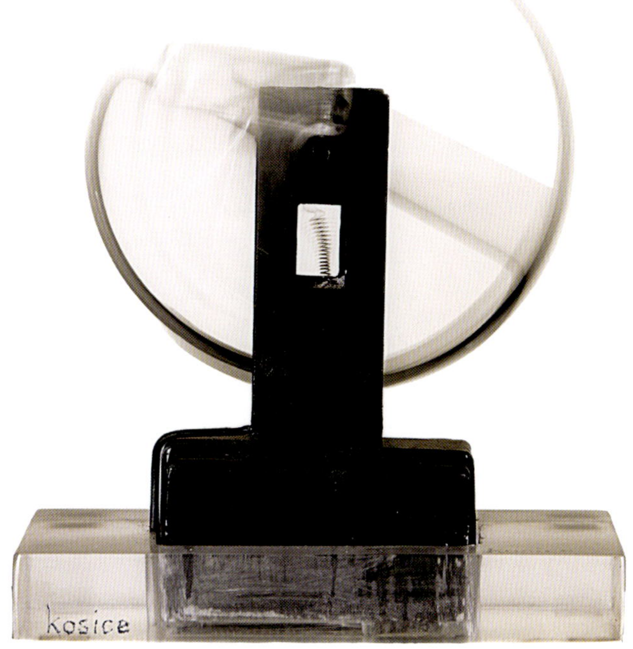

simply excluded it from the catalogue, even though it won a handful of international jury awards. In a further irony, the obscurity of his historic accomplishment trailed him for a time, since he did not fully perfect the workings of his portable *Kinechromatic Devices* until some years after the biennial. Furthermore, like many of the other kinetic artists, Palatnik had a strong penchant for creating non-kinetic work, as well as kinetic work unrelated to *Kinechromatic Devices*, and his oeuvre includes a wide cross-section of electric mobiles that are much closer in spirit to the whimsical playfulness of a Calder than to the enigmatic shadows and biomorphic shapes that emanate from his shadow-boxes. In some ways, Palatnik's greatest achievement has been his success working in an artistic context in which his practice was unquestionably sui generis. The very core of Brazil's artistic development from the 1950s onward lay in fully reconstituting European movements and tendencies using characteristically local elements, which does not occur in Palatnik's output. He has never lacked for a loyal following, especially among younger artists captivated by his seeming autonomy from the vicissitudes of artistic taste, but neither has his example spawned a successor. In that sense, Palatnik is one of Latin American Kinetic Art's first real trailblazers, and possibly its greatest iconoclast.

Another point that becomes clear in hindsight is that in the wake of *The Responsive Eye*, most U.S. interest in Latin American art centered on a loosely expressionist model of making art. Typical of these is *The Emergent Decade* (1966), a survey of the art of Latin American countries that was also an institutional collaboration between Cornell University and the Guggenheim Museum, with Thomas Messer serving as curator. Of fifty-five artists whose works are illustrated in the *Emergent Decade* exhibition catalogue, an overwhelming majority produced work in a loose, brushy style derived to varying degrees from Expressionism, Surrealism, Primitivism, and/or folk art. Soto is the only bona fide kinetic artist to have made the cut, and only in a section devoted to expats in Paris. The same year, the University Art Museum at Berkeley presented *Directions in Kinetic Sculpture*, with Peter Selz as curator of what was billed as the first U.S. survey of the subject. None of the participating artists in Selz's survey was from Latin America, but considerable effort was spent linking Americans like Fletcher Benton, Robert Breer, Len Lye, and George Rickey to their European contemporaries and immediate predecessors: Pol Bury, Gianni Colombo, Takis, and Jean Tinguely. In view of these examples, it is clear that to the degree a renewed conversation about Kinetic Art can be situated relative to the U.S. art world of the 1960s, it was strictly conceived of as taking place between Western Europe and the rest of the world, with North and South America as distant bystanders.

In short, at the precise historical moment when the artists included in *Kinesthesia* were at the height of their creative powers, and just as the example set by *The Responsive Eye* — which had after all included Carlos Cruz-Diez, Luis Tomasello, and GRAV— had begun to reverberate through the museum and critical establishment, one major U.S. museum hosted an exhibition about contemporary South American painting that downplayed its kinetic component to the point of near invisibility, while another major U.S. museum exhibition about Kinetic Art completely excluded Latin American artists. How might such a dramatic informational lacuna have occurred? The likely answer in Messer's case is twofold: he saw the art his handlers wished him to see on his research trips and made his selections accordingly; and he was likely uncomfortable with Latin American art that didn't conform with established stylistic categories in the U.S. Selz's starting premise was probably narrower to begin with: a scholar of German Expressionism, he apparently considered first those European examples of Kinetic Art closest to his field of vision — his prioritizing German over French artists bears that out — and then grafted on a hodgepodge of artists from his adopted country, none of whom turned out to be a major figure. At the very least, it can be presumed that little incentive existed for either museum to seriously research either Kinetic Art or recent Latin American artistic developments, even though by 1966, Denise René had already presented solo exhibitions of Boto, Kosice, Soto, Vardánega, and Tomasello in her Paris gallery; and that summer, Julio Le Parc would win the Golden Lion at the Venice Biennial, to be followed by another kinetic artist, Nicolas Schöffer, in 1968.

The overall reluctance of the American art world to embrace Kinetic Art during its heyday, while related to its Parisian and South American roots, also appears to have been pragmatic. After Calder, relatively few artists in the U.S. were directly employing movement in their work, and those who did tended to find themselves relegated to the outer fringes of the art world. Of the six Americans that Selz included in his 1966 exhibition, four stopped making kinetic works within a few years of the exhibition, and only Rickey continue to occupy a niche in American art history for having dedicated his professional career to concealing motorized infrastructures that animated his otherwise conventional welded steel sculptures. In fact, an odd but uncontested reality of twentieth-century American art is that despite fervent celebration by mass culture of all things new and technological, the incorporation of motorized movement and/or light has never been a prominent feature of American sculpture. Even those artists based in the U.S., from Nam June Paik in the 1970s and 1980s to Jennifer Steinkamp or Leo Villareal in our own era, who have gleefully exploited the metamorphic visual potential of new digital technologies, have tended to do so in the service of their imagery, not as a means of questioning the visual authority of the object itself. For better or worse, the U.S. never produced the equivalent of a Schöffer (1912–1992), the Hungarian-born sculptor who moved to Paris in 1936 and dazzled the art world with experiments using the spatial dynamics of light and color, eventually producing room-scale installations of whirling machines whose movements were captured on continuous video feeds.[8] While such artists as Robert Whitman experimented with multiple projections, and Andy Warhol's *Exploding Plastic Inevitable* (1966–67) transformed the Happening into a sound and light spectacle, the closest American art ever came to a Schöffer was the Danish-born inventor-artist

8. Nicolas Schöffer was the subject of numerous monographs published during his lifetime, including a book published in 1963 by Éditions du Griffon in Switzerland as part of the series *The Sculpture of the Twentieth Century.*

Thomas Wilfred (1889–1968). His *Lumia* projections were written about admiringly as far back as 1922 by László Moholy-Nagy, and he showed at MoMA alongside Pollock and Rothko in Dorothy Miller's 1952 *Fifteen Americans* exhibition. Despite MoMA's commission of the large-scale work *Lumia Suite, Op. 158* in 1964 for long-term display in the museum's lobby and a survey exhibition devoted to Wilfred in 1971,[9] his work passed into obscurity soon after his death, until American director Terrence Malick included passages of it in the opening and closing scenes of his 2011 film *Tree of Life*.

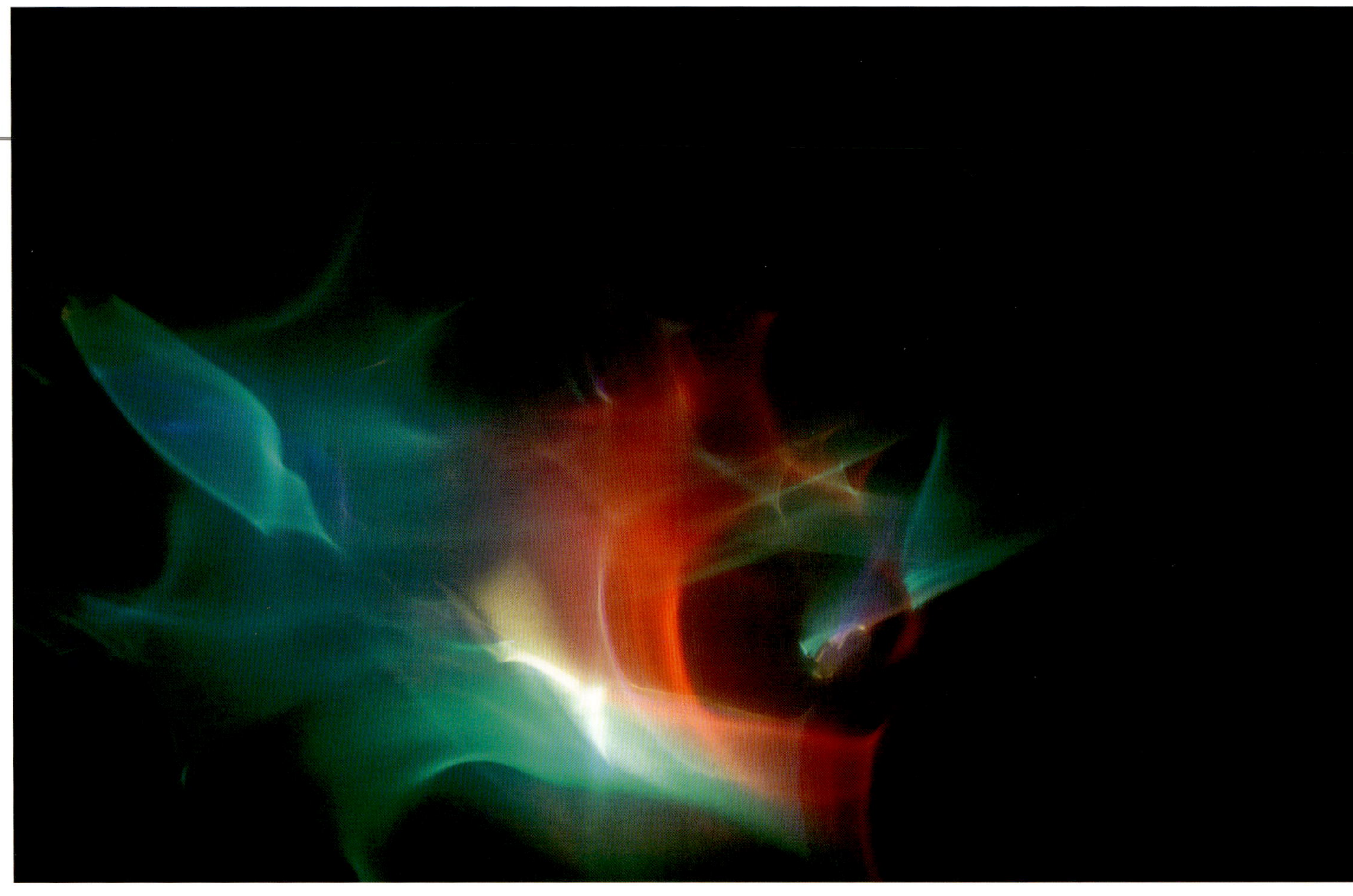

Thomas Wilfred, *Lumia Suite, Op. 158*, 1963–64. Projectors, reflector unit, electrical and lighting elements, and a projection screen. Museum of Modern Art, New York, Mrs. Simon Guggenheim Fund, 582.1964

9. MoMA's August 9, 1971, press release for the exhibition described Wilfred as "the first artist of this century to use light as the sole means of expression."

The case of Thomas Wilfred provides an unexpected point of connection between Latin American Kinetic Art from the mid-1950s through the late 1960s and West Coast Light and Space art of the late 1960 and 1970s. One future artist who saw Wilfred's work in MoMA as a boy was the Light and Space pioneer James Turrell, who years later recalled being fascinated by the work's combination of engineering gadgetry and high-minded aesthetics. Setting aside such paeans, however, Wilfred's career serves just as easily as a cautionary tale: although he was championed after years of struggle by such discerning patrons as Miller and Katherine Dreier, Wilfred left New York City shortly after World War II and settled in West Nyack, where he worked in relative isolation for the last two decades of his life. Despite his late-career embrace by Howard Wise, the visionary dealer in electronic art, there was little critical or curatorial enthusiasm for Wilfred's work after he died, presumably because it had never been accepted as art by the art market, which tended to favor oil paintings and cast-metal sculptures rather than opaque black boxes that blinked and flashed when their buttons were pushed and could be repaired by any competent electrician. The paradigm shift in art's materiality that Wilfred's work implies was likely a step too far for the New York market — a situation not unlike that faced by a generation of Southern California artists a few years later.

It was suggested at the outset of this essay that the works in *Kinesthesia* might have something meaningful to express to the inhabitants of our time and place, and that conjecture is at least partly intended as a reference to the emergence of the Light and Space movement in Southern California in the 1960s and 1970s, just as the heyday of Kinetic Art was winding down several thousand miles away. Just as the international acceptance of the importance of Light and Space has emerged only over the past two decades, its gestation as a movement reflected the ongoing struggle that the movement's pioneers experienced in their efforts to attract national attention to their collective achievements, or at the very least a recognition of the geographical and cultural particularities of Southern California that fed these artists' creative evolution. The work of Turrell and Irwin, certainly, but also Craig Kaufmann, Eric Orr, DeWain Valentine, and Doug Wheeler successfully challenged the material limits and perceptual boundaries of sculpture in ways that baffled a broad swath of East Coast viewers, while consolidating regional artistic principles set in motion in the 1950s by such abstract painters as Frederick Hammersley and John McLaughlin. In this way, with New York's general indifference as its backdrop, Southern California's first truly international style was birthed.

Since the advent of a globalist paradigm for considering the history of twentieth-century art, conventional ideas of historical succession and influence are beginning to be understood more fluidly. Antecedents sometimes come to light long after the fact, and connections that might appear abundantly clear in retrospect may not have seemed anything of the sort at the time. This seems the best way of framing any discussion of a relationship between Latin American kinetic artists of the 1950s and 1960s and the surge of interest in light as both material and subject in the Light and Space generation. Just as Thomas Wilfred with his *Lumia* in New York almost certainly had no direct influence on his younger contemporaries Gyula Kosice in Buenos Aires or Abraham Palatnik in Rio de Janeiro, it is worth considering the premise that in the mid-1960s, almost nobody in Los Angeles would have been paying close attention to the program at Instituto Di Tella in Buenos Aires, the Galeria Bonino in New York, or even Galerie Denise René in Paris. Even after Julio Le Parc's Golden Lion award at the 1966 Venice Biennial and a lifetime of accolades, a full fifty years would pass before a museum in the U.S. — the Pérez Art Museum Miami — would give him a one-person exhibition, and very few significant examples of Le Parc's work have been shown on the West Coast. Despite the likelihood that such resemblances are little more than coincidence, it is worth considering how, with the advent of Thomas Wilfred's first luminous inventions and Naum Gabo's spinning machines, a trajectory of high-tech artistic creativity was launched that would help define the middle years of the century until the digital age swept the 1970s and stunned any visionary remnants of the analog age into a protracted spell of suspended animation.

What Latin American Kinetic Art of the 1950s and 1960s is capable of articulating for a twenty-first-century public is the shared desire to understand how our imaginations have always been transported by the elementary combination of movement, color, and light. We are so accustomed to experiencing the manipulation of visual imagery through the use of digital tools whose workings we don't need to grasp that the elaborate manual transformation of mechanical and optical parts that went into producing Kinetic Art's abstract visual sensations seems nearly as distant and primordial to us as cave paintings viewed by a campfire's light. The ghostly forms and shifting palettes that we experience through the *Kinesthesia* artists operate as a coded message sent to us by our analog forebears, who after all had no awareness of the boundary-less realm of digital information storage that was about to burst open the world. They achieved, through a fusion of private invention and traditional techniques, a hybrid state of feeling in which the humming and blinking machines all around us seem to be like other species, attempting to communicate sublime messages if only we could break through the barrier that prevents us from understanding them. The realm of mechanization, which loomed large in art's background for much of the twentieth century, might seem impoverished and hokey when held up alongside the visceral clarity, speed, and intensity with which today's screens and projections can whisk us to other worlds. But there is nothing that inspires a reconsideration of the archaic tools and formulas of the recent past quite like the realization that the most sophisticated digital visualizing tools in the world cannot compare to witnessing the remarkable visions that may be conjured through the precise use of a simple motor, a single colored light bulb, and a translucent screen just thick enough to camouflage the moving parts and frame the flickering shadows.

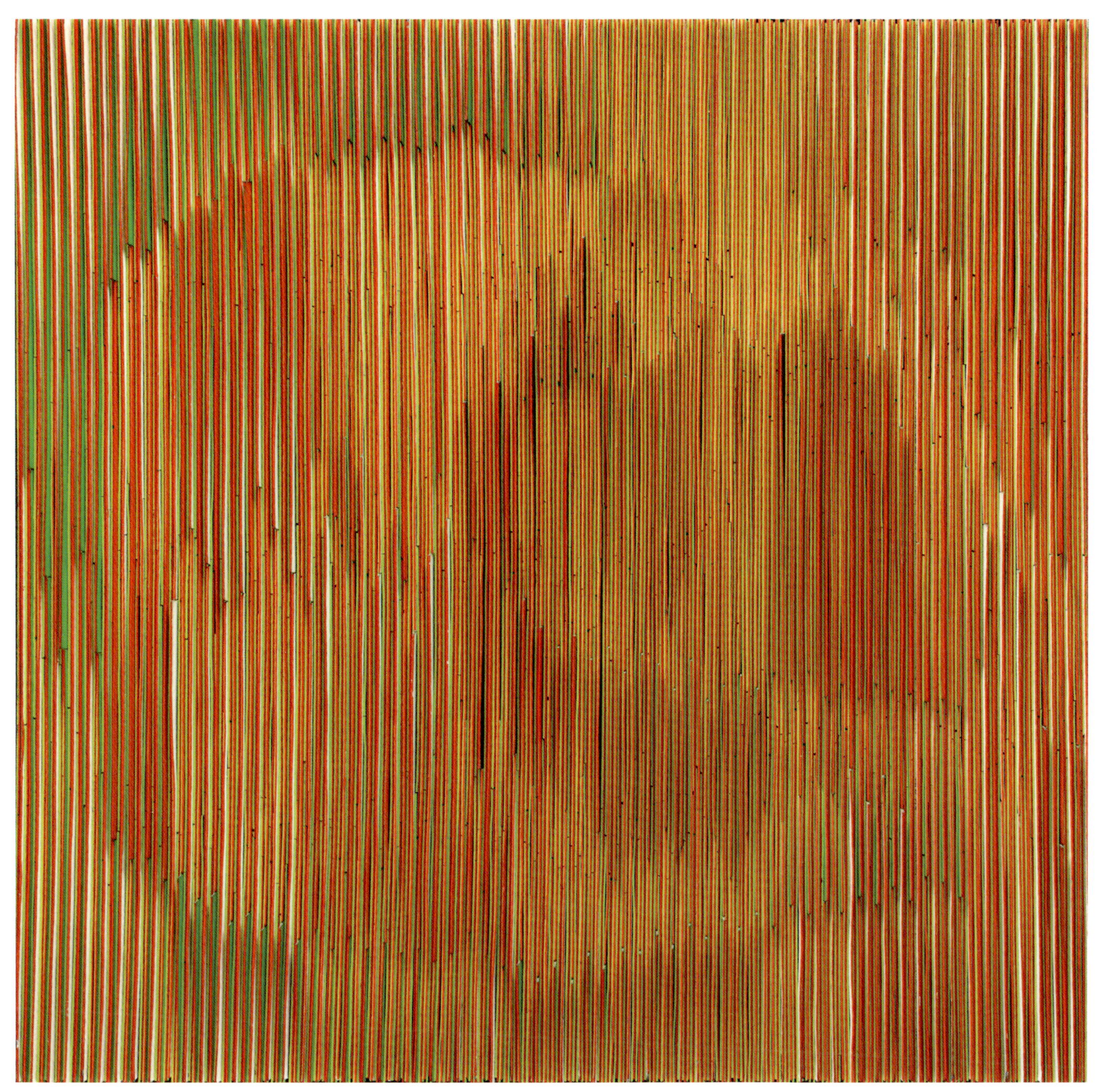

CARLOS CRUZ-DIEZ   *Physichromie 48*, 1961
Cardboard (Celloderme), casein (Plaka) mounted on plywood with
painted wood frame and aluminum strip frame, 35 ¾ × 35 ¾ × 2 in. (90.8 × 90.8 × 5.1 cm)
The Museum of Fine Arts, Houston. Museum purchase funded
by the 2005 Latin American Experience Gala and Auction, 2005.322

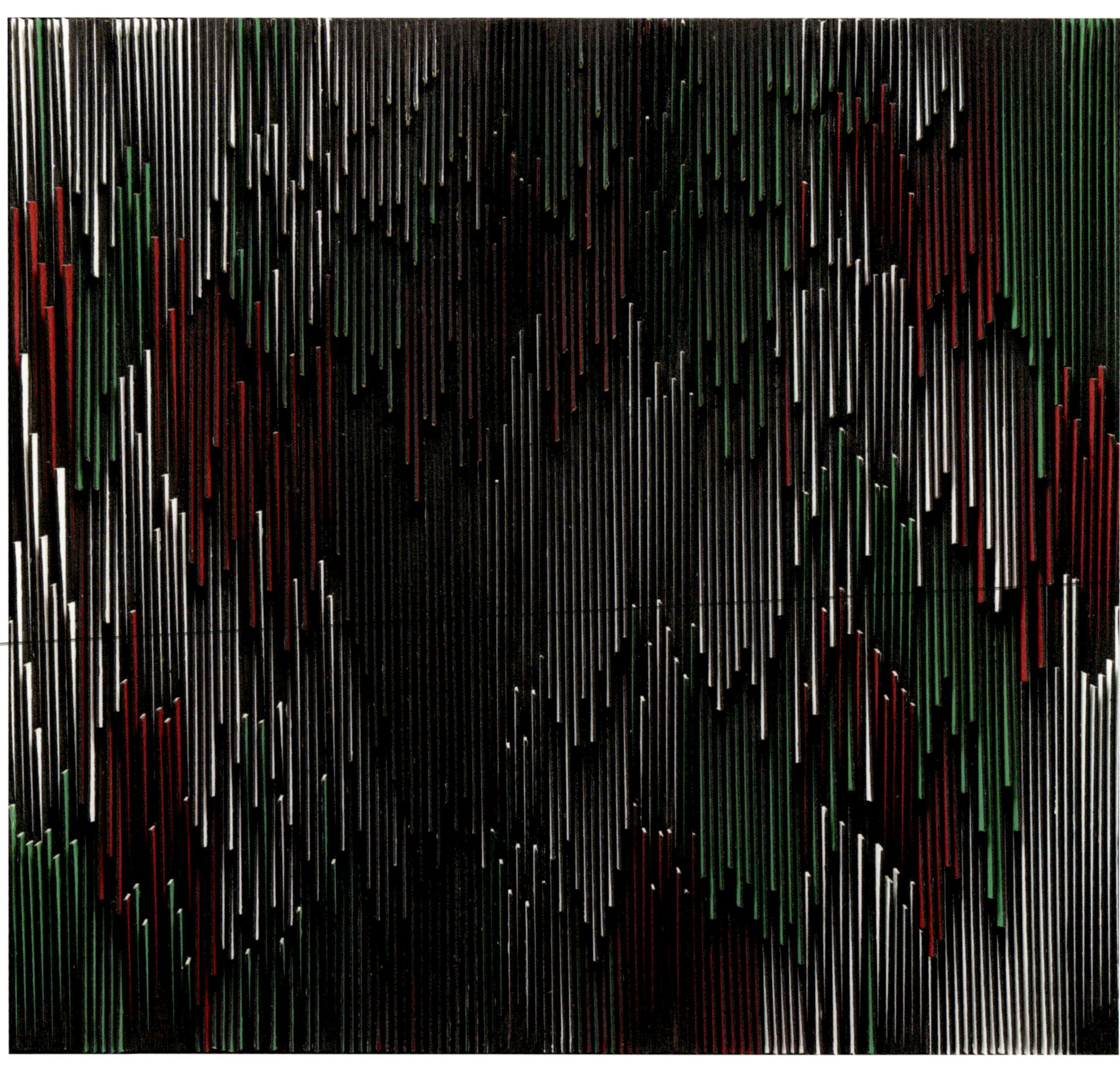

CARLOS CRUZ-DIEZ *Physichromie 23*, 1961
Cardboard, casein (Plaka) on plywood inserted in wood with aluminum strip frame, 26 × 27 ¾ in. (66 × 70.5 cm)
The Museum of Fine Arts, Houston. Museum purchase funded by the
2005 Latin American Experience Gala and Auction, 2005.323

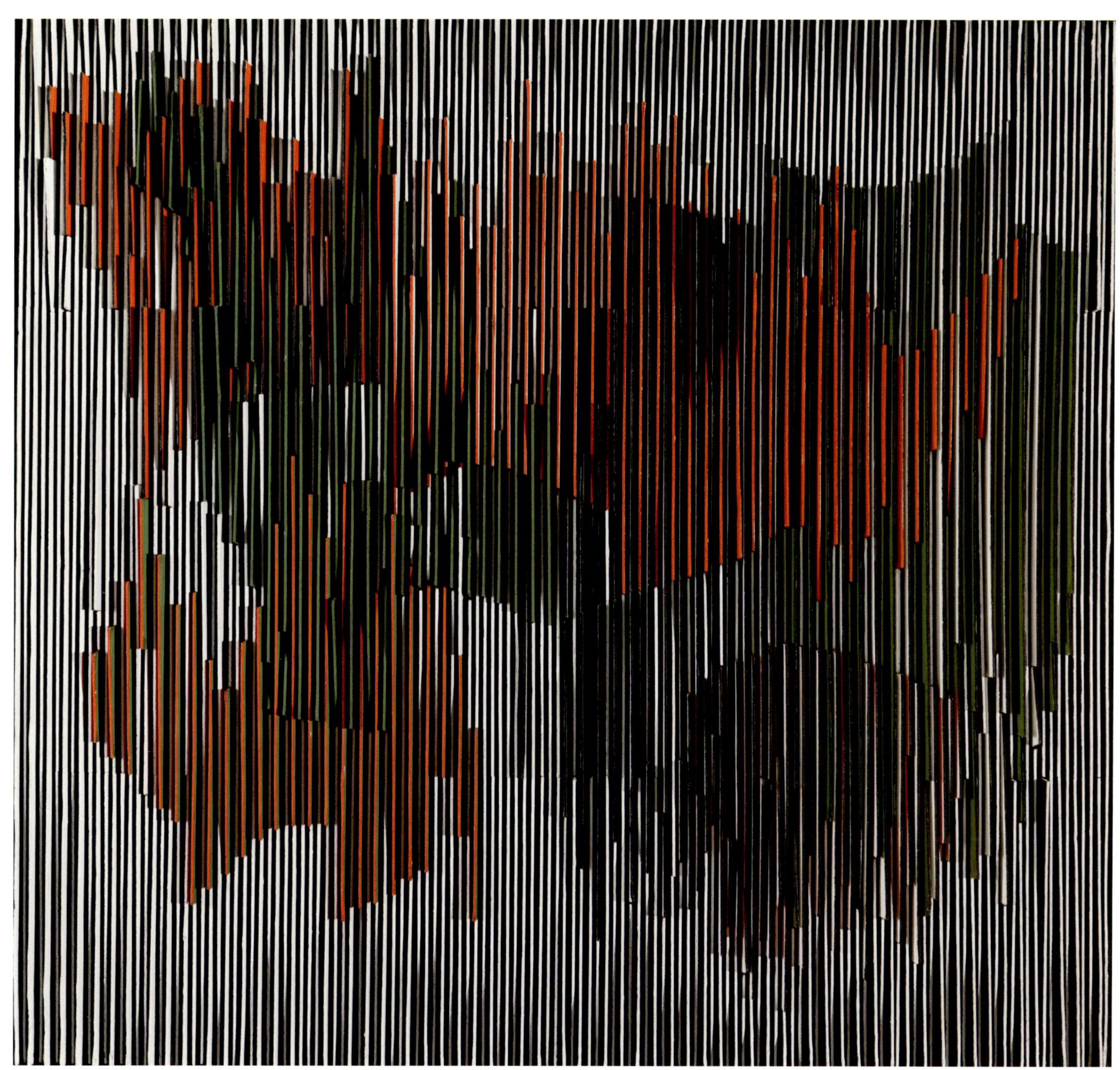

CARLOS CRUZ-DIEZ *Physichromie 21*, 1960
Casein on plywood and cardboard, 40 ⅝ × 41 ⅞ × 2 ½ in. (103.3 × 106.4 × 6.5 cm)
Colección Patricia Phelps de Cisneros. Promised gift to The Museum of Modern Art through
the Latin American and Caribbean Fund

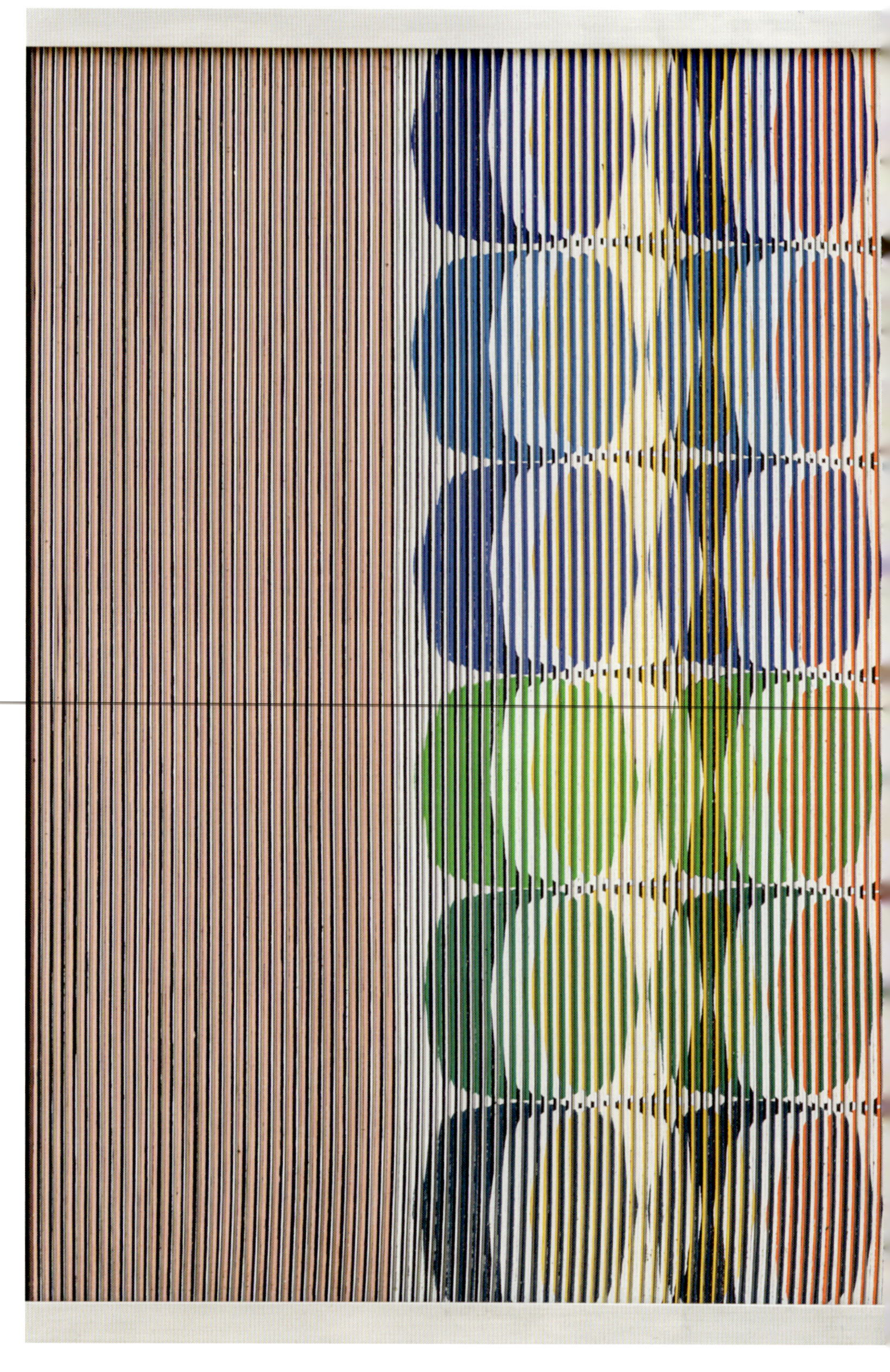

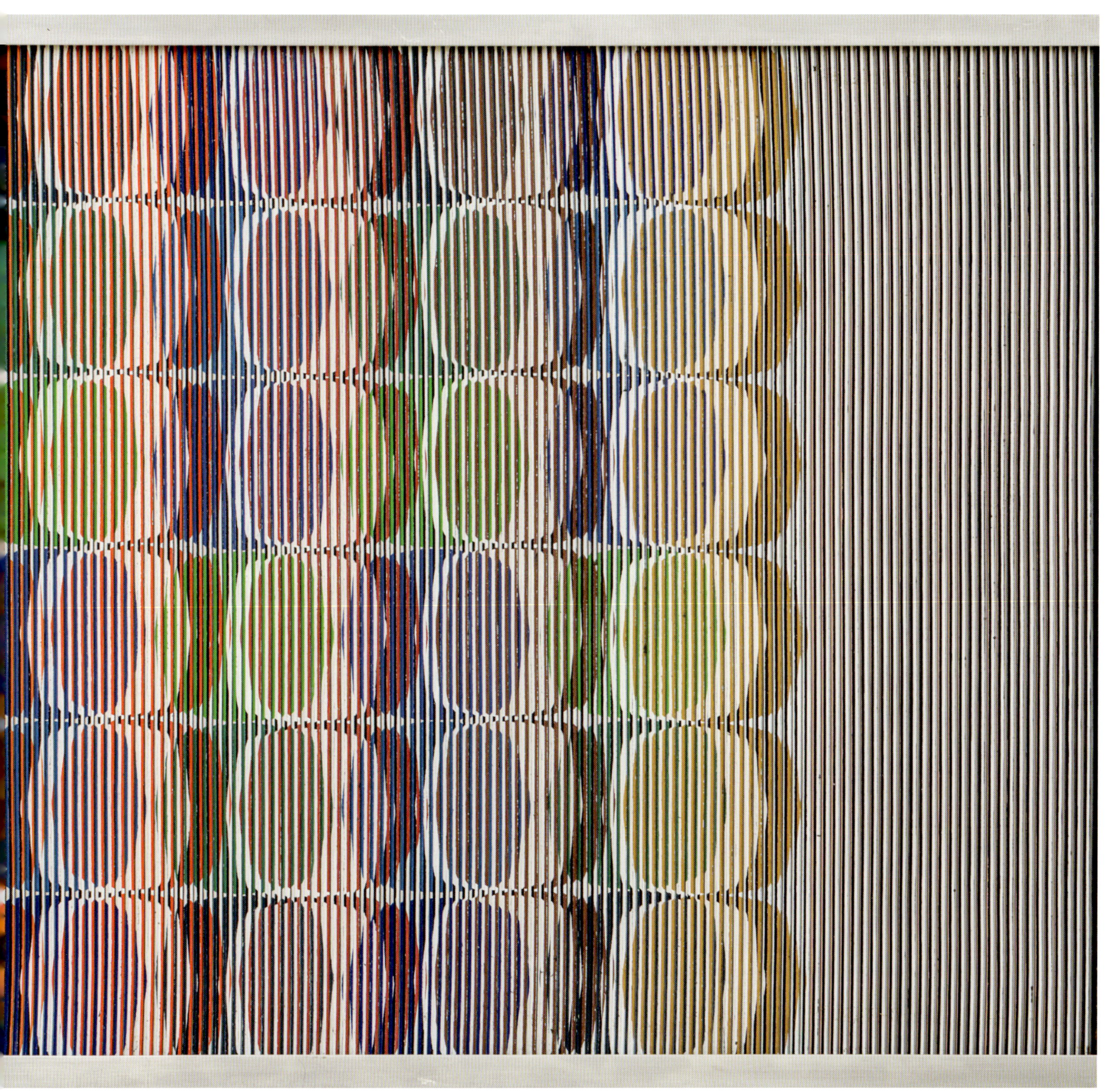

CARLOS CRUZ-DIEZ *Physichromie 228*, 1966
Cardboard, casein, PVC inserts (in replacement of cellulose acetate) mounted on plywood
with aluminum strip frame, 23 ⅝ × 39 ⅜ in. (60 × 100 cm)
Collection of Don and Martha Freedman, Houston. Courtesy of Sicardi Gallery, Houston

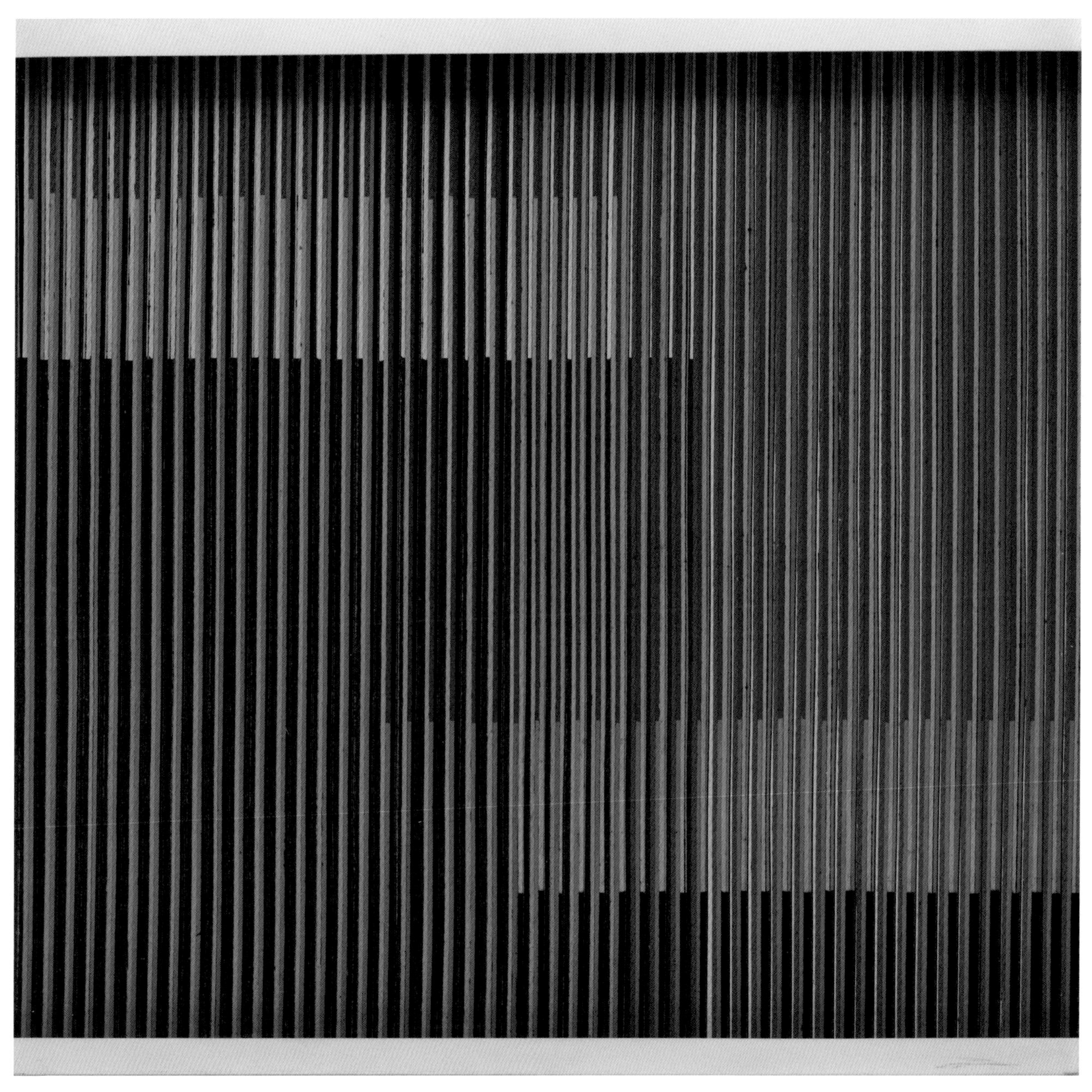

CARLOS CRUZ–DIEZ *Physichromie 261*, 1966
Acetate sheets and painting on PVC, 12 × 12 × 1 ¾ in. (30.5 × 30.5 × 4.3 cm)
Colección Patricia Phelps de Cisneros

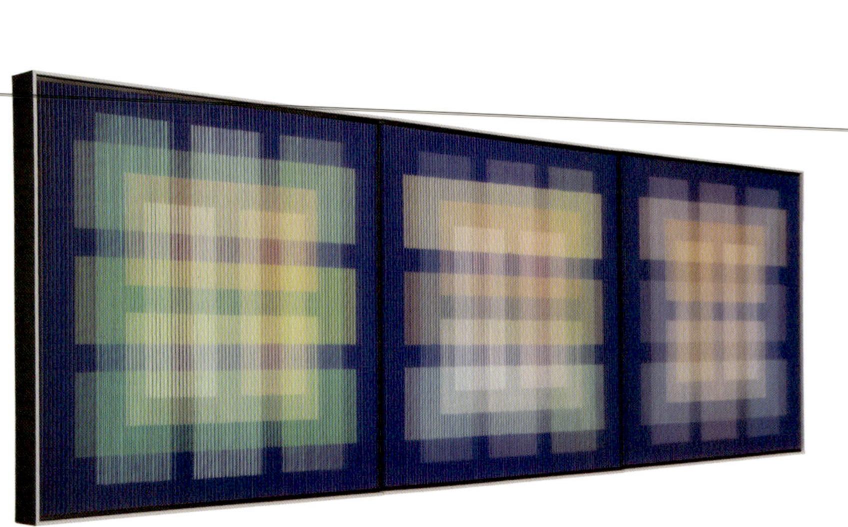

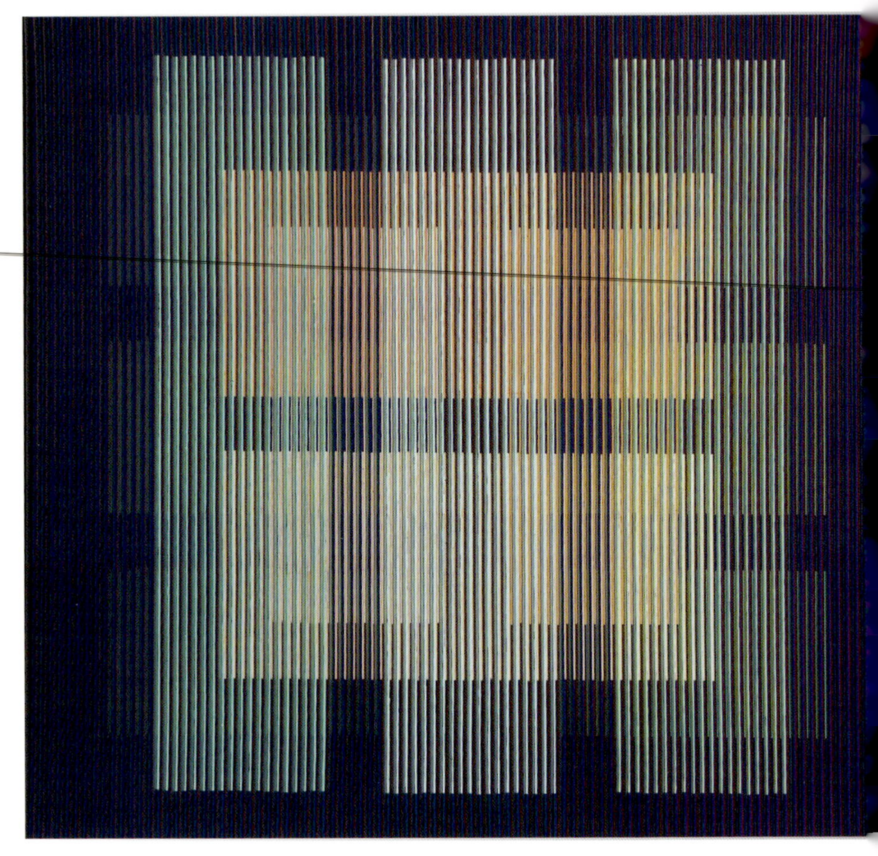

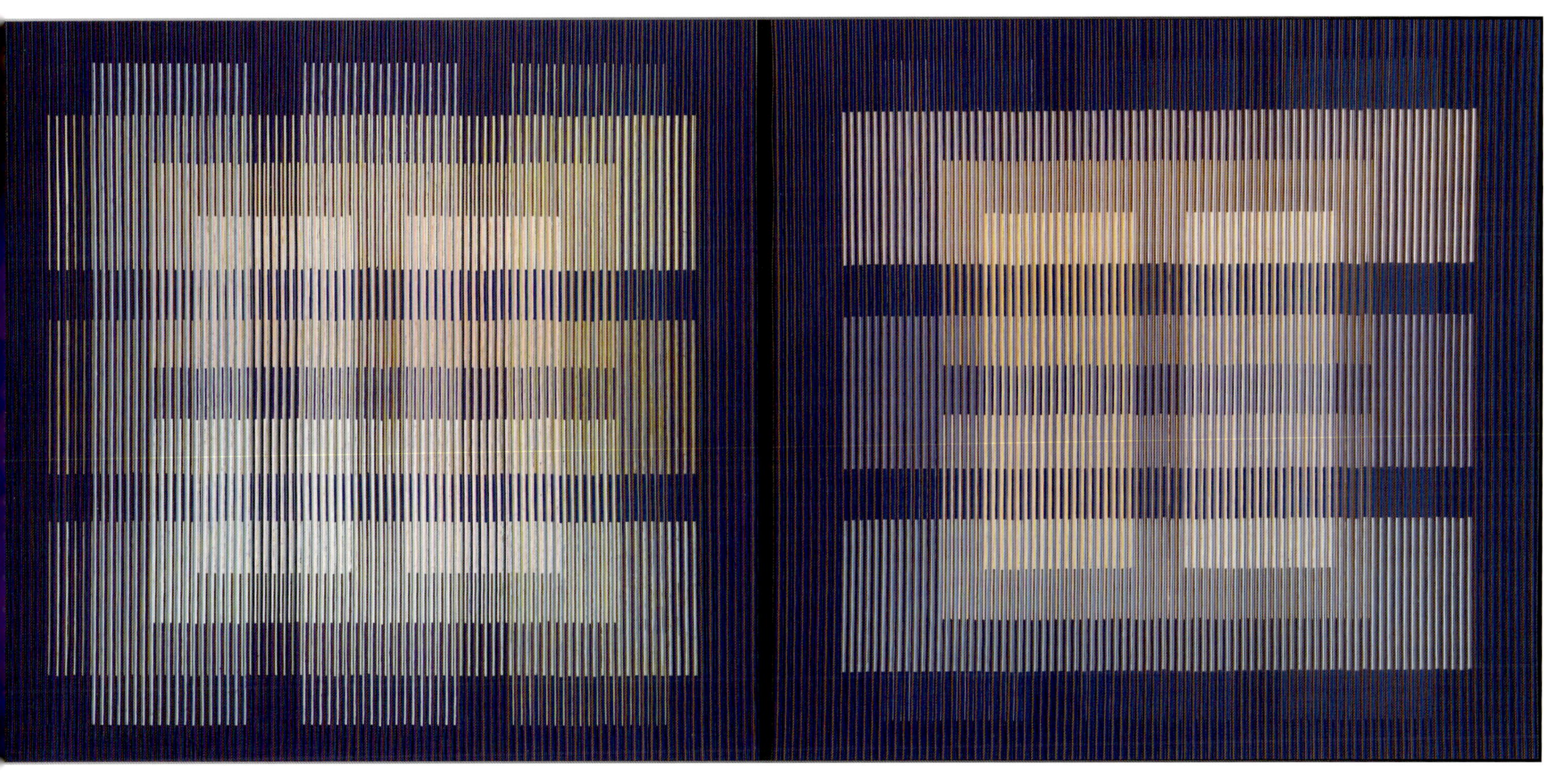

CARLOS CRUZ-DIEZ   *Physichromie 402*, 1968
Three units bolted together. Cardboard (Celloderme), casein (Plaka), sandblasted plastic inserts
mounted on wood with white plastic strip frame, 28 ½ × 73 ⅝ in. (72.2 × 187 cm)
Collection of Mary and Tom Lile, Houston. Courtesy of Sicardi Gallery, Houston

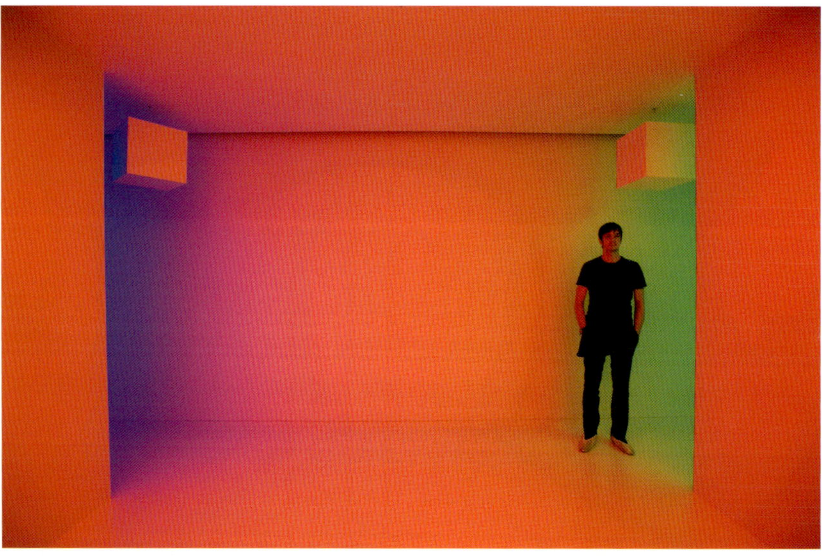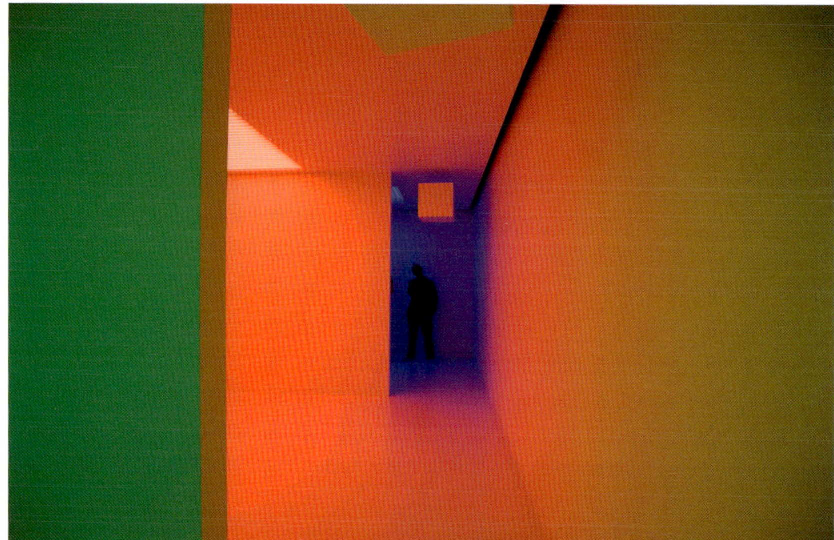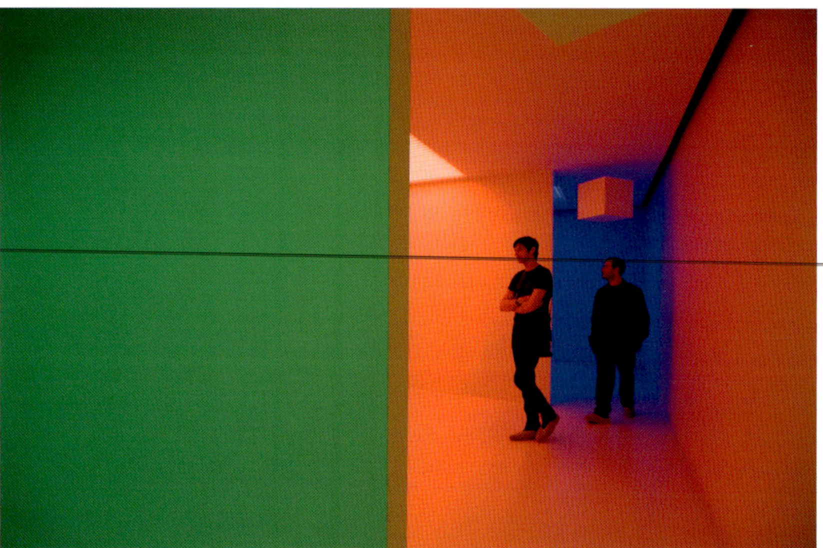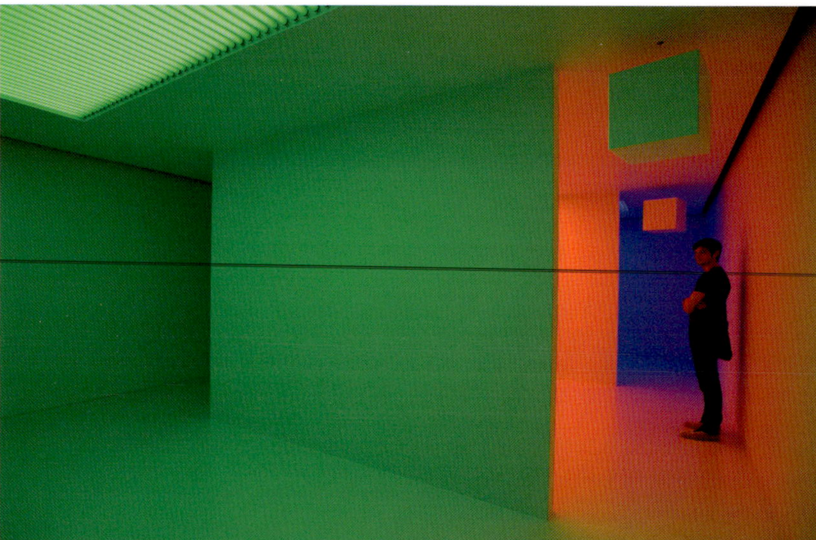

Opposite: CARLOS CRUZ-DIEZ, *Chromosaturation*, 1965/2010. Installation view from the exhibition *Suprasensorial: Experiments in Light, Color, and Space*, The Geffen Contemporary at The Museum of Contemporary Art, Los Angeles, December 12, 2010–February 27, 2011 Collection of The Museum of Contemporary Art, Los Angeles, and Hirshhorn Museum and Sculpture Garden, Washington, D.C.

Above: Installation views from the exhibition *(In)formed by Color* at Americas Society Visual Arts Gallery, New York, September 10–December 13, 2008

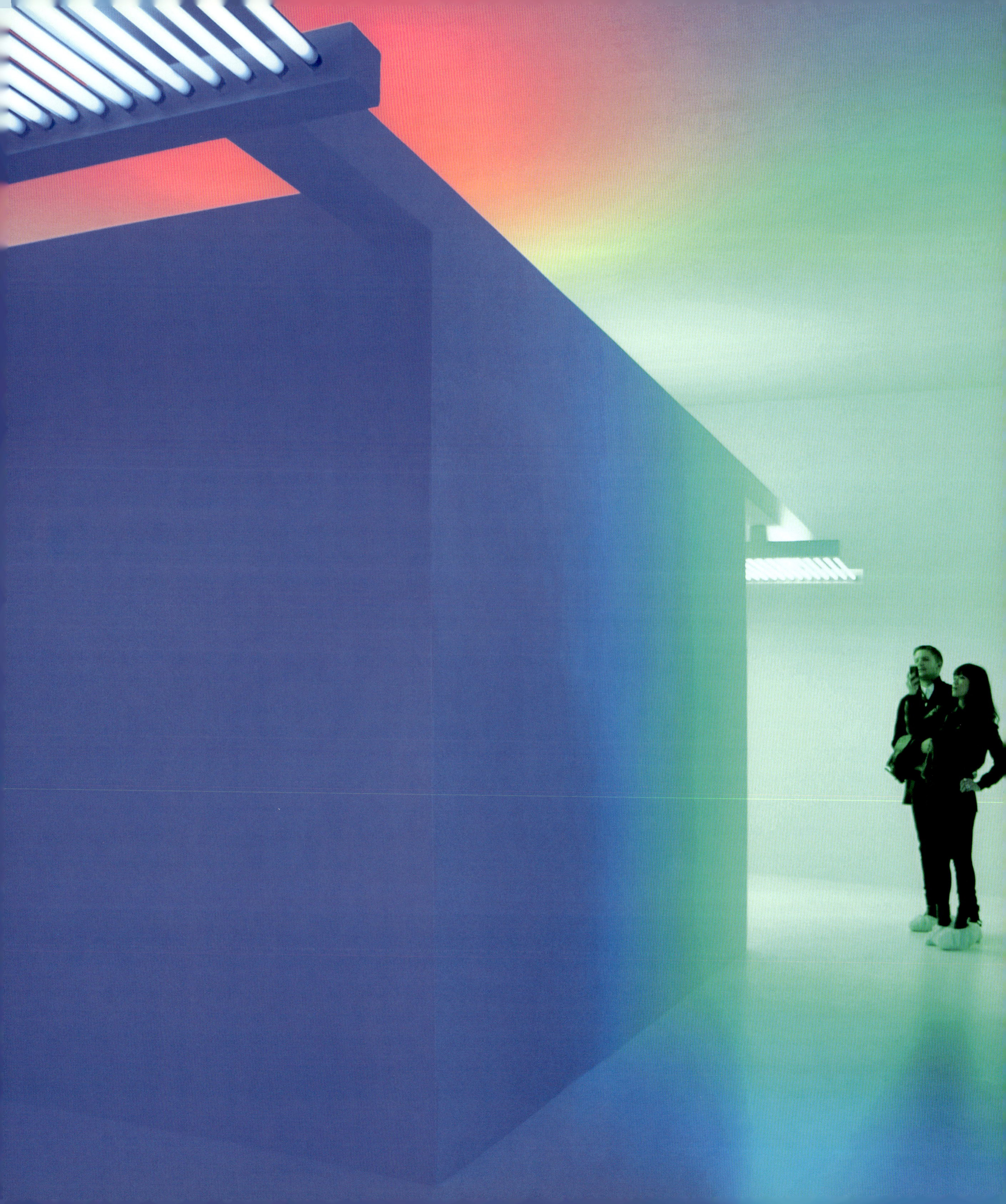

INVENTION AND MOVEMENT

Cristina Rossi

1. The rejection of Tomás Maldonado's neo-Cubist rendering of a model who posed in his first-year class provided a starting point for the student rebellion. For more information, see Cristina Rossi, "Escritos y testimonios: El caso del Manifiesto de cuatro jóvenes." Consulted June 2016 at http://sedici.unlp.edu.ar/bitstream/handle/10915/38786/Documento_completo.pdf?sequence=1.

THE ARGENTINE ARTISTS WHO SET ABOUT exploring optical-kinetic art in the late 1950s followed in the footsteps of previous responses to the Concrete Art movement from the Río de la Plata region. The need to break with the canon of "representational" figuration and establish a paradigm for a new, inventive, "presentational" and autonomous language required this avant-garde movement arising in the 1940s to employ every means possible. From the initial steps that eventually led to the creation of the Concrete Art groups, these young artists made their intentions and assertions known through manifestos, articles, lectures, and pamphlets. Afterward, when conditions in postwar Europe allowed them to travel there and become directly acquainted with modern art, many of them sought to put their experiences to the test by visiting museums as well as the studios of artists influenced by the various avant-garde movements that arose in the early twentieth century.

It is our intention to trace both in the works and in the oral and written discourse of the avant-garde Concrete Art movement the tracks of their commitment to break with traditional forms and to incorporate virtual or real movement. Furthermore, we will analyze testimonies and documents from the 1950s that bear witness to the exchanges between the European artists who fomented an interest in destabilizing the gaze, orienting it toward a new type of art that sought to open up on to a cosmic space and incorporate optical and kinetic effects.

A DECISIVE BREAK

One of the first texts that reflected the desire for a break with the past surfaced in Buenos Aires, specifically at an art school that not only required its students to practice drawing by copying plaster models but also rejected any interpretations of an avant-garde nature.[1] Conversely, in Montevideo, the teachings of Joaquín Torres-García were opposed to this method of imitation and instead promoted a form of constructive art supported by structure and symbols, as the synthesis of an idea.

MANIFIESTO DE CUATRO JOVENES

En nosotros, hoy, sólo está la pasión y el verbo: la obra no existe, no puede existir todavía. No nos pidais que mostremos la creación como precio de nuestro atrevimiento. Esa es una añeja táctica para acobardarnos; pero en esta ocasión nada logra, pues es mas fuerte el *deseo de decir la verdad* que el *temor de ser* acusados por los picapedreros del arte argentino. Por el momento, solo exigimos; nada podemos dar porque nada tenemos: estamos en la edad desnuda de nuestras vidas, quizás las mas propicias para exigir sin ofrecer. Venimos a decir que los que tengan que irse que se vayan, a obligar a suicidarse a los señores de la "panza moral", del centimetro y del Haber.

La osadia de los filisteos en arte ha llegado al colmo este año al reconocer como máximo talento pictorico oficial al Agakhan de los mediocres. Sin embargo, no es precisamente el destino que se le pueda dar a esos calmantes estomacales lo que nos preocupa; no venimos a defender ningun estomago. Por el contrario creemos con Cocteau que la unica cosa de que puede uno enorgullecerse es de haber hecho la obra de tal modo que nadie pueda pensar en concedernos una recompensa oficial. Lo que verdaderamente nos rebela es la existencia del tipo cretino y tartufo en arte, es la orientación artistica que pretenden imponer estos señores al consagrarse a sí mismos.

Y acusamos de indignidad a los "vanguardistas" participantes del jurado que, al no renunciar como les correspondia, se hicieron solidarios a las resoluciones de la crápula artistica; acusamos tambien a todos los pintores vanguardistas de la pasada generación por haber traicionado las inquietudes de sus primeras épocas, de aceptar hoy complacientes los sillones y las cátedras, de estrangular, en suma, las ilusiones de una juventud, quizás demasiado crèdula, que tuvo fè en ellos. Y si hay todavia alguno no del todo manchado, sepa que la juventud espera al artista de conducta insobornable para àyudarlo a quebrar todos los limites

JORGE BRITO — CLAUDIO GIROLA
TOMAS MALDONADO — ALFREDO HLITO

"Es necesario suprimir a los imbéciles en el arte"
CARLO CARRÁ

Jorge Brito, Claudio Girola, Alfredo Hlito, and Tomás Maldonado, "Manifiesto de cuatro jóvenes," 1942

In Europe, Torres-García had encountered such artists as Theo van Doesburg, Piet Mondrian, and Georges Vantongerloo, and he shared these experiences with Argentine artists when he returned, but some of them, such as Lucio Fontana, Emilio Pettoruti, and Juan Del Prete, had also established contacts in Europe and had created their own dissenting principles. Consequently, in the 1940s Argentine students had various means for accessing the ideas of the early twentieth-century avant-garde movements. Nevertheless, they insisted on challenging the academic focus that still prevailed in the country's art schools.

The decision by the jury of the 1942 Salón Nacional art show to award a prize for an oil painting by Raúl Mazza — which represented a traditional composition of the painter and his model — was enough to launch a period marked by vocal dissidence. Jorge Brito, Claudio Girola, Alfredo Hlito, and Tomás Maldonado signed and printed their "Manifiesto de cuatro jóvenes" (Manifesto by Four Young Men), which discredited both the winner and the jury (all professors at the Prilidiano Pueyrredón National School of Fine Arts, which they attended). The manifesto concluded with a phrase from Carlo Carrà: "Es necesario suprimir a los imbéciles en el arte" (In art it is necessary to eradicate the imbeciles.)[2] Although they expected that their peers would join the protest after they distributed leaflets on the day that the president of Argentina officiated at the inauguration of the Salón Nacional, the result was merely that the school's director, Pío Collivadino, demanded that they defend or retract their statements. Far from swaying their opinion, this demand led the four men to decide to leave the school once and for all.

Even though they never subscribed to the principle of Constructive Universalism, it is apparent in this context why they were attracted to Torres-García — both for his rejection of naturalist or representational painting and for his style of anti-academic teaching. Mobilized to produce an avant-garde publication, Carmelo Arden Quin solicited Torres-García's collaboration, and together with Edgar Maldonado Bayley he sought the support of the Brazilian poet Murilo Mendes and the Chilean poet Vicente Huidobro. It was in the first and only issue of the magazine *Arturo: Revista de artes abstractas* that the Uruguayan Rhod Rothfuss proposed structuring the framework in keeping with the composition of the painting, in order to avoid the suggestion that the theme extends beyond the limits established by the setting.[3] Soon, the young men who had come together around *Arturo* founded two groups: the Asociación Arte Concreto-Invención, and Madí, which from the very start worked on the idea of the *marco recortado*, or cut frame, which echoed the geometric forms contained in the work. Afterward, members of these groups became interested in abstracting these forms from the context of the composition in order to place them directly on the space of the wall.

The coplanar works of the Madí artists — as they called these types of configurations placed directly on the wall — were different from those created by the members of AACI. The AACI group sought to control the final composition, connecting the geometric shapes painted with

2. "Manifiesto de cuatro jóvenes" [September 1942], signed Brito, Girola, Hlito, and Maldonado; the text is attributed to Maldonado. Consulted June 2016 at http://icaadocs. mfah.org/icaadocs/ELARCHIVO/ RegistroCompleto/tabid/99/doc/733193/ language/es-MX/Default.aspx.

3. Rhod Rothfuss, "El marco: Un problema de la plástica actual," *Arturo: Revista de artes abstractas*, no. 1 (Summer 1944).

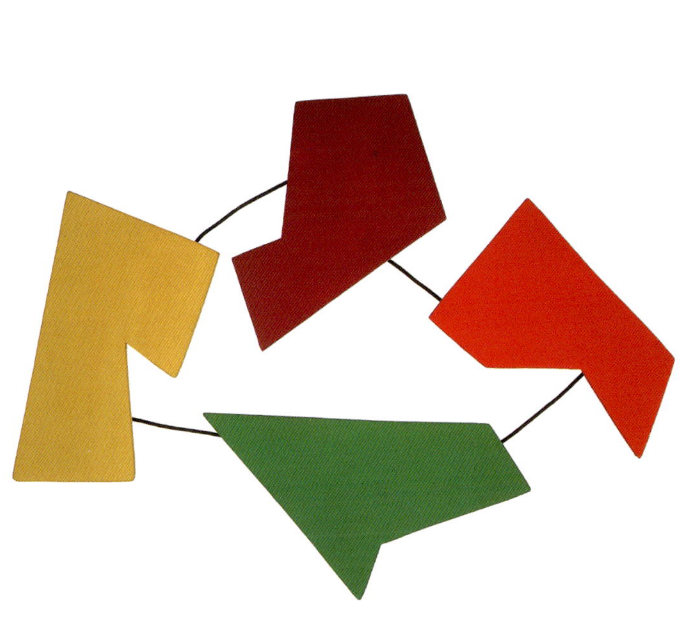

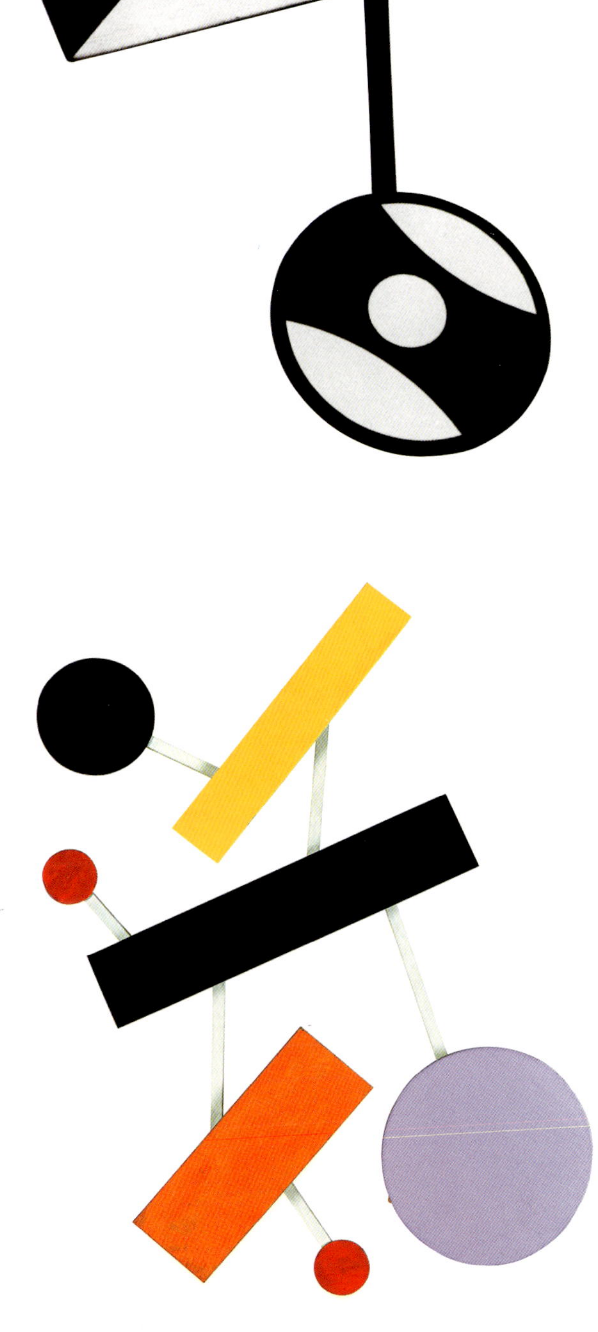

clockwise from above

Raúl Lozza, *Relieve N° 30*, 1946, oil on hardboard and painted metal, 16 ½ x 21 x 1 in. (41.9 x 53.7 x 2.7 cm). Colección Patricia Phelps de Cisneros

Carmelo Arden Quin, *Coplanal a geométrie variable*, 1945, oil varnish on wood and mixed media. Private collection

Diyi Laañ, *Pintura articulada MADI*, 1946, enamel on plywood and mixed media. Private collection

solid colors by means of wood, metal, or acrylic joints, once they felt that the composition was finished. Conversely, the Madí artists, who were more liberal in the treatment of color, allowed for movement of these joints in order to facilitate the participation of the viewer in the perpetual transformation of the work.

Some members of Madí, such as Rothfuss and Arden Quin, had become familiar early on with the works that Torres-García referred to as "plastic objects," made with wood cuttings adapted to the designs painted on them or engraved with etchings or with wood reliefs, as well as toys designed specifically for children. In fact, when Arden Quin sent Torres-García a copy of *Arturo*, the Uruguayan master, responding by letter, compared the *marco recortado* works and his own "frame-objects":

> The idea of the frame-object is explained in many chapters of C. U. [Constructive Universalism]. Thus, I am in total agreement. There are many works that I have created within that theory.[4]

Since childhood, Rodolfo Ian Uricchio and Rothfuss had shared an enthusiasm for the possibilities offered by the "Meccano" games, features that endured in the articulated metal sculptures that Uricchio created when joining the Madí group. Some of Arden Quin's mobile works made use of the random movements produced by the suspended pieces, and in other cases, their parts were arranged in a way that was open to interaction. The possibility of participating in the transformation of the work naturally implies a degree of playfulness, apparent in the first Madí articulated and mobile works, in particular *Röyi*, an emblematic piece created by Gyula Kosice in 1944, which allows for manipulation.

4. Letter from Joaquín Torres-García to Carmelo Arden Quin, Montevideo, August 28, 1944, published in J. A. García Martínez, *Arte y enseñanza artística en la Argentina* (Buenos Aires: Fundación Banco de Boston, 1985), 32.

5. Excerpt from the "MADI Manifesto," read during the first Madí Art Exhibition, August 3, 1946. *Revista MADI Nemsor*, no. 0, Buenos Aires, 1947.

6. Juan Melé, *La vanguardia del 40: Memorias de un artista concreto* (Buenos Aires: Ediciones Cinco, 1999), 110.

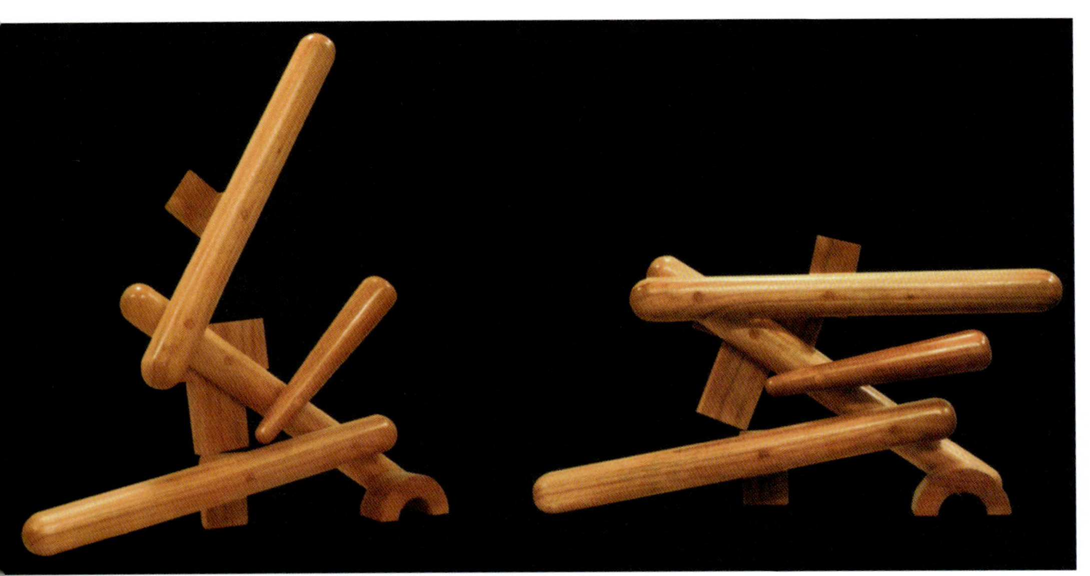

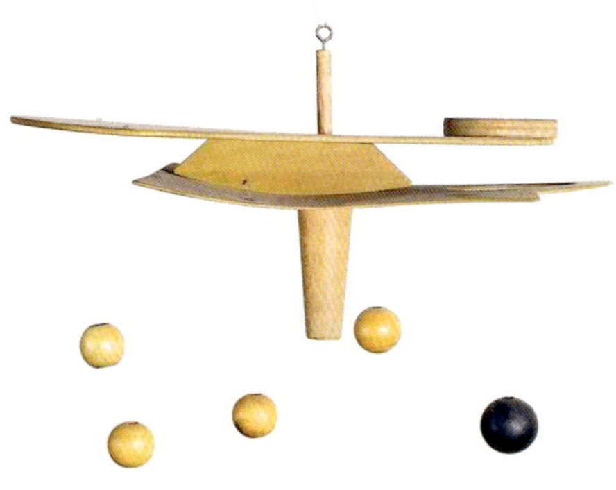

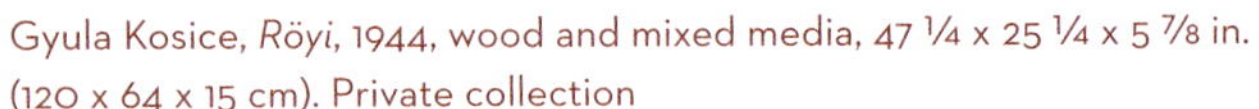
Gyula Kosice, *Röyi*, 1944, wood and mixed media, 47 ¼ x 25 ¼ x 5 ⅞ in. (120 x 64 x 15 cm). Private collection

Carmelo Arden Quin, *La boule noire*, 1949, wood, 10 ⅜ x 16 ⅞ x 11 ½ in. (26.5 x 40.5 x 29.5 cm). Fundación Costantini, Colección Museo de Arte Latinoamericano de Buenos Aires

Moreover, movement and playful interaction were tenets included in the Madí Manifesto, which stated:

> MADI art (Nemsorismo) can be identified by the organization of elements peculiar to each art in its continuum.
>
> It contains presence, a movable, dynamic arrangement, development of the theme itself, playfulness and plurality as absolute values . . .
>
> MADI painting, color and two-dimensionality . . . Articulated surfaces with linear, rotating and changing movement.
>
> MADI sculpture, three-dimensional, no color. Total form and solid shapes with contour, articulated, rotating, changing movements, etc.
>
> MADI architecture, environment and mobile, movable forms.[5]

Conversely, for AACI the concept of coplanar works was quite different, as noted in Juan Melé's account:

> The concrete version, despite also employing forms that are liberated within space, was based on a very different concept. The forms were separate yet attached, since they were conceived as parts that are dependent upon one another for an overall composition. They were a set of juxtaposed surfaces that could not change positions without destroying the established composition. Every form, every quantity, was painstakingly thought out with regard to color, proportion and the field of separation between its parts, so that it was impossible to move the surfaces even one millimeter without destroying the harmony created by the artist.[6]

During meetings that took place at Maldonado's house to discuss their principles, the members of AACI considered *Die Kunstismen: 1914–1924,* published by Arp and Lissitzky, the *Abstraction, création, art non-figurative* catalogue (1932), *Cubism and Abstract Art* (1936), and *Constructive Universalism* by Torres-García, among other works. From discussion of these materials they drew conclusions about the perception of space and time, pointing out issues that were not yet satisfactorily resolved. Maldonado wrote, for example, that while László Peri had relativized painting, he had not yet called into question the traditional function of painting as a "content organism" in which an event unfolded. The Constructivists had advocated an exaltation of space, and had viewed the relationships between different materials, following the Bauhaus movement, but had not addressed the problems related to aesthetic structures. The group studied the mobile creations of Calder, Gabo, Giacometti, Moholy-Nagy, Pevsner, and Rodchenko in terms of the concrete plenitude of space and time, concluding that these artists had not yet solved the problems of two-dimensional composition and aesthetic structure.

Maldonado then detailed the reconsiderations they had discussed together. First, they had already broken from the traditional form of painting by means of spatializing the surface via the *marco recortado*, yet they noted that space penetrated the painting as though it were an additional element. Second, while they had made figures three dimensional (like Nicholson and Domela), they also felt that it was a mistake to adopt a three-dimensional approach to tackle a two-dimensional problem. Last, while seeking to grant more importance to penetrating space, they separated within space the constitutive elements of the painting, without abandoning its coplanar arrangement. As such, Maldonado emphasized "maximum discovery," and consequently he stressed: "Today, for the first time, non-representational art finds in itself the possibility of approaching space and movement from an absolutely concrete point of view."[7]

However, these artists soon noted that while coplanar works allowed them to present a concrete form and to emphasize the real opposition between figure and background, the wall had an active role as well. Based on its characteristics, it assumed an unforeseeable operative value for the painter. In order to separate the forms from the coplanar works, Melé recalled, "Maldonado proposed the use of glass or plastic sheets, which, when separated from the surface, supported colored forms that appeared as if floating in space, and they were complemented by other conventional ones."[8] The group continued discussing the problem of painting's subjection to architecture — the necessity of presenting concrete forms on surfaces and in space — but because the solutions were not satisfactory, Maldonado wrote in 1948: "Based on all of this, the consideration of this possibility was postponed until a later time. We again reconsidered the problem of figure versus background upon a surface."[9]

While these artists sought solutions for the presentation of concrete forms on surfaces and in space, they were also incorporating new materials. Gregorio Vardánega affixed wooden and glass forms to the flat background of the painting, as seen in *Relieve* (Relief; 1948). In this work the painted lines on the back of the glass result in an interplay of shadows, due to the thickness of the transparent material, which underscores the third dimension and calls into question the surface of the painting. Because the artists from AACI sought to exalt emptiness in sculptural works, Melé, through the translucid quality of acrylic, created *Objeto espacial o planos en el espacio* (Spatial Objects or Planes in Space; 1947), in which he availed himself of the transparency of acrylic to hold two concrete forms that thereby appear to be suspended within actual space.

7. AACI, "Lo abstracto y lo concreto en el arte moderno," *Arte Concreto*, no. 1 (August 1946).

8. Melé, *Memorias de un artista concreto*, 99–100.

9. Tomás Maldonado, "El arte concreto y el problema de lo ilimitado: Notas para un estudio teórico," Zurich, 1648 [1948], in *Ramona: Revista de artes visuales* (Buenos Aires, 2003), facsimile edition. The brothers Raúl and Rembrandt van Dyck Lozza chose to develop this working method further, which later came to be known as Perceptismo (Perceptism).

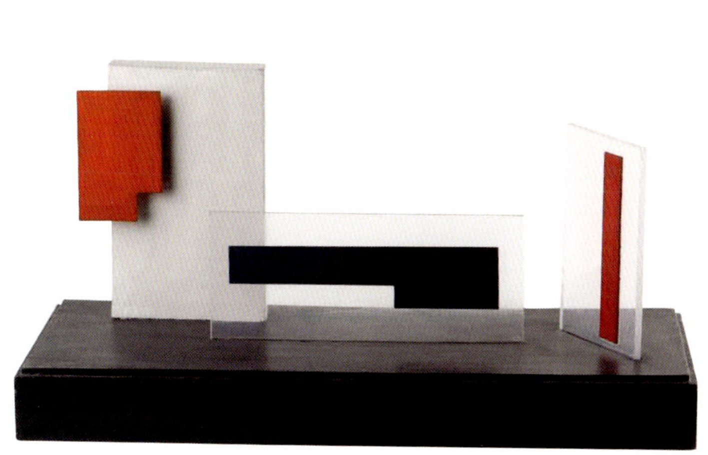

Juan Melé, *Objeto espacial*, 1947, paint on wood and transparent acrylic, 10 x 19 ⅛ x 7 ⅞ in. (25.5 x 48.8 x 20 cm). Fundación Costantini, Colección Museo de Arte Latinoamericano de Buenos Aires

Gregorio Vardánega, *Relieve*, 1948, oil on wood and glass, 29 ¼ x 20 ½ x 4 ⅝ in. (74.5 x 52 x 4.4 cm). Fundación Costantini, Colección Museo de Arte Latinoamericano de Buenos Aires

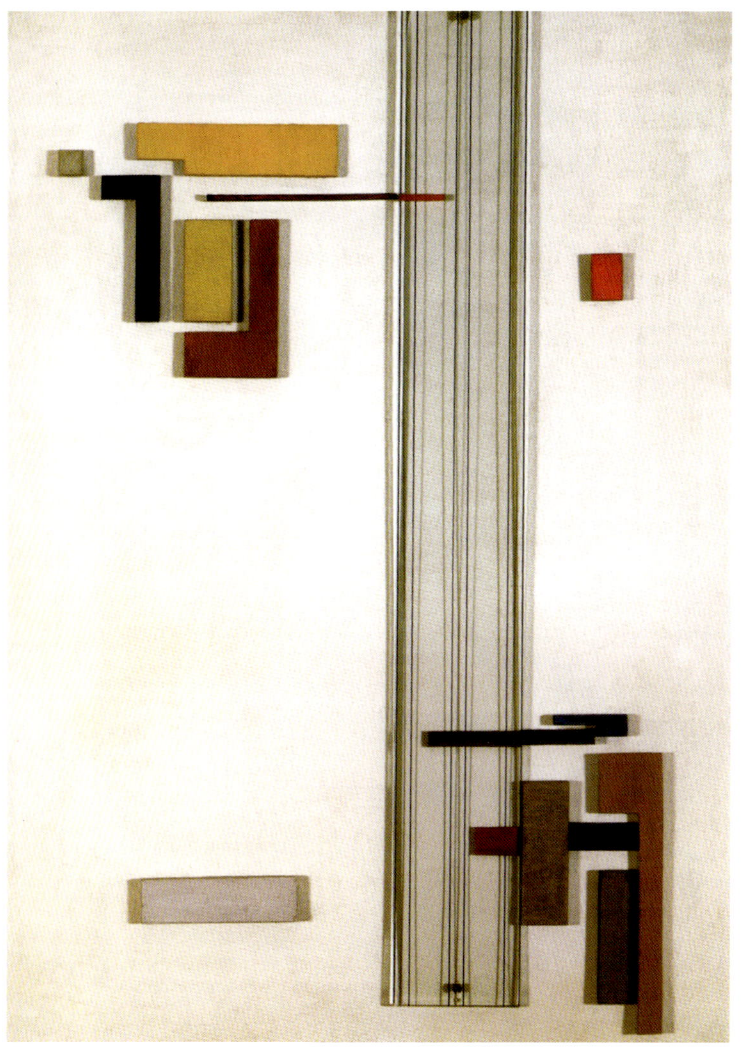

Although the sculptures by the brothers Ennio Iommi and Claudio Girola explored directional issues through the use of wood or metal rods, in some cases they used other materials to alter the perception of direction. To exploit the characteristics of particular materials, Girola created a piece in 1946 with reflective metal plates, underscoring the opposition of the base to the spatial trajectory, and evoking a broken metal bar. The viewer, when circling the sculpture, can see the bar suspended in space and, simultaneously, its mirrored replica on the metal base, which appears to be continually changing and unstable. Iommi also used acrylic or glass plates that interrupted the trajectory of directions and altered the viewer's perception of them.

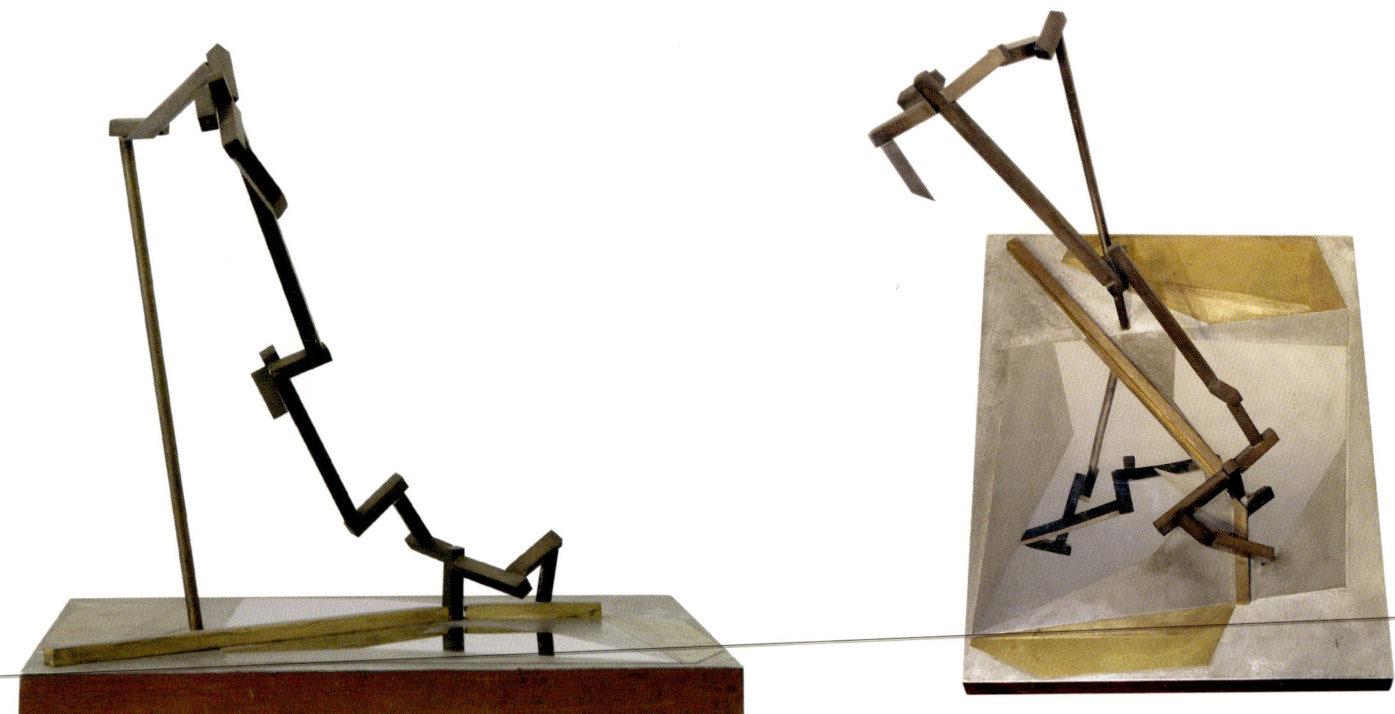

Claudio Girola, *Sin título*, 1946, metal bars and plates, 17 ¼ x 19 ⅝ x 15 in.
(44 x 50 x 38 cm). Gallery De Sousa

Ultimately, however, for the Concretism of the Río de la Plata region, the function of art was related to political militancy, as evident on the first page of the magazine *Arte Concreto*:

> We have written previously that we hoped to contribute, with our art, to the progress of our era . . . Our works have a revolutionary commitment; their purpose is to help transform everyday reality through the effective involvement of each reader or viewer within the aesthetic experience.[10]

The Concrete artists' faith in the power of one's imagination to promote social and technological progress was also key for those who in the 1960s created groups of visual artists seeking to incite change while adopting a political stance.

In summary, the avant-garde movement's disruptive intentions in the 1940s resulted in a radical break from traditional forms through the use of the *marco recortado* and the subsequent liberation of forms on the wall. Along with the particular features we have analyzed, this was promoted by the Madí artists as well as the members of AACI. As for the inclusion of "movement," it is clear that it was incorporated within the Madí group. We have observed this in the discourse promulgated through their manifestos and other writings, and in the works that

10. AACI, "Nuestra militancia," *Arte Concreto*, no. 1 (August 1946).

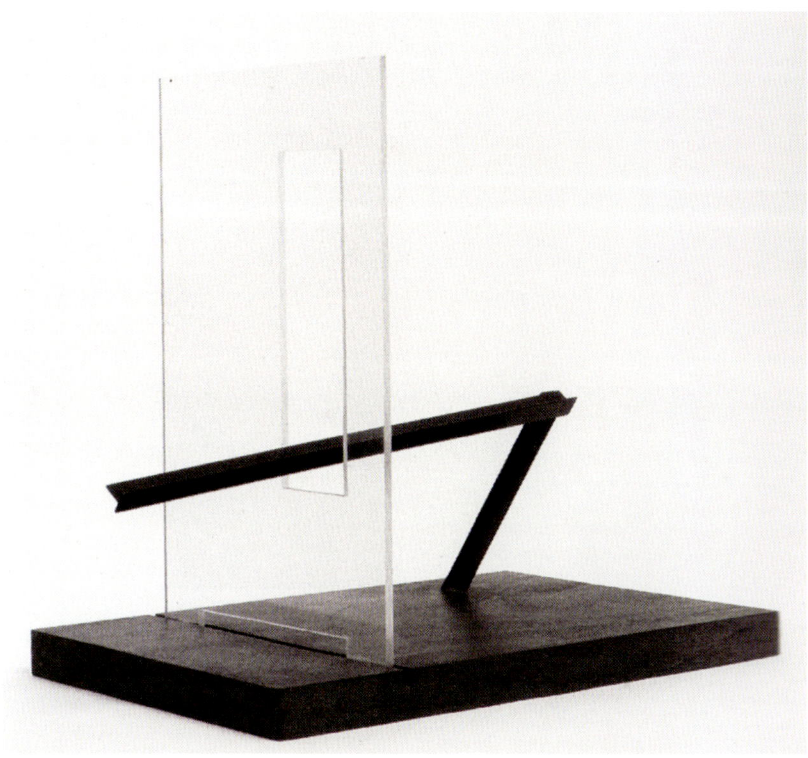

Ennio Iommi, *Construcción sobre el espacio*, 1946, metal, wood, and acrylic, 27 x 19 ⅝ x 27 in. (70 x 50 x 70 cm). Susana Schneider de Girola, Claudia Girola, and Rafael Girola

incorporated random movement, as is the case with mobiles, or in works whose articulations were open to manipulation and participation by the viewer. The initial programs of AACI did not prescribe movements and modifications within the composition of a work; nevertheless, the spatialization of the concrete form was moving toward experimentation with unconventional materials that engendered new shifts and fissures. Moreover, by taking into account the active role of the viewer in the aesthetic experience — as an action promoting the political transformation of reality — another path was opened toward the notion of viewer as participant.

POSTWAR ITINERARIES

If up until 1948 this avant-garde movement had worked in its own "splendid isolation" — to use the words of Maldonado — but beginning that same year they were able to travel to compare their investigations with European experiences. Maldonado was the first one to go to studios in Italy, Switzerland, and France, where he interacted with Max Bill, Piero Dorazio, Gillo Dorfles, Gianni Dova, Camille Graeser, Max Huber, Verena Loewensberg, Richard Paul Lohse, Bruno Munari, Achille Perilli, Diego Peverelli, and Georges Vantongerloo. After his trip, he shared his contacts so that Arden Quin, Girola, Melé, and Vardánega could undertake their own exploratory missions, followed by Manuel Espinosa, Lidy Prati, and Kosice. In any event, each itinerary was based on personal possibilities and affinities; for example, Girola used his time in Milan to forge a friendship with the Concrete Art group, while Espinosa was the first who was able to interact directly with Vordemberge-Gildewart in Amsterdam, and Melé and Vardánega extended their visits with Vantongerloo at his studio in Paris at 7, impasse du Rouet.

Prior to his departure, Vardánega had already started to interpret the cosmic phenomena revealed by scientists through various works he created in plaster spheres, in which the concavities held strands of thin threads. The time he spent in Vantongerloo's studio, along with Melé, had a very strong impact on both men, as can be seen in the travel memoir written by the latter:

> He says that he wants to travel throughout infinite space. To do so he takes one point and then he makes it traverse a surface, the shape that results isn't important, he says that it is always a spatial voyage. As such he creates paintings where, for example, there is a spiral form that changes colors every 2 or 3 centimeters: red, blue, yellow, etc. . . . He also has wire objects in spiral forms, in the center of which there is a wooden sphere, for example. He says that there shouldn't be any rules, that there shouldn't be any dogmas, that there shouldn't be any prohibitions, and that the painter should do what he feels, although it must always be guided by his brain.[11]

This shows, first, the liberties Vantongerloo took in imagining these works, especially in view of the restrictions that had been imposed by the aesthetic principles of Concrete Art established in Buenos Aires. In addition, both Vantongerloo and Vardánega were able to reaffirm the possibilities opened up by new materials, such as plastics. Meanwhile, the conversations concerning the perception of continuous cosmic movement served as an incentive for Vardánega, who redoubled his previous efforts, as he recalled:

> My interest and observation of universal space led me to use it as a material for aesthetic and educational purposes. In fact, my first light sculpture in 1950 was an attempt to represent the universe . . . Electric colors, transparent colors, colored space, the diffraction of light, spectral decomposition, the transmission of light within solids, liquids and gases; all of these are infinite sources for a new aesthetic and type of education. The aesthetic of movement and electronics, the aesthetic of light and electric color are elements for a new formal education. My *Universo electrónico* [Electronic Universe] from 1958 allowed the viewer to directly interact in order to change the environment by transforming the background color.[12]

During the 1940s, Vantongerloo's work had forgone the geometric phase associated with the orthogonal system — which, in his opinion, was measurable, "finite," and a limited case — instead

11. Juan Melé, *Notas de viajes 1*, manuscript, n.p.; Juan Melé Archives.

12. Gregorio Vardánega, "Statements by Kineticists Working in Paris," *Studio International* (October 1970): 141. Reproduced in *Palabra de artista: Textos sobre arte argentino 1961–1981*, comp. Roberto Amigo, Silvia Dolinko, and Cristina Rossi (Buenos Aires: Fundación Espigas and Fondo Nacional de las Artes, 2010), 118.

embarking on a new phase understood as unlimited, in correspondence to the infinite universe. Beginning in 1949, he started to use unconventional materials such as Plexiglas. Based on this notion of "finite-infinite," points ceased to be fixed within space without the support of geometry, and bodies no longer had measureable dimensions, instead existing as energy in eternal transformation. These investigations related to "free space," and the acrylic objects Vantongerloo produced in connection with this concept had a strong impact on many Latin American artists, such as Víctor Magariños D., who wrote:

> G. Vantongerloo is the only one who at that time, in 1950, was interested in the *universe and the laws that govern it,* which is why the vocabulary he uses to explain his thoughts related to the art he creates is closer to the field of astronomy or physics than that of the psychological speculations, which up until that time had been disseminated through

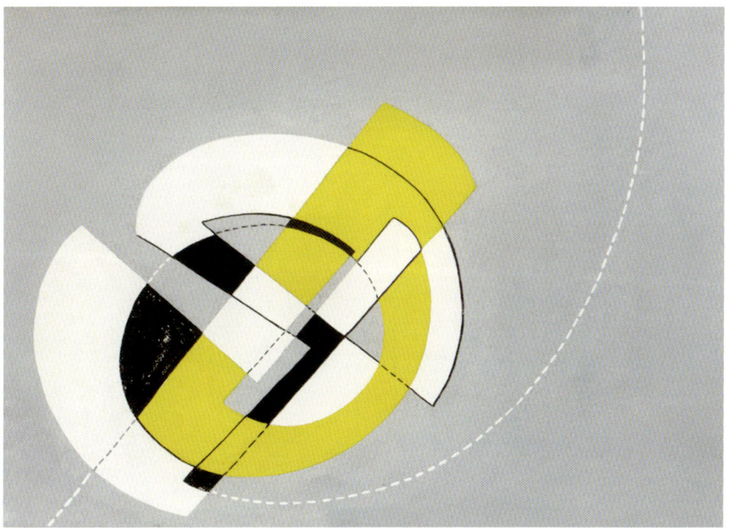

Víctor Magariños D., *Sin título*, ca. 1950, tempera on paper, 9 1/4 x 12 5/8 in. (23.5 x 32.2 cm). Private collection

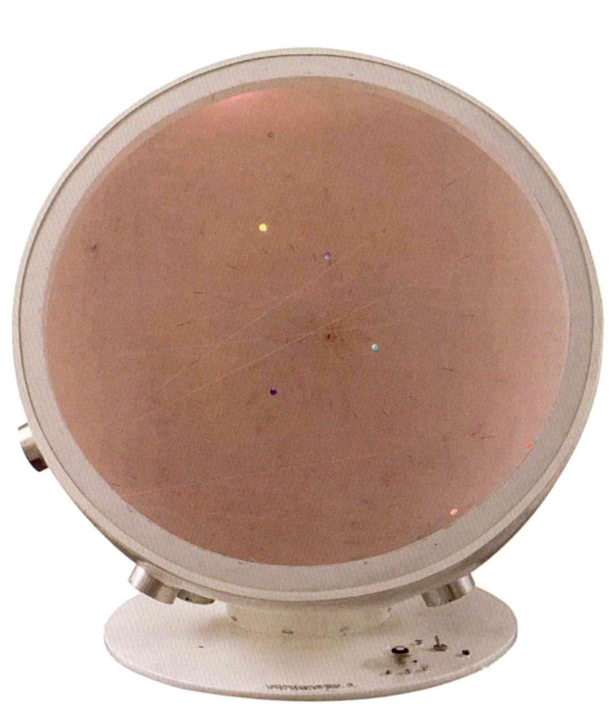

Gregorio Vardánega, *Universo electrónico*, 1958, enamel on plaster hemisphere, painted cotton threads, aluminum cylinders, colored acetate and vinyl, wood, plastic, and a lighting system, 30 1/2 x 29 x 22 3/8 in. (77.5 x 74 x 57 cm). Fundación Costantini, Colección Museo de Arte Latinoamericano de Buenos Aires

manifestos or in theories about art. Terms like action and reaction, poles of attraction and repulsion, belong to Newton's theories of gravity and to the cosmological constant introduced by Einstein. The "Theory of Relativity" published in 1905 and the "General Theory of Relativity" from 1915, in which Einstein transforms all pre-existing thought about cosmological laws, must have been something fundamental for G. Vantongerloo, because it is there — more than in Cubist paintings — that Euclidean three-dimensional space loses the importance it had held since the Renaissance.[13] Since then, time and space have been inseparable in the entire conception of the cosmos, and the notion of the "space-time continuum" would be the primary motif in all the works by Vantongerloo.[14]

Arden Quin was also strongly influenced by Vantongerloo's ideas. After a visit to his Paris studio at Place d'Alésia, he stated:

> When arriving in Paris, I hadn't understood Mondrian, or Malevich, and even less so the Malevich of *White on White*. It was by observing the work of Vantongerloo that, for the first time, I was aware of that problem. Currently, with the creation of the MADI scientific movement I have blankness as an artistic basis for this new experience. For me, blank space isn't a relationship like it is for Mondrian, nor the way emptiness is for Vantongerloo, but rather art's essence, function and creation.[15]

In addition to the visit with Vantongerloo, for Girola the Italian art scene was very important. It was there that he established contact with the founders of the Movimento per l'arte concreta (MAC; Concrete Art Movement), which was supported by the Galleria Bergamini and the Salto bookstore, a space that also housed an exhibition of Girola's art during his time in Italy. Girola formed what was to be a longstanding relationship with Bruno Munari, whose passionate use of varied materials and incorporation of playful elements were illuminating for the young Argentine artist, as Munari was then creating "useless machinery," "illegible books," and "found objects." Later on, Girola not only maintained the connection but also promoted an exhibition of the Milan-based MAC movement at the Galería Krayd in Buenos Aires and in Chile (in Viña del Mar and Santiago), with a prologue by Gillo Dorfles and a "useless machine" by Munari on the cover of the catalogue.

For Maldonado, the relationship established with Max Bill was particularly significant.[16] After returning from Europe, he examined together with Hlito the principles governed by algebraic equations (consistent with the geometric phase of Vantongerloo's work from 1930 to 1936). Paintings such as *Composición* (ca. 1950) by Maldonado and *Ritmos cromáticos III* (1949) by Hlito

13. In 1917, two years after the publication of "General Theory of Relativity," Vantongerloo created a sketch for his painting titled *Points in Space*, depicting a series of stars in the Milky Way. In 1947, two years after the dawn of the atomic age, he decided to return to the theme and to finally complete this painting. This work belongs to the collection of Ignacio Pirovano in Buenos Aires.

14. In the conception of the universe, time and space are inseparable, from which the notion of the "space-time continuum" arises. To describe the position of a galaxy, not only are the three dimensions of space required, but also a fourth dimension, which corresponds to time. In this regard, it can be said that the universe is four-dimensional and that time is the fourth dimension. The excerpt is from Víctor Magariños D., "El Arte Cosmológico: El proceso creador en pintura, más allá de las últimas tendencias" (Pinamar, 1977); reproduced in *Palabra de atista*, 130.

15. Michel Seuphor, *Dictionnaire de la peinture abstrait*, s.v. "Arden Quin" (Paris: Hazan, 1957).

16. María Amalia García, *El arte abstract: Intercambios culturales entre Argentina y Brasil* (Buenos Aires: Siglo Veintiuno Editores, [2011]), 123–32.

17. *Feria de América: Vanguardia invisible*, ed. Wustavo Quiroga (Mendoza: Fundación del Interior, 2012).

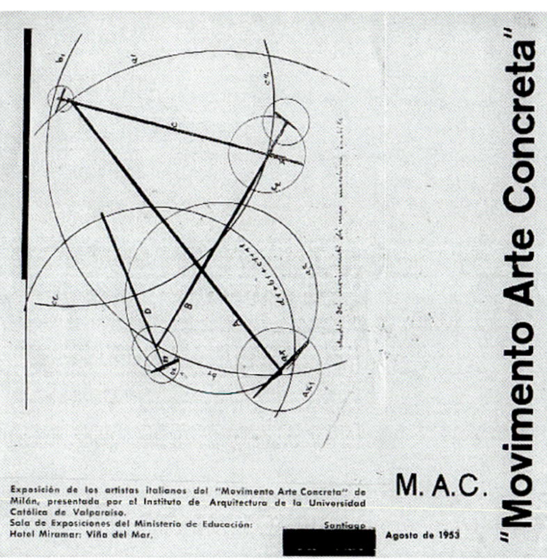

Cover of the catalogue from the exhibition *Movimento Arte Concreta*, Hotel Miramar, Viña del Mar, 1953

Tomás Maldonado, *Torre alegórica, Feria de América*, Mendoza, 1954

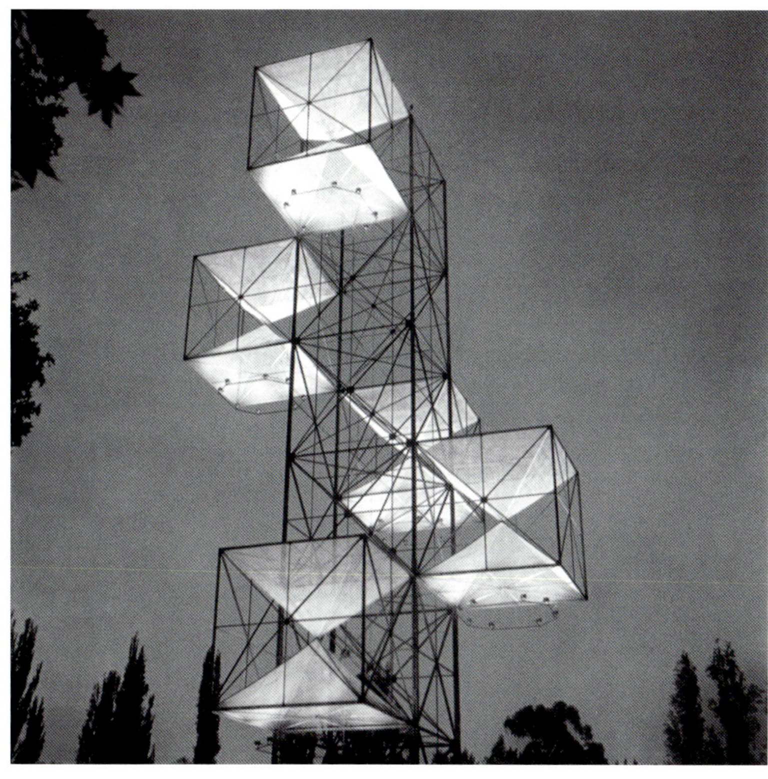

make the supporting background vibrate by means of the rhythm of linear sequences. In 1951, the arrival of Max Bill's work in São Paulo had a strong impact on the artists from the region. A solo exhibition was held in March and by October he had received, for *Tripartite Unity,* the highest praise from the first biennial in São Paulo. Among those influenced was Iommi, who explored the trajectory of the endless strip and variations on these continuous forms, whose mathematical properties had been established by Moebius and Listing. In 1953, Maldonado designed the *Torre alegórica* for the entrance to the Feria de América (Americas Fair), based on the pyramid sequences that Bill had created in his metallic constructions from the 1930s. The fair was held one year later at the Parque San Martín in Mendoza, Argentina, based on the architectural design of César Jannello. The entry tower, designed by Maldonado, reached fifty meters in height and included a program of sounds and changing lights that transformed it into a cinematic work, in line with the spatiodynamic towers created by Nicolas Schöffer.[17]

In the mid-1950s, art students took the three major Buenos Aires schools to task, demanding that they revamp their academic programs, comprehensively reorganize their instruction, and achieve inclusion in the university system. They organized themselves through the Centro de Estudiantes de Artes Plásticas (CEAP; Center for Students of the Fine Arts) — which was chaired by Julio Le Parc — and they undertook alternative curricular proposals so as not to interrupt their studies while the process was underway. Among the measures they adopted were integrated and open workshops offered by professors who supported their struggle and who, in general, promoted the integration of the various disciplines and experimentation.[18] The courses that garnered the most interest were those related to vision, taught by Héctor Cartier and structured around an understanding of the creative process as a vital experience. Also compelling were classes that discussed the Bauhaus movement and Gestalt theories, the ideas of Moholy-Nagy, György Kepes, and Vantongerloo, and even the concept of the artist's multiple.

Among those who took part in the student movement, Antonio Asís was the first to travel to Paris, where he came into contact with Galerie Denise René, and by 1956 he had met the Hungarian artists Vasarely and Schöffer, the Swiss artist Jean Tinguely, the Israeli artist Yaacov Agam, the Belgian artist Pol Bury, and the Venezuelan artists Narciso Debourg and Jesús Rafael Soto. With Soto he collaborated on solo exhibitions in Holland, Paris, and New York. By 1957, Luis Tomasello had also established himself in Paris, and soon Denise René could count him as one of her exhibitors, and the *Art MADI International: Groupe Argentin* show also included his works in the 1958 program. By the time that Kosice embarked on this voyage, he was already far advanced in his own experimentation, which he discussed in a series of interviews — compiled in a publication at the time — in which he put his own results to the test.[19] When Tomasello visited Vantongerloo in 1958, he was surprised by the use of Plexiglas in his works, especially the indeterminate forms that he sought within the material and the vibrations that he achieved with visible colored points and lines. Meanwhile, by April of 1960 Tomasello had managed to present his own work in the form of hydrokinetic sculptures at the Galerie Denise René.

If the student demands were partially met at the start of the 1958 school year — when the new curriculum was approved — the controversial period had nonetheless pushed students toward new ways of exploring the image, optical phenomena, and multiple works. This created the backdrop for Vasarely's exhibition at the Museo Nacional de Bellas Artes in Buenos Aires in August of that year, where he received an enthusiastic response. Le Parc traveled to Paris through a grant by the French government that same year, and he soon met Francisco Sobrino. Later, Hugo Demarco, Francisco García Miranda, Horacio García-Rossi, and Sergio Moyano had arrived as well. Mobilized by the same influence, many artists in Argentina were then working with Kinetic Art;[20] as such, Miguel Ángel Vidal and Eduardo Mac Entyre developed, at the suggestion of Ignacio Pirovano, what they called Generative Art, creating forms while starting from a single point.

Once in Paris, Sobrino and Le Parc continued their research into Concrete Art. When studying the book *kalte Kunst? zum Standort der heutigen Malerei,* published by the Swiss artist and designer Karl Gerstner in 1957, they were able, as Le Parc put it, to thoroughly analyze the work

18. Leopoldo Torres Agüero — in his double role of painter and musician — the theater professor Fasulo; Magariños D., Vardánega, the sculptor Antonio Pujía, the architect Rafael Onetto, the engravers Fernando López Anaya, Aída Carballo, and Albino Fernández, among many others.

19. Gyula Kosice, *Geocultura de la Europa de hoy* (Paris: Losange, 1959).

20. Artists who were interested in working with the serialization of a concrete form, visual effects, intervention of real movement, graphic design, and the notion of systems include Perla Benveniste, Ary Brizzi, Armando Durante, Jorge Luna Ercilla, Olga Gerding, Alicia Orlandi, Rogelio Polesello, Eduardo Rodríguez, and Carlos Silva, all based in Buenos Aires; Mario Casas, Gonzalo Chaves, Hugo De Marziani, Raúl Mazzoni, Jorge Pereira, Héctor Puppo, Roberto Rollié, and Juan Carlos Romero, based in La Plata; Eduardo Serón in Rosario and Abdulio Giudici in Mendoza, among many others.

21. CRAV was founded by Hugo Demarco, García-Rossi, Le Parc, Francisco García Miranda, Moyano, Sobrino, and the Europeans François Molnar, François Morellet, Nadine Servanes, Joël Stein, and Jean-Pierre Yvaral.

22. Cf. GRAV (García-Rossi, Le Parc, Morellet, Sobrino, Stein, and Yvaral), "Basta de mitificaciones," Paris, October 1963.

23. AACI, "Nuestra militancia," *Arte Concreto,* no. 1, August 1946.

of Max Bill, Camille Graeser, Verena Loewensberg, and Richard Paul Lohse. However, for them, the European concrete artists' emphasis on purely mathematical aspects seemed excessive, particularly with regard to the scant attention paid to the eye of the viewer. Moreover, they noted that these artists still had a manual method of creation, in which they tended to be part of the final arrangement of the form. On the contrary, they proposed a system that would govern the surface through a previous design, which could not be interrupted by the interference of the artist. It was in this context that in July 1960 they created the Centre de Recherche d'Art Visuel (CRAV),[21] and afterward founded the Groupe de Recherche d'Art Visuel (GRAV), which resolved to eliminate the static nature of traditional work and to involve the public in this action. A viewer cognizant of his power of action and tired of so much abuse and mythification could himself create the true "revolution within art," putting into practice the guidelines:

Prohibited not to participate.

Prohibited not to touch.

Prohibited not to break.[22]

For the Argentine artists, these tenets reflected the utopian notions of an avant-garde movement that firmly believed its art could "help to transform everyday reality, through the effective involvement of each reader or viewer within the aesthetic experience."[23]

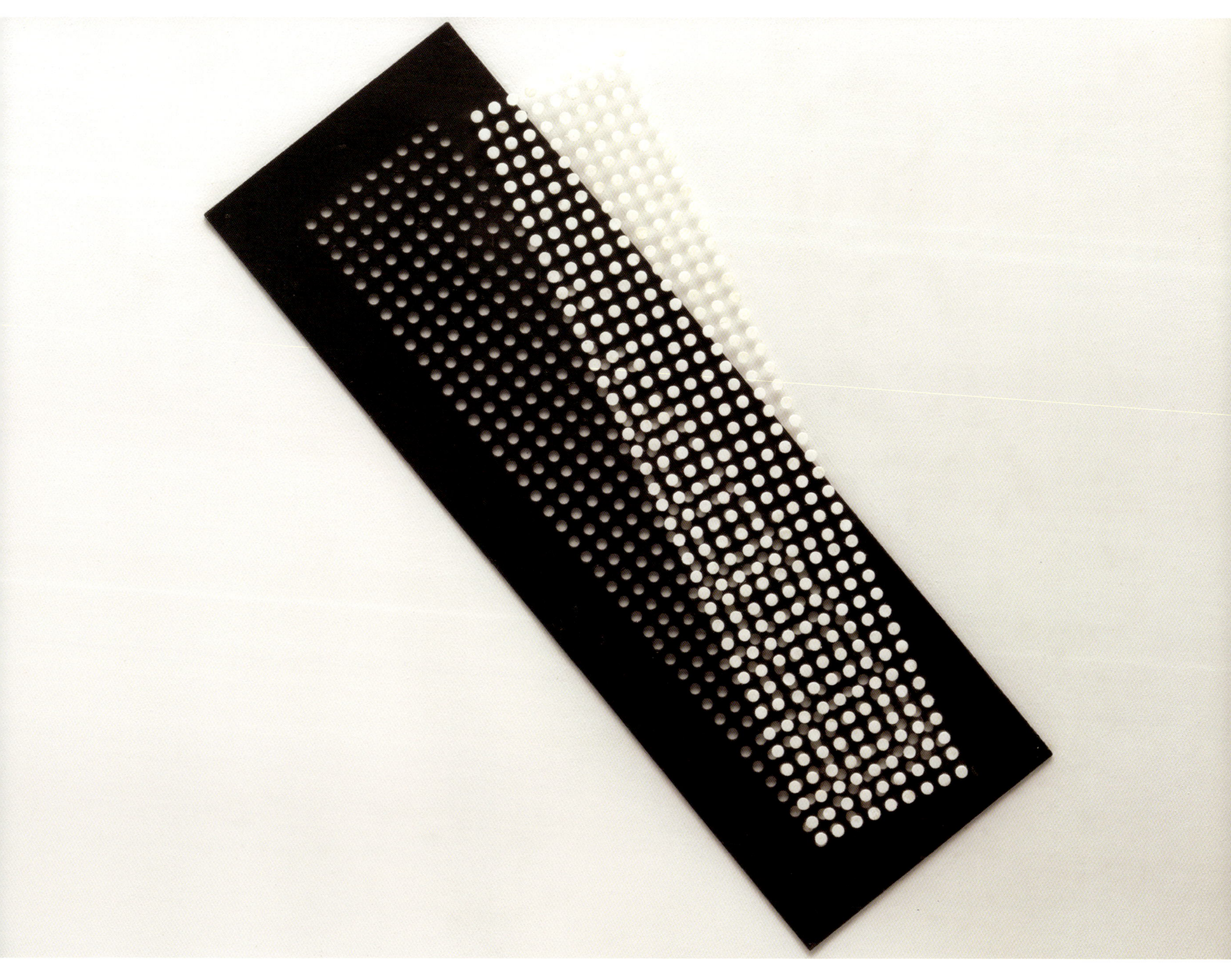

JESÚS RAFAEL SOTO   *Desplazamiento de un elemento luminoso, 1954*
Vinyl dots on acrylic over board and wood, 19 ¾ × 31 ½ × 1 ¼ in. (50 × 80 × 3.3 cm)
Colección Patricia Phelps de Cisneros. Promised gift to The Museum of Modern Art through the
Latin American and Caribbean Fund in honor of Susana & Ricardo Steinbruch

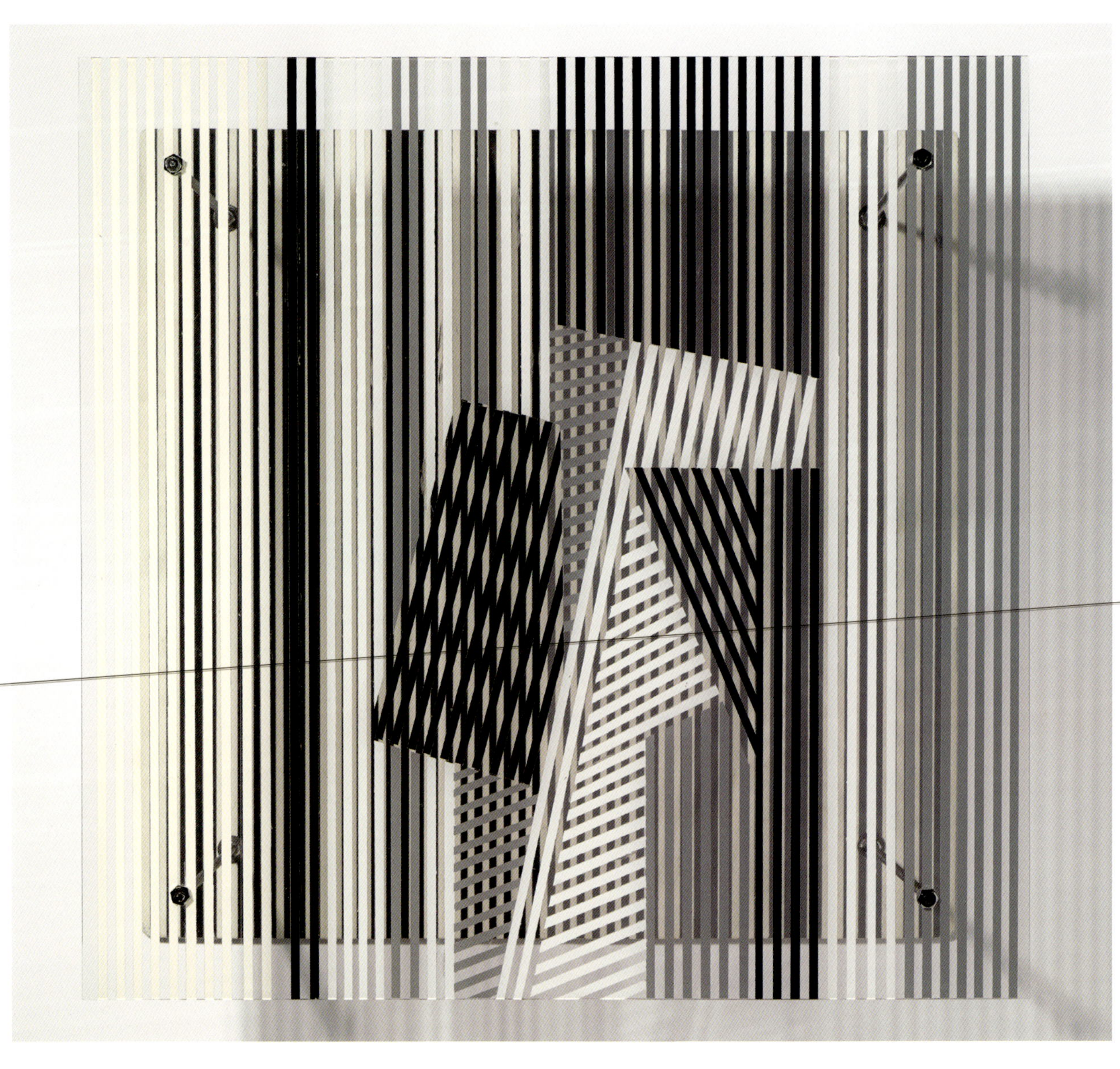

JESÚS RAFAEL SOTO   *Sin título (Estructura cinética de elementos geométricos)*, 1956
Paint on Plexiglas and wood with screws, 21 ¾ × 21 ⅞ × 13 in. (55.2 × 55.6 × 33 cm)
The Museum of Fine Arts, Houston. Museum purchase
funded by the Caroline Wiess Law Accessions Endowment Fund, 2010.76

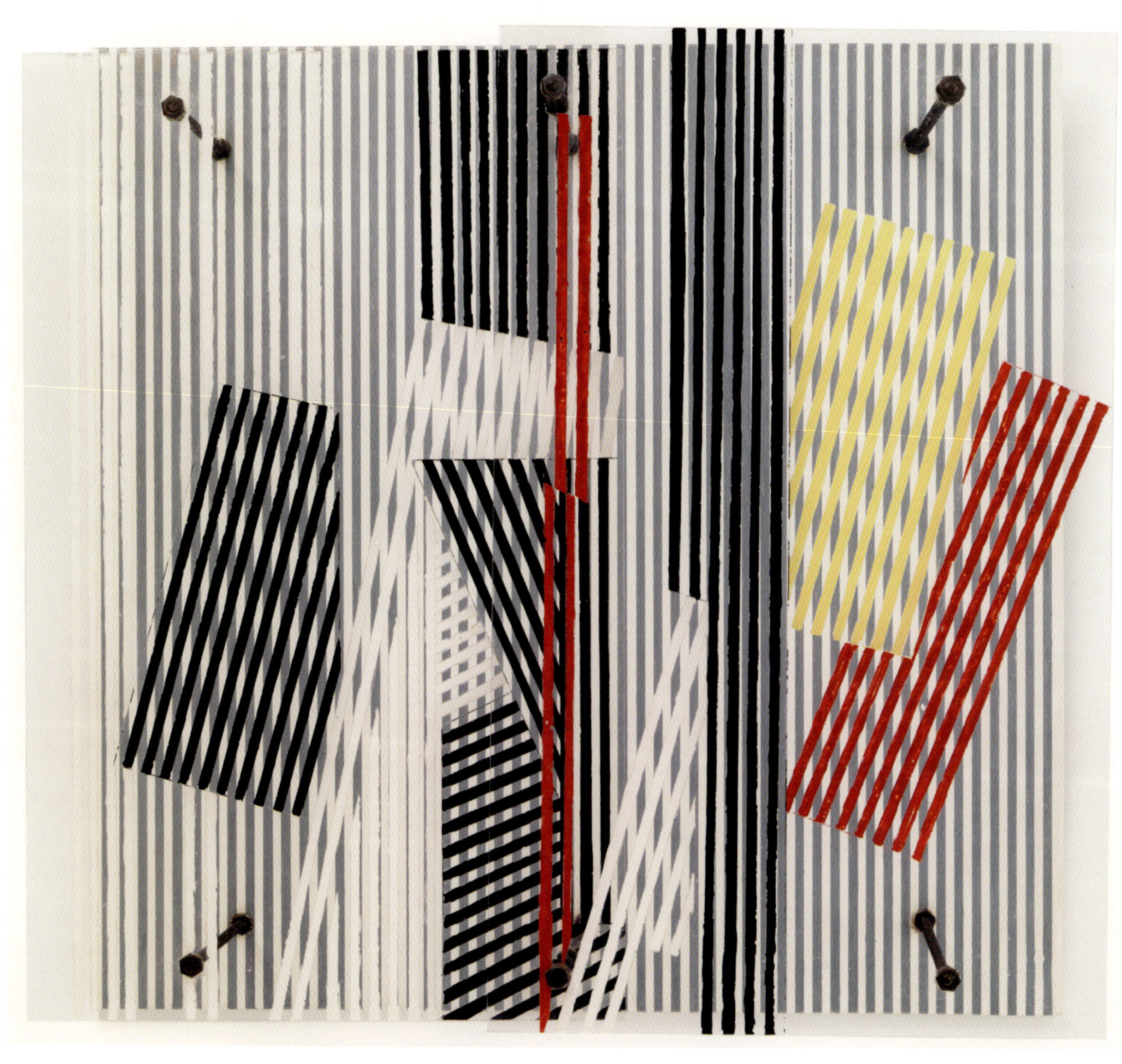

JESÚS RAFAEL SOTO   *Doble transparencia*, 1956
Oil on acrylic and wood, 21 ⅝ × 21 ⅝ × 12 ⅝ in. (54.9 × 54.9 × 32.1 cm)
Colección Patricia Phelps de Cisneros. Promised gift to The Museum of Modern Art through
the Latin American and Caribbean Fund in honor of Ana Teresa Arismendi

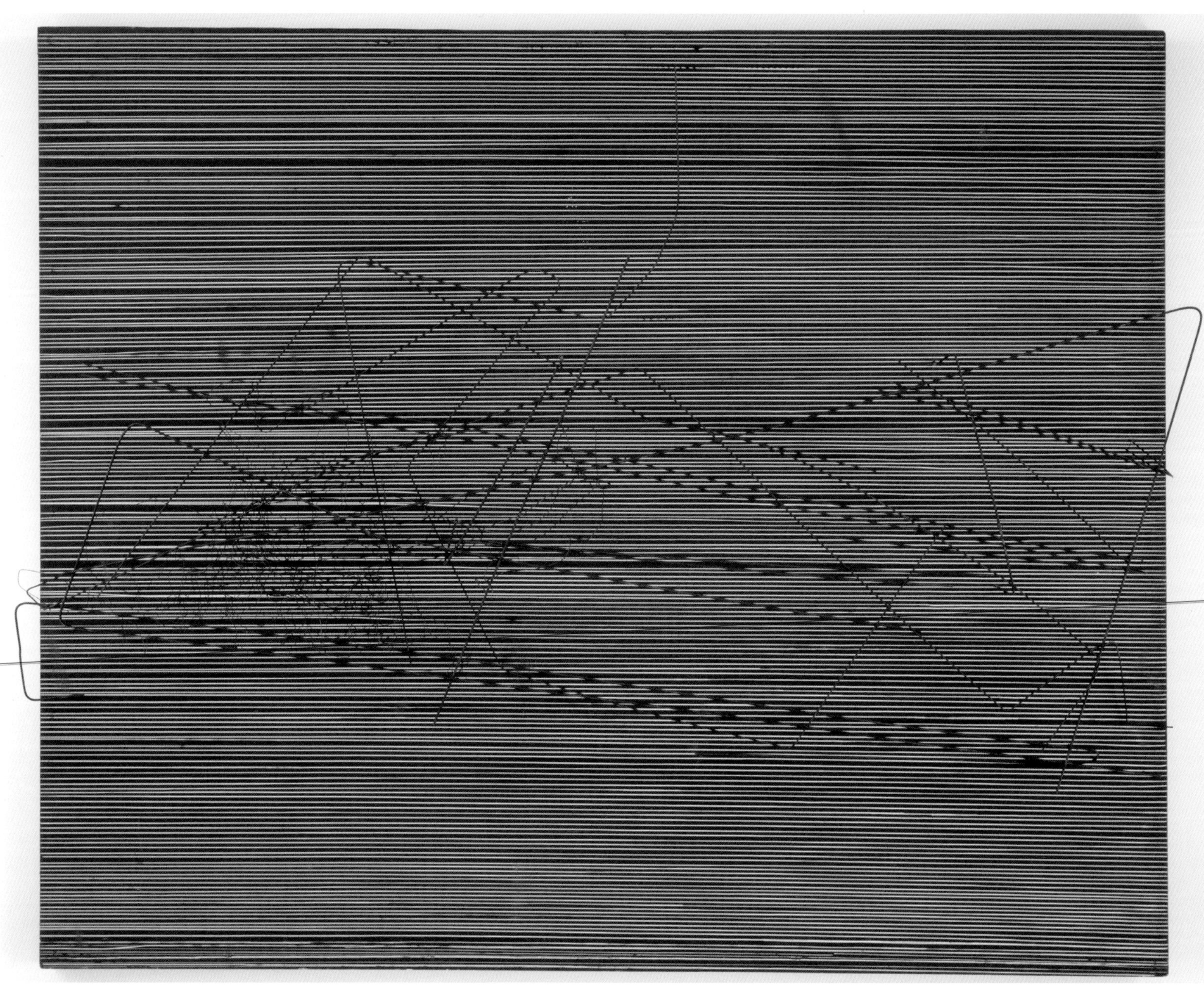

JESÚS RAFAEL SOTO *Vibración*, ca. 1959
Acrylic on plywood and wire paint, 53 ¾ × 63 × 15 ½ in. (136.5 × 160 × 39.5 cm)
Colección Patricia Phelps de Cisneros

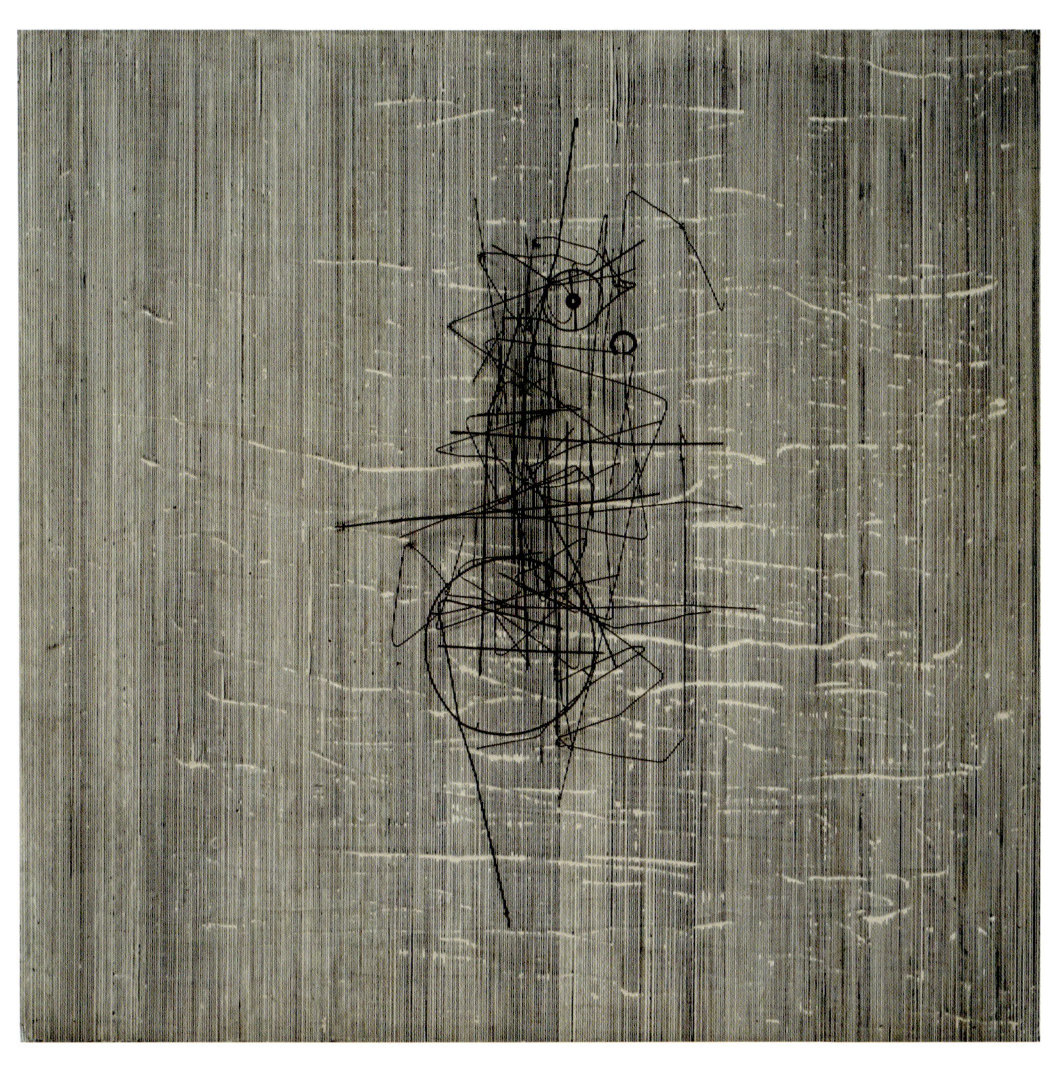

JESÚS RAFAEL SOTO   Vibration, 1961
Wood, plaster, and metal, 39 3/8 × 39 3/8 × 6 in. (100 × 100 × 15.2 cm)
The Ella Fontanals-Cisneros Collection, Miami

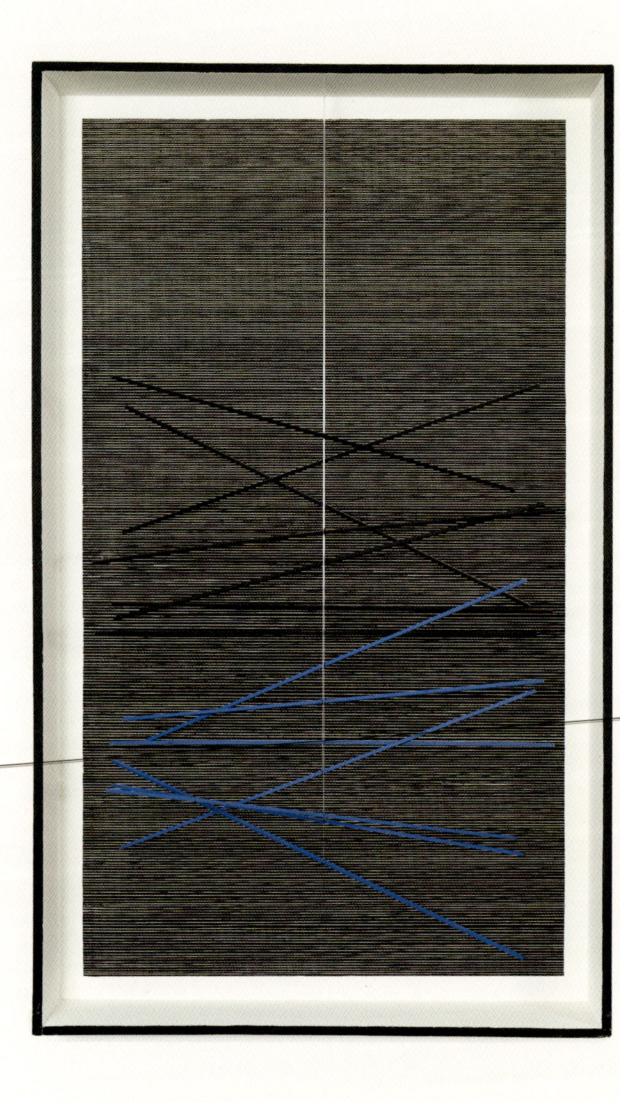

JESÚS RAFAEL SOTO   *Vibraciones*, 1963
Paint on wood and metal, 41 × 24 ⅞ × 5 ⅛ in. (104.1 × 63.2 × 13 cm)
Collection of René and Paula Brillembourg. Courtesy of Sicardi Gallery, Houston

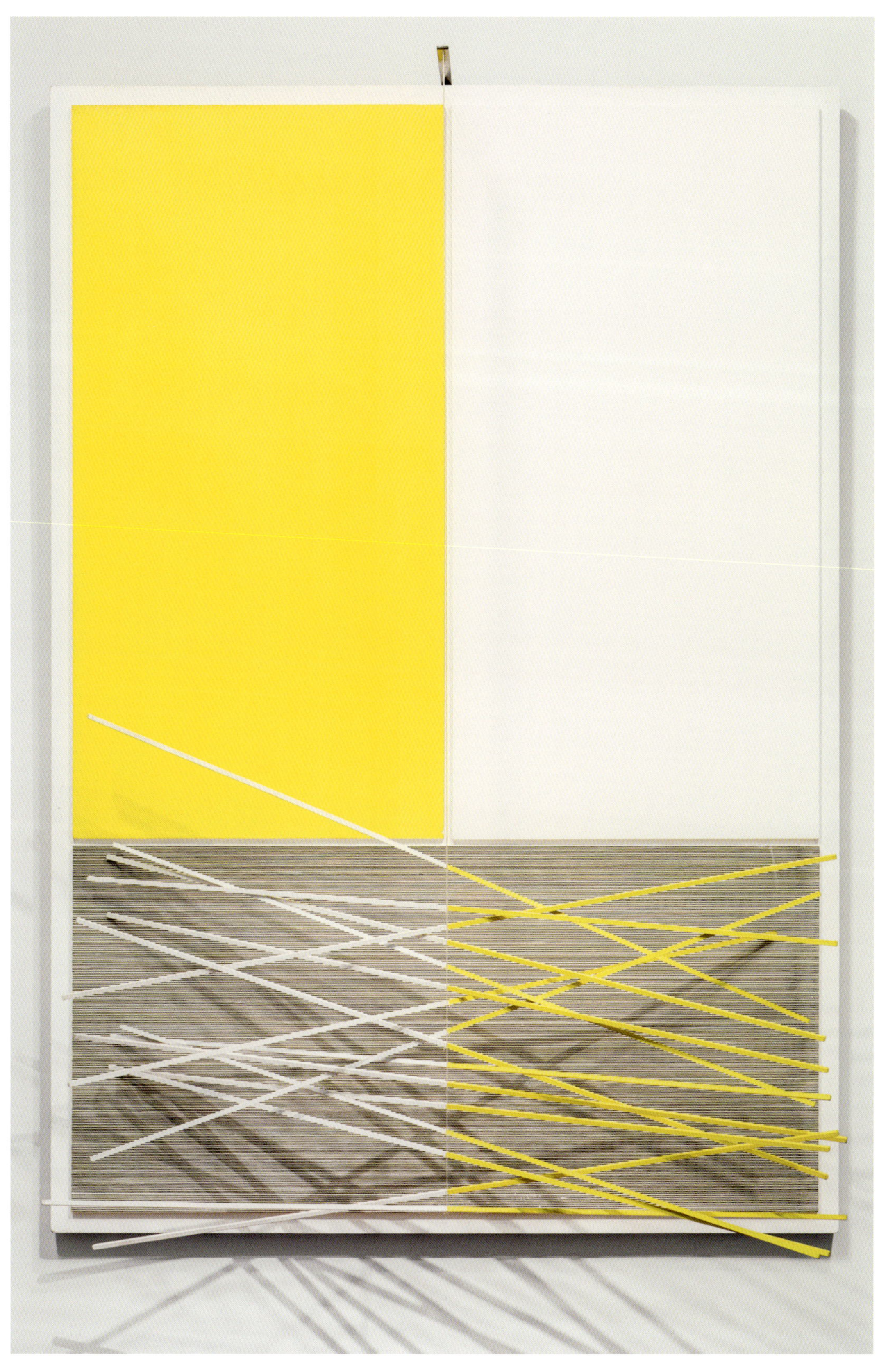

JESÚS RAFAEL SOTO   *Barres et rectangles jaunes et blancs*, 1965
Acrylic on board with aluminum rods and nylon wire, 62 × 42 ½ × 23 in. (157.5 × 108 × 58.4 cm)
Private collection. Courtesy of Sicardi Gallery, Houston

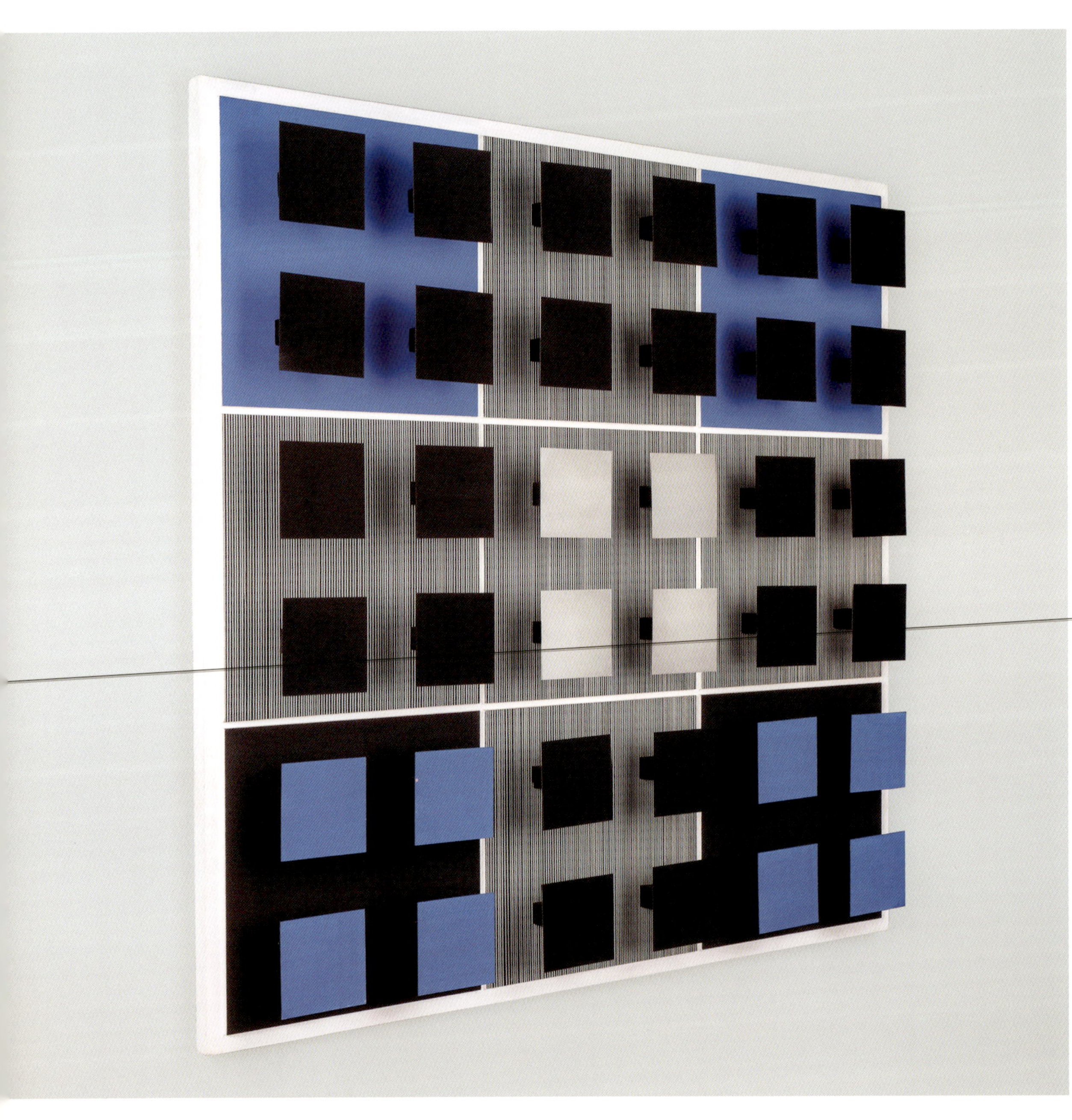

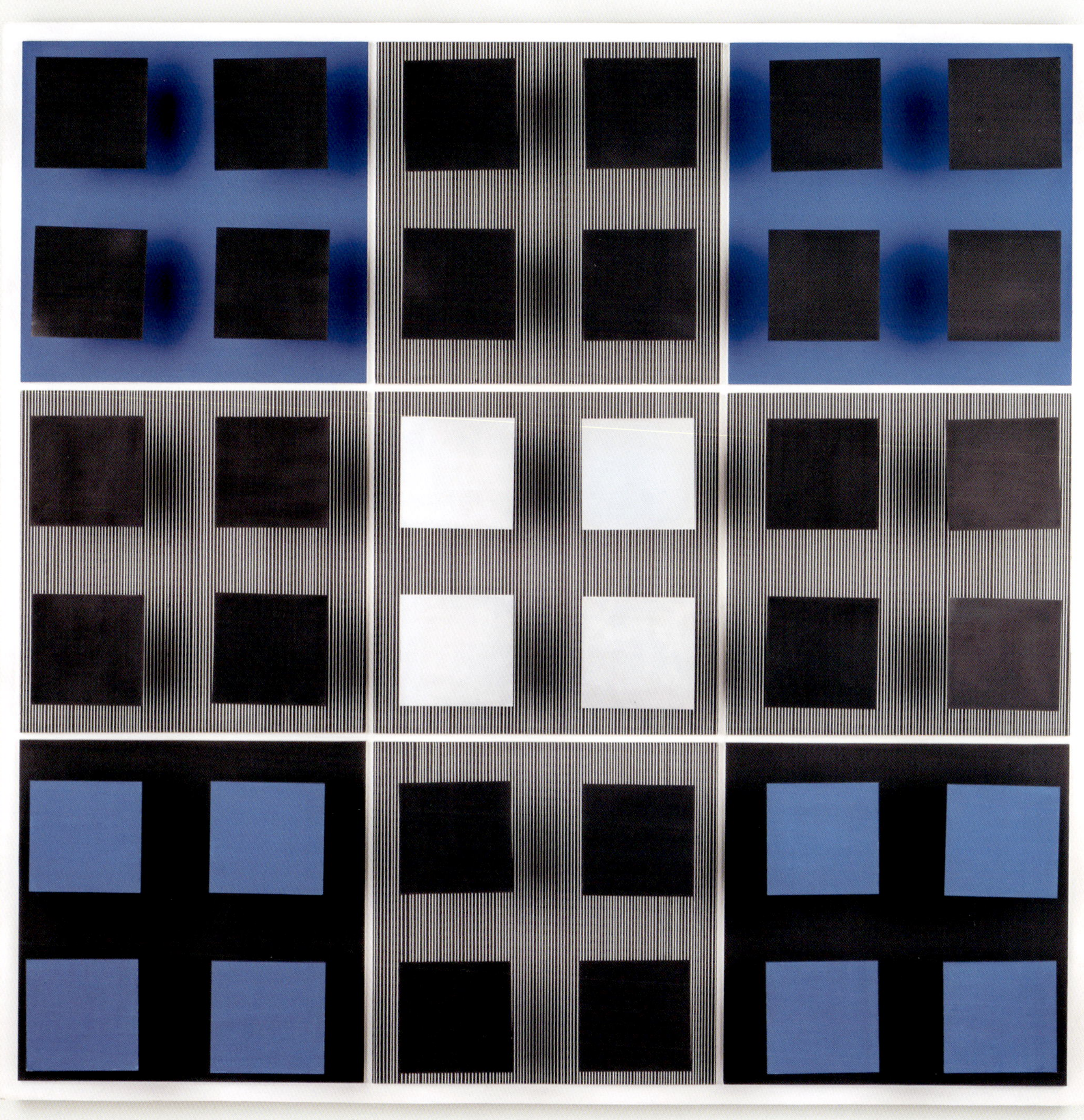

JESÚS RAFAEL SOTO   *Cuatro modulaciones*, 1969
Paint on metal and wood, 60 ¾ x 60 ¾ x 6 ⅞ in. (154.3 × 154.3 x 17.46 cm)
Collection of Palm Springs Art Museum. Gift of the Estate of Sigmund E. Edelstone

ARGENTINA'S "TANDEM SCENE" OF KINETIC ART

María José Herrera

INTRODUCTION

Kinetic Art's genealogy stretches back to early twentieth-century avant-garde movements and Constructivism in Europe, and Concrete Art from the 1930s and 1940s. In Argentina, the artists who strived for renovation by way of abstraction were influenced by the poetics of these movements. Artists in the Concrete, Madí, and Perceptism groups sought the end of representation in a practice that would transcend metaphor, illusion, and the literary anecdote: there would be only pure form, developed on a two-dimensional plane. The "shaped canvas" dealt the coup de grace to the last vestiges of illusion harbored by the "window-frame canvas." Forms gained independence from the stretcher frame to interact directly with their immediate surroundings in Raúl Lozza's "perceptismo" and "coplanar" compositions, which gave plastic relevance to the space around the forms in a way that traditional geometry had not. The Madí manifesto, in a parallel formulation, called for "dynamic, mobile ordering and playfulness," characteristics that take shape in the first transformable work, a sculpture by Gyula Kosice titled *Röyi* (1944).

Argentine artists traveled to Europe in the early 1940s, where they could compare their concerns with those of Max Bill, Constantin Brancusi, Bruno Munari, Antoine Pevsner, and Georges Vantongerloo, among others.[1] Artists on both sides of the Atlantic shared the ideas of modern physics, non-Euclidean geometry, and the conquest of infinite space as sources of inspiration. A new strain of geometrical discourse was thus emerging, whose lexicon included notions like object, environment, light, experience, perception, and movement. This extension of the modernist impulse would have to adapt to the postwar era's new political and cultural conditions. Several utopias had been left behind, and new ones were being generated at the same pace as the exponential acceleration in communication, with corresponding consequences in perceptions of time and space.

1. See Cristina Rossi, "Imágenes inestables: Tránsitos Buenos Aires-París-Buenos Aires," in María José Herrera, *Real/Virtual: Arte cinético argentino en los años sesenta* (Buenos Aires: Museo Nacional de Bellas Artes, 2012).

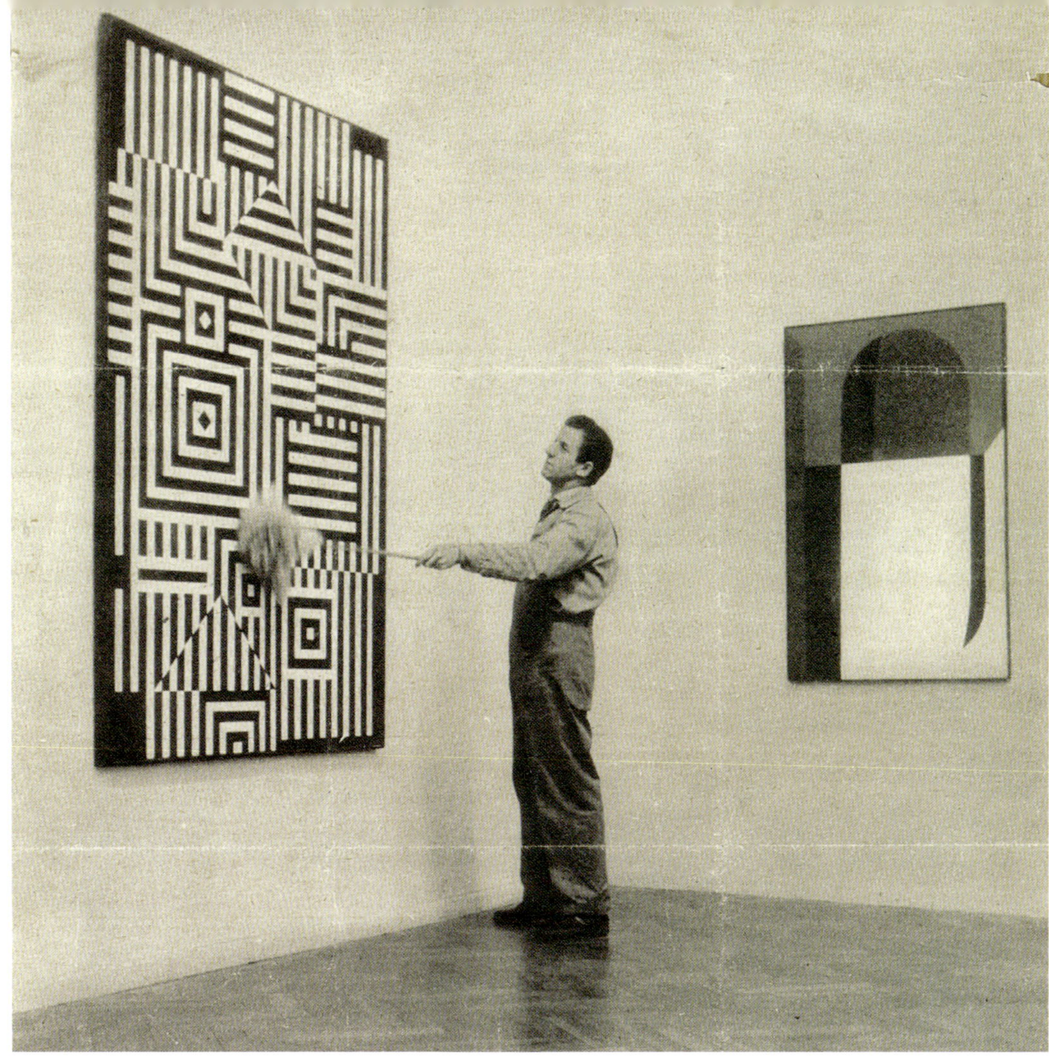

Work by Víctor Vasarely for the August 1958 exhibition at the Museo Nacional de Bellas Artes, Buenos Aires

2. Guy Habasque, "Les expositions: Mortensen et Vasarely," *Aujourd'hui: Art et architecture* (January 1957), 37.

3. Maurice Merleau-Ponty, *Fenomenología de la percepción* (1945; Barcelona: Planeta-Agostini, 1984), 88–89.

In the French avant-garde magazine that made the rounds among artists in Buenos Aires, *Aujourd'hui: Art et architecture,* French-Hungarian artist Victor Vasarely stated the need for a "tabula rasa": "at some point and without any consideration for the old values in our possession, we need to wipe the slate clean . . . and take a leap into the void." Vasarely enjoyed great prestige at the time, and his ideas also reached the port city by way of bulletins distributed by the Asociación Arte Nuevo — founded by Carmelo Arden Quin and Aldo Pellegrini — a group that brought together abstract artists with different allegiances to debate the current state of "modern" art in Argentina and abroad. Vasarely explained that "painting and sculpture became two anachronistic terms . . . it is more precise to speak about two, three and multi-dimensional plastic art. It is no longer a question of different manifestations of creative sensibility, but of developing one single plastic sensibility in different spaces."[2] At the same time, theories such as Gestalt and perceptual phenomenology were also circulating in Argentina. Philosopher Maurice Merleau-Ponty observed that "to look at an object is to inhabit it, and from this habitation to grasp all things in terms of the aspect which they present to it . . . In this way each object is a mirror of all others." Similarly, in relation to time, he indicated that an object is seen from all time-frames (past, present, and future), just as it is seen from everywhere and through the same means — the structure of the horizon.[3]

Toward the end of the 1950s, then, Argentina's art was being nourished along various lines, both locally and from Europe, which sought to erase the boundaries between disciplines, leading to experimentation with environments, objects, and geometry in terms of exploring virtual movement. This experimentation was followed by optical art and art incorporating real movement — or Kinetic Art, featuring optical machines, as the most outstanding example. These manifestations were based on the shared premise that they were aimed at a type of person who would no longer be merely a spectator but an active participant in the aesthetic experience the artists had to offer.

In Paris in 1955, Vasarely organized *Le Mouvement* at Galerie Denise René, an exhibition that was seminal in the formation of the Kinetic Art movement. Artists from different countries experimented with works that could be transformed, involving light as well as real and virtual movement, thus marking the beginning of a trend that would become international in scope. The show's catalogue included a statement, "Le Manifeste jaune" (the Yellow Manifesto), made public on the occasion of the show and published later in the Asociación Arte Nuevo's bulletin in Buenos Aires in 1958. Vasarely stated that the new plastic arts would both receive and provide a place for a range of activities, including fashion, publicity, stage design, urban design, and film. They would address "sensibility," an "intrinsically human faculty," making access to the realm of aesthetics more democratic. This would bring "craft management" to an end, along with the "myth of the unique work," while it would foment the work "of RECREATION, MULTIPLICATION and EXPANSION . . . The majestic chain of **still images** in two dimensions spans from Lascaux to abstract artists . . . in the future, satisfaction awaits us within this new plastic, mobile and emotive beauty."[4] An entire generation of Argentine artists — many of whom worked professionally as graphic designers — experimented with geometry's language, finding inspiration in these ideas, which also allowed for a broader distribution of their work by way of a cultural industry that was blossoming during the early years of *Desarrollismo*.[5]

Vasarely's work finally came to be known in Buenos Aires in 1958, when an exhibition that had been part of the São Paulo Biennial was presented at the Museo Nacional de Bellas Artes. The show inspired different artists — some only briefly — to employ the serial methodology and the laws of vision applied by Vasarely to develop their own works. Antonio Asís, Martha Boto, Ary Brizzi, Hugo Demarco, Armando Durante, Manuel Espinosa, Horacio García-Rossi,

4. The boldface type and capital letters appear in the original.

5. *Desarrollismo* was the policy implemented during Arturo Frondizi's presidency, a political theory that encouraged industrialization. During this period, Argentina enjoyed unprecedented levels of internal capitalization, and an era of great prosperity and increased per capita consumption.

Julio Le Parc, Eduardo Mac Entyre, Francisco García Miranda, Rogelio Polesello, Carlos Silva, Francisco Sobrino, Luis Tomasello, Gregorio Vardánega, and Miguel Ángel Vidal all formed part of this new tradition in Argentine art associated with the figure of Vasarely. Many emigrated to France and went on to become the so-called "Paris Argentineans," artists who enjoyed success and recognition while giving Kinetic Art an international dimension, in Europe as well as in Argentina.

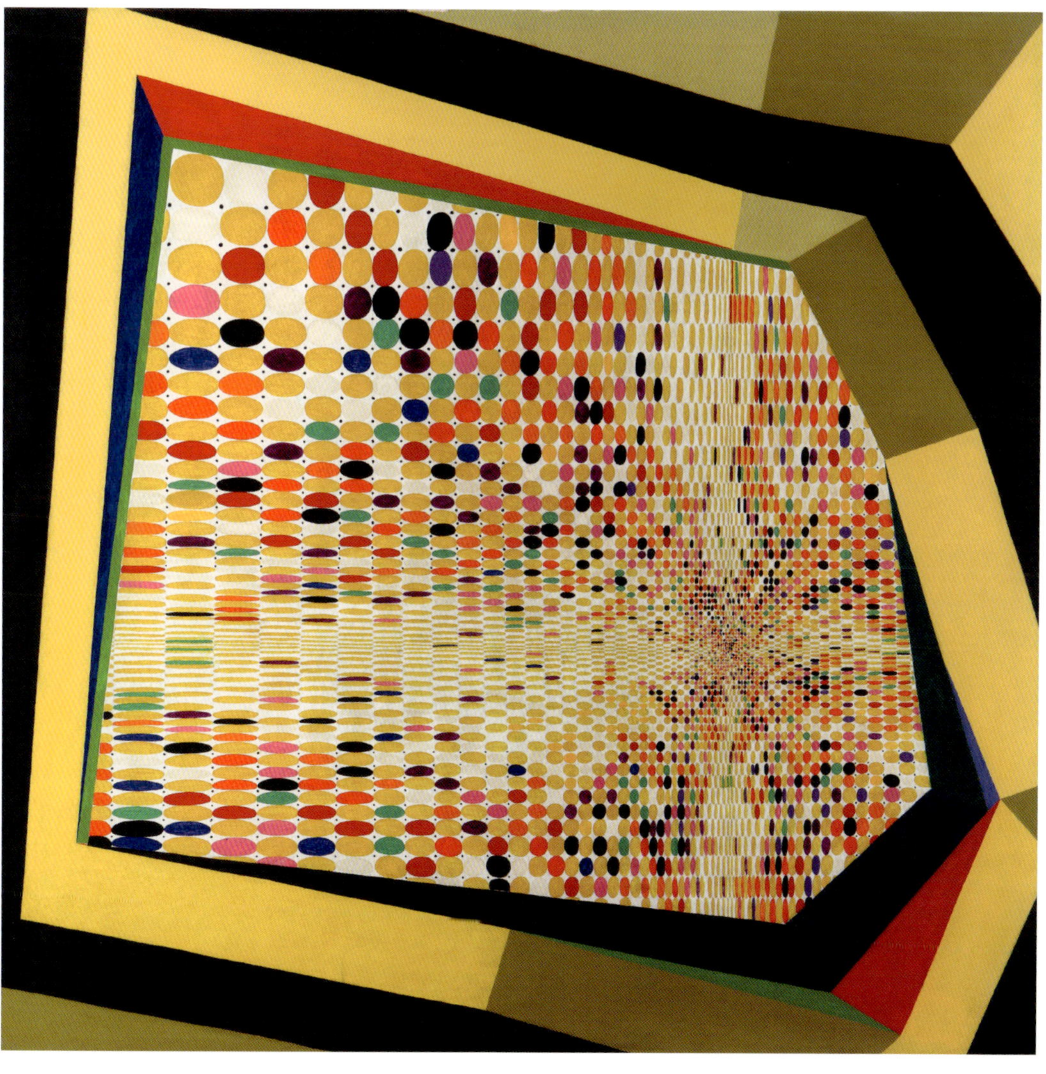

Carlos Silva, *Ibus II*, 1968, oil on canvas, 47 ³/₈ x 47 ³/₈ in. (120.5 x 120.5 cm). Private collection

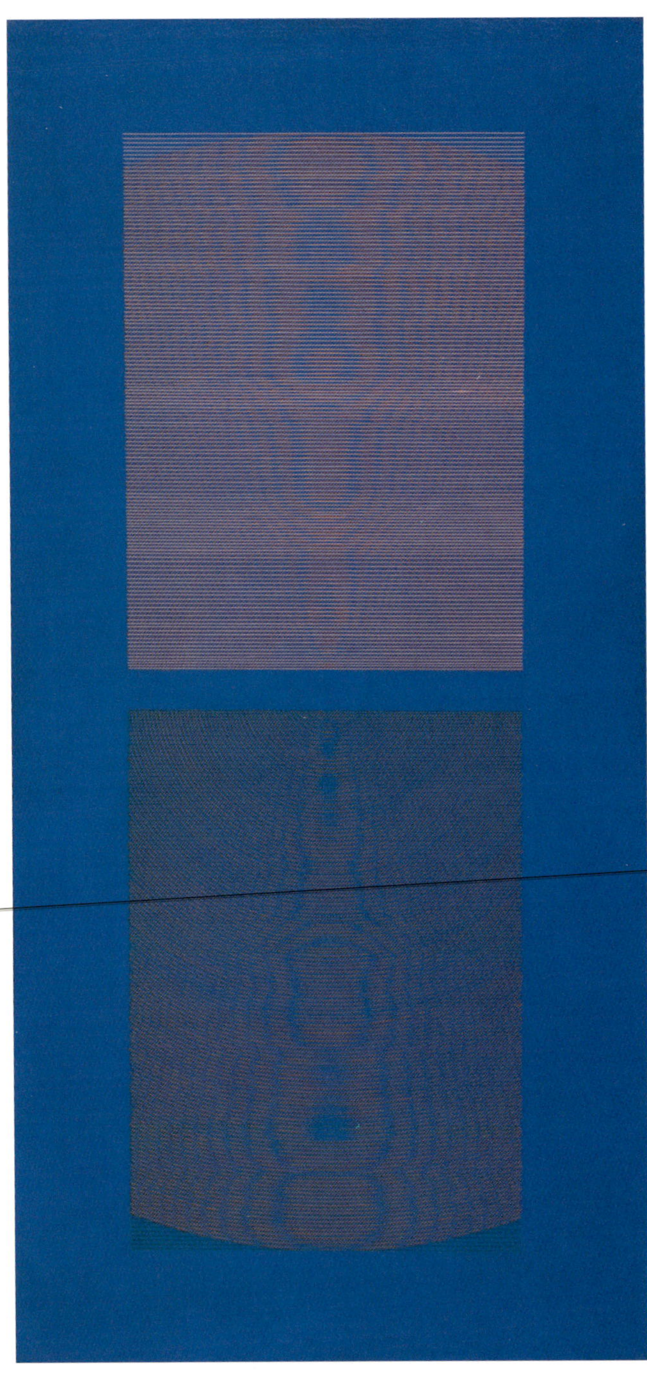

Eduardo Armando Mac Entyre, *Tramas*, 1961/1964, oil on canvas, 53 x 25 in. (135 x 63.5 cm). Colección Museo Nacional de Bellas Artes, inv. 7275, acquired through a grant from the Fondo Nacional de las Artes 1964

In Buenos Aires, Eduardo Mac Entyre and Miguel Ángel Vidal founded the Arte Generativo (Generative Art) group in 1959, a local strain of optical art, or Op art. Joined by Ignacio Pirovano as the group's theoretician, they explained that with formal art as their point of departure, they had been able to set points and lines in motion, engendering other forms through turns, shifts, and vibrations, always on the two-dimensional plane. Mac Entyre worked with curves that were superimposed to create vibration, and from there, new configurations. In Vidal's work, straight lines were deployed to generate the illusion of movement. Both asserted that they had "created new forms of beauty" containing energy and strength, "identified with the present and with the future."[6]

When Julio Le Parc arrived in Paris in 1958 to settle there, he brought his "plastic experiences" with him, along with his ideas of rebellion against traditional art and its elitist circulation. He had forged these notions along with his fellow participants in the Movimiento estudentil (Student Movement) in Buenos Aires, some of whom had also emigrated.[7] As a result, exchange between the artists active in kinetic experimentation in Paris and Buenos Aires began very early on.[8]

Le Parc made his first mobile pieces in 1960, using metal plates hung on threads and illuminated with external artificial light. This marked the outset of an interest that would bring about the formation of the Groupe de Recherche d'Art Visuel, known as GRAV, in 1961, where he was joined by Argentine Horacio García-Rossi and Europeans François Morellet, Francisco Sobrino,[9] Joël Stein, and Jean-Pierre Yvaral. They would gain a high level of visibility on the art scene after exhibiting at Galerie Denise René. The group aspired to shape a new relationship with viewers, eliminating the traditional category of the unique work of art by a single author. In accord with this viewpoint, they abandoned painting and took up constructions, making prototypes that would allow multiple examples to be produced like print editions, thus broadening access to art objects.

At the opening for the second Paris Biennial in 1961, members of the group handed out a manifesto titled "Assez de mystifications" (Enough with the Mystifications), in which they held that "the stable, unique, definitive and irreplaceable work of art goes against the evolution of our era." In their creations and in these texts, the group members reflected on the artist's role in society, and they spread these ideas throughout other important international art centers in the years that followed, including at Documenta in Kassel, the Venice Biennial, and through other artists' groups associated with Kinetic Art. In addition to these international initiatives, an exhibition by GRAV titled *La Inestabilidad* (Instability) was presented in Buenos Aires in 1964. The overall image was contemporary, marked by the predominance of technology, viewer participation, and "multiples," as well as the introduction of environments, mobile pieces, ceilings, and relief murals. To an unusual extent, the exhibition provoked repercussions in the Argentine public and press.

6. *Arte generativo*, exhibition catalogue (Buenos Aires: Salón Peuser, 1960).

7. During the reordering of institutions following the fall of President Juan Domingo Perón in 1955, students took over the fine arts schools. Le Parc was actively involved in these events, which led to the formation of the Movimiento estudantil group, which sought to transform and update art education and communication. See Cristina Rossi, "Tránsitos Buenos Aires-París-Buenos Aires."

8. See Isabel Plante, *Argentinos de París: Arte y viajes culturales durante los años sesenta* (Buenos Aires: Edhasa, 2013).

9. Born in Spain in 1932, he moved to Argentina in 1949 and attended the School of Fine Arts there. In 1958, he finally settled in Europe.

Production of optical and kinetic artworks in Argentina was already growing, with the support provided by prizes and exhibitions. Julián Althabe, Fioravanti Bangardini, Jacques Bedel, Perla Benveniste, Ary Brizzi, Davite, Manuel Espinosa, César A. Fioravanti, Gyula Kosice, Eduardo Mac Entyre, Rogelio Polesello, Eduardo Rodríguez, Carlos Silva, and Miguel Ángel Vidal, among others, worked with light and movement. They created mechanisms or objects that made the most of peripheral vision's retinal instability by means of deforming lenses, superimposed layers of glass or acrylic, and movement generated through simple devices, such as hot air circulation with light bulbs. Meanwhile, other Argentine artists were arriving in Paris, the mecca for Kinetic Art, where the numerous international artists working there included Venezuelan artists Carlos Cruz-Diez and Jesús Rafael Soto. Antonio Asís, Martha Boto,

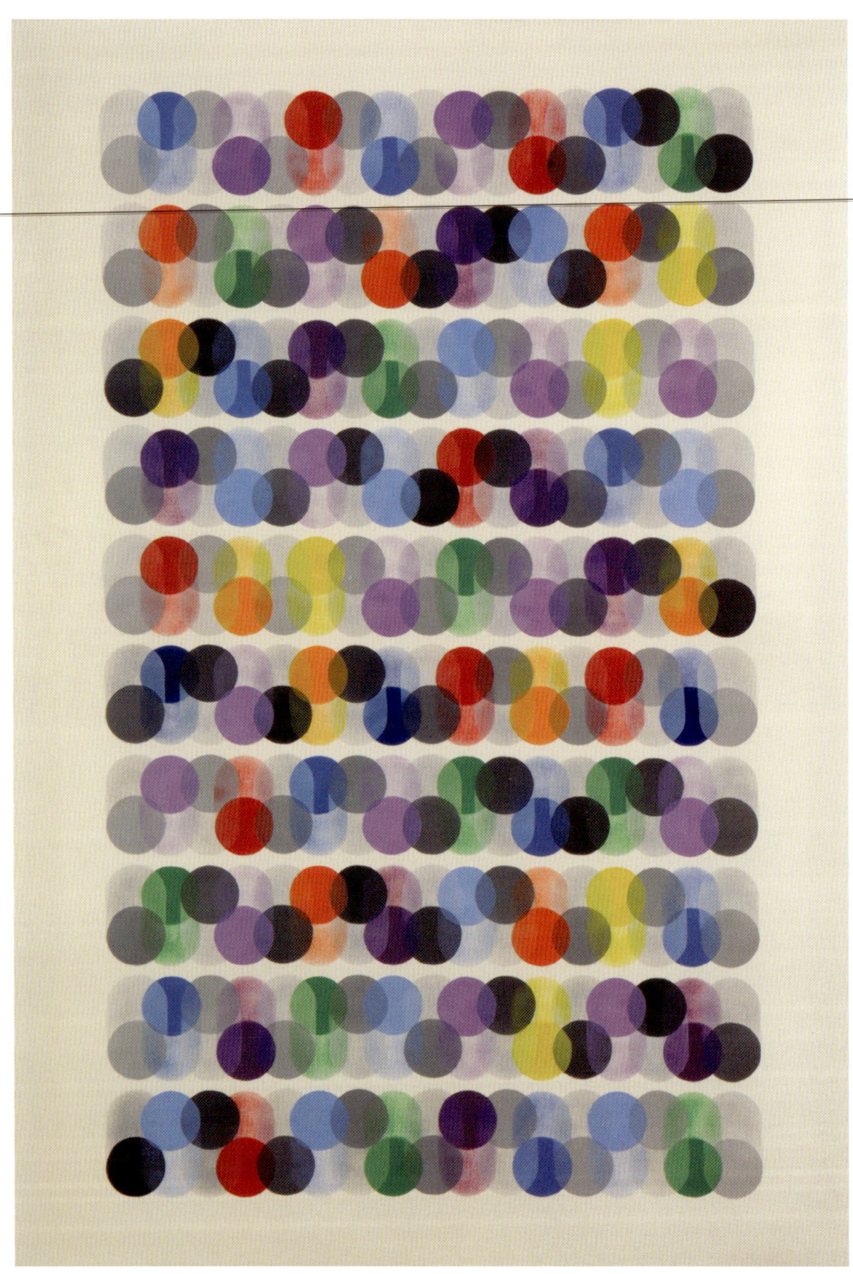

Manuel Espinosa, *Agarnixg*, 1966, oil on canvas, 59 x 39 ¼ in. (150 x 100 cm). Colección Espìnosa, ET616

Hugo Demarco, Armando Durante, Gregorio Vardánega, and Luis Tomasello settled in France and figured among the artists forming part of Galerie Denise René. These artists also had a marked presence in Buenos Aires, however, by way of their works, which were shown in solo exhibitions in local galleries, as well as participation in juries for prizes. In the case of Luis Tomasello, the 1962 exhibition titled *Tomasello: Relieves* (Tomasello: Relief Pieces), held at the Museo Nacional de Bellas Artes, was an opportunity to acknowledge the important contribution he made to optical art known as *cromoplastía* (chromoplasty).[10] This clearly demonstrates the fluid contact and feedback taking place between Paris and Buenos Aires at the time: the Kinetic Art that blossomed in both cities had its roots in the same artistic tradition.

10. Tomasello pointed out that color is born out of form and transforms "vision" into "sensation." His chromoplasties, or chromoplastic atmospheres, are produced by the reflection created by vibrant colors on the white surface of background planes.

In 1966, Julio Le Parc was awarded the Golden Lion in Painting at the Venice Biennial, leaving no doubt about Kinetic Art's success and Argentina's contribution to the movement, which promised to make access to aesthetic enjoyment more democratic. One year later, Le Parc reiterated the call to a broader public in a retrospective show held at the Instituto Di Tella in Buenos Aires, which met with acclaim. The year 1968, however, would be GRAV's final year of activity as a group. Le Parc's individual distinction with the Venice award, as it contradicted the tenet that work and recognition should be undertaken and received collectively, produced tensions within the group, while differences in political views and artistic strategies among members only hastened the process of disintegration.

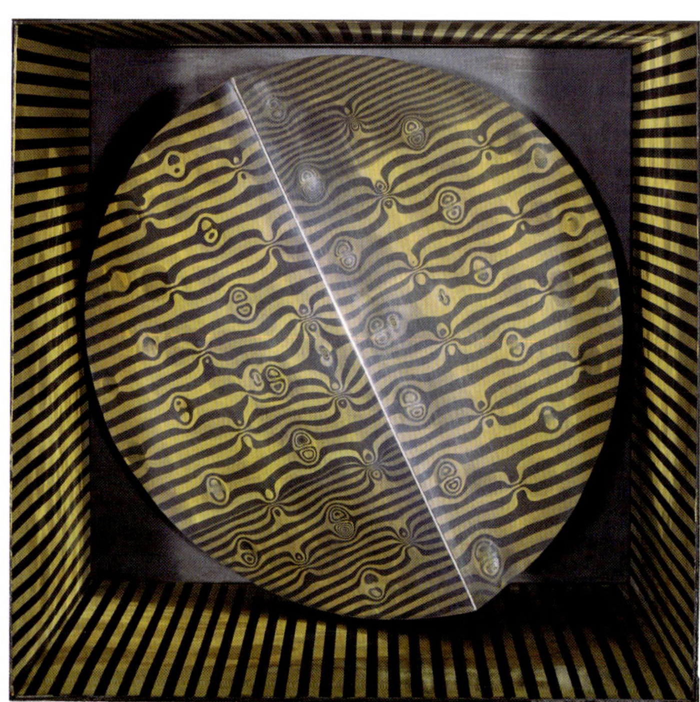

Julio Le Parc, *Trames altérées (caja)*, 1968, artist's proof (Éditions Denise René), steel and 220V motor in metal box with silkscreened paper interior, 11 ⅞ x 11 ⅞ x 11 ⅞ in. (30 x 30 x 30 cm). Fundación Costantini, Colección Museo de Arte Latinoamericano de Buenos Aires

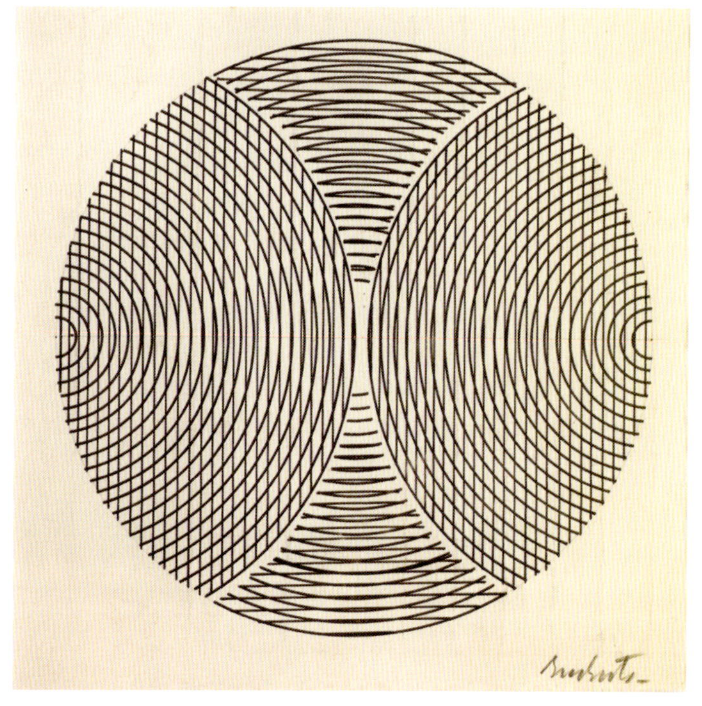

Eduardo Armando Mac Entyre, *Untitled*, 1962/1964, ink on paper, 5 ½ x 5 ½ in. (14 x 14 cm). Private collection

Today's concept of art is generated in parallel with the notion of industry . . . Industry thus becomes entirely the instrument of a new humanism. Art does not ignore that the capacity for social communication that used to pertain to it during the pre-industrial era now eludes it. And industry, in turn, has learned to accept artists' capacity for exploration, which is found only within the individual, and needed by any social enterprise. —Basilio Uribe

Desarrollismo's economic-political project during the mid-1950s brought with it a rare phase of industrial expansion, with an increase in jobs and an overall rise in the standard of living. The middle class in Argentina was the largest in all of South America, and its consumer habits were being transformed. A mass society was coming into being, with the help of communications technology. A blossoming cultural industry disseminated film, music, theater, and, to an unprecedented extent, the visual arts in the cosmopolitan centers of Buenos Aires, Rosario, and Córdoba.

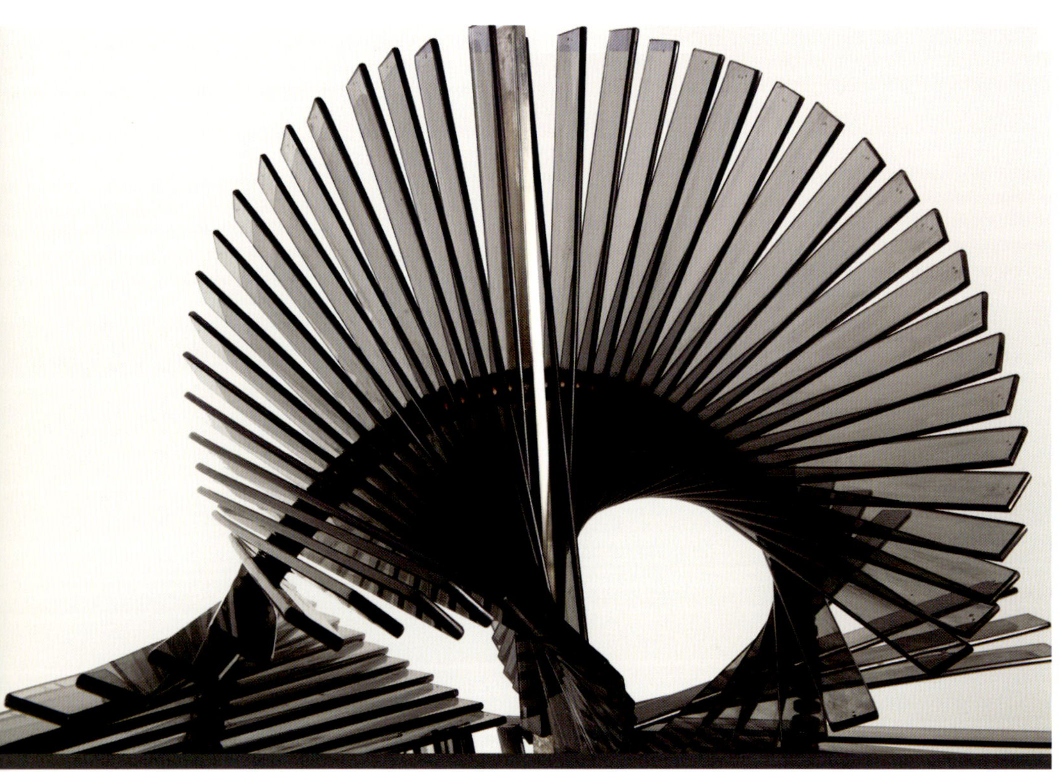

Ary Brizzi, *Construcción a partir de una circunferencia*, n.d. (detail), glass and metal, 40 ⅛ x 39 ⅛ x 23 in. (102 x 99.5 x 60.5 cm). Colección Museo Nacional de Bellas Artes, inv. 7210, gift 1964

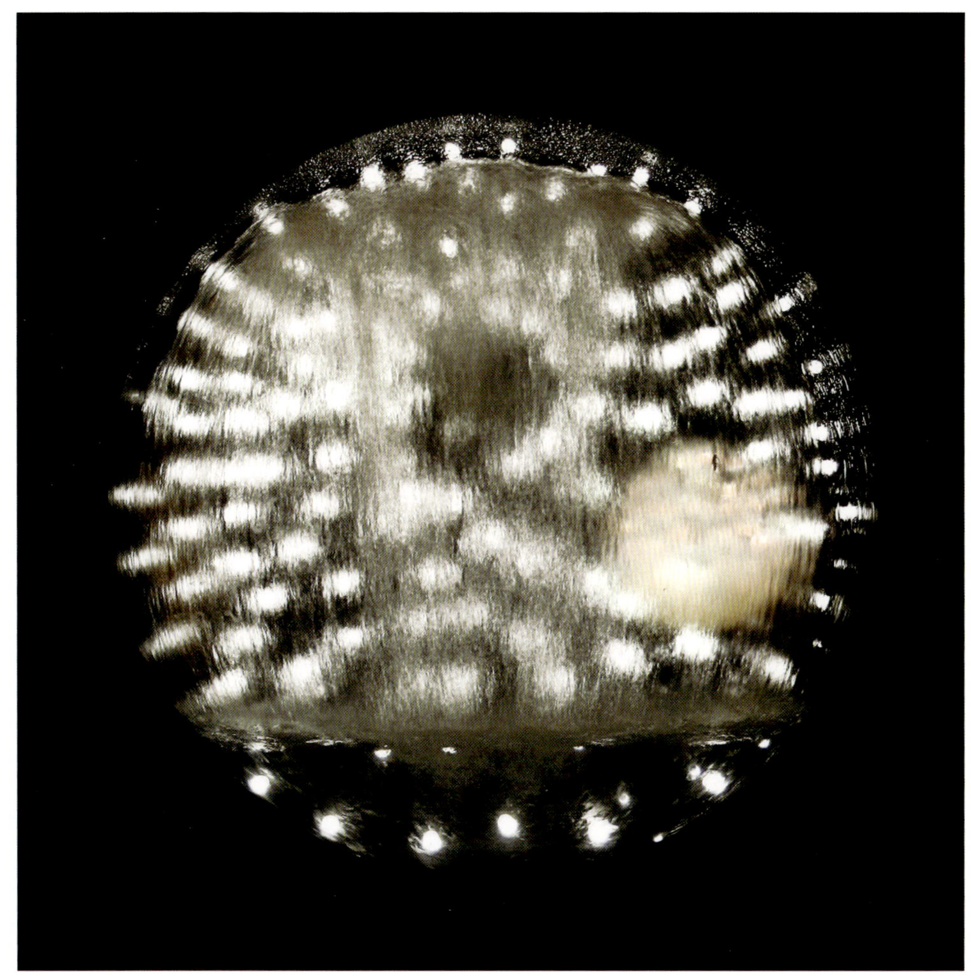

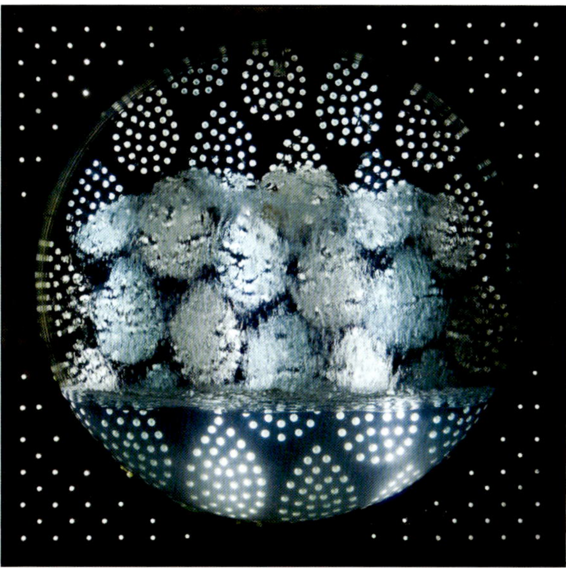

Left: Gyula Kosice, *Hidroactividad (caja)*, 1966, acrylic, wood, water, lights, and motor, 82 ¼ x 61 ⅜ x 35 ⅜ in. (209 x 156 x 90 cm). Private collection

Above: Gyula Kosice, *Hidroactividad, H-13*, 1965, acrylic, water, lights, and motor, 27 x 27 x 16 ⅞ in. (69 x 69 x 43 cm). Colección Museo Nacional de Bellas Artes, inv. 9819, acquired 1996

Part of this modernizing project involved a renewed collaboration between art and industry. In Buenos Aires, the creation of the Instituto Di Tella — a project undertaken by a company dedicated to the automotive and home appliances industry — aimed to promote science and the arts, as did Kaiser, another automotive company, in Córdoba. They organized prizes and biennial exhibitions; other companies also joined them in providing cultural incentives. The itinerary of Kinetic Art in Argentina reached an additional landmark during the mid-1960s: institutional recognition and the creation of a new discipline, Investigaciones Visuales (Visual Research).

11. A French painter, critic, and director of Lirolay gallery in Buenos Aires. Derbecq was married to sculptor Pablo Curatella Manes.

In 1966, the exhibition *Plástica con plásticos* (Plastic Arts Using Plastic) invited participants to work with "the material of the future." An international jury was appointed to award prizes, comprising Germaine Derbecq,[11] Thomas Messer (director of the Guggenheim Museum in New York), Michel Ragon (a French critic), and Aldo Pellegrini (Argentine poet, essayist, and art critic), all well versed in the international art scene. Gyula Kosice presented a piece titled

Hidroactividad (Hydroactivity), an expression in his kinetic vein featuring water in movement. During his Concrete phase in the 1940s, Kosice had been among the first to make use of acrylic. Fioravanti Bangardini showed *Estructuras con color-energía* (Structures with Color-Energy), which experimented with chromatic changes in neon light. Both Ary Brizzi and Rogelio Polesello focused on acrylic's transparent quality and the corresponding incidence of light interacting with it. Eduardo Rodríguez exploited the heat emitted by electric light bulbs as energy that generated movement in small pieces of celluloid, which reflected on to an acrylic column, in *Estructuras luminodinámicas* (Luminous-dynamic Structures).

In the *Materiales, nuevas técnicas, nuevas expresiones* show (Materials, New Techniques, New Expressions), organized by the Unión Industrial Argentina and held two years later, in 1968, the union's member companies contributed a wide range of innovative materials, including metal alloys, tempered glass, and plastics. Almost 50 percent of the pieces shown in the *Materiales* exhibition were kinetic by definition. At that time, Kinetic Art seemed to be part of the established canon, so that artists who may not have habitually cultivated the practice ventured into it, given the availability of materials and opportunities offered by these "thematic" competitive salons. The results included a distinctive type of kinetic works produced by Argentine artists, with interactive mechanisms employing "poor," or elementary, technology.

One of the prizes was awarded to optical-kinetic artist Ary Brizzi for *Interacción luz color* (Light Color Interaction), a large-scale light sculpture. The *Materiales* exhibition also featured mechanical pieces by kinetic artists who had emigrated to Paris (Boto, Demarco, Durante, García-Rossi, Sobrino, and Vardánega), and demonstrated the synchronicity of the Argentines'

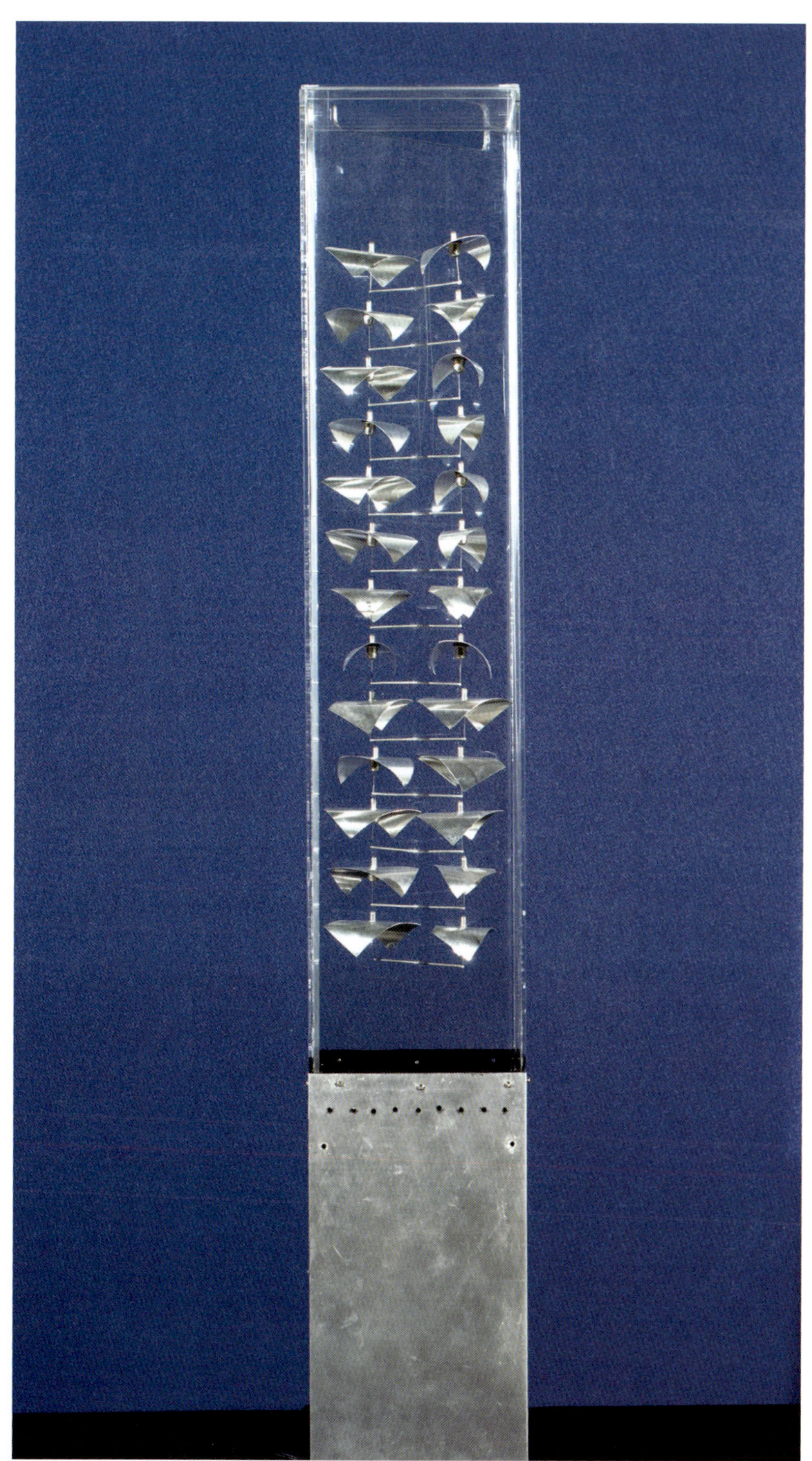

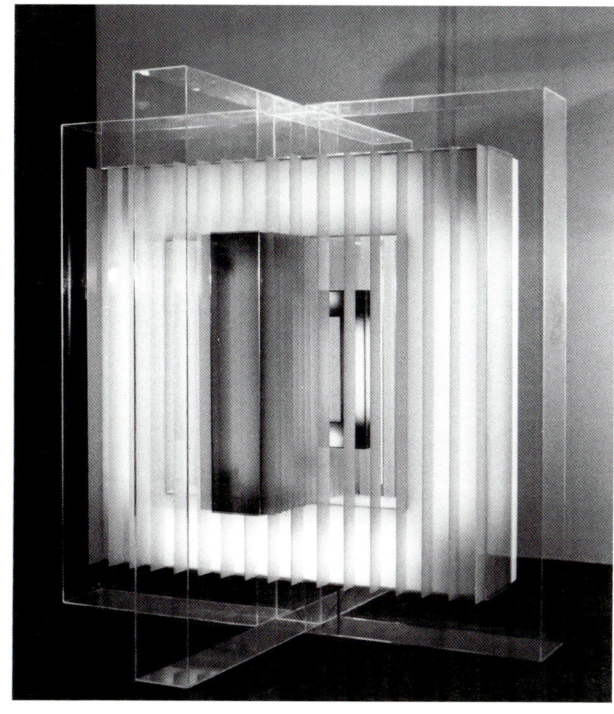

Left: Eduardo Rodríguez, *Columna luminosa*, ca. 1970–2011, acrylic, aluminum, light, and motor, 39 x 6 x 6 in. (99.5 x 15 x 15 cm) . Colección Museo Nacional de Bellas Artes, inv. 7796, gift of Jorge Romero Brest 1971

Above: Work by Ary Brizzi for the 1968 exhibition *Materiales, nuevas técnicas, nuevas expresiones*, organized by the Unión Industrial Argentina

research and techniques: a shared penchant for mechanical devices in which boxes and screens concealed motors, mirrors, and lights, with ingenious applications of elementary technology to achieve sophisticated aesthetic effects. For some critics, the exhibition was an Argentine version of the E.A.T. project (Experiments in Arts and Technology), founded in New York in 1966 by artist Robert Rauschenberg and engineer Billy Klüver. That group's aim was clearly "to create within the technological world in order to satisfy the traditional involvement of the artist with the forces that shape society."[12]

The intention of turning art into a participative practice for viewers was a way of putting the notion of "inhabiting the object" into effect, which GRAV had proposed in Paris, along with diverse artists in Buenos Aires. Le Parc, García-Rossi, and their French colleagues were reconsidering "the relationship between the work and the human eye," and together they created "new visual situations," postulating that a work "only exists in this relationship."[13] The viewer was consequently as much a physical reality as a social one, the protagonist of the discourse articulating the era's diverse poetics.[14] In this sense, the kinetic works produced by Argentines were typically characterized as participative, playful, and dedicated to reversing the alienation of everyday life: the aim was to broaden individual perception in the same way that technology does. The same thesis was advanced by the so-called media guru Marshall McLuhan in his book *Understanding Media: The Extensions of Man* (1964), which enjoyed wide international circulation at that time.[15]

Kinetic art objects — not paintings or sculptures — were the subject of debate in exhibition regulations, particularly in cases such as the Salón Nacional, which resisted modernizing change, yet its success was undeniable. The Salón thus decided to broaden its range of disciplines, incorporating Investigaciones Visuales in 1968 to provide a place for kinetic machines. As Ana Longoni points out, the creation of this specific section, Julio Le Parc's distinction in Venice and his celebrated exhibition at Di Tella in 1967, the GRAV's show at the Museo Nacional de Bellas Artes

12. *E.A.T. News* 1, no. 2 (New York, 1967).

13. *Basta de mistificaciones*, GRAV (Paris, 1961).

14. In Buenos Aires in 1961, Rubén Santantonín wrote "A mis mirones" (To My Voyeurs), in which he pointed out that art is "devotional, existential participation." That same year, in his manifesto "Arte cosa-rodante" (Art Thing-on-Wheels), he referred to a viewer who is "converted into an active participant." The "Vivo dito" manifesto by Alberto Greco appeared in 1962, followed by the happenings and environments, which required active participation by the public.

15. Marshall McLuhan, *La comprensión de los medios como las extensiones del hombre*, 2nd ed. (Mexico City: Editorial Diana, 1969).

16. Ana Longoni, "Investigaciones Visuales en el Salón Nacional (1968–71): La historia de un atisbo de modernización que terminó en clausura," in *Tras los pasos de la norma*, coordinated by Marta Penhos and Diana Wechsler, Archivos del CAIA 2 (Ediciones del Jilguero, 1999), 198.

17. Susana Castillo composed the music that accompanied the piece, and it was produced at the electronic music lab at the Universidad de Córdoba, Argentina.

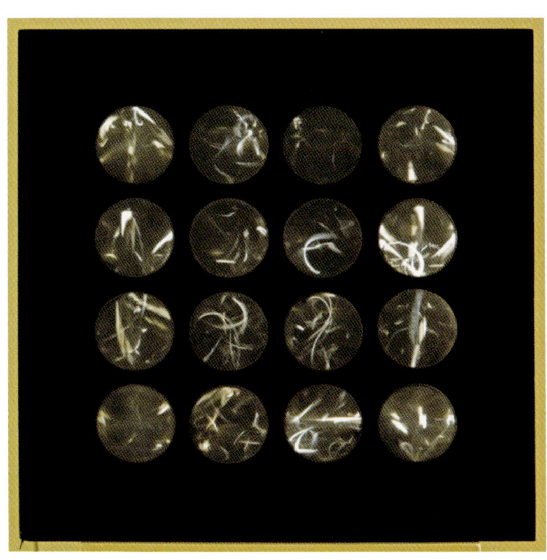

Martha Boto, *Microlux (caja)*, wood, acrylic, lights, and motor, 25 ⅝ x 29 ½ x 18 ¼ in. (65.3 x 75 x 46.5 cm). Colección Museo Nacional de Bellas Artes, inv. 7418, acquired through a grant from the Fondo Nacional de las Artes 1967

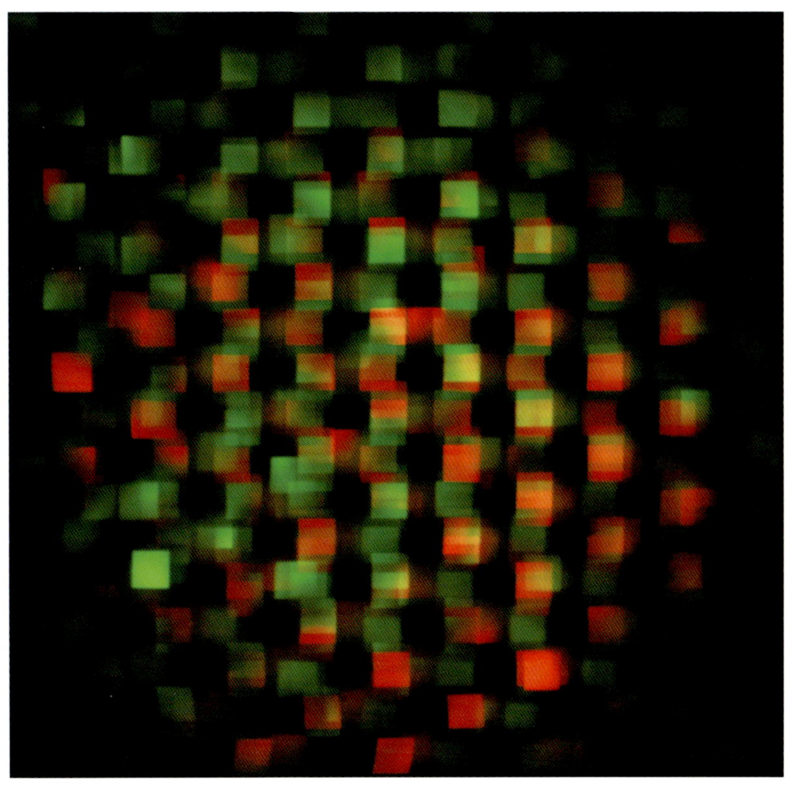

Horacio García-Rossi, *Boîte lumineuse D*, 1964/1967, acrylic, wood, lights, celluloid, paper, and motor, 70 ⅞ x 70 ⅞ x 28 in. (180 x 180 x 73 cm). Colección Museo Nacional de Bellas Artes, inv. 7510, gift of the artist 1969

prior to that, and the prizes awarded to Soto and Cruz-Diez in the Kaiser Biennials in Córdoba all confirm the supposition that in the Argentine context, "the experimental tendency that was most quickly incorporated by institutions, critics and the public during the second half of the decade was kinetic art."[16] In effect, by the late 1960s, Kinetic Art's visibility and influence were part of a cultural industry in full bloom. In the country's most important cities, "multiples" circulated in art galleries and design boutiques, with an aesthetic identified with a modern world to which many sought entrée.

The single prize the Salón Nacional offered in the newly created Investigaciones Visuales category was awarded in 1968 to Eduardo Giusiano and Jorge Schneider for their jointly created piece *Generador de imágenes* (Images Generator), a complex apparatus combining optical devices (magnifying glasses and mirrors), light (from light bulbs), and mechanical means to produce three-dimensional images, where the iconic reference to a television screen could be discerned. Its mechanisms were exposed, in plain view, and accompanied by music.[17] The machine was not a symbol of progress as much as the wonder of the automaton, the marvel that results from form-creating imagination.

In 1970, the Investigaciones Visuales section of the Salón Nacional was spun off to become a competitive exhibition all its own, the Certamen Nacional de Investigaciones Visuales (National Visual Research Competition). Only two exhibitions for this prize were held, with fewer participants than had been expected. Eduardo Rodríguez was the winner of the first Certamen with the work *Espacio temporalizado* (Space Made Temporal), an illuminated box with clear acrylic disks painted with different colored concentric circles in order to generate a variety of visual patterns when set in motion.

One year later, in 1971 — at a particularly agitated moment in our recent history — the competition was "taken over" by artists who had little to do with Kinetic Art — the usual habitués of these salons — with the aim of undermining an art form that they already saw as formalist, "canonical art," emptied of any significance. Using its imprecise regulations as an excuse, a group of artists presented works with markedly political content, denouncing persecution and torture. The action appears to have been a statement directed at their fellow artists involved in kinetic practice, that the time for "play" and "narcotic" expansions of perception had come to an end. It was time to take action on urgent realities, where the very figure of the artist was becoming a contradiction.[18]

The issue of art's function in society had developed into different controversies. Along with the "dematerialization of art" that conceptual art proposed, art's traditional disciplines were retracting and genres were being hybridized. The "death of art" was a prevalent prediction among critics at the time. One route was a fusion between art and design, and the art or design option could be seen reflected in exhibitions like *Objetos útiles e inútiles con Acrílicopaolini* (Useful and Useless Objects with Acrílicopaolini) in 1970, with an abundance of kinetic mechanisms.[19]

That same year, *Panorama de experiencias visuales argentinas* (Panorama of Argentine Visual Experiences) was held at the Fundación Lorenzutti. The catalogue pointed out that these experiences were an "aesthetic proposition that has reached a relevant level of development in our midst."[20] In effect, the Salón Nacional, and its prize, the Festival de las Artes held in Tandil (1968 to 1970), and the exhibitions mentioned above had all established Visual Research as a particular type of experimentation. As previously mentioned, it was at the heart of

18. Among the works presented, there was a "picana," a notorious instrument of torture invented in Argentina that delivers an electric shock to the prisoner's body. The piece was made of acrylic (Kinetic Art's favorite material) and like the real version, had electric current. It was a kinetic object *sensu stricto*, and the title of the piece was *Made in Argentina*.

19. There was an extensive open call that brought together *useful* objects, such as doors, privacy screens or room dividers, jewelry, and tables, as well as *useless* ones, sculptures and different pieces of three-dimensional art.

20. *Panorama de experiencias visuales argentinas*, exhibition catalogue (Buenos Aires: Fundación Lorenzutti, 1971), 11.

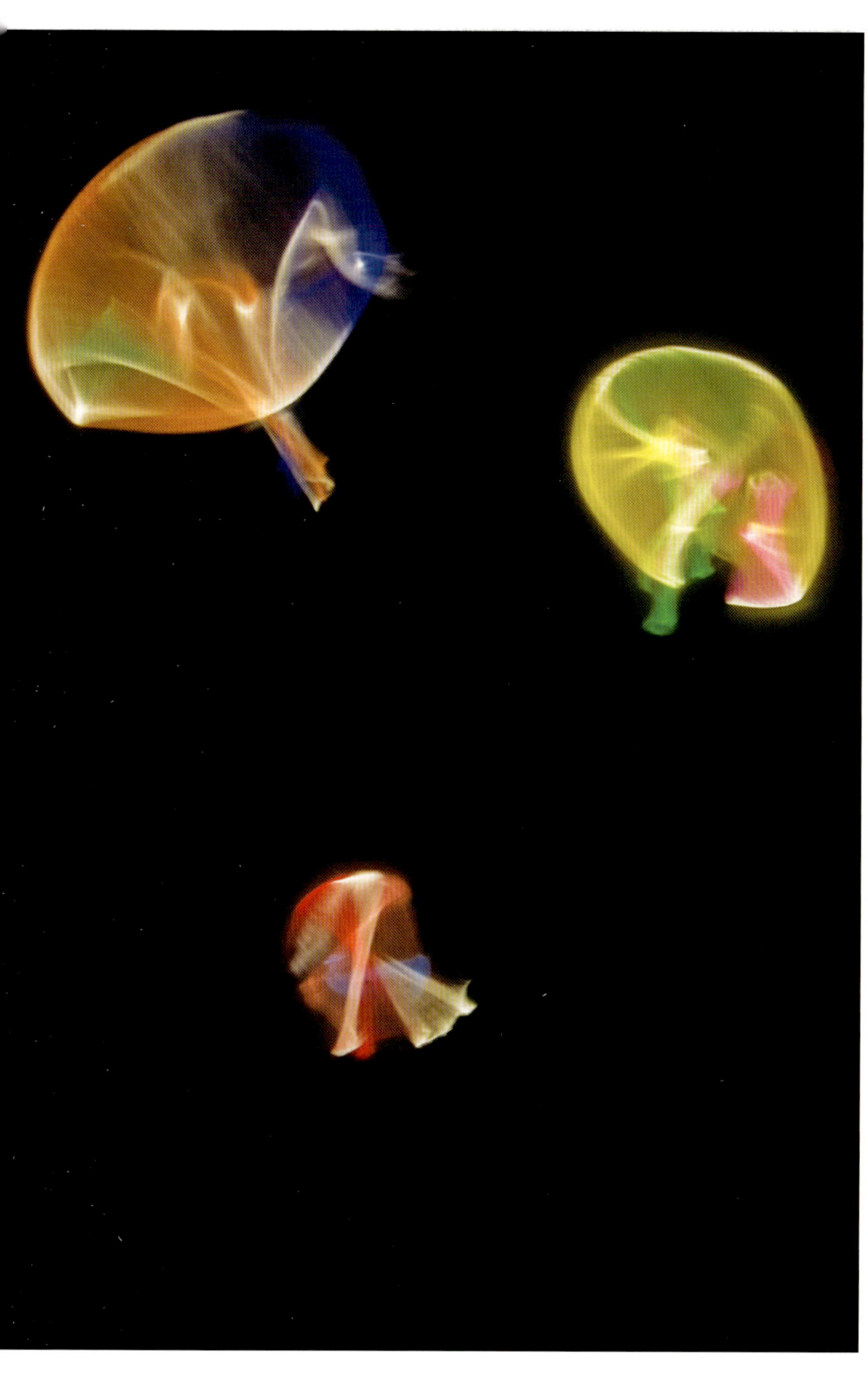

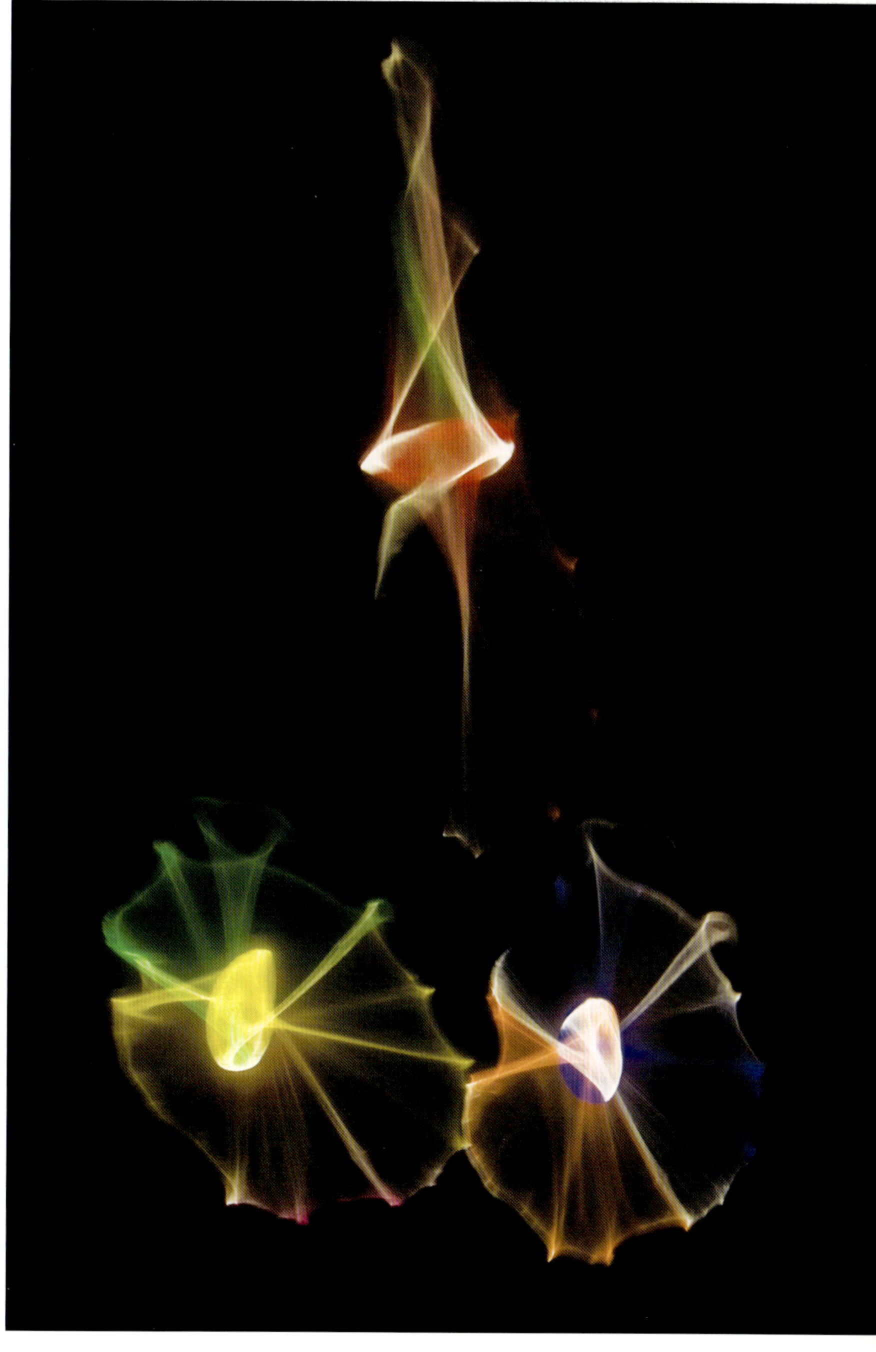

Eduardo Giusiano and Jorge Schneider, *Generador de imágenes*, ca. 1968, wood, mirrors, lenses, metal, acetate, lights, and motor, 29 x 31 ½ x 13 ⅝ in. (73.5 x 80 x 35 cm). Colección Museo Nacional de Bellas Artes, inv. 7693, acquired 1968

Desarrollismo's industrial optimism that Kinetic Art was able to unfold and to grow. This same optimism was now being severely questioned and would show its utopian facet during the oil crisis soon to come.

In this sense, Gyula Kosice's participation in *Panorama,* with *La ciudad hidroespacial* (The Hydrospatial City), is emblematic of art's projection of life as an urban, environmental initiative that combines poetry and technology. Artists established in both Paris (Boto, Demarco, Durante, García-Rossi, Le Parc, Sobrino, and Vardánega) and Buenos Aires (Julián Althabe, Fioravanti Bangardini, Ary Brizzi, Davite, César A. Fioravanti, Jorge Gamarra, Rogelio Polesello, and Eduardo Rodríguez) came together in this extensive roll call of the "experiences" that had been carried out during the previous decade.

VARIOUS CONCLUSIONS

What were the most characteristic aspects of the Kinetic Art produced in Buenos Aires? What works produced in Paris could be found in circulation? In an overall sense, Kinetic Art in Buenos Aires was more directly related to its immediate context, responding, first, to the opportunities provided by economic prosperity, and toward the end of the decade, deliberating between differing critical perspectives, often assimilating itself to design and the cultural industry. Art by Argentines in Paris circulated on the local scene in exhibitions, through an ongoing exchange of correspondence and personal contact. It must be pointed out, however, that Kinetic Art in Argentina was undoubtedly less specific from the outset than it was in Paris, where galleries such as Galerie Denise René were particularly dedicated to its sustenance and dissemination. In addition, the group dynamic that kinetic artists had adopted (founding groups and international associations) meant that its presence was imposed in a different way, allowing for very rapid conceptual growth. In Europe, GRAV and independent kinetic artists would attend international events (biennials and group exhibitions) and present clearly defined, programmatic profiles. This was rarely the case during the early years in Buenos Aires, where the size of the art scene could not offer the same conditions found in a mature, diversified market. Nevertheless, by the late 1960s, in the categories of visual "research" and "experiences," an ample, flexible group of works were developed in Buenos Aires in relation to Kinetic Art, employing shared concepts of "open work," an interest in viewer participation, and signaling time and space — or, as Umberto Eco would say, regarding that which pertains to contemporary life. This was so to the extent that the Salón Nacional, whose delineation of disciplines had hardly been modified since 1911, created a section specifically for the exhibition of mechanisms, and then a prize. Many kinetic artists in Buenos Aires enjoyed extensive circulation on a regional level, with noteworthy, influential exhibitions in different countries throughout the continent, particularly in Venezuela, and in shows organized with national representation, such as those held at the Americas Society in New York, the Organization of American States in Washington, D.C., and biennials in São Paulo and Costa Rica. Similarly, works of kinetic artists are found in important collections, especially of Latin American art in the United States.

It is somewhat surprising that both artists and critics refer to Kinetic Art as intimately linked to technology, when only very basic resources, like clock gears and simple electric circuits, were actually used. Nevertheless, this evidently "poor" character, present in the works produced in both Paris and Buenos Aires, in no way diminishes Kinetic Art's attractiveness or lessens its appeal to futuristic poetics. Art taking place right before your eyes, as you watched, was a virtue that managed to reintroduce the wonder of the machine into art, a metaphor for the modern world, where automation would also in the future contribute to aesthetic experience.

Argentina's "tandem scene" of Kinetic Art, as we have called it, was also permeated by the artistic and political tensions of a tumultuous period on both local and international levels. In the late 1960s, a process that had begun with the 1966 military coup and accelerated exponentially subjected the artistic avant-garde and its supposed social repercussions to harsh questioning. In Néstor García Canclini's opinion, the avant-garde found itself in a "blind alley" that was the result of disparity between "modernism" and "modernization," a situation that laid the ground

rules of cultural relations in Latin American countries.[21] The disparity that García Canclini
identifies resulted on the one hand in the elites associated with the developmental project
blowing the reach of cultural phenomena entirely out of proportion, and on the other in
reluctance to accept the impulse for innovation.

Two contemporary voices from the era, Oscar Masotta and Marta Traba, also criticized Kinetic
Art's technological optimism. Masotta pointed out the "myth dragged along by a large part of
today's avant-garde [particularly] kinetic, abstract-geometric and neo-geometric [artists]":

> As the myth goes . . . visual artists would have to abandon their role as professionals of
> anguish and subjectivity in order to join, once and for all, the industrial process that
> defines the vocation and the progressive, collective-forming reality of today's societies.[22]

In her 1973 book *Dos décadas vulnerables en las artes plásticas latinoamericanas 1950–1970* (Two
Vulnerable Decades for Latin American Visual Art 1950–1970), Traba analyzes how Pop Art
and Kinetic Art encoded their communicative power in playfulness. In a critique of avant-garde
art as an expression of submission to outside fads, she wrote: "the instructions would seem to
be play, forget, let yourself go, detoxify yourself." In this context, play is an ally of "alienating
systems" that keep spectators away from their real problems.[23]

Following radical initiatives by GRAV in Paris in 1968, and Le Parc's participation in the Atelier
populaire d'affiches while events were going forward in May that year, he was deported from the
country. Five months later, the sanction was lifted, but the group broke up. Even so, projects in
Paris continued.

In Buenos Aires, the "tandem scene" gives reciprocal feedback, and Kinetic Art takes diverse
paths. One of these focuses on electronic technology and introduces a new institution
that is growing, even while the Instituto Di Tella's close is imminent: the Centro de Arte y
Comunicación (CAYC; Center for Art and Communication). Founded in 1968, it took the

21. Néstor García Canclini, *Culturas
híbridas* (Mexico City: Grijalbo, 1989).

22. Oscar Masotta, *Conciencia y
estructura* (Buenos Aires: Editorial Jorge
Álvarez, 1968), 205.

23. Marta Traba, *Dos décadas
vulnerables en las artes plásticas
latinoamericanas 1950–1970* (Buenos
Aires: Siglo Veintiuno Editores,
1973/2005), 100.

24. This exhibition took place just one
year after *Cybernetic Serendipity*,
the paradigmatic show organized
by Jasia Reichardt at the Institute of
Contemporary Arts (ICA) in London.

25. Jorge Glusberg et al., *Primera
muestra del Centro de Estudios en Arte
y Comunicación*, exhibition catalogue
(Buenos Aires: Galería Bonino, 1969).

lead in experimentation from the very start. An exhibition titled *Arte y Cibernética* (Art and Cybernetics) was held in 1969, bringing together artists from Argentina and abroad who were exploring the creative possibilities of computers.[24] Among the eclectic group convened, the local artists coming from generative-kinetic art were the ones most familiar with the machine's operations, since they were able to repeat operations in series involving variables that could be controlled in a determined pattern. With this experience, Jorge Glusberg took a position aligned with several of the tenets of Kinetic Art, "a new, dynamic art with a commitment to the social context to which it pertains, and to the interplanetary era, reaching beyond institutionalized techniques." He also encouraged the notion of the "death of painting" and its replacement with "lights and motors and information instead of brushes."[25]

That same year, *Argentina Inter-Medios,* shown at the Ópera theater in Buenos Aires, fulfilled this commitment to technology. It was a show created as an integrated environment, with electronic music, experimental theater and film, poetry, dance, and kinetic sculpture. Continuing along the lines of the tradition of Kinetic Art, the piece sought to enrich audiovisual perception by way of light and sound devices controlled by computers.

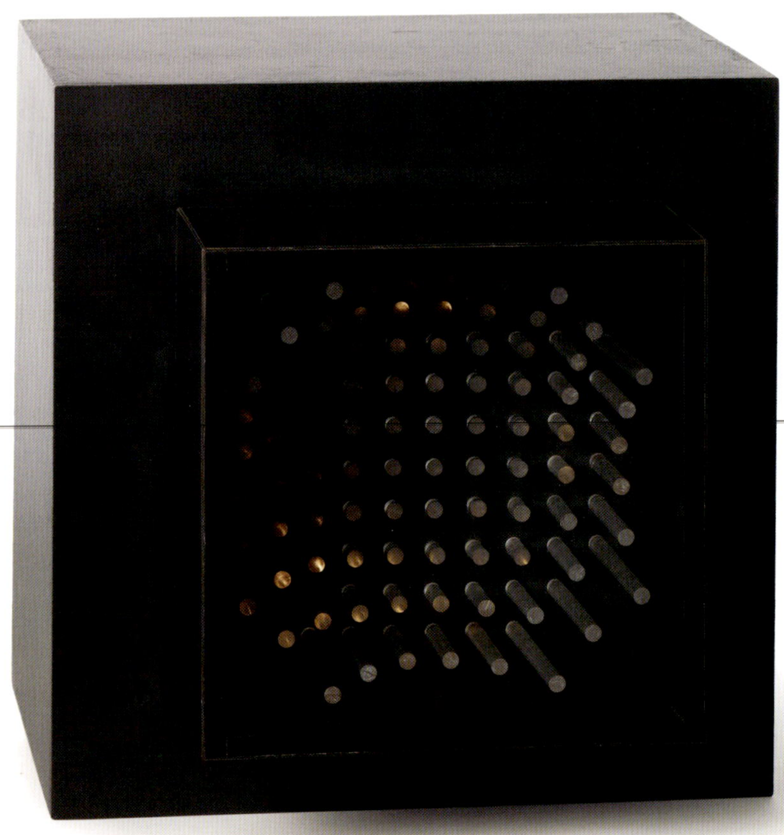

110

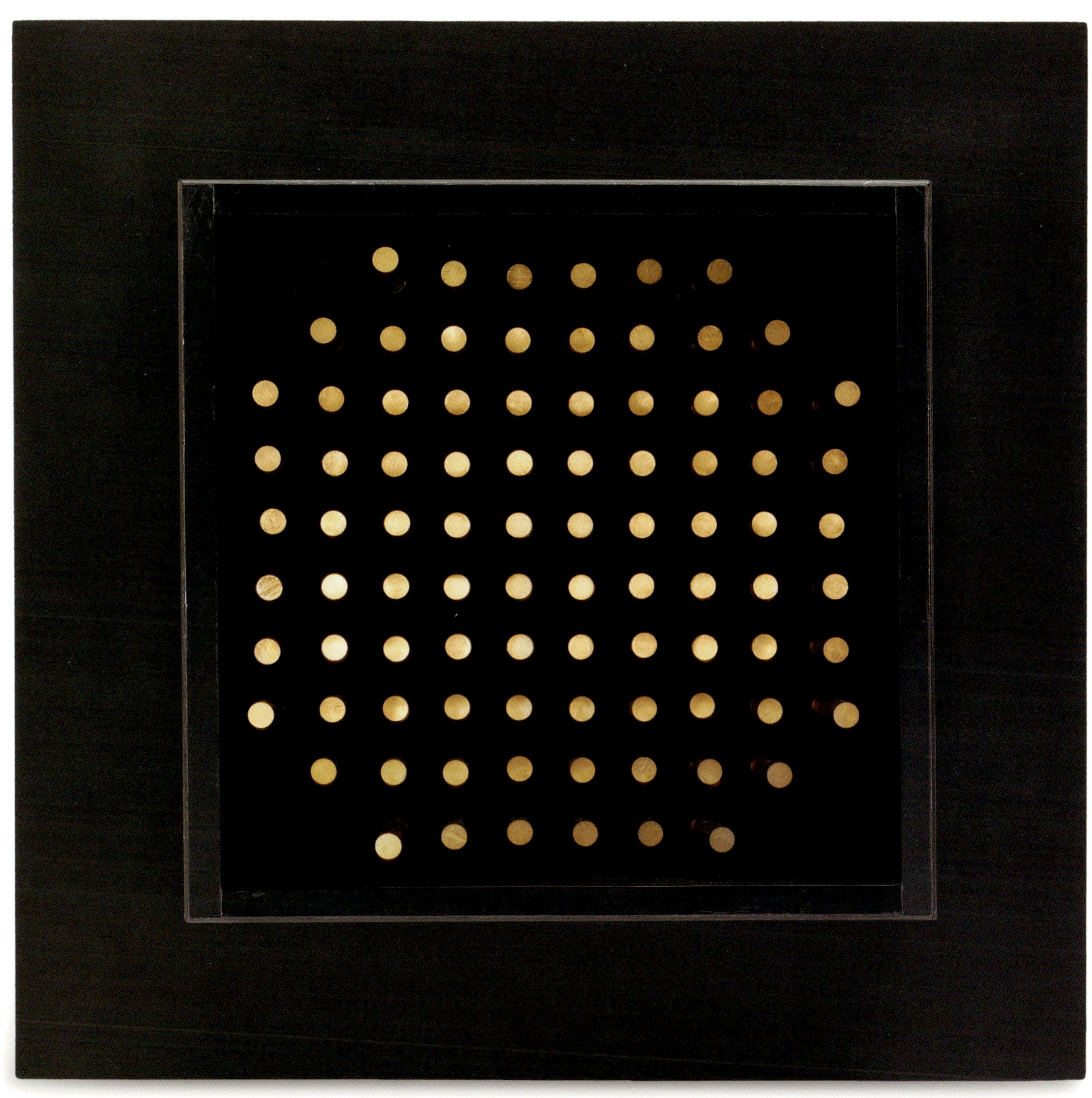

HORACIO GARCÍA-ROSSI   *Relief à lumière instable*, 1965
Acrylic on wood, Plexiglas, aluminum, and light bulbs, 13 ⅞ × 13 ⅞ × 16 ¾ in. (35.1 × 35.1 × 42.5 cm)
Courtesy of Sicardi Gallery, Houston

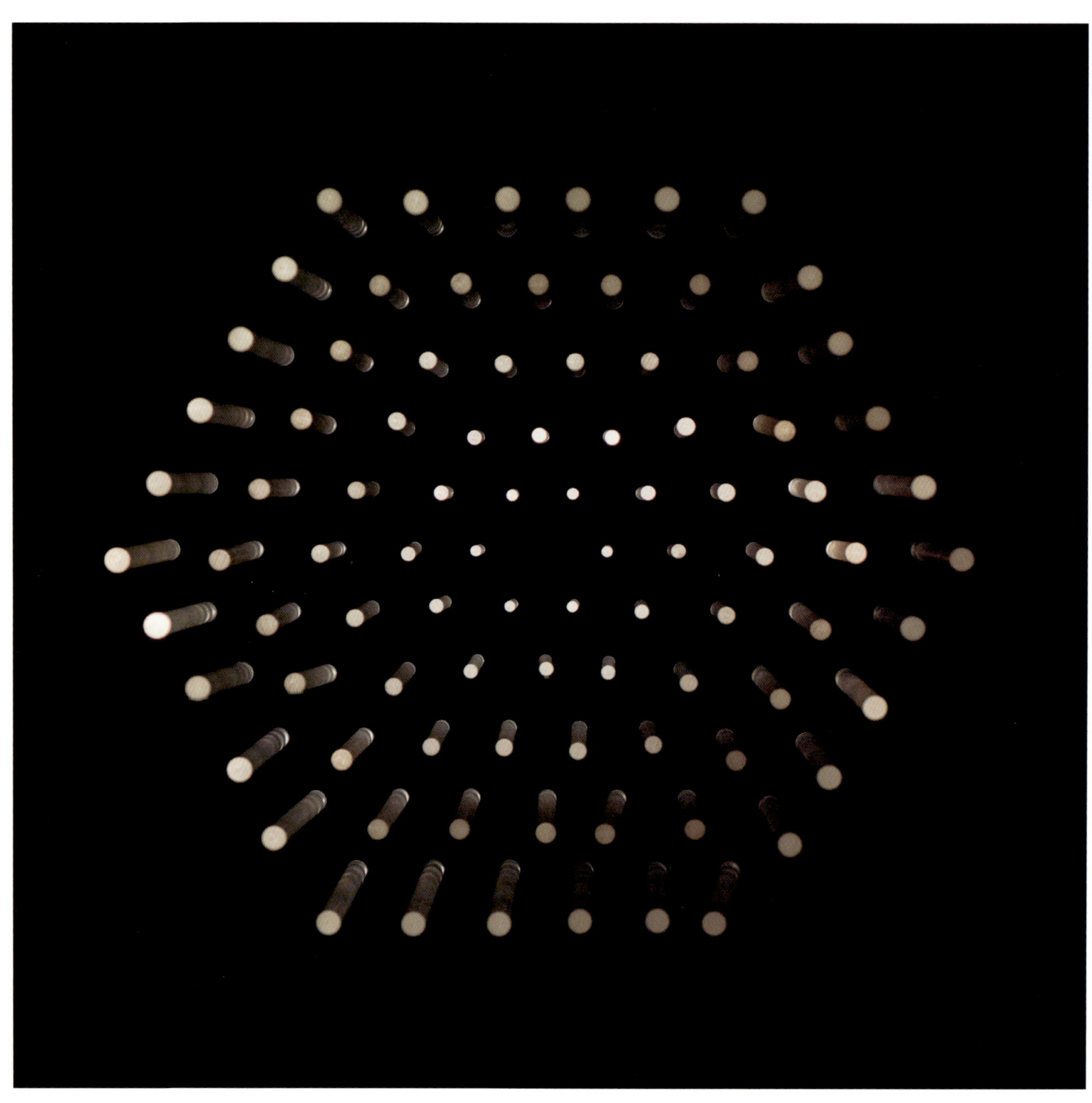

HORACIO GARCÍA-ROSSI *Structure à lumière instable no. 29, 1966*
Painted wood, Lucite rods, electric motor, and lights, 23 ⅝ × 23 ⅝ × 19 ¼ in. (59.9 × 59.9 × 48.9 cm)
The Museum of Fine Arts, Houston. Gift of Benbow and Jean Bullock, 2004.1618

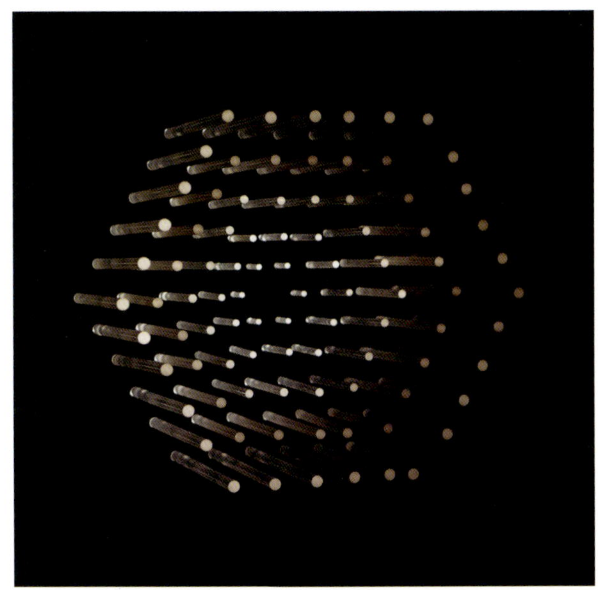

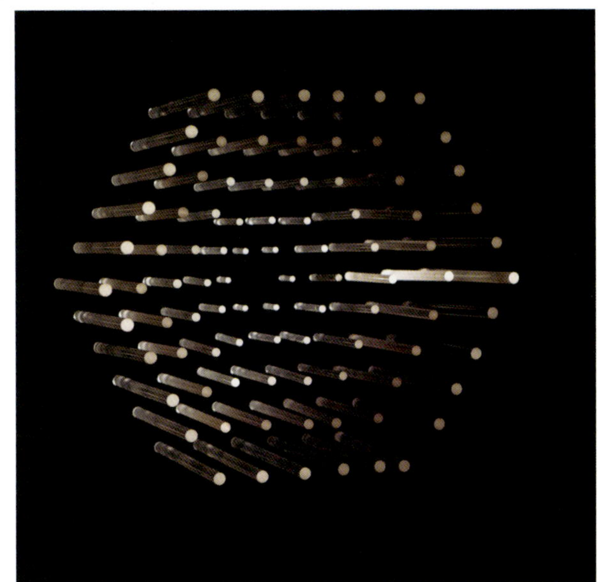

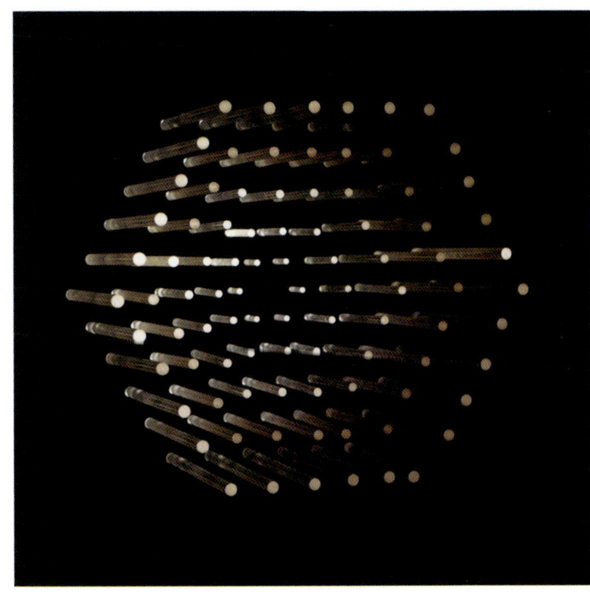

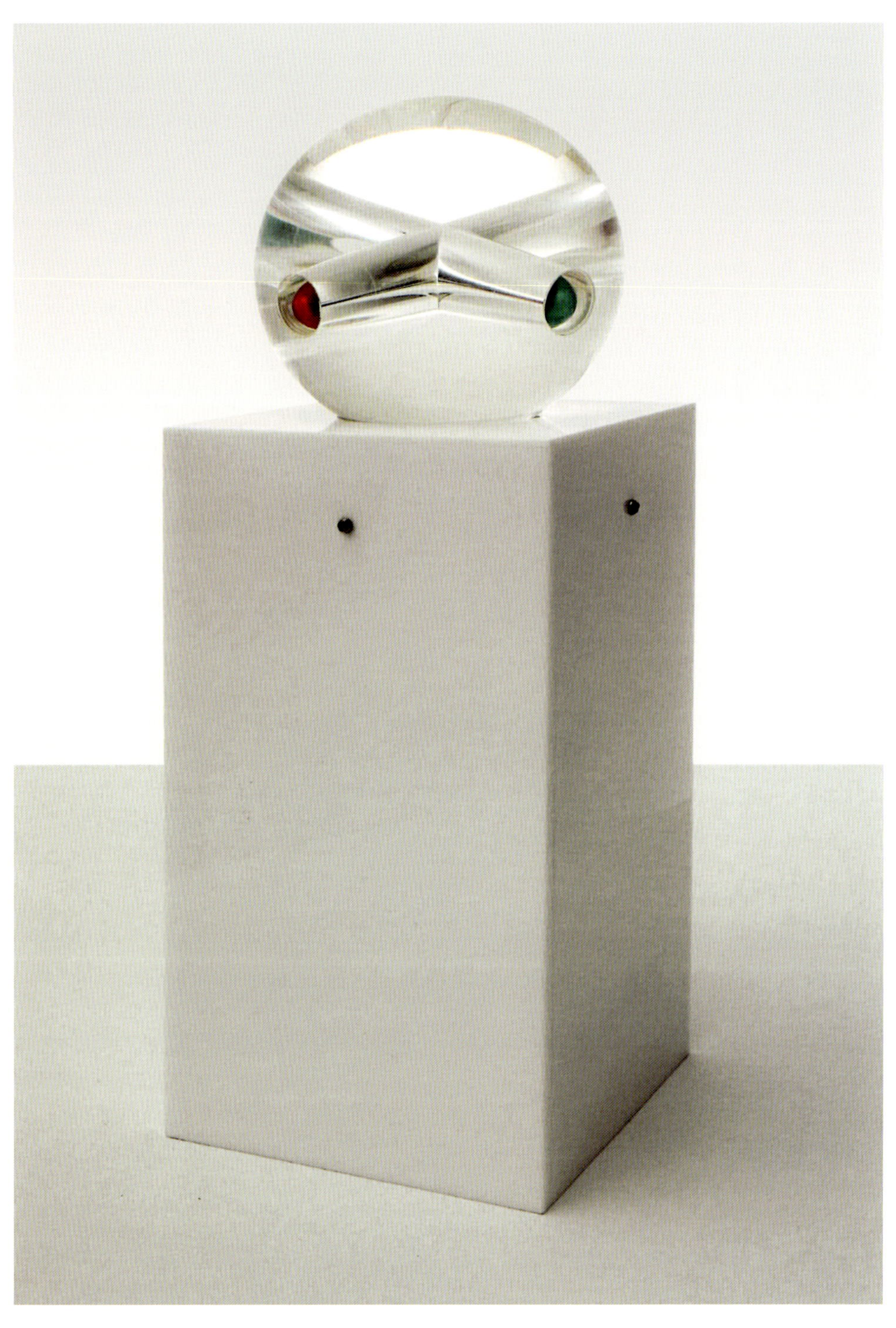

HORACIO GARCÍA-ROSSI   *Esfera en rotación*, 1969
Plexiglas and electric motor, 11 × 4 × 4 in. (28 × 10 × 10 cm)
The Ella Fontanals-Cisneros Collection, Miami

JULIO LE PARC *Continuel-lumière cylindre, 1962/2013*
Painted wood, stainless steel, motor, metal disk, and light
Diameter: 157 ½ x 35 ½ in. (400 x 90 cm), box: 15 ¾ x 15 ¾ x 15 ¾ in. (40 x 40 x 40 cm)
Collection: Famille Le Parc, Paris

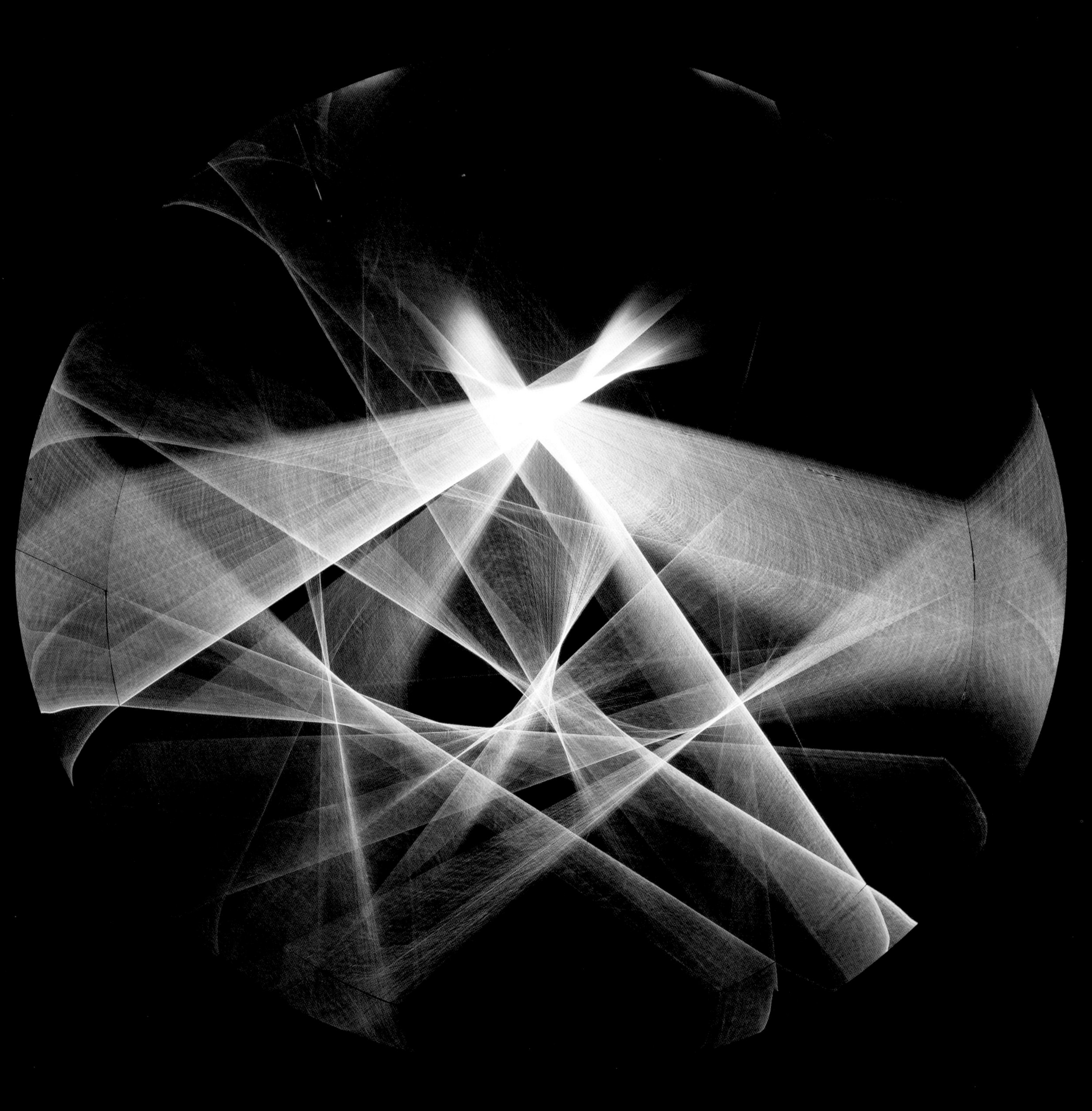

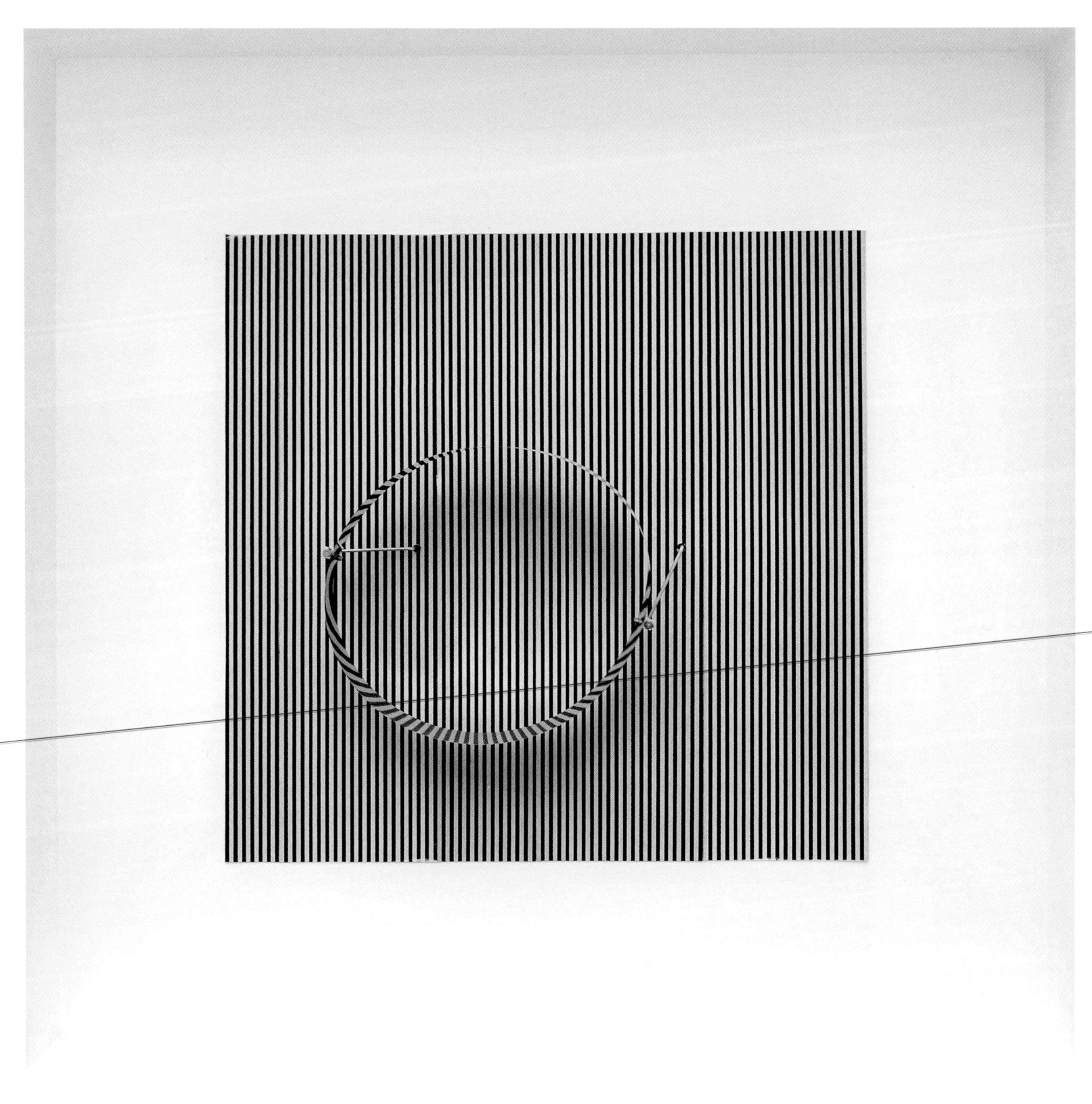

JULIO LE PARC *Cercle en contorsion sur trame*, 1966
Wood, stainless steel, motor, screenprint, and paint, 48 ⅜ x 48 ⅜ x 7 ⅞ in. (123 x 123 x 20 cm)
Collection: Famille Le Parc, Paris

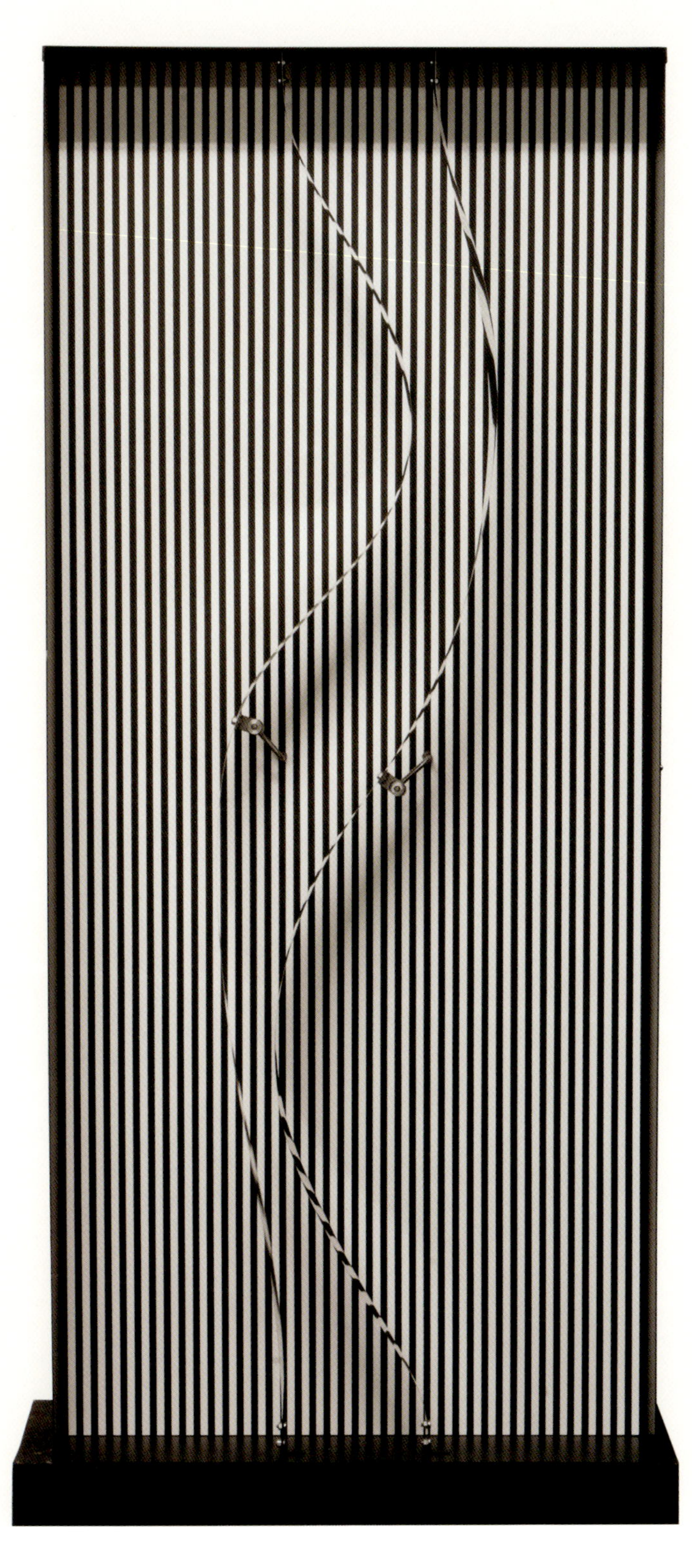

JULIO LE PARC   *Formes en contorsion sur trame*, 1966, 47/250 (Édition Denise René)
Serigraph on cardboard, stainless steel, aluminum, and motor, 40 3/8 x 18 x 6 3/8 in. (102.6 x 47 x 16.2 cm)
Collection of Leslie and Brad Bucher, Houston. Courtesy of Sicardi Gallery, Houston

JULIO LE PARC   *Lumière sur resort*, 1964/1996
Wood, metal, springs, mirrors, motor, and light, dimensions variable
Collection: Famille Le Parc, Paris

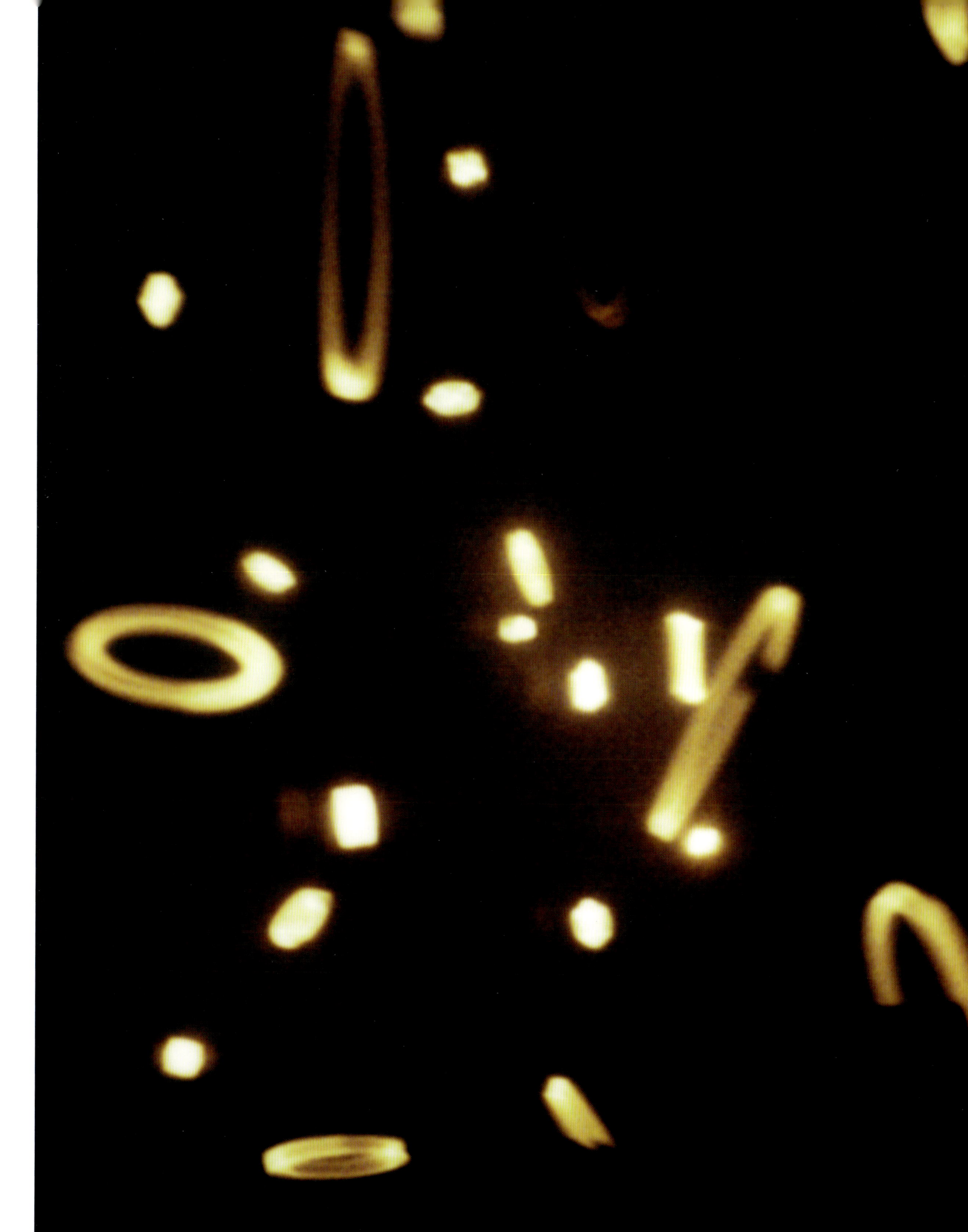

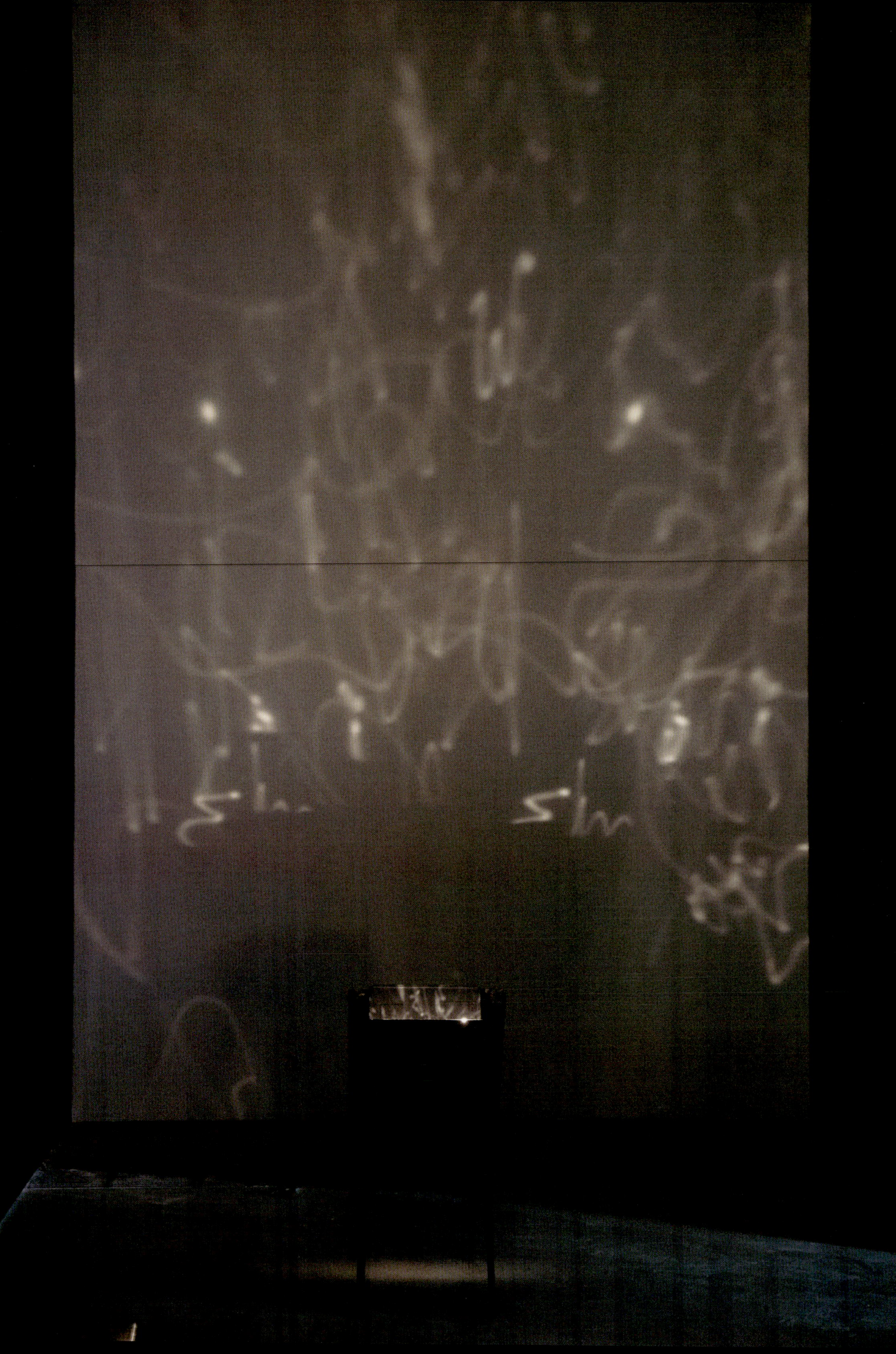

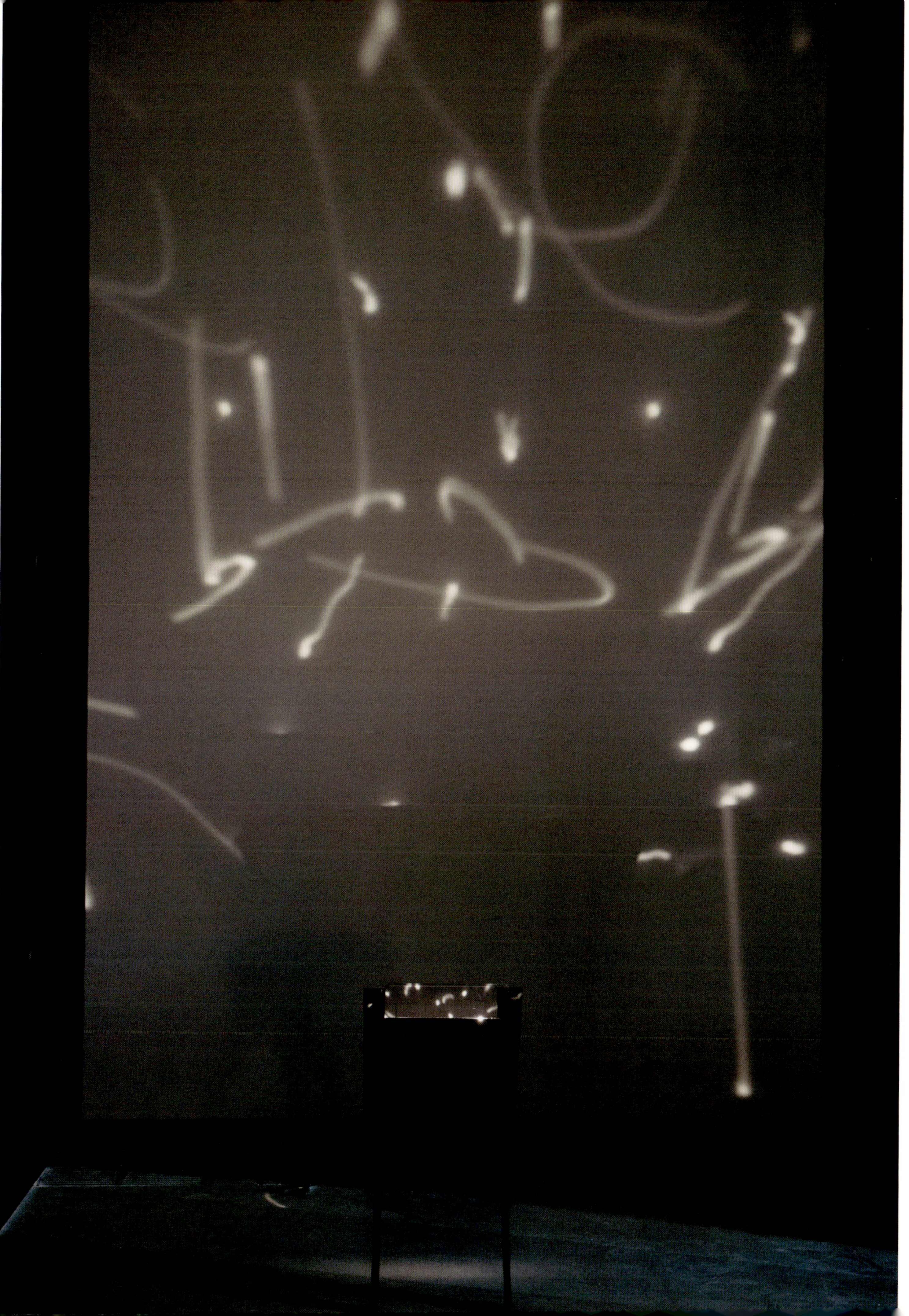

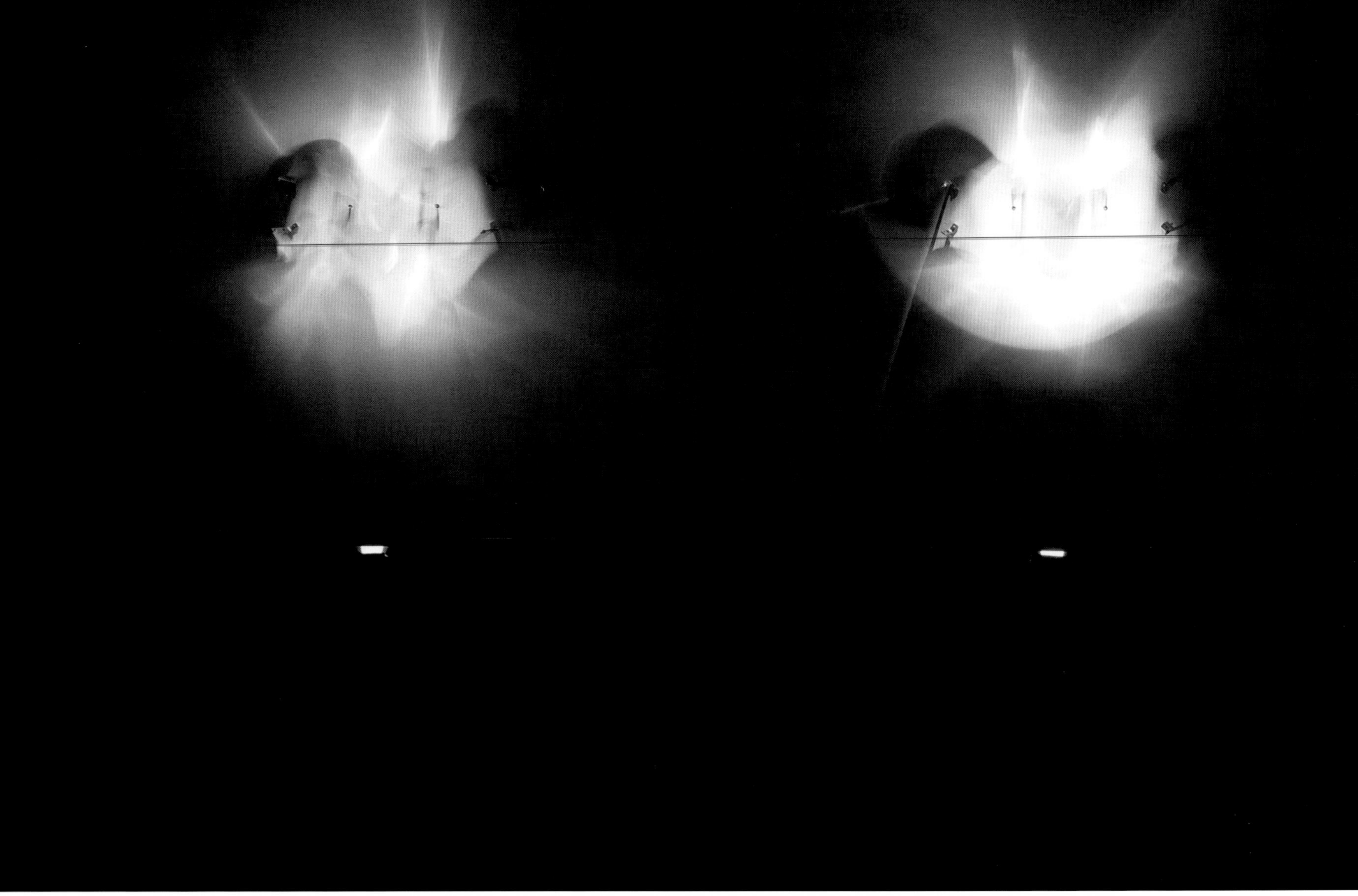

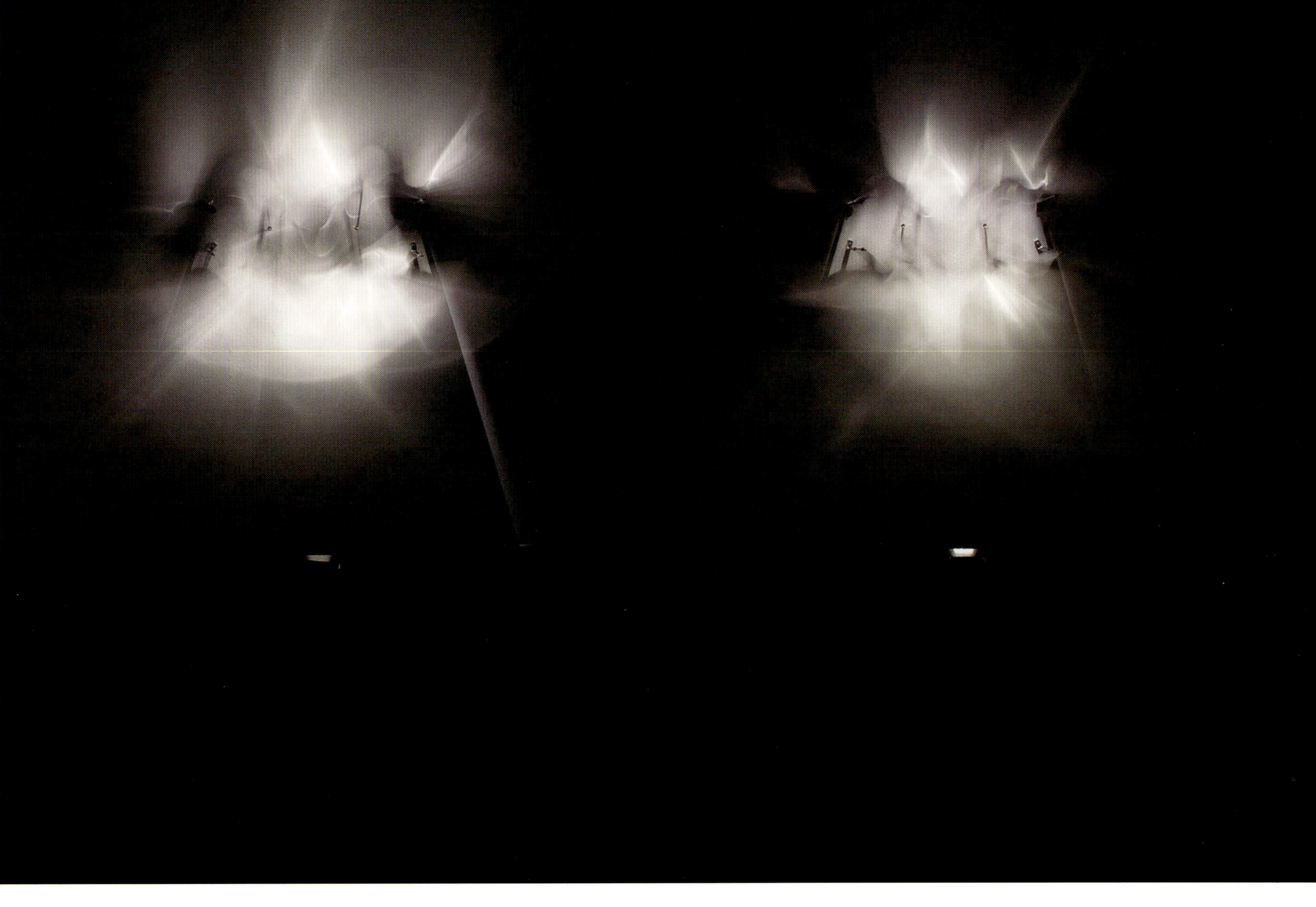

JULIO LE PARC   *Continuel-lumière avec formes en contorsion*, 1966/2012
Wood, plastic, light, and motor, 95 ¾ x 237 ⅜ x 14 ¼ in. (24 x 603 x 36 cm)
Collection: Famille Le Parc, Paris

JULIO LE PARC
Cloison à lames réfléchissantes, 1966/2005
Steel, 91 x 109 x 31 ½ in. (231.14 x 276.86 x 80 cm)
Collection: Famille Le Parc, courtesy Galeria Nara Roesler

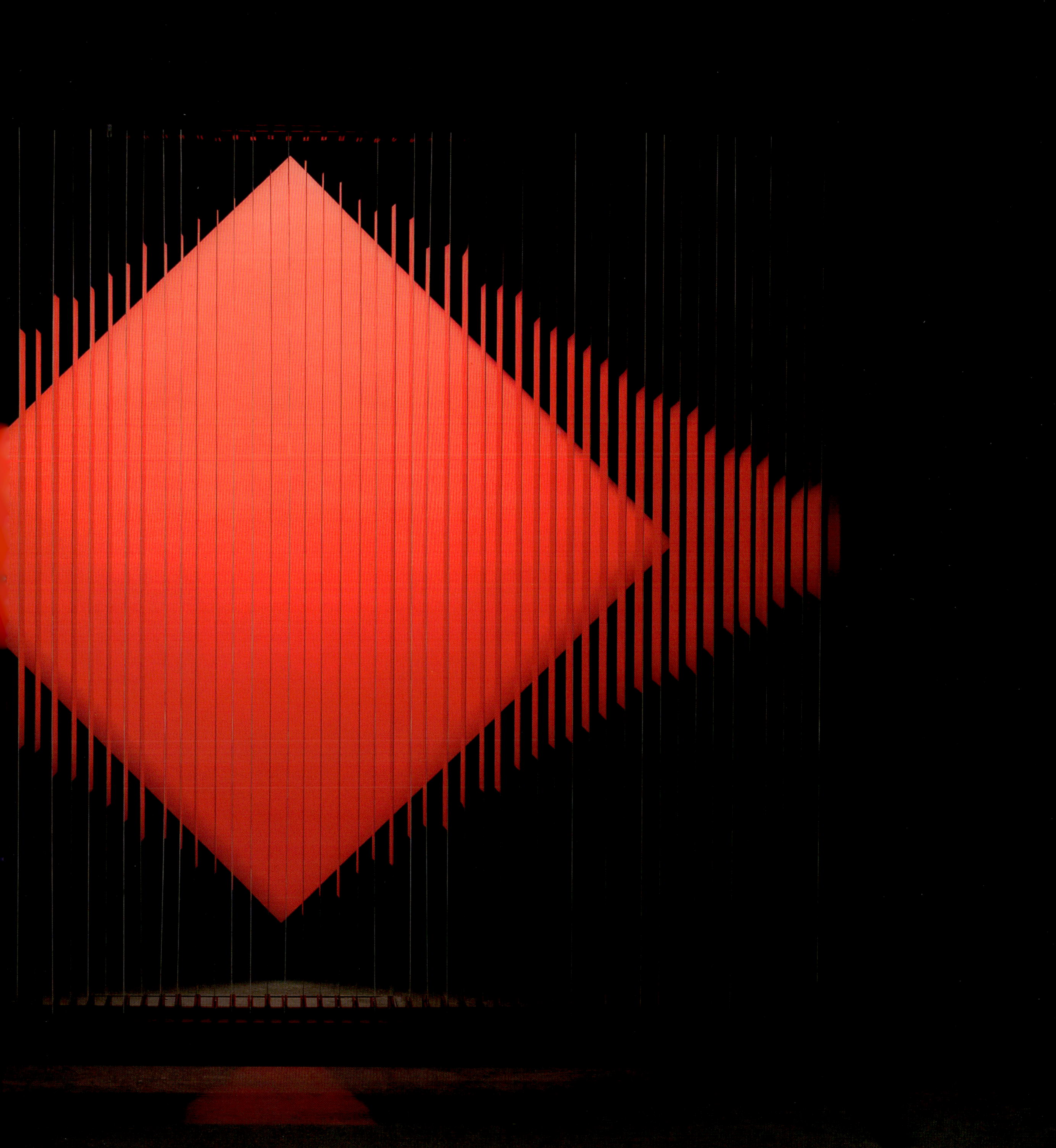

PARIS AS A CULTURAL ARENA
FOR SOUTH AMERICAN GEOMETRIC ABSTRACTION
FROM THE POSTWAR PERIOD TO THE 1960s

Isabel Plante

Gregorio Vardánega, che cosa fai adesso?

    Sono preparando l'exposizione de Popper al musée d'art moderne de la ville de Paris.

Antonio Asis, que haces tu en este momento?

    Yo preparo la exposición de Popper para el musée d'art moderne de la ville de Paris.

Carlos Cruz-Diez, que en este momento?

    Yo preparo la exposición para Popper en el musée d'art moderne de la ville de Paris

Narciso Debourg, che haces tu momento?

    Yo la exposición para en el musée art moderne

Yacob Agam, que are machen adesso momento?

    Yo bereites on Popper exposicion al musée d'art moderne de la ville de Paris

Luis Tomasello, tu en este?

    Para Popper art moderne de la ville de Paris.

Martha Boto, che haces tu?

    Preparo en el musée d'art moderne

Victor Vasarely, tu en ce moment?

    Je l'exposition de Popper au musée . . .

Et toi, Blaine, que fais-tu?

    Moi je questionne

    Julien Blaine, *"dialogues de la fin d'avril," Robho,* 1967 [1]

1. Julien Blaine, "dialogues de la fin d'avril," *Robho*, no. 1 (June 1967): 5.

2. "Réponses à un questionnaire rédigé par Véronique Wiesinger: Frank Popper," in *Denise René l'intrépide: Une galerie dans l'aventure de l'art abstrait 1944–1978* (Paris: Centre Georges Pompidou, 2001), 160–63.

3. There are no counts of visitors on record, but the press material in the museum archives includes more than thirty reviews.

4. USCO (an abbreviation for "the Company of Us") was a media art collective founded by Michael Callahan and Gerd Stern that was active in New York in the 1960s and 1970s.

5. Pascal Rousseau, "'Folklore planétaire': Le sujet cybernétique dans l'art optique des années 1960," in *L'œil moteur: Art optique et cinétique, 1950–1975* (Strasbourg: Musée d'Art Contemporain de Strasbourg, 2005), 142.

THE JUMBLE OF LANGUAGES JULIEN BLAINE USED for this poetic intervention in the first issue of the magazine *Robho* played with the serial work of Kinetic Art, its international profile, and with the problem of Esperanto — or geometric abstraction — as a shared language. The piece was also in tune with the Parisian news: in April 1967 all of the artists mentioned were preparing their works for an exhibition of Kinetic Art at the Musée d'Art Moderne de la Ville de Paris, by invitation of Frank Popper. Opening in May and titled *Lumière et mouvement*, the exhibition featured a strong Latin American presence (fourteen of the thirty-nine participants): Antonio Asís, Martha Boto, Sergio Camargo, Carlos Cruz-Diez, Narciso Debourg, Hugo Demarco, Armando Durante, Horacio García-Rossi, Ana María Gatti, Gyula Kosice, Julio Le Parc, Jesús Rafael Soto, Luis Tomasello, and Gregorio Vardánega. According to Popper, the exhibition included only those foreign artists who were residing in France, so they wouldn't be limited to sending in already completed works. Artists, curators, architects, and Popper himself worked together for a year on various installations for the available space.[2] As it turned out, such a large number of people attended that the museum authorities decided to extend the exhibition for several months.[3]

In the mid-sixties, Kinetic Art was an international phenomenon comprising the activities of individual artists as well as interconnected groups such as the Groupe de Recherche d'Art Visuel (GRAV) in France, Gruppo T and Gruppo N in Italy, Zero in Germany, Dvizjenije in Moscow, and USCO in New York.[4] In 1964, the exhibition *Nouvelle tendance* at the Musée des Arts Décoratifs in Paris brought together some fifty artists from eleven countries. In the words of Pascal Rousseau, Kinetic Art was conceived "as a sort of Esperanto through which each individual could communicate with the world in the ecstatic inebriation of optic vibration."[5] Rousseau argued that Kinetic Art aspired to a universal language, one that looked ahead to a future marked not only by the eradication of cultural and linguistic borders but also by the evolution of cognitive perceptions of a humanity transformed by contact with communication technologies.

The magazine *Robho,* in which Blaine published his multilinguistic dialogue, can clearly be considered an index of the South American kinetic artistic presence in the City of Light. Published from 1967 to 1971 by Blaine, Jean Clay, and Christiane Duparc (a visual poet as well as an art critic and a cultural journalist), *Robho* was not a current events magazine. It selected cultural work as indices of the cultural resistance, coming mainly from France, to the expansion of the logic imposed by American-style capitalism. In its six issues, figures such as the French Daniel Buren, the German Hans Haacke, the Philippine David Medalla, the Swiss Daniel Spoerri, and the Greek known as Takis, among others, were central. Also featured were the Venezuelans Soto and Cruz-Diez, the Uruguayan Carmelo Arden Quin, the Brazilians Lygia Clark and Sergio Camargo, the Argentine Le Parc, and the collective project that emerged in Argentina in 1968 under the title *Tucumán Arde.* Although the rebellious horizon marked out in *Robho* was representative of the cosmopolitan cachet that Paris still exerted in the sixties, the presence of the Latin American kinetic artists in the first issues of a magazine dedicated to anti-establishment art was quite significant.[6]

The first issue of *Robho*, in June 1967, began with Clay's editorial "La peinture est finie" and featured on the cover two of the artists responsible for sending painting into extinction. Photos of Soto and Le Parc, who had resided in Paris since 1950 and 1958, respectively, shared the cover, which was designed by another Venezuelan kinetic artist who lived in Paris, Cruz-Diez.[7] Their works had not only ceased to be perspective windows, presented as objects with their own internal logic, but by means of Kinetic Art also turned toward viewers, casting doubt on their certainties about perspective. The mention of Pop and neo-Dada as offshoots of "consumer society," in its fetishization of both the art object and the industrial product, reveals the political dimension that Clay valued in Kinetic Art: the absence of fixed forms and the transmutation of the object into art installations, which also involved a cultural wager on a system that would be an alternative to neoliberalism.

The initiative taken by these figures to try their luck in Paris during the sixties created a continuity with previous cultural forays but also presented different nuances. It was not a matter of apprentices traveling to the undisputed mecca of the arts to study and then returning to file reports, but of artists who lived as foreigners in this cosmopolitan city and developed innovative works that received recognition both inside and outside their countries of origin. Aware that

6. See Isabel Plante, "*Les Sud-américains de Paris:* Latin American Artists and Cultural Resistance in *Robho* Magazine," *Third Text,* vol. 24, no. 4 (July 2010): 445–55.

7. Cruz-Diez, who moved to Paris in 1960, was a typographer and designer at the Creole Petroleum Corporation, artistic director at the McCann-Erickson advertising agency, and an illustrator at the newspaper *El Nacional* in Caracas.

8. Serge Guilbaut, *How New York Stole the Idea of Modern Art* (Chicago: University of Chicago, 1983).

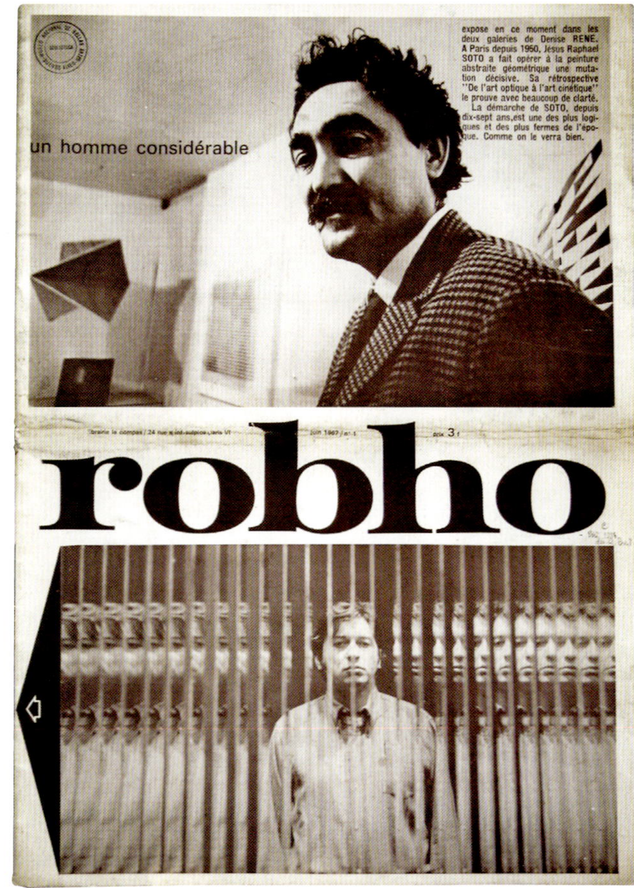

Robho no. 1, June 1967. Cover: Soto and Le Parc

9. Several of the Argentine kinetic artists — Armando Durante, Julio Le Parc, and Gabriel Messil — arrived in Paris either with a grant from the French government or by means of the Premio Braque awards that the French Embassy offered in Argentina between 1963 and 1969.

10. The editorial board of *Arturo*, whose sole issue was published in January 1944, also included Rhod Rothfuss, the brothers Tomás Maldonado and Edgar Bayley, and a very young Gyula Kosice. See María Amalia García, "Capítulo 1: La revista "Arturo" y la relocalización de la vanguardia en el cruce regional," *El arte abstracto: Intercambios culturales entre Argentina y Brasil* (Buenos Aires: Siglo Veintiuno, Fundación Costantini, 2011), 25–53.

New York had already stolen the idea of modern art (paraphrasing Serge Guilbaut),[8] these artists were undoubtedly attracted by what Paris implied in terms of cultural traditions and art markets, but the city was also significant to them in political terms. In the mid-sixties, anti-Americanism reached unprecedented virulence, and in France it was fueled by President Charles de Gaulle's attacks on U.S. foreign policy and the opposition to the Vietnam War as well as the political radicalization that exploded in France in May 1968. The choice of France was mediated by both concrete opportunities[9] and aesthetic issues, which were linked to geometric abstraction itself, considered to be the opposite of U.S. stridency. But for some, the decision to live and work in Paris was also the result of the French left's embrace of the Third World.

AN ALTERNATIVE HISTORY FOR KINETIC ART: MADÍ ART

The contents of the third issue of *Robho*, published in the tumultuous European spring of 1968, were devoted to Carmelo Arden Quin, the Uruguayan artist who had settled in Paris in 1948 after launching Invencionismo in the Río de la Plata region with the magazine *Arturo: Revista de artes abstractas*.[10] This issue of *Robho* displayed the archive of photographs and documents of Madí's first art initiatives, which had been created in 1946 in Buenos Aires and Montevideo, and later on in

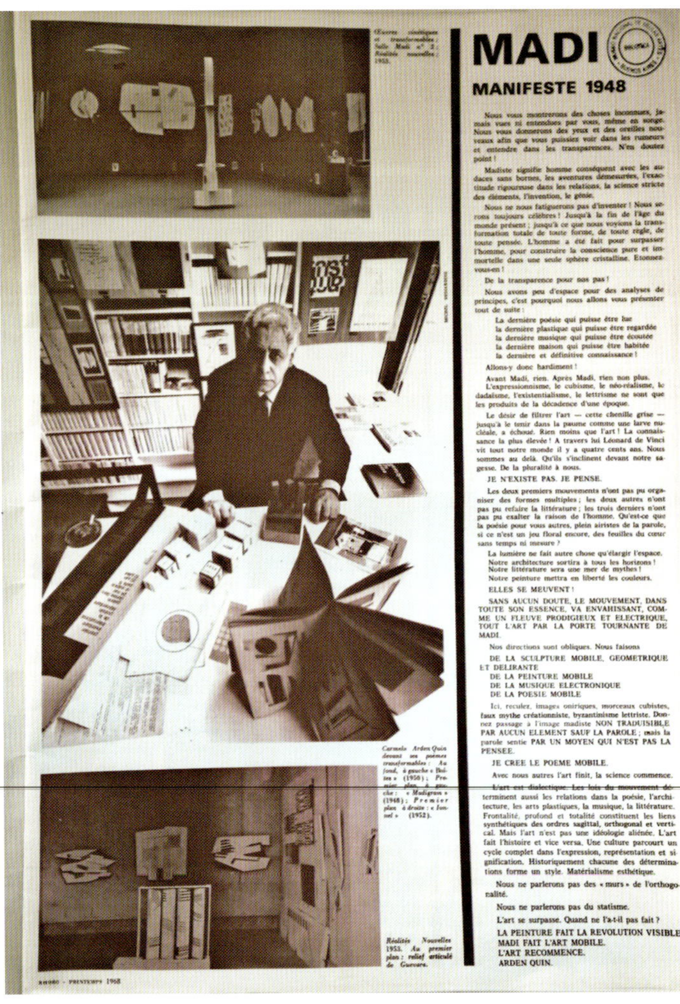

Robho no. 3, second quarter, 1968. Issue devoted to Arden Quin and Madí.

Europe.[11] A short text titled "Arden Quin précurseur" placed him at the beginning of Kinetic Art:

> The archaeology of kinetic art remains to be written. Arden Quin, since the beginning of the post-war period, posed the problem of movement in art, first in Argentina and then in France . . . It has been somewhat forgotten since that time and today we tend to think that Kinetic Art was developed in Paris in 1955. This is false.

If the first issue of *Robho* gave new visibility to Kinetic Art, it also recirculated information on Arden Quin and his career going back more than twenty years, while also stating that it was necessary to revise the established idea that the initial kickoff for Kinetic Art had been the exhibition *Le Mouvement,* organized by Galerie Denise René in Paris in 1955. Highlighting the figure of Arden Quin meant going beyond Paris, while also correcting what Clay himself had argued a couple of years earlier, in 1966, in an article firmly situating the rise of Kinetic Art in Paris.[12] Pointing to some early artistic experiments with movement (from Antoine Pevsner to Alexander Calder), Clay indicated that such experiments had proliferated around 1950. Yaacov Agam,

Pol Bury, Frank Malina, Bruno Munari, Abraham Palatnik, Nicolas Schöffer, Soto, Takis, Jean Tinguely, and Victor Vasarely then produced a series of works that Denise René assembled for exhibition in 1955. From there would come the experiments of the next generation, Clay continued, which would be more numerous and also organized in groups. Here, he pointed to Soto as a turning point, because in 1954 the Venezuelan artist had gone from optical to kinetic works, unfolding the pictorial surface between two sheets of Plexiglas, superimposed and painted with different geometric frames. By moving the gaze of spectators from the work itself, the superimposition of drawings varied and gave the illusion that what was moving was the image. But two years later, when *Robho* drew attention to Arden Quin and Madí, the first postwar experiments with Kinetic Art were pushed back in time and southward to the city of Buenos Aires.

11. Reconsidering the place of Madí in the history of Kinetic Art is the course proposed by Cristina Rossi in "Imágenes inestables: Tránsitos Buenos Aires-París-Buenos Aires," in María José Herrera, curator, *Real/Virtual: Arte cinético argentino en los años sesenta* (Buenos Aires: Museo Nacional de Bellas Artes, 2012), 47–67.

12. Jean Clay, "L'art du mouvement," *Réalités* (June 1966): 88–93.

13. Agnès de Maistre, *Carmelo Arden Quin* (Nice: Éditions Demaistre, 1996).

14. "Chronologie," in *Soto* (Paris: Galerie Nationale Jeu de Paume/Réunion des Musées Nationaux, 1997), 179.

In the period immediately following World War II, the avant-garde in the Río de la Plata region had advocated an art of "invention," whose debut had occurred in *Arturo* magazine. It explored the relationship of form and color, the vibration of dots and lines on the plane, and spatial rhythms, as well as the possibility of randomization and interaction by means of the inclusion of mobile parts. The two groups that arose from the nucleus of *Arturo* — Madí and the Asociación Arte Concreto-Invención — created coplanar structures composed of cut geometric forms painted with flat colors and placed directly on the wall. By 1946, the coplanar structures and articulated sculptures by the artists of the Buenos Aires Madí group, led first by Arden Quin and then by Gyula Kosice, had incorporated transformation into the works.

The series *Reliefs amovibles*, developed by Arden Quin in Paris between 1949 and 1950, had continued those experiments with modifiable coplanar structures. For Agnès de Maistre, these works were direct predecessors of Kinetic Art, in particular the *Meta-mécaniques* of Tinguely, the mobile planes of Bury, and the *Assemblages mouvants* of Agam, all executed in Paris in 1953.[13] The arguments put forth in *Robho*'s third issue were moving in this direction: Arden Quin's experiments not only anticipated those of the kinetic artists of the mid-fifties, they also inspired them. The magazine overlooked one detail about early contact between Arden Quin and Soto. In 1950 Soto, a newcomer to Paris, sought out the emerging group of Madí artists, which included the Venezuelans Luis Guevara and Rubén Núñez, and in late 1951 had participated with them in the exhibition *Espace-Lumière* that Arden Quin organized at the Suzanne Michel gallery.[14]

This view of Arden Quin's importance in the development of Kinetic Art, as acknowledged in this French account of 1968, may possibly be due to Julien Blaine, co-editor of *Robho*.[15] His relationship to the Uruguayan artist dated back to the beginning of the decade when, along with Jacques Sénelier and Godofredo Iommi,[16] Blaine had performed "poetic acts" at various sites, such as reading from Guillaume Apollinaire alongside the poet's tomb in the Père Lachaise cemetery. Shortly thereafter, Blaine and Sénelier had become editorial colleagues of Arden Quin in the magazine *Ailleurs* (1963–66), which included representations of the kinetic artworks of Antonio Asís, Julio Le Parc, François Morellet, Francisco Sobrino, Joël Stein, and Gregorio Vardánega.[17] In this context, the figure of Arden Quin linked not only Madí to Kinetic Art but also visual arts to poetry, an area of aesthetic production given continuity in *Robho* by the efforts of Blaine and Cruz-Diez, its designer.

GEOMETRIC ABSTRACTION AS A UNIVERSAL ART

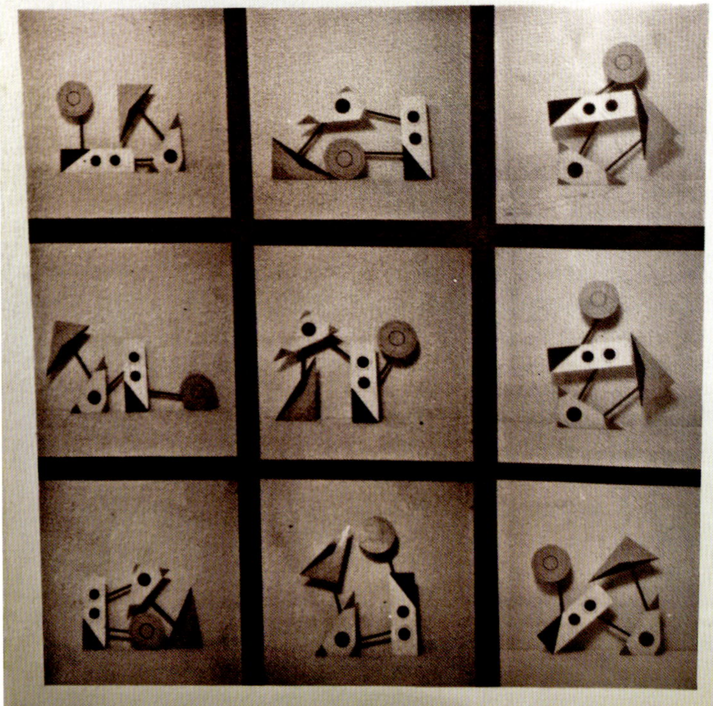

Robho no. 3, second quarter of 1968. *Structure articulable* by Carmelo Arden Quin

15. Shelley Goodman attributes to Blaine the content on Arden Quin in *Robho*. See her catalogue *Carmelo Arden Quin: When Art Jumped out of Its Cage* (Dallas, 2004), 253.

16. Arden Quin had met this Argentine poet in the mid-forties in Buenos Aires.

17. Sénelier appeared as part of the editorial team beginning with the first issue and Blaine with the second. See *Ailleurs*, no. 1 (third quarter, 1963) and no. 2 (first quarter, 1964).

18. Between July and August 1948, before arriving in Paris, Arden Quin (under the pseudonym Ramón Rasas Pety) also participated in the Salon des Réalités Nouvelles as part of the shipment of Madí art organized by Kosice from Buenos Aires.

19. Pierre Nora specifically gave the name "invention of France" to the role of Paris in the nineteenth century, giving it a national identity; *Les lieux de la mémoire* (Paris: Gallimard, 1984).

The many documents related to Arden Quin reproduced by *Robho* included a page from the magazine *Arturo;* a series of photographs of the various positions of an "articulable structure" dated 1946; a photograph of a motorized "electric mobile" dated 1952; views of the 1950 and 1953 Madí exhibitions at the Salon des Réalités Nouvelles, which began assembling abstract, geometric, and constructive productions in 1946;[18] a photograph of the artist in his Paris studio, surrounded by his poetic creations; the brochure printed on the occasion of the "Matinée madiste" in April of 1948; and the transcription of the manifesto published in French in the same brochure.

20. Raymond Williams, *La política del modernismo* (1989; Buenos Aires: Manantial, 1997), 66.

21. While Laurence Betrand Dorleac speaks of a "Republic of the arts," Pascale Casanova thinks of a "World republic of the arts," and both authors locate the capital of this republic in Paris. Laurence Bertrand Dorleac, "De la France aux *Magiciens de la terre:* Les artistes étrangers à Paris depuis 1945," Antoine Marès and Pierre Milza, *Le Paris des étrangers depuis 1945* (Paris: Publications de la Sorbonne, 1994), 403–28. Pascale Casanova, *La República mundial de las Letras* (Barcelona: Anagrama, 2001).

22. I have borrowed the expression from María Amalia García, "La revista 'Arturo' y la relocalización de la vanguardia en el cruce regional," 41.

Announced in French, this soirée took place in Ramos Mejía, a suburb of Buenos Aires, at the home of Elías Piterberg, a homeopath who was a patron of the group. But why publish the announcement in French in a Spanish-speaking country? One answer could be that he had already bought his ticket, had Paris on his horizon, and wanted to disseminate his writings in France. Another reason might be a certain eccentric and playful approach that inspired the Madí artists, their work and their pseudonyms. Another possibility may lie in the universal vocation of their artistic inventions. While geometric abstraction could be considered a sort of visual Esperanto, the language used by people who spoke different languages, the "international" language was still French. (Who in South America would have written a manifesto in English in the forties?) And if there had been a city that identified itself as universal, that city was Paris.[19]

However, the case of Arden Quin, unlike that of Soto for example, does not appear to correspond to the migratory dynamics of modernism, as proposed by Raymond Williams in a well-known book published in 1989. According to Williams, migration to the metropolis opened up, through the experience of visual and linguistic strangeness, a "decisive aesthetic effect,"[20] a distance in respect to national or provincial cultures and a communion with a sort of republic of the arts governed by the rules of the practice itself.[21] Arden Quin was already a promoter of Madí before leaving Buenos Aires, but it was beginning to be acknowledged in Paris only twenty years later, due to the visibility attained by the South American kinetic artists working in Europe during the sixties.

On September 25, 1948, Arden Quin set out for Europe with the Peruvian José Bresciani and two members of the Asociación Arte Concreto-Invención, Juan Melé and Gregorio Vardánega. For these young South American artists, interwar Paris had been a sort of "constructive Eden,"[22] where the leading activists of abstract constructive experiments came together. In 1930, the Uruguayan Joaquín Torres-García, along with Theo van Doesburg, Piet Mondrian, and Michel Seuphor, had launched the Cercle et Carré group. The Parisian prominence of Torres-García confirmed the receptivity toward foreign artists, and revealed that it was not necessary to be Russian or Dutch to have a place in Paris. The universal language of geometric shapes united artists coming from different places who spoke different languages.

Once these young South American artists arrived in the French capital, contact with Georges Vantongerloo helped to reorient their work. Vantongerloo had been part of legendary movements such as De Stijl, Neoplasticism, Cercle et Carré, and Abstraction-Création. His work had been part of the selection carried out in the framework of the magazine *Arturo,* and after the war he experimented with Plexiglas, one of the materials that was very dear to the kinetic artists of the sixties. Meanwhile Vardánega had also experimented with plastics in the mid-forties, and in 1948, shortly after arriving in Paris, he exhibited his work along with Vantongerloo himself, the Italian Bruno Munari, and the Swiss Max Bill at the Galerie Denise René. Between 1949 and 1950, Vardánega and Melé returned to Buenos Aires.[23] From 1956 onward, Vardánega explored the possibilities of Kinetic Art using mobile ribbons of celluloid and devices enabling the viewer to modify the works,[24] and the end of the decade found him back in Paris, this time in the company of the artist Martha Boto.

23. Arden Quin traveled to South America in 1953 and returned in 1956. During his stay in Buenos Aires, he formed the group Arte Nuevo together with the critic Aldo Pellegrini, Tomasello, and Vardánega, among other artists.

24. Frank Popper, *Naissance de l'art cinétique* (Saverne: Gauthier-Villars, 1967), 144 and 161.

Martha Boto and Gregorio Vardánega's shared exhibition card, ca. 1969

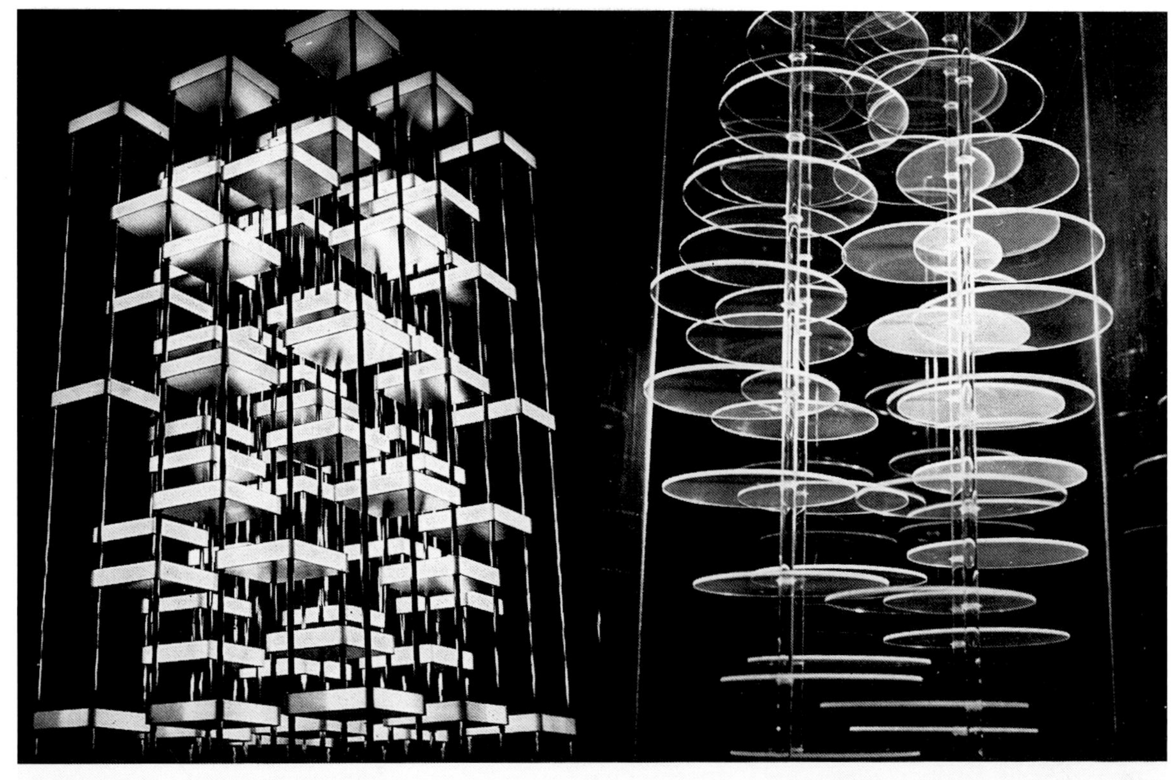

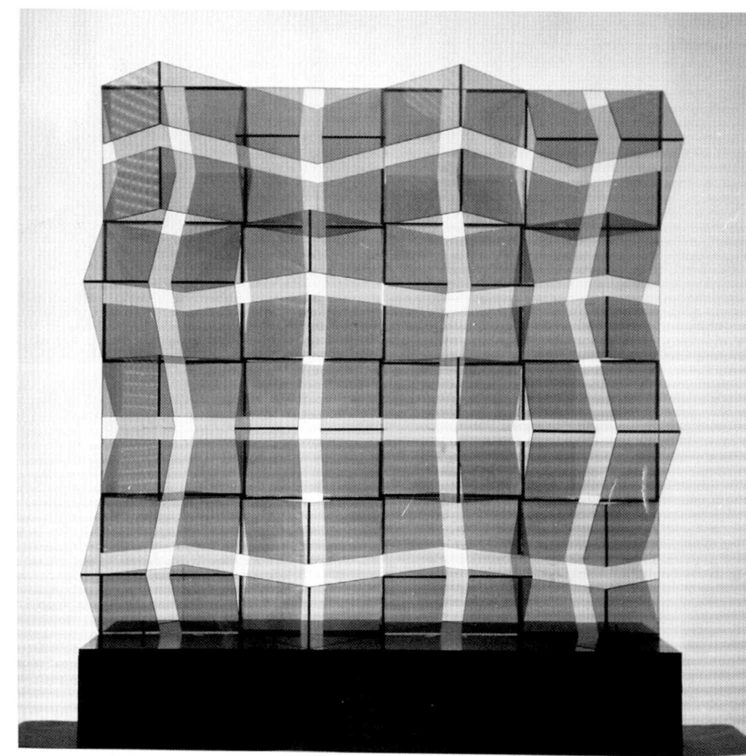

Francisco Sobrino, *Espacios indefinidos F*, 1963, plastic, 21 ½ x 17 ⅝ x 6 ½ in.
(54.5 x 45 x 16.5 cm). Museo Nacional de Bellas Artes

25. While Le Parc has said that the Vasarely exhibition in 1958 at the Museo Nacional de Bellas Artes served to stimulate travel to Paris, the migration of this group of artists began earlier: Asís, Kosice, and Tomasello left in 1957, and other artists, such as Antonio Berni, Lea Lublin, Antonio Seguí, and Nicolás García Uriburu, who followed different aesthetic paths, also migrated. See my book *Argentinos de París: Arte y viajes culturales durante los años sesenta* (Buenos Aires: Edhasa, 2013).

26. See my "The Multiplication (and Rebellion) of Objects: Julio Le Parc and the European Triumph of Kinetic Art," in Isabel Plante and Cristina Rossi, *XIII Premio Fundación Telefónica a la investigación en historia de las artes plásticas en la Argentina* (Buenos Aires: FIAAR-Fundación Espigas, 2011), 173–215.

Between 1957 and the mid-sixties, a greater number of Argentine artists began journeys to Paris.[25] Among those who were inclined toward Kinetic Art, in addition to Vardánega and Boto, were Kosice (another pioneer in the incorporative experiments that were part of the movement from the mid-forties), Antonio Asís, Hugo Demarco, Armando Durante, Horacio García-Rossi, Julio Le Parc, Francisco Sobrino, and Luis Tomasello. In 1966, the Argentine press noted that at the crowded opening of the second Denise René gallery, which was dedicated to the exhibition and sale of kinetic multiples, the Spanish language was mixing with French on all sides. The prize for painting at the Venice Biennal (the most prestigious prize at the international level),[26] which Le Parc had received that year, was still fresh news, and the press emphasized the encouraging effects the award would have in the highly competitive Parisian artistic field:

Facing reality is very difficult in the terrible marathon that has always been art in Paris. The troop, as everyone knows, is tightly packed, the race is grueling and without immediate prospects. The grants have run out and there is no choice, if nothing else happens, other than painting walls. And they paint . . .

But, suddenly something does happen, and the situation improves for everyone. Things begin to sell. Some museums of modern art buy and the meager remuneration of galleries increases considerably. And now Zagreb, New York, London and Buenos Aires are buying "mobiles" from Le Parc, and the Musée de la Ville de Paris includes those by Martha Boto; the Pompidou and Rockefeller ladies choose works of Tomasello and various institutions bring home the echoing towers of Vardánega and the gigantic complexes of Sobrino.[27]

The tension between collective production, group membership, and individual legitimacy coursing through the production and marketing of multiples in the Argentine artistic community of Paris reached its apex with the 1966 Venetian prize for Le Parc. The members of GRAV (García-Rossi, Le Parc, Sobrino, and the French artists François Morellet, Joël Stein, and Jean-Pierre Yvaral) also had individual works and exhibitions, but the Venetian prize radically modified the symmetry among them. For the French press (with some exceptions, such as Clay), Le Parc emerged from the obscurity of group production and was then defined as a figure on a more prominent plane. On the other hand, because of the prize, Kinetic Art as a whole gained visibility.

27. Miguel Alfredo D'Elia, "El mendocino que triunfó en Venecia," *La Nación*, July 10, 1966. Le Parc Archive.

28. Housing constructed by the French government and rented at subsidized prices.

29. Le Parc, in Christiane Duparc, "Julio Le Parc: Voulez-vous jouer avec lui?," *Le Nouvel Adam*, December 1966. Le Parc Archive.

30. Umberto Eco, *Obra abierta* (1962; Buenos Aires: Planeta, 1992), 98. Emphasis in the original.

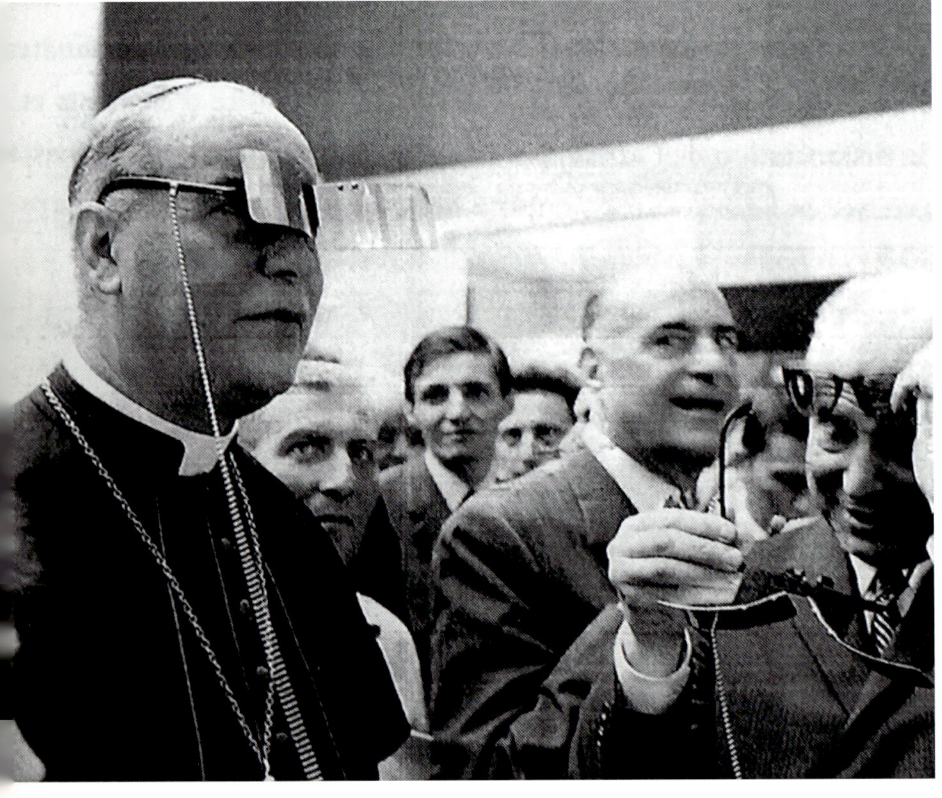

Le Parc's exhibition room at the Venice Biennal, 1966. Denise René Archive

Le Parc. *XXXIII Bienale di Venezia, Italia*, 1966. Design and cover of catalogue by Rogelio Polesello

A cognitive conception of perception allowed kinetic artists to argue that optical and kinetic resources did not come down to a simple play of illusion. Altering visual and synesthesic perception involved literally — and above all, symbolically — modifying the way in which participants saw themselves and the world. The resources they implemented were intended to question the naturalness of everyday perceptions, and once they were put in doubt, not only the system of fine arts but also a society that could be seen as automated were subject to fundamental questioning. The fact that a large number of these art objects were not unique works, but multiples susceptible to reproduction without limit, made it possible to imagine the expansion of their destabilizing effects on a wide audience. In fact, the formal and material qualities of kinetic works favored broad public visibility. The volumetric presence and attractiveness of new materials with shiny surfaces, such as Plexiglas or stainless steel, with an interactive opening toward the viewer, were among the properties of Kinetic Art that drew large numbers of visitors to exhibitions. Le Parc took advantage of the Venice Biennal interviews to disseminate the principles of GRAV regarding the virtues of the kinetic productions, which were to be at once collective, multiple, and eccentric within the field of art:

> One has to lean toward the "collective multiple," the game room, the public demonstration where groups of spectators are involved simultaneously, where each one becomes both the actor and object of the spectacle at the same time. These mazes, these game rooms have to be located in barracks, in schools, in H.L.M.s,[28] to overcome the loneliness of the crowd and to recapture, in some way, conditions for participation found among primitive societies.[29]

If modern society plunged individuals into the crowd, into routine, if it reduced them to cogs in the great capitalist machine to the point of making them long for "primitive" times, it simultaneously offered them tools to combat an inertia that had nothing to do with immobility but rather with automated and unreflexive velocity. Kinetic artists expressed confidence that with an effective combination of art and technology, it would be possible to modify modernized life.

This ambitious objective was to be pursued in two ways. First, through an art increasingly sensitive to the participation of the viewer, which Umberto Eco defined in terms of open works, "works *in movement*" characterized by "the invitation to *make the work* with the author."[30] The tactile intervention of the viewer became a central concern for GRAV, which investigated it through mazes and through journeys, during which the visitor wandered, manipulated objects, and was subject to optical and tactile stimulation of all kinds. Furthermore, however, Kinetic Art proposed blurring the aura of the work and the art market through the serial production of artistic objects that did not correspond to the requirement of rarity or of manual touch by the artist.

At the end of 1967, the critic Otto Hahn gave an overview of their commercial success in Paris: "Multiples are multiplying. The word is now 'Open Sesame.' Even lithographs are vested with the sweet name of Multiples."[31] The options and the prices were varied. The Givaudan gallery, opened in 1966, took the model of the publishing industry: large-scale reproduction with the same price for famous and unknown artists. In this way, Givaudan aspired to moralize an art market that was growing at the pace of French modernization without modifying its elitist logic. In July of the same year, Denise René opened her gallery dedicated to the exhibition and sale of multiples; and a little later, she patented the denomination "multiple" with the hope of using it exclusively.[32] In her case, the works were executed under the supervision of the respective artists. René favored limited editions of kinetic multiples, under the supervision of the artists, in disagreement with the wishes of most South American kinetic artists, who wanted unlimited multiples. "Art must preserve its 'aura'" — René held — "and continue being a high quality product that bears witness to a reflection on the world."[33] With this in mind, in the following years she organized individual exhibitions for her artists, whose respective catalogues had a section reserved for multiples. With more affordable prices, René intended to disseminate modern art among people who could otherwise not acquire unique works. The point was democratizing access to the ownership of art objects (and increasing sales).

By 1966, Clay was imagining a near future in which galleries would cede their place to "organizations conceived on an industrial scale,"[34] which would disseminate the "artistic product" in the same way that books and LP records were sold. But these visual artifacts were fraught with the tension between their industrial vocation and their effective insertion into the exclusivist logic of an art market that did not expand at the desired pace. By 1969, in the context of a roundtable on kinetic multiples organized by *Robho*, Clay expressed some reservations. In regard to the initiative to sell multiples by the FNAC — a shop devoted to marketing photographic, cinematographic, and phonographic materials, which was beginning to expand its offering to

31. Otto Hahn, "Les multiples à Paris," *Art International,* vol. 12, no. 1 (January 1968): 47–49.

32. Jean Clay, "An interview with Denise René," *Studio International,* vol. 175, no. 899 (April 1968): 192–95.

33. Ibid.

34. Clay, "L'art du mouvement," 88.

35. La FNAC (Fédération nationale d'achats) was founded in France in 1954 by André Essel and Max Théret, two former Trotskyite militants. In 1969, the second Paris store was opened. "Décès de Max Théret, fondateur de la Fnac," *La Tribune.fr,* February 25, 2009.

36. "La fin de l'objet et du lieu culturel : Débat organisé par la revue *Robho* avec Jean Clay, les artistes présents et le public," program brochure of the Centre culturel Noroit, Arras 8, March 24, 1969, Le Parc Archive.

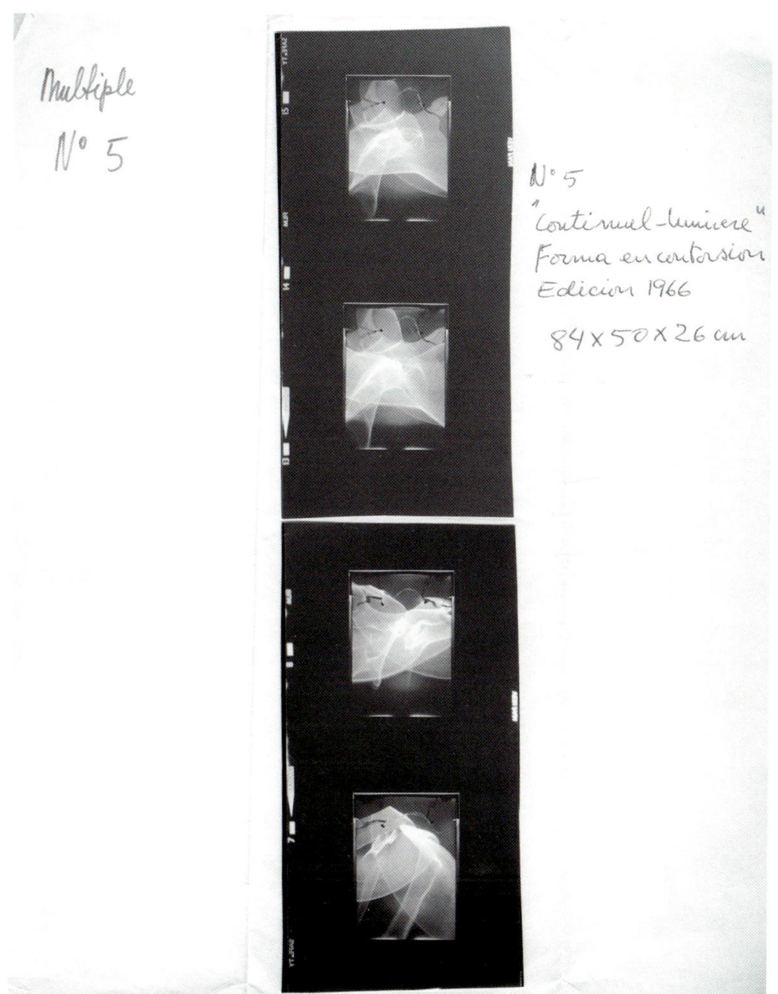

Julio Le Parc, *Múltiple No. 5. Continuel-lumière. Forma en contorsión*, 1966, 33 x 19 ⅝ x 9 in. (84 x 50 x 23 cm). Di Tella Archive, Torcuato Di Tella University, Argentina

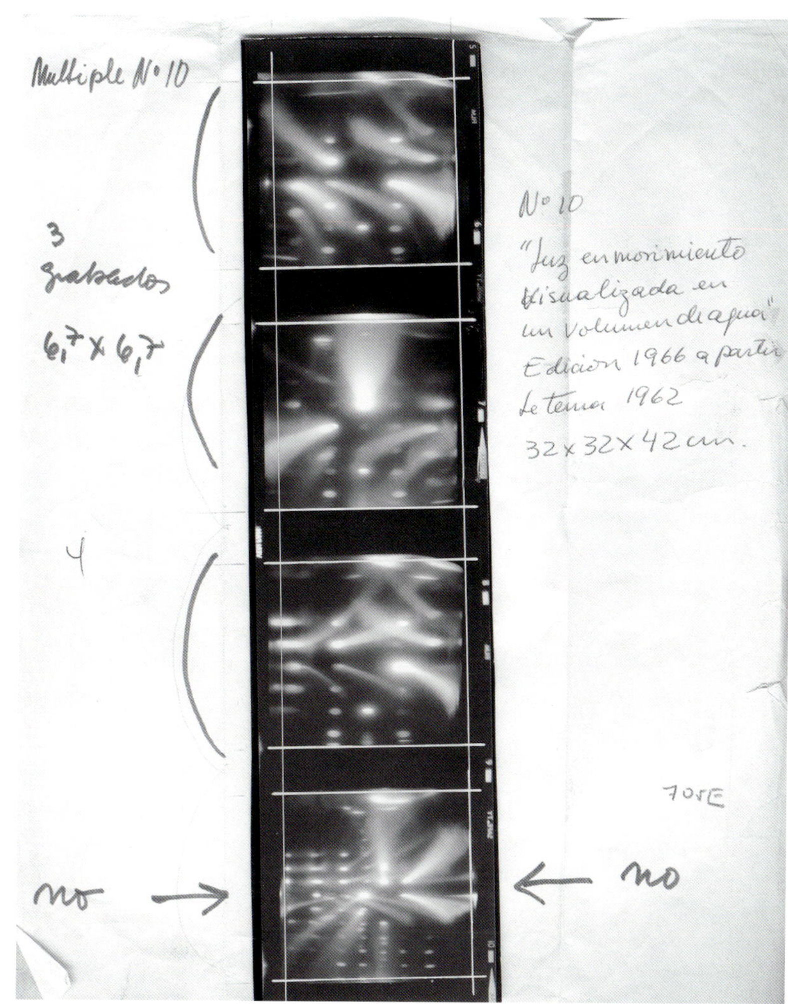

Julio Le Parc, *Múltiple No. 10. Luz en movimiento visualizada en volumen de agua*, 1966, 12 ⅝ x 12 ⅝ x 16 ½ in. (32 x 32 x 42 cm). Di Tella Archive, Torcuato Di Tella University, Argentina

multiples

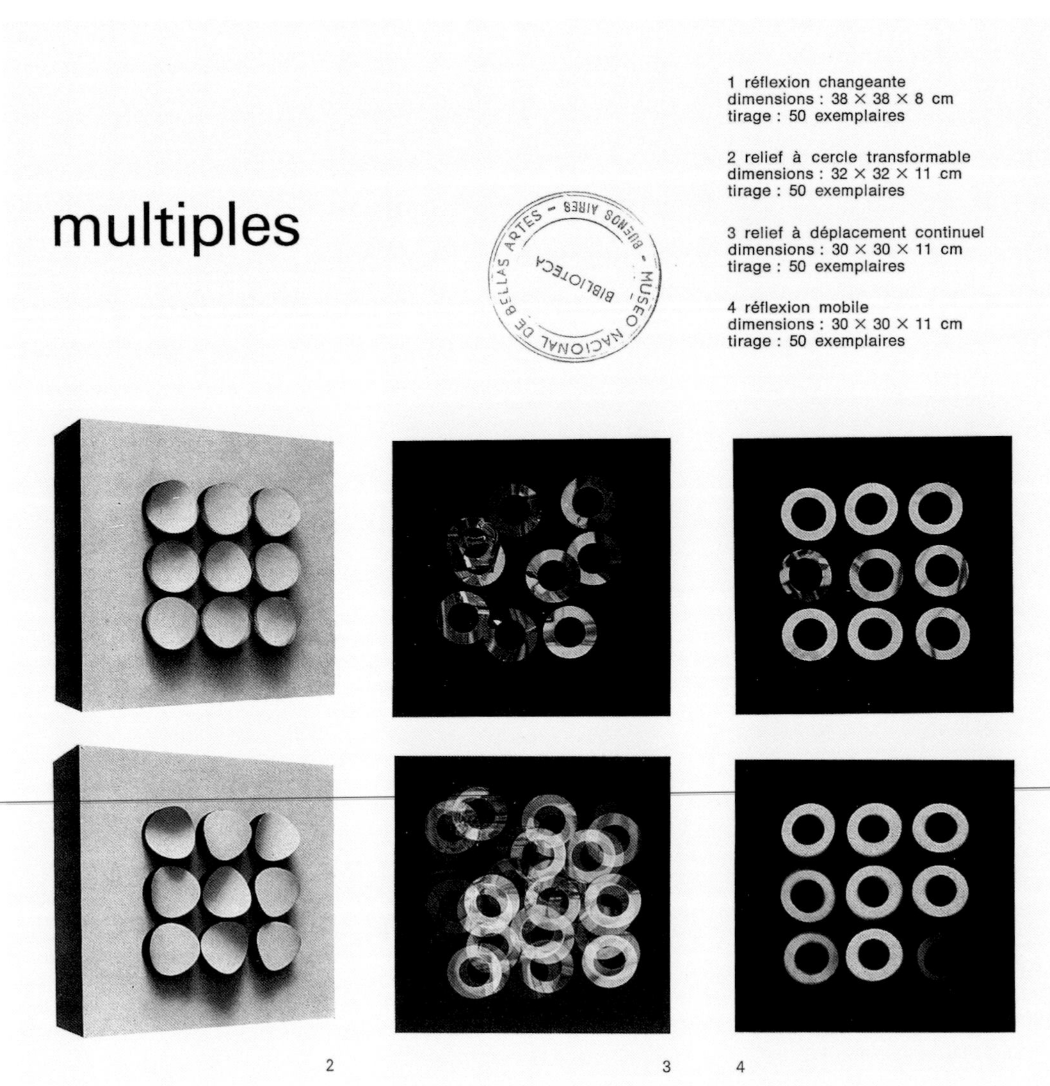

Demarco: Dynamique de l'image, 1968. Multiples by Hugo Demarco. Galerie Denise René, Paris

other products[35] — this critic asserted that it was a mistake to offer these objects along with all types of artifacts.[36] For multiples to preserve their meaning, they had to be displayed in such a way that people would understand that they were artistic statements and not just gadgets.

In the context of an unprecedented abundance of small objects designed with ingenuity — which Jean Baudrillard described with suspicion in his book *The System of Objects* (1968) — the bright and colorful kinetic multiples ran the risk of becoming simply "one more gadget." Paradoxically, if kinetic artists produced their work with the main goal of dragging viewers out of their passivity in modernized society, these same works, which could pass for artifacts — just as Baudrillard had seen it — reduced users to viewers of a technical imaginary displayed in an indeterminate group of consumer goods.

37. For example, issues of the British magazines *Art and Artists*, vol. 4, no. 3 (June 1969) and *Studio International*, vol. 180, no. 926 (October 1970) each dedicated their contents to the phenomenon of multiples, with information about Germany, the United States, France, Holland, England, Italy, and the Soviet Union. In Paris, Denise René and many of the kinetic artists we discussed were key figures.

38. See my paper, "Afiches del Mayo Francés: Gráfica, autoría y alteridad sudamericana en 1968," *Revista VIS*, vol. 15, no. 1, Universidad Nacional de Brasilia (September 2016); http://periodicos.unb.br/index.php/revistavis/index.

Kinetic Art reached its European zenith in the mid-sixties, but in France discovered its limitations and contradictions in discussions about culture, standardization, and consumption toward the end of the same decade. At this point, the events of May 1968 in France brought a symbolic break and an aesthetic turning point: Demarco, Le Parc, and Sobrino were active participants in collective and anonymous poster production at the Atelier populaire, the printmaking workshop of the École nationale supérieure des beaux-arts, which was taken over by artists and students in mid-May of that year. In support of a student protest that escalated to a strike of nine million workers, and that actually paralyzed France, these posters shared walls with the famous graffiti echoing the hopes that imagination would then take control.

Withdrawing from geometric abstraction, the Argentine kinetic artists saw the opportunity to fight side by side with students and workers identified, in many cases, with the figure of Che Guevara. They also found a way to radicalize the demythization of art that they had been promoting since the beginning of the decade. The posters, like the kinetic multiples, were visual artifacts from large print runs with high visual impact, but they inhabited the streets with greater naturalness than the kinetic works. This did not imply that the artists abandoned the production and promotion of their kinetic work or that the proliferation of multiples would suddenly cease, from one day to the next. The Boto, Demarco, Cruz-Diez, Le Parc, Sobrino, and Vardánega solo shows at the Galerie Denise René took place between 1968 and 1970; the aforementioned debate about multiples organized by the magazine *Robho* took place in 1969, and the European press continued analyzing the phenomenon of the multiple.[37] But that confidence in the universal vocation of Kinetic Art was no longer in one piece. In the context of what the crisis of May 1968 meant for the artistic field and its autonomy, the participation of the Argentine artists in the Atelier populaire was interpreted in relation to a Latin American subject whom the European Third World movement identified with collective and politicized production.[38] In that identification with the Third World, which was being delineated around the Cuban Revolution and the independence of Algeria, the emergence of these "collective voices" in Paris drowned out the grand aspirations for a universal art.

GREGORIO VARDÁNEGA *Multiplication electronique II*, 1966
Plexiglas, wood, light bulbs, and motor, 35 3/8 × 35 5/8 × 9 7/8 in. (89.9 × 90.5 × 25.1 cm)
Collection of Gérard and Maria Rose Guilbert, Paris. Courtesy of Sicardi Gallery, Houston

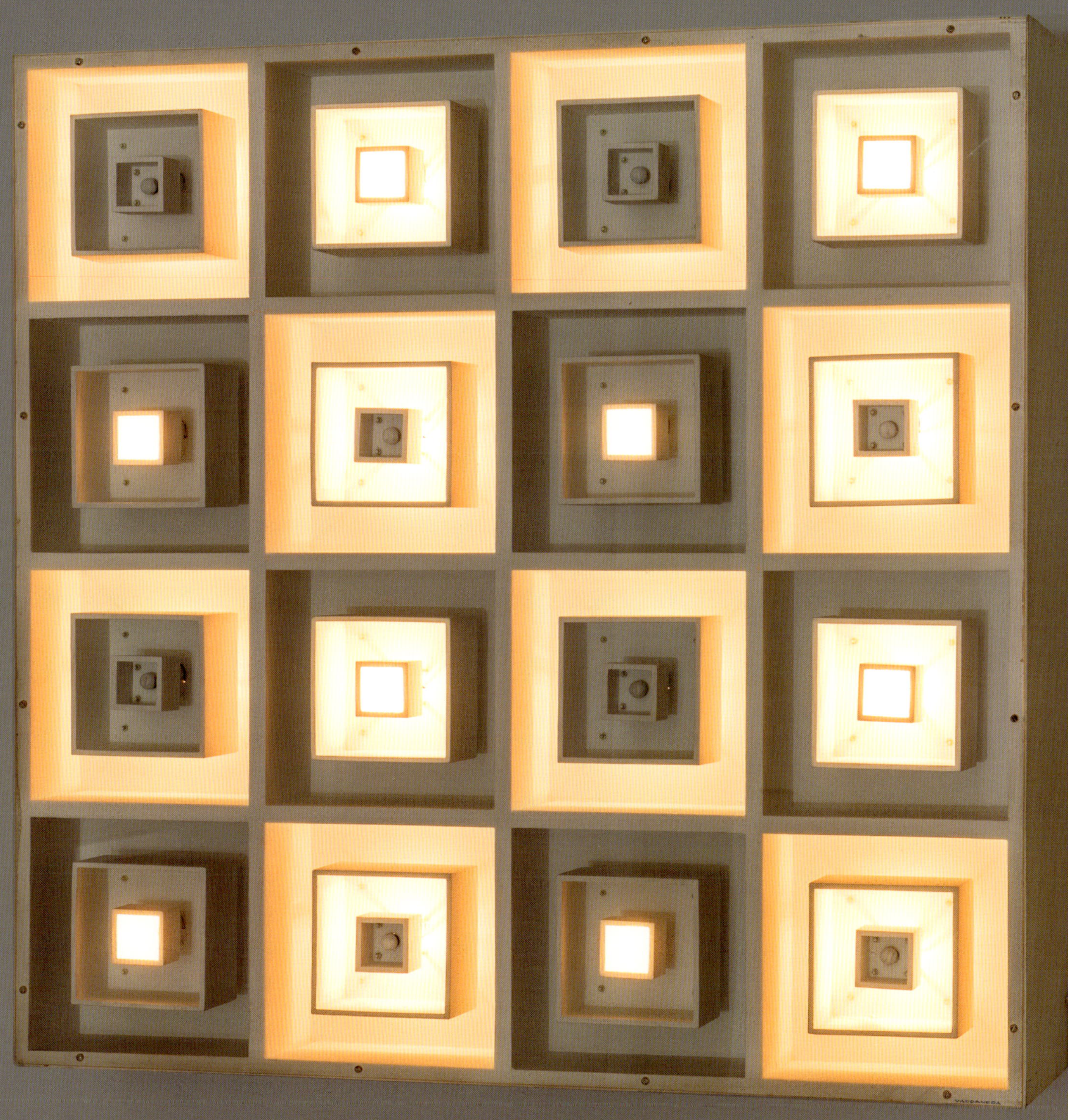

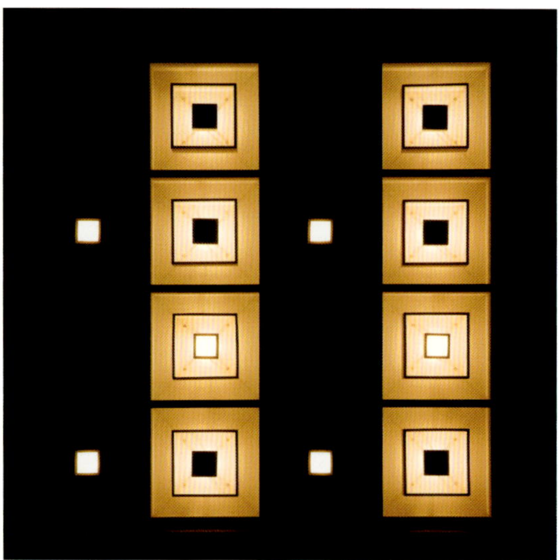
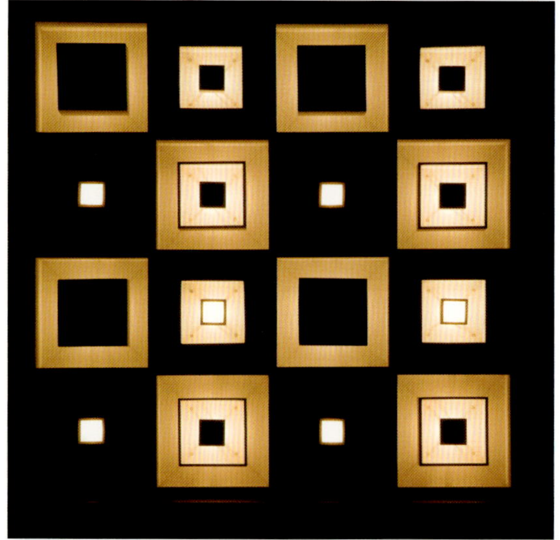
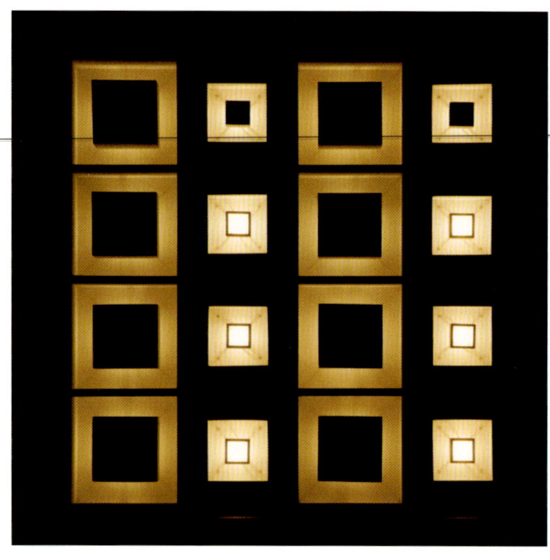
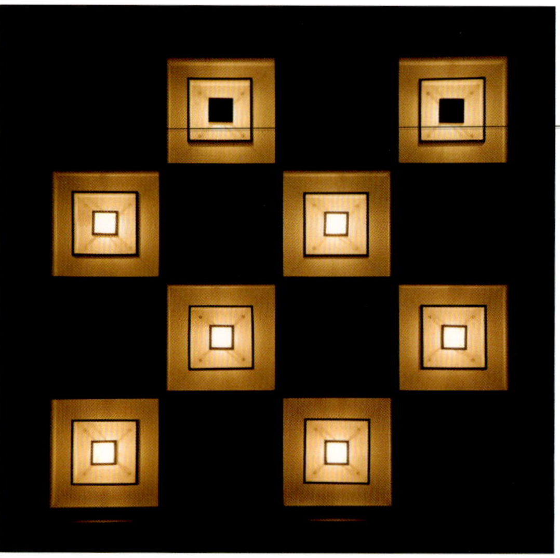
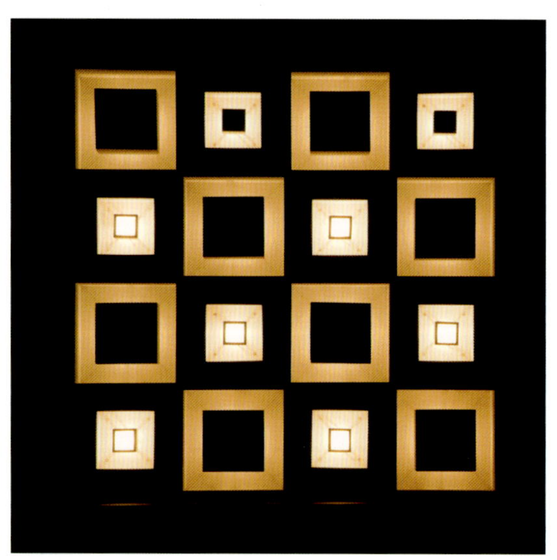
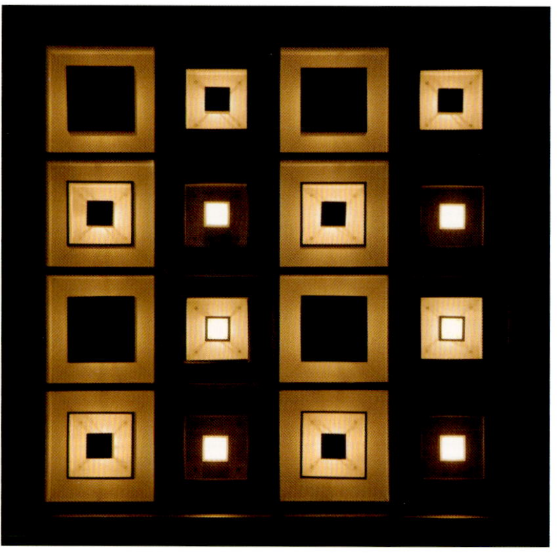

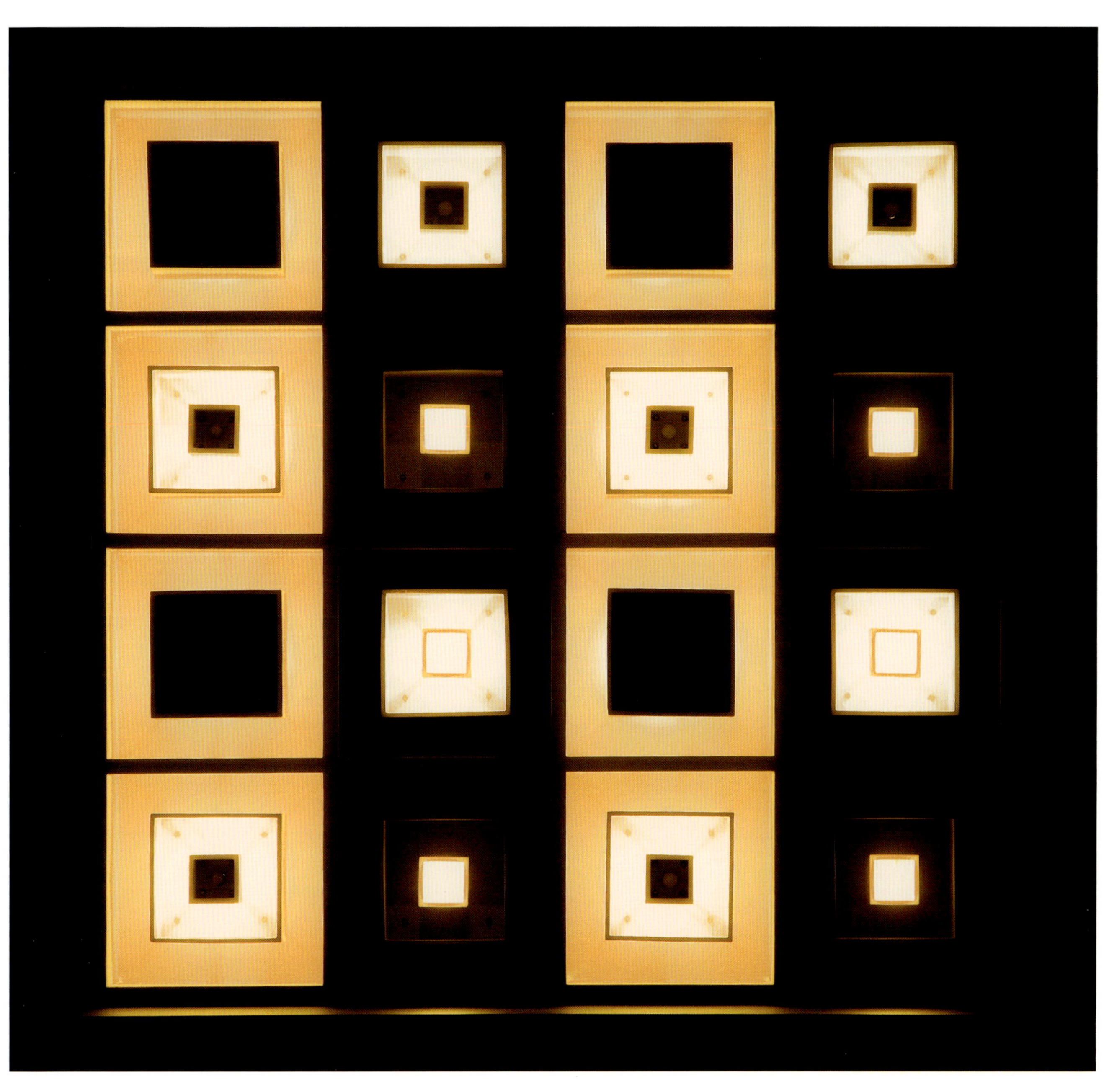

GREGORIO VARDÁNEGA *Multiplication electronique III*, 1966
Wood, Plexiglas, and motor, 35 x 35 x 10 in. (88.9 x 88.9 x 10.16 cm)
The Ella Fontanals–Cisneros Collection, Miami

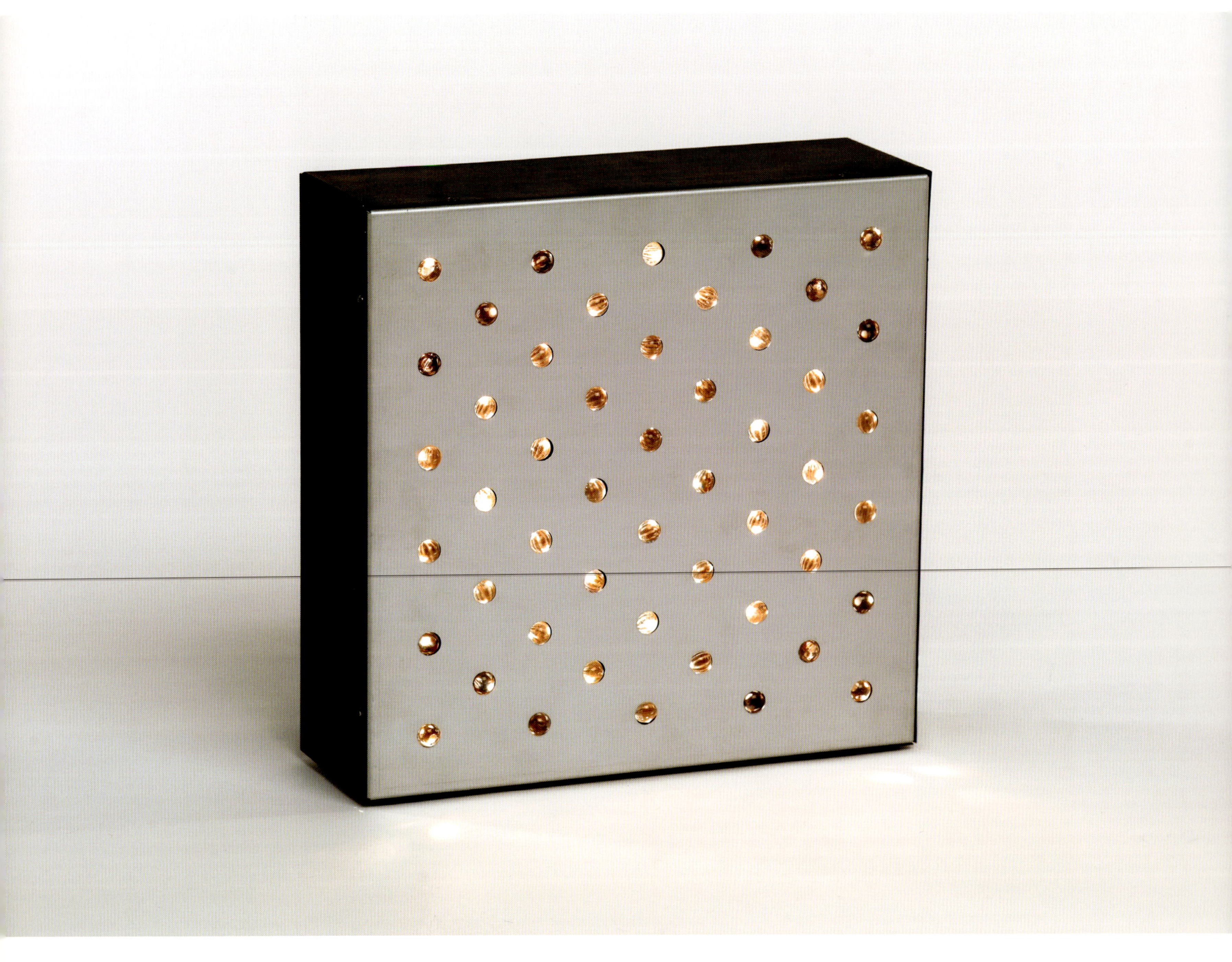

GREGORIO VARDÁNEGA   *Scintillement electronique*, 1969
Metal and motor, 13 × 13 × 4 1⁄8 in. (33 × 33 × 10.5 cm)
Collection of Gérard and Maria Rose Guilbert, Paris. Courtesy of Sicardi Gallery, Houston

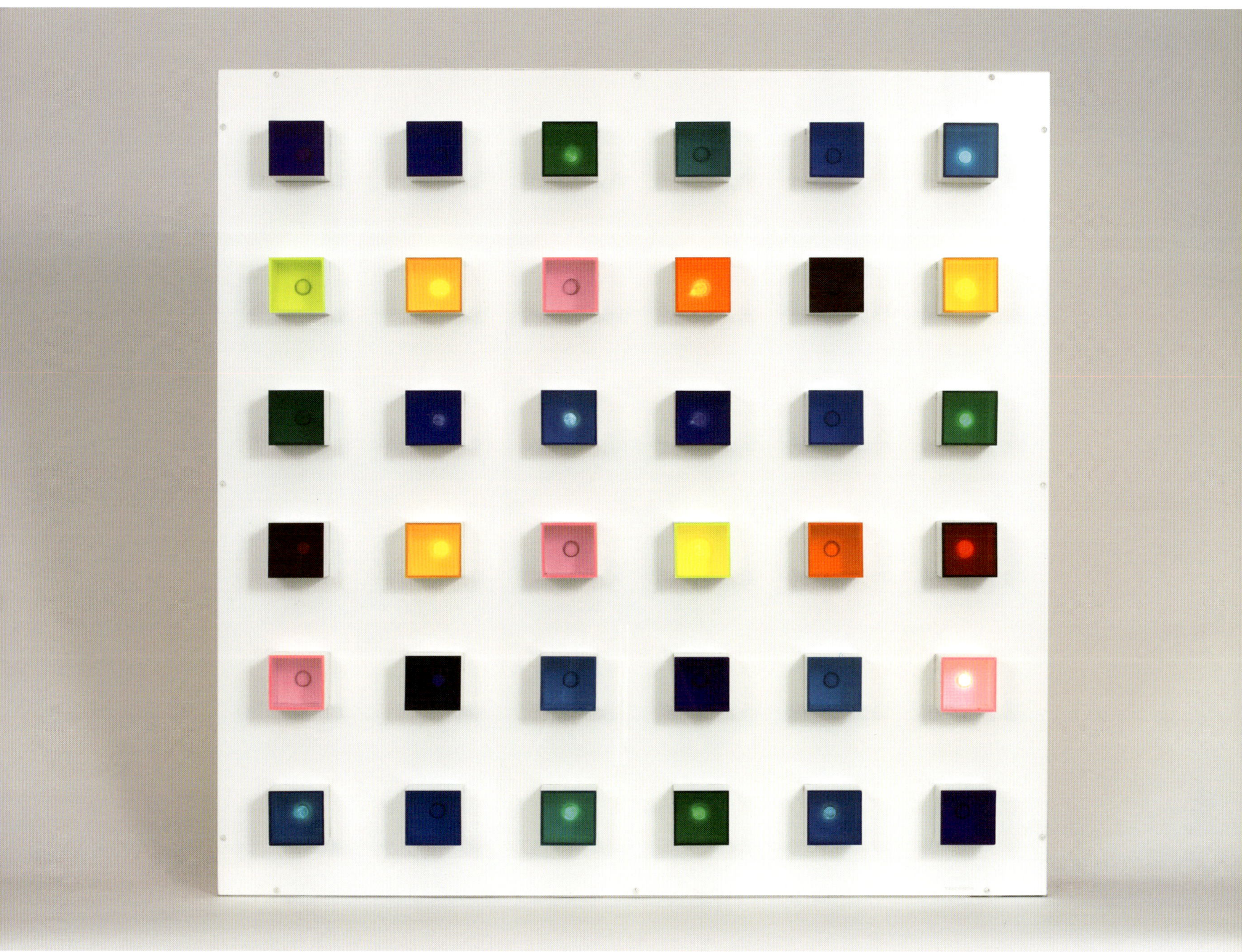

GREGORIO VARDÁNEGA   *Polychromie electronique I*, 1965–70
Plexiglas, wood, light bulbs, and motor, 39 ⅝ × 39 ½ × 7 ⅝ in. (100.6 × 100.2 × 19.5 cm)
Courtesy of Sicardi Gallery, Houston

GREGORIO VARDÁNEGA *Espaces chromatiques carrées en spirale*, 1968
Plexiglas, light bulbs, and electric motor, 39 ¾ × 49 ⅛ × 18 ⅛ in. (101 × 124.8 × 46 cm)
The Museum of Fine Arts, Houston. Museum purchase funded by the Latin Maecenas, 2010.173

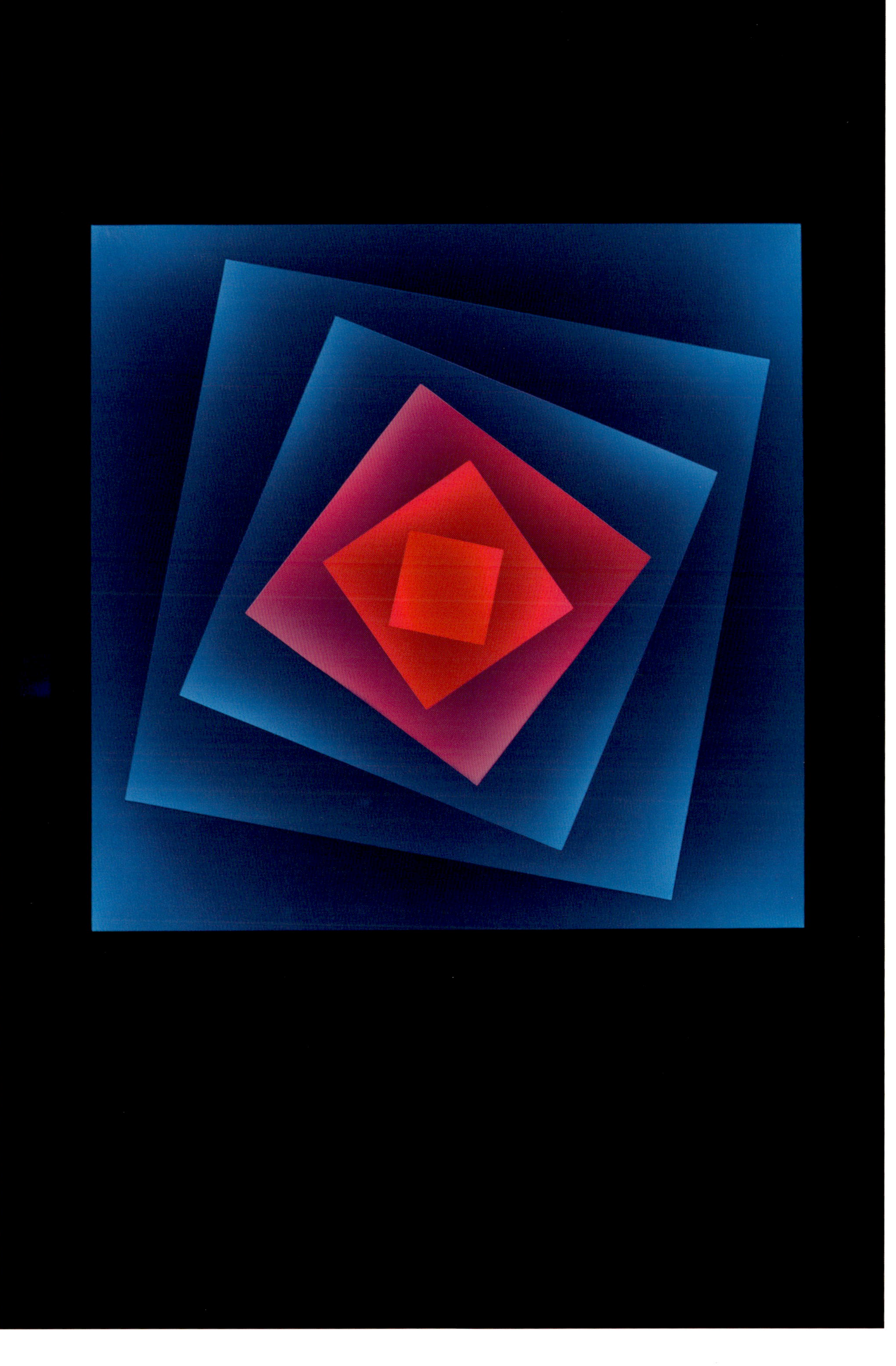

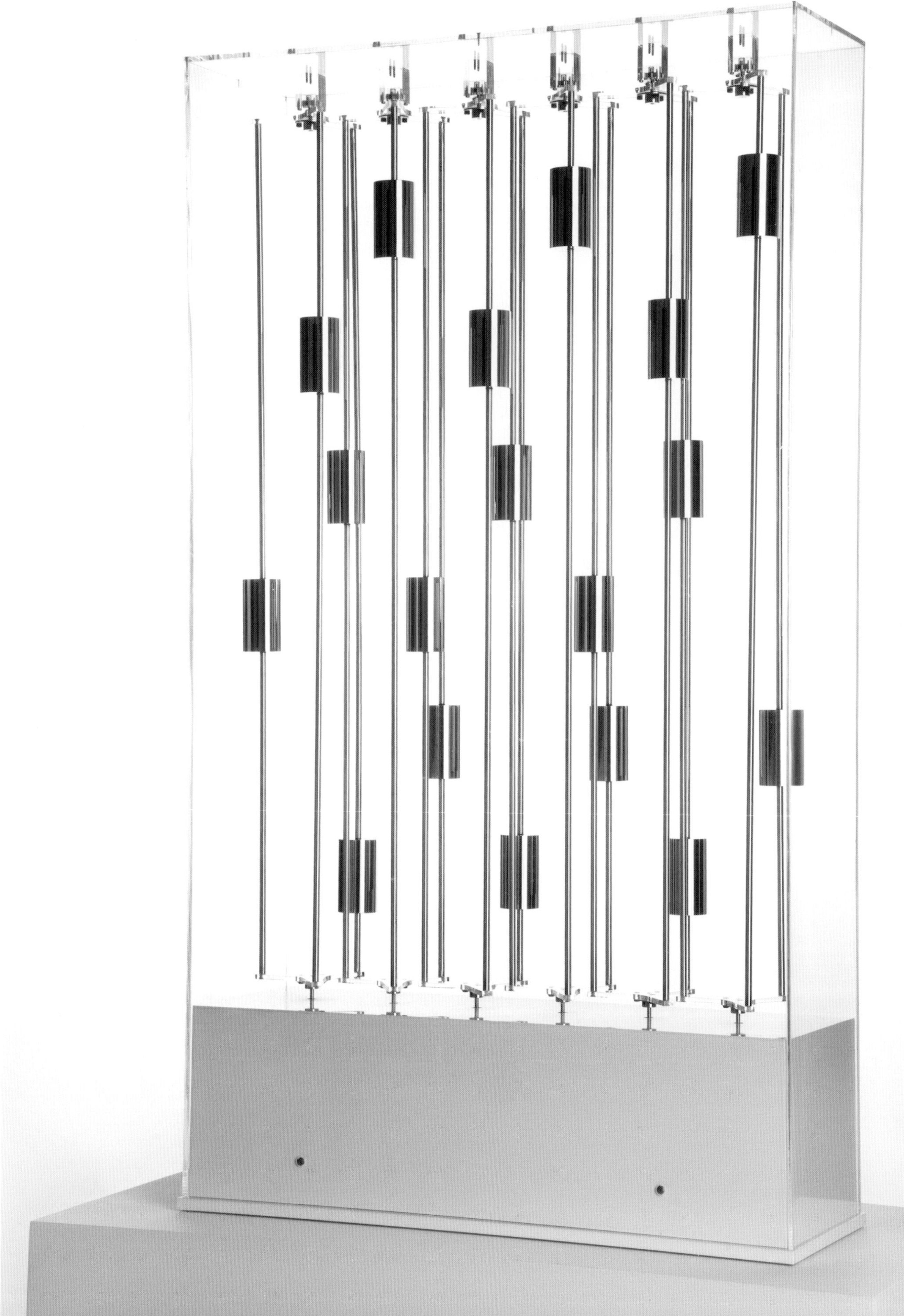

GREGORIO VARDÁNEGA *Sans titre*, 1969
Aluminum, glass, metal, wood, light bulbs, and motor, 39 ³/₈ x 15 ¼ x 15 ¼ in. (100.01 x 38.7 x 38.7 cm)
Collection of Gérard and Maria Rose Guilbert, Paris. Courtesy of Sicardi Gallery, Houston

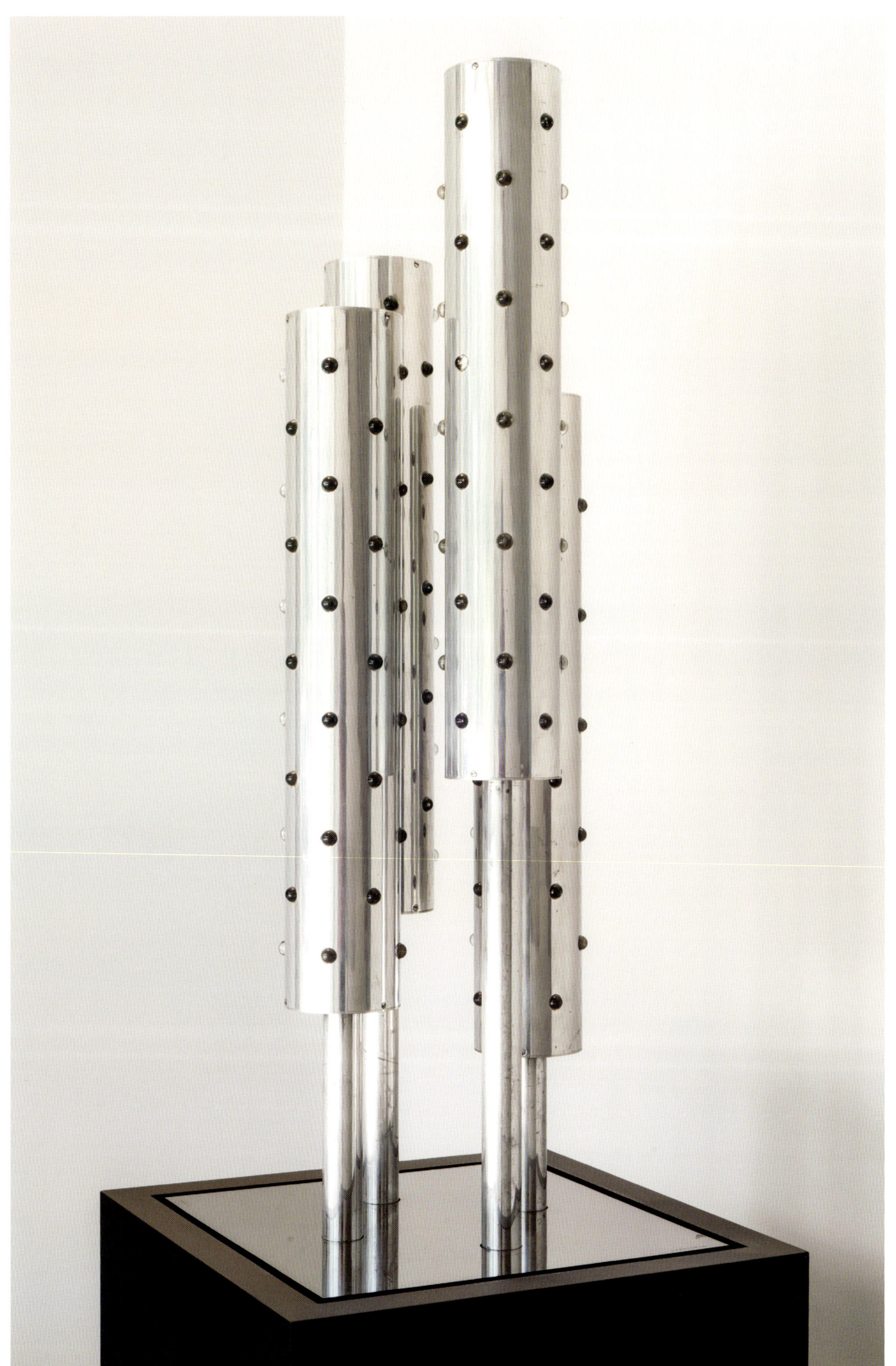

Frederico Morais

Abraham Palatnik was born in 1928 in Natal, Rio Grande do Norte, to a family of Russian Jews who had settled there in 1919. At that time Natal was a small city, and the local economy was based on agriculture. His father and uncles were among the first to develop trade and industry on a systematic basis in Natal, and they introduced new business methods and manufacturing techniques. Over several decades they were active in eight different branches of industry, from furniture and ceramics to sugar refining. Palatnik himself, even today, doubles as plastic artist and industrialist.

When he was four years old, Abraham Palatnik went to Palestine, now Israel, with his family, and it was there that he got his primary and secondary schooling. He went on to take courses in mechanics and physics and specialized in internal combustion engines. He had been drawing since early childhood and spent four years at an atelier studying drawing (with live models), painting, and aesthetics. He painted landscapes, still lifes, portraits and self-portraits. The line in his pencil drawings is lively, fluent, and almost lyrical, while his charcoal drawings portraying his classmates feature a heavy and dark line that is strong, solid, and realist, at times almost expressionist. In his painting he stripped his representation of all that was superfluous and rhetorical.

Palatnik returned to Brazil in early 1948 and settled in Rio de Janeiro. Two decisive encounters took place that year that radically transformed his creative work in the field of art: his acquaintance with art critic Mario Pedrosa, and his first visit to the Occupational Therapy Department at the D. Pedro II Psychiatric Hospital in the nearby town of Engenho de Dentro, which had been founded by Nise da Silveira two years previously.

Mario Pedrosa had by then become a leading Brazilian intellectual and was active in both art and politics. In a 1947 lecture to the Brazilian Press Association, he was the first Brazilian critic to support art created by schizophrenics. Two years later, seeking the nomination as History of Art and Aesthetics Professor at the National School of Architecture, Pedrosa defended a thesis called

"On the Affective Nature of Form in Works of Art." This was the first text published in Brazil, and one of the first internationally, to analyze artworks using Gestalt theory.

Together with the artist Almir Mavignier, Palatnik was a frequent guest at the home of Pedrosa, at that time constantly crowded with more politicians than artists. He described those encounters in an interview granted to Wilson Coutinho (*Jornal do Brasil*, December 5, 1981): "With all our talk of art, we soon got rid of the politicians. Pedrosa talked a great deal about psychology of the form and Gestalt. But he didn't just talk. He was also a great listener. We were attempting to understand the nature of the creative processes and the function of the artist. I reached the conclusion that the artist's work is to order the chaos of perception. I still believe in perception being linked to intuition. Without it, nature would be no more than chaos."

Palatnik was introduced to the Psychiatric Hospital in Engenho de Dentro by Mavignier, who had been running the painting workshop there. "When I saw the artistic output of some of the inmates, my preconceived notions were shattered. I knew how to handle paint and brushes, I felt secure in my knowledge and, suddenly, I met these people, who had never had any kind of training, producing works using complex and profound language." The powerful impression made by this and several successive visits, together with the conversations with Pedrosa, "demolished my ideas and convictions in relation to art." He decided to drop painting and spent two years at home creating his first kinechromatic device.

Palatnik felt sure that by adopting a different technique, using the latest technology, he could bring to "pictorial art the potential of light and motion in time and space." He built his first two kinechromatic devices as experiments in 1949 and 1950. On a plastic screen covering the front of his devices, he projected colors and forms driven by electric motors, creating a luminous effect with its own timing. Using motors and light bulbs, he replaced paint as a material dimension with refracted light. The timing of the lighting was controlled from a console with switches for each lamp. The viewer sees only the colored shapes projected onto the front of the kinechromatic device. Inside there were about 600 meters of electric wires in different colors, linking 101 lamps of varying voltages, rotating several cylinders at varying speeds. Light is projected through a set of lenses and shapes and a prism to refract colors.

The first kinechromatic device was called *Azul e roxo em primeiro movimento* (Blue and Purple in First Movement). It was shown at the first São Paulo Biennial in 1951 but was not well received. The Brazilian jury ruled it out on the grounds that it did not fit in any of the categories foreseen in the regulations. However, the Biennial committee allowed it to be shown in a room allocated to Japanese artists who failed to appear. Nevertheless, Palatnik was excluded from the catalogue. The work was then seen by another jury composed of international visitors, who considered it to be an important manifestation of modern art, worthy of presentation at the Museu de Arte Moderna de São Paulo, and his apparatus eventually won an honorable mention. The Argentine critic Jorge Romero Brest, master of several generations of Latin-American critics, published a long commentary on the first São Paulo Biennial in number 26 of the *Ver y Estimar* review (Buenos Aires, 1951), and enthusiastically praised the "singular machine created by Abraham Palatnik and based on the kaleidoscopic principle," in which "diverse shapes are composed, enlivened by intense coloring that can be very soft and subtle, emerging as compositions that paintings as such would like to achieve but cannot."

The term "kinechromatic" was coined by Pedrosa, who, not accidentally, published the first critical-analytic text on Palatnik's invention. His article in *Tribuna da imprensa* (1951) refers to Palatnik's "chromatic plastic dynamism" in leaving aside painting and figuration to paint directly with light, attempting, for the first time in Brazil, to materialize Moholy-Nagy's "artistic utopia." This involved the creation of "frescoes of light brightening entire buildings or walls with the plastic dynamism of artificial light under the control of the artist's creative powers and inspiration. In the houses of the future a special place would be reserved for the installation of these luminous frescoes, as is already the case for radio and television." After looking at some of the technical aspects of the first kinechromatic device as well as several aesthetic implications, Pedrosa concluded that it was "the true art of the future," and "an excellent introduction to the Biennial."

Pedrosa wrote another two pieces on Palatnik's invention: in 1953, on the occasion of the presentation of his third device at the Museu de Arte Moderna do Rio de Janeiro, and again in 1960. In the first of these two texts, he highlights the fact that the new apparatus, entitled *Paralelas em azul-laranja numa seqüencia horizontal* (Parallels in Blue-Orange in a Horizontal Sequence), was an advance on previous versions "because of its precision lighting, and chiefly due to the control of the creative concept over the movement of the forms." He concludes, "through the sequence of his forms and development of chromatic chords, the artist has imposed his will on the machine, enabling it to produce artworks."

By 1959, Palatnik had built about twenty kinechromatic devices, nine of them in that year alone. The eighth, with a four-minute sequence of green-orange images, was shown in 1960 at the Museu de Arte Moderna do Rio de Janeiro, and introduced several technical modifications: controls were smaller and there was less wiring (down to 60 meters) and fewer lamps (down to 51); it featured a new automatic control console and two independent switches for light and movement. Observing that the technical improvement had not modified the formal repertoire, Pedrosa demands of the artist, "with his God-given inventive genius . . . a new technical and aesthetic revolution, using electronics to attain greater freedom and variation in his kinechromatic experiments."

Palatnik went on to show his kinechromatic devices at the São Paulo Biennials in 1955, 1957, 1959, 1961, and 1965, and at the Venice Biennial in 1964. The success of the "painting machine" in Venice brought invitations to show in both one-person and group exhibitions in Germany, France, Switzerland, England, the United States, and Israel. By 1964, Palatnik was showing alongside some of the leading names in the world of Kinetic Art at the second *Mouvement* exhibition organized by the Denise René Gallery in Paris, with an introduction to the catalogue by Jean Cassou. It then traveled to the Tel Aviv Museum of Art. Critic Juergen Morschel, in a long article for the *Kulturspiegel* newspaper of Ulm, commented on Palatnik's one-person show at the Hochschule Museum, Saint Gallen, in 1964, saying that the "visitor to the exhibition meets an artist who does not execute objects, but rather stages events. He is a régisseur." Two years later Palatnik was to take part in another leading international Kinetic Art event, *Kunst-Licht-Kunst*, at the Museum of Art in Eindhoven, the Netherlands. Jean Leering wrote a preface to the catalogue, followed by a long introductory text by Frank Popper, in which for the first time he referred to Palatnik's "luminous mobiles," highlighting the poetic vein in his inquiries. In 1967, Popper confirmed Palatnik's advances in the field of research into light and motion in his book *Naissance de l'art cinétique*. In another review, highlighting the importance of the Eindhoven exhibition, Pierre Cabanne wrote in *El arte del siglo veinte* (1983), "Here mention must be made, above all, of Palatnik's kinechromatic boxes, which are picture-boxes of electrically driven changeable chromatic combinations." In a book written jointly with Pierre Restan in 1969, *L'Avant-garde au XXe siècle*, Cabanne had already emphasized Palatnik's important pioneering role in relation to Nicolas Schöffer's inquiries into spatial dynamism. And Tomás Maldonado, the leader of the Argentine concretists-inventionists, as dean of the Ulm Higher School of Form in 1967, greeted his Brazilian colleague as "the most important forerunner of the recent return to the aesthetics of light and motion."

In the United States, Palatnik held one-person exhibitions at the Howard Wise Gallery in New York and at the Pan-American Union in Washington, D.C., both in 1965, and soon after he took part in numerous group exhibitions, among them *Light and Motion*, at the Worcester Art Museum, Massachusetts, in 1967.

Meanwhile, Palatnik had already held his first Brazilian one-person exhibition in 1965 at the Petite Galerie in Rio de Janeiro, and had won an award at the third Biennial of Córdoba, Argentina, with his kinechromatic device titled *Visual Sequence S-81*. It should be emphasized that the international jury at the Córdoba Biennial consisted of Alfred Barr, director of the Museum of Modern Art, New York, and one of the first supporters of abstract art in the United States; Sam Hunter, director of the Jewish Museum, New York; Arnold Bode, creator of the Documenta in Kassel; Carlos Villanueva, the architect for the National University, in Caracas, where he initiated the movement for synthesis across the arts; and finally, Aldo Pellegrini, one of the first Argentine critics to support concretist art. By this time, therefore, Palatnik was one of the most widely known Brazilian artists internationally, and most of the kinechromatic devices he made during his career are to be found in major public and private collections around the world.

In 1959, after his kinechromatic devices, there followed some works in which he explored the aesthetic potential of magnetic fields, including, in some cases, ludic audience participation. In *Mobilidade IV* (Mobility IV), wooden beads are silently moved by electromagnets. In 1983, he again took up this line of inquiry, creating a ludic object consisting of a circular glass base supporting geometric forms in different colors, directly driven by viewers controlling a magnetized rod. The positive and negative poles are used to attract or repel geometrical forms constituting fragments of a larger structure to be assembled by the viewer using the magnetized rod. This work is, in fact, a game.

In 1964, he started his work on "kinetic objects," which consisted of metallic rods or wires attached to wooden disks in several colors and to shapes slowly and silently rotated by motors or, in some cases, by electromagnets. There is nothing but movement in these works. In the kinechromatic devices the electromechanical part is entirely invisible: the spectator sees only the rhythmic movements of the colored light. However, the mechanical equipment is visible in these objects, as Palatnik points to the aesthetic dimension of the mechanism itself.

What are the characteristics of Palatnik's kineticism and what position does he occupy in the world of kinetic movement? There are many interpretations of the meaning of Kinetic Art and they do not always converge. Frank Popper talks about an aesthetic of motion, tracing a course from the moving image to the art of movement. For Jean Clay, however, kineticism is not just that which moves, but it is rather becoming aware of the instability of "the Real." Guy Brett, in his book *Kinetic Art: The Language of Movement* (1968), goes further and relocates the idea of movement to the field of biology, seeing Kinetic Art as a broadening of perception, as a deepening of the biological act of living itself.

As an "aesthetic of motion," kineticism does have predecessors in the history of art. After all, the expression of motion, which is the essence of kinetic artworks, was already being taken up by artists in Egypt and Greece, during the Renaissance and Baroque periods, and so forth, through to the emergence of modern art. These predecessors can also be found in the history of technology, in some mechanical inventions that were quickly appropriated by artists for aesthetic purposes: clocks, musical boxes, Scriabin's lux, Rimington's colored organ, experimental movies by Leopold Survage, Viktor Eggeling, and Hans Richter, among others. Richter was a member of the Dada movement and later became one of its leading historians. In his films *Rythme 21* and *Rythme 23*, he speaks of an "orchestration of time" and sees movies as "visual art above all."

In his kinechromatic devices, Palatnik took up the binomial "light and motion" while his kinetic objects focused on movement, and his ludic and rotative objects and games featured viewer participation within set rules. This work, therefore, is pure kineticism and part of the constructivist tradition. The remotest predecessors of Palatnik's kinetic creation are those mentioned above, and also Gabo and Calder. However, from the 1950s onward, we see him constantly advancing, sometimes ahead, sometimes a little behind, but never far removed from artists such as Pol Bury, Takis, or Jean Tinguely, to mention just three of the most outstanding contemporary kineticists.

abraham PALATNIK

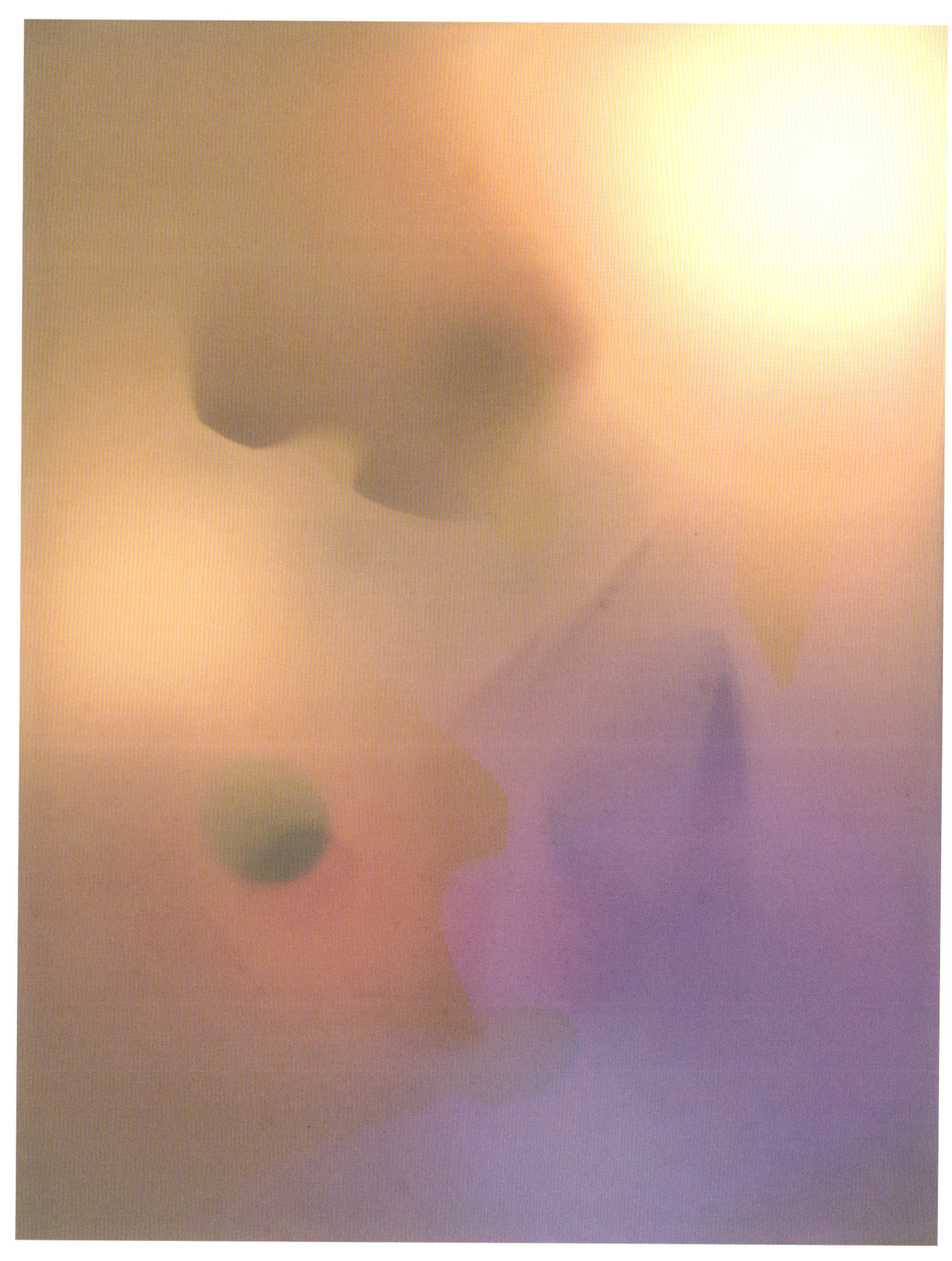

ABRAHAM PALATNIK *Kinechromatic Device S–14*, 1957–58
Wood, metal, synthetic fabric, lightbulbs, and motor, 31 ½ × 23 ⅝ × 7 ⅞ in. (80 × 60 × 20 cm)
The Museum of Modern Art, New York. Latin American and Caribbean Fund
through a gift of Patricia Phelps de Cisneros in honor of Marnie Pillsbury, 2008

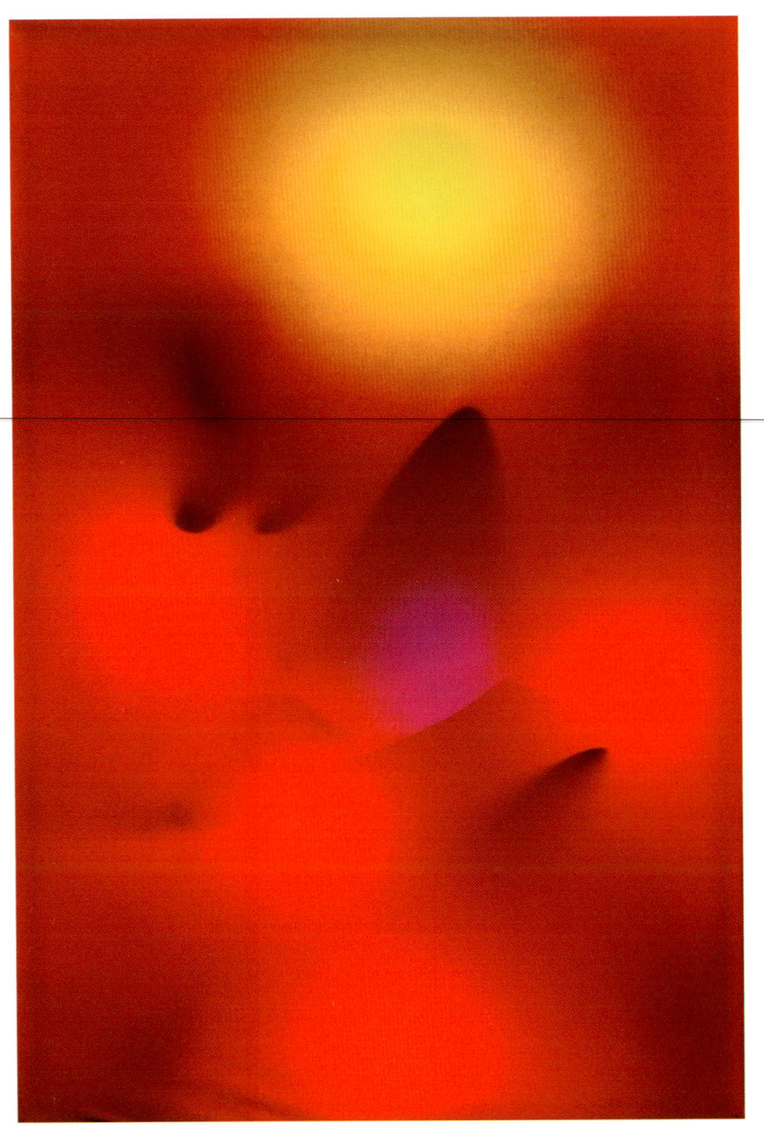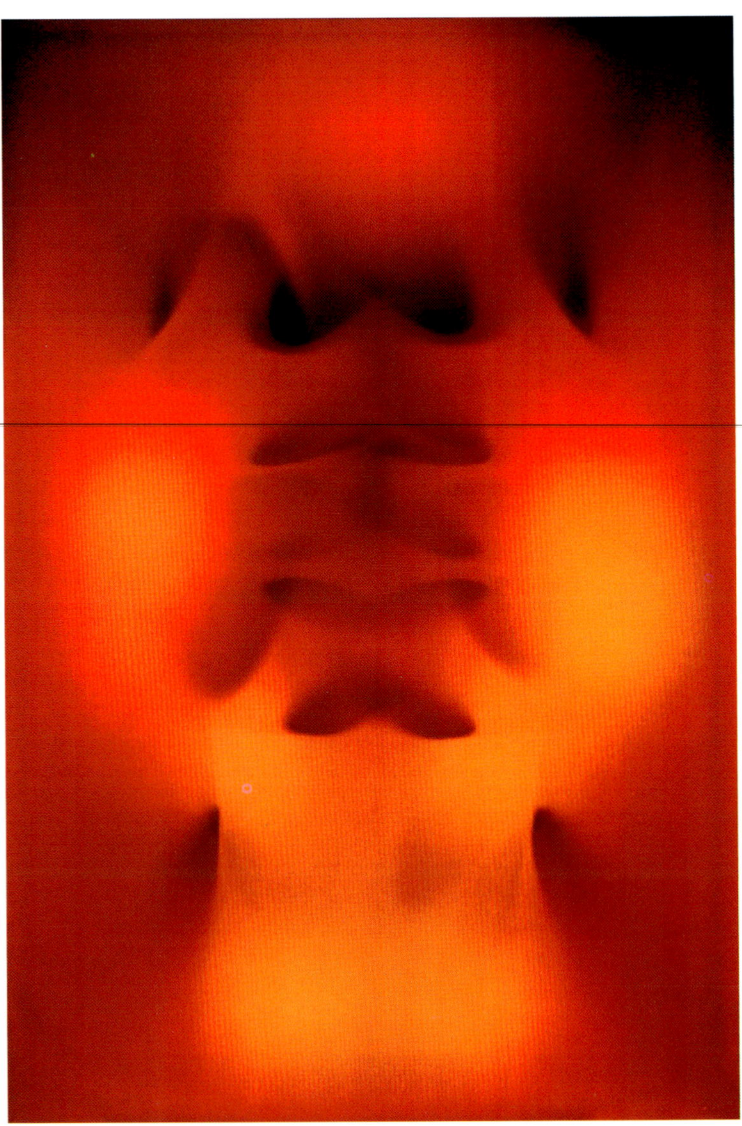

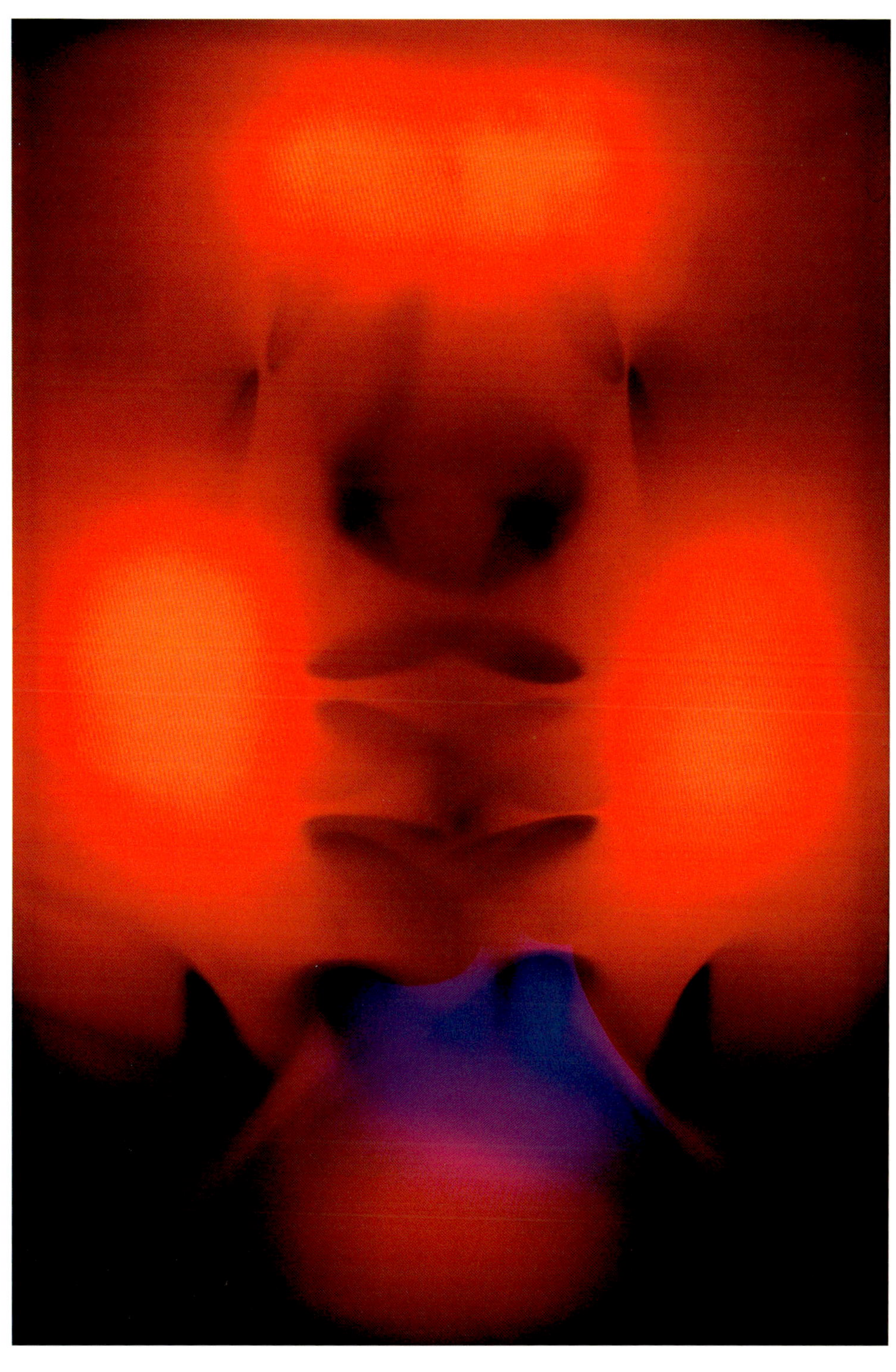

ABRAHAM PALATNIK   *Aparelho cinecromático*, 1955
Wood, metal, synthetic fabric, light bulbs, and motor, 48 1/16 × 29 3/8 × 7 7/8 in. (122 × 74.5 × 20 cm)
Private collection

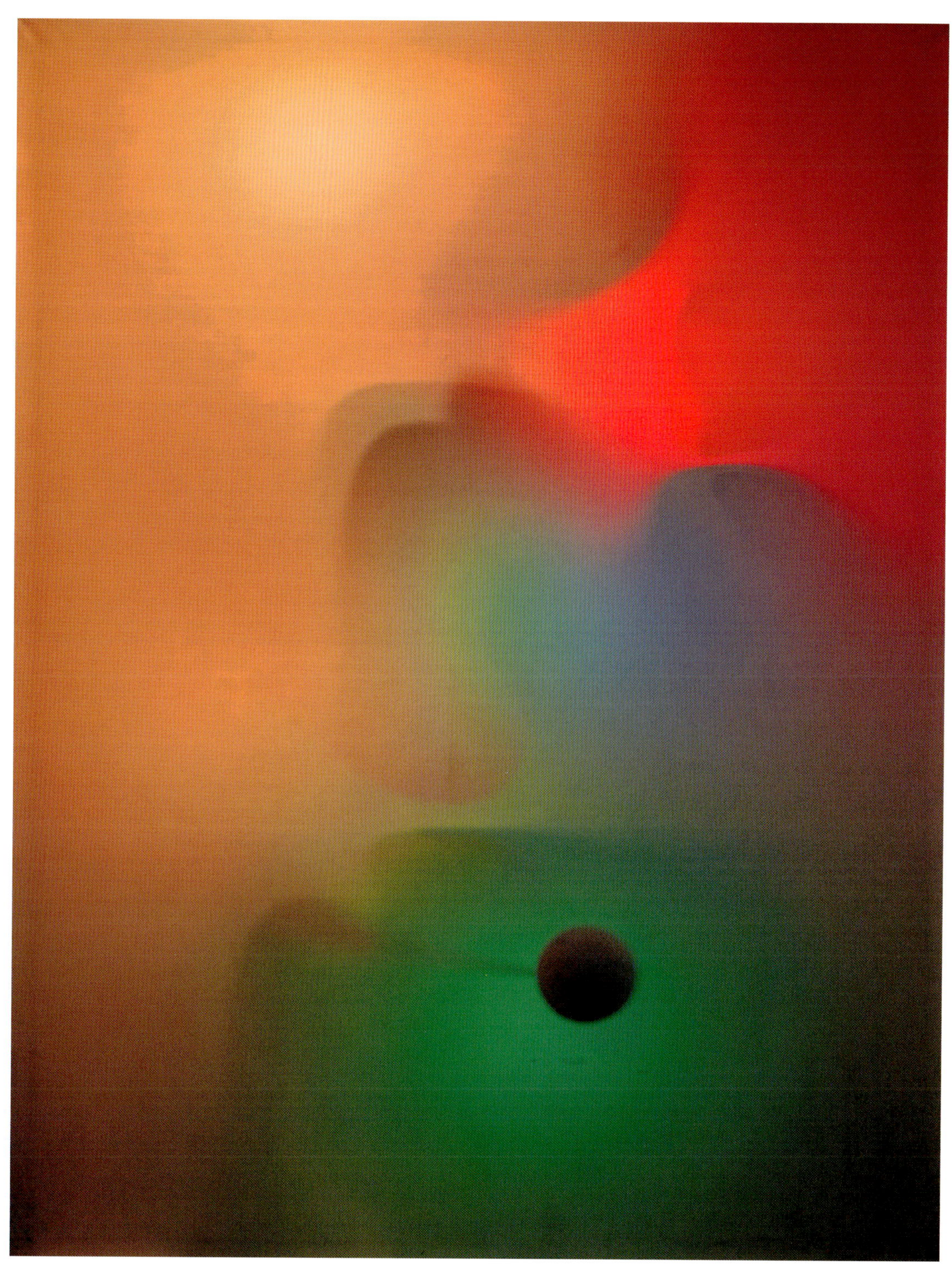

ABRAHAM PALATNIK   *Aparelho cinecromático*, 1962
Wooden box with plastic cover, electric motor, colored light bulbs linked to a programmed
electric circuit and cardboard paddles, 38 1/8 × 28 3/4 × 7 1/2 in. (96.8 × 73 × 19.1 cm)
The Museum of Fine Arts, Houston. The Adolpho Leirner Collection of Brazilian Constructive Art,
museum purchase funded by the Caroline Wiess Law Accessions Endowment Fund, 2007.21

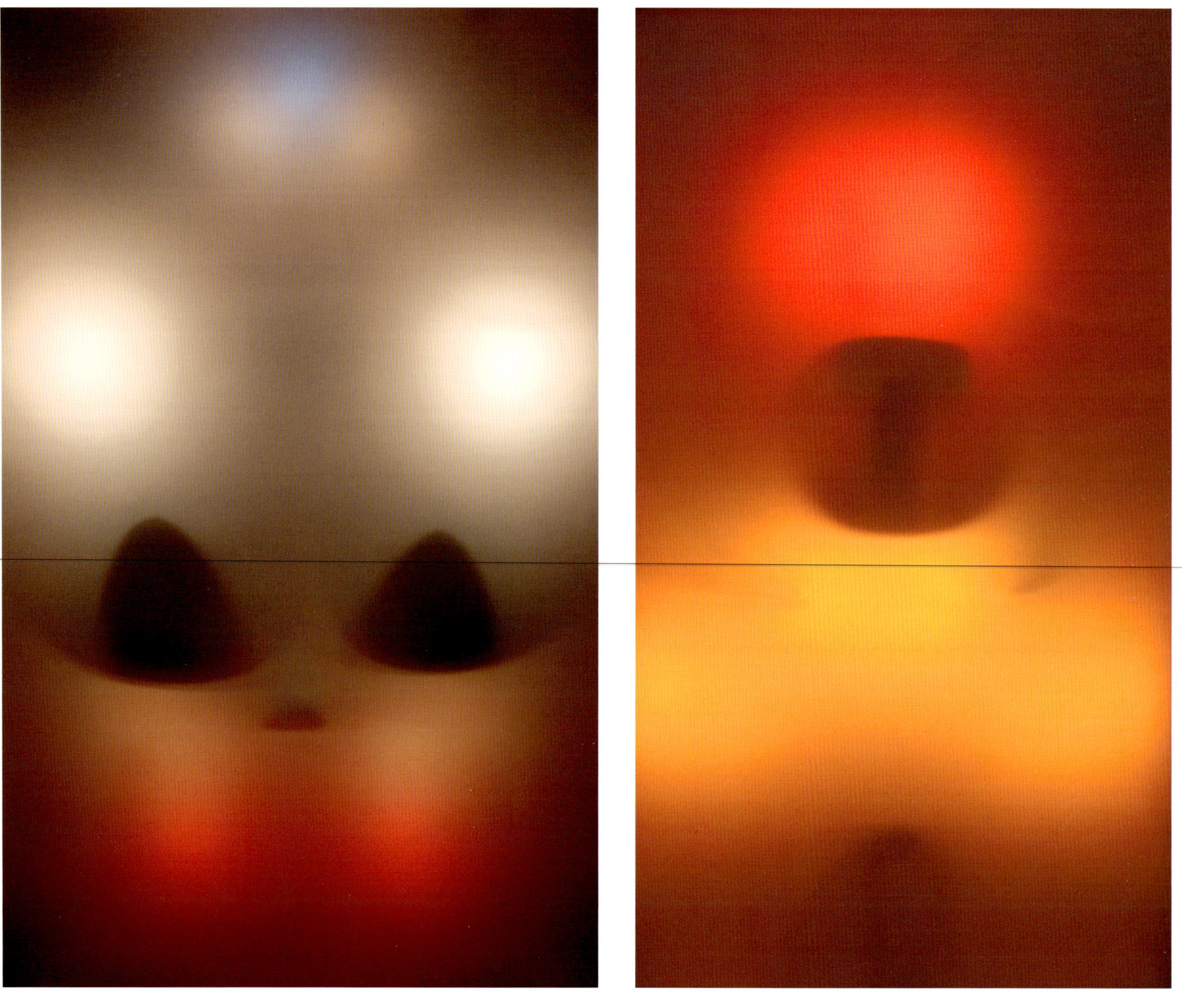

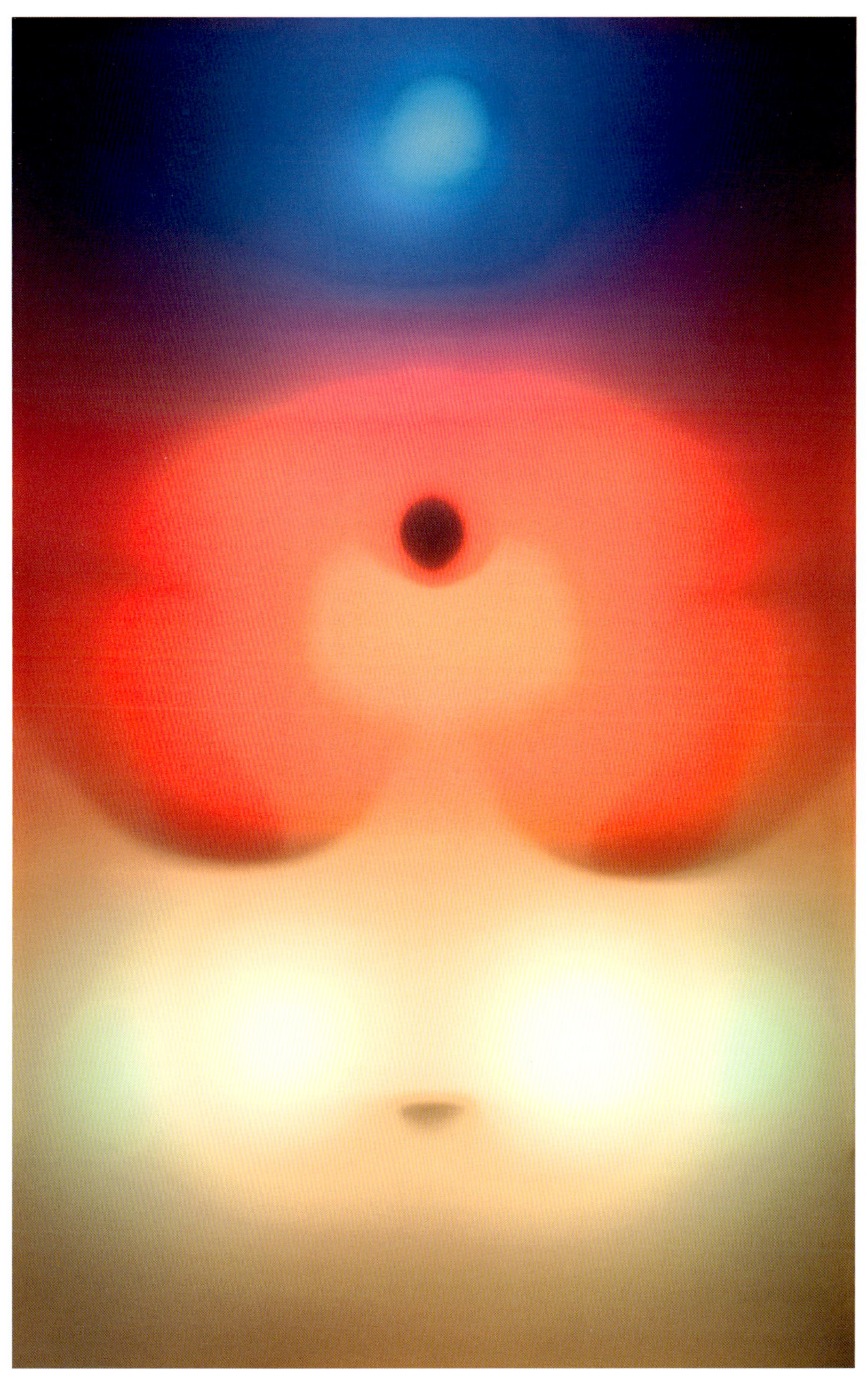

ABRAHAM PALATNIK   *Aparelho cinecromático*, 1969/1986
Wood, metal, synthetic fabric, light bulbs, and motor, 44 3/8 × 27 3/4 × 8 1/16 in. (112.5 × 70.5 × 20.5 cm)
Courtesy of the artist and Galeria Nara Roesler, São Paulo, Rio de Janeiro, and New York

Héctor Olea

HYDROKINETICS, OR WHAT IS HYDROSPATIALITY?

In the mid-1940s, the founder of Madí, an art movement that straddled both banks of the Río de la Plata, abandoned canvas to begin experimenting with neon gas and water. In 1948, there was a significant international exhibition by the Argentine faction of this group at the Salon des Réalités Nouvelles in Paris, featuring the display of "cut-out frames," which anticipated shaped canvases by two decades. A year later, Gyula Kosice developed his concepts of "hydrokinetics" and "hydraulic sculpture," in which, instead of pigment on canvas, the artist made use of water, light, and movement as essential elements. Nevertheless, the great bet on the *Hydrospatial City* was already underway, while the author questioned himself about "coming to terms with his own contradictions, creating 'hydrosculptures' and 'hydro-neon' reliefs for an architecture that I am attacking at a fundamental level."[1] The proposal of a "hydrospatial citizen" did not just mean starting out from a planet (Earth) that should properly be called "Water"; it also entailed a higher, bolder step, the transition from considering water as an *object* to letting it emerge as a *subject* in a specific place, far from earthly gravity: the *Hydrospatial City* in undefined outer space. Kosice supports his thesis, stating: "It is not audacious to enter into and investigate the absolute, through the possible, starting from a deliberate, imaginative chain interaction."[2] The *absolute* is what is imagined by science; the *possible* simply refers to the links arising from his poetic sensitivity.

1. Kosice, "Manifiesto" (2010), 10.

2. Ibid., 11.

Gyula Kosice, *Fotomontaje de la ciudad hidroespacial*, 2010 (detail). Courtesy of Museo Kosice, Buenos Aires, Argentina

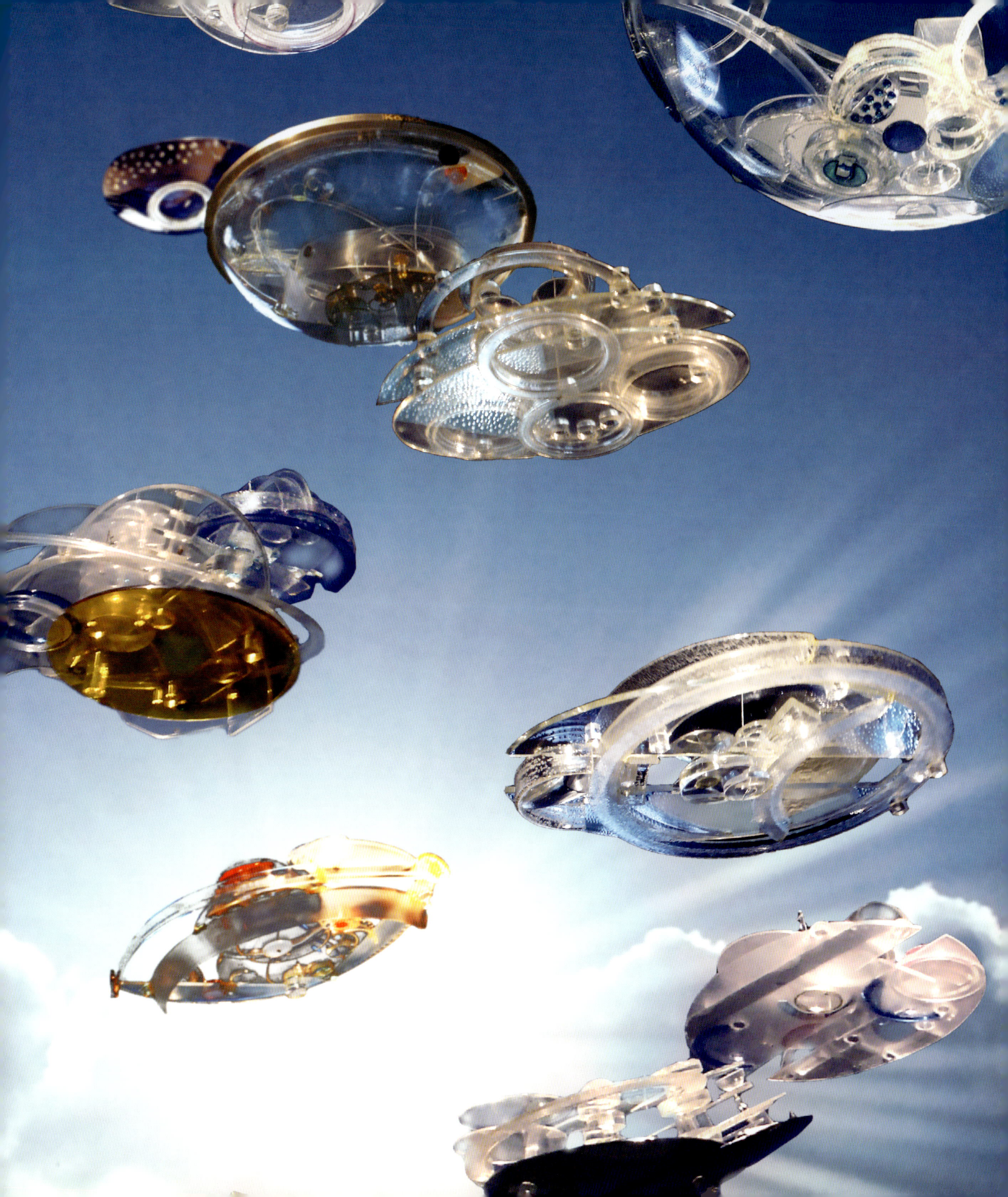

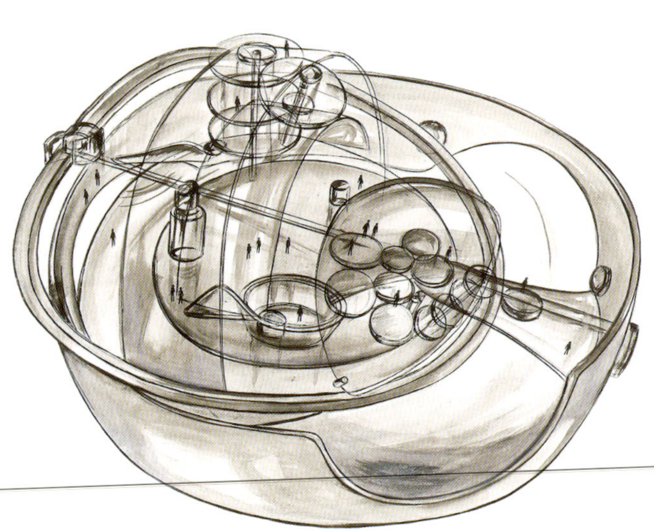

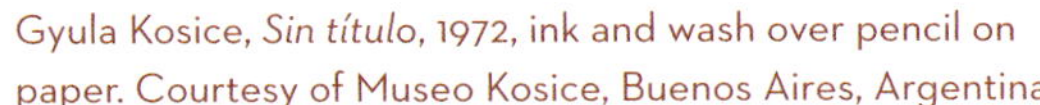

Gyula Kosice, *Sin título*, 1972, ink and wash over pencil on paper. Courtesy of Museo Kosice, Buenos Aires, Argentina

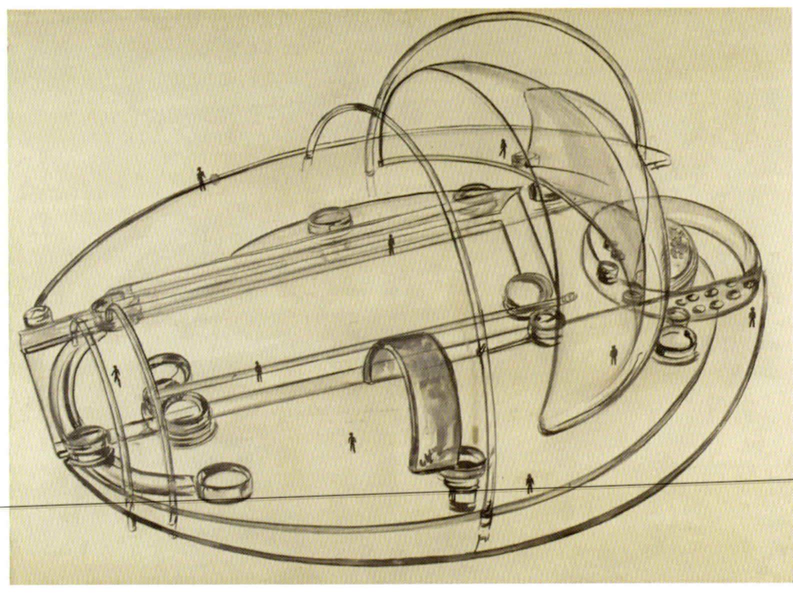

Gyula Kosice, *Hábitat hidroespacial, maqueta R*, 1948, ink on paper. Courtesy of The Museum of Fine Arts, Houston, 2009.1791

The artist conceives works with water, but there is also an idea that surpasses the idea of an artwork: a proposal that "aims at opening up art," in which it is not only *a place* in space but also *habitable*. Therefore, the work he postulates exists where "the places conceived with a sense of synthesis and community life are its extension. In that case, why painting, why sculpture, in short, why 'the object,' if all this is already contained in the dwelling occupying space, volume, color, movement?"[3] Here Kosice identifies the *new* existential *subject*; here the *object* will come to be an intermediary rather than an end in itself. At this time he made his first sketches, then developed them into nineteen oval, acrylic models measuring approximately 8 by 14 inches and some 6 inches high. These were related to a complex project that would take decades of conceptualizing and execution — that is, of metaphysical thinking and physical making. Although the project was not a joint effort, Kosice referred to it with the plural, seeing himself as an integral part of humanity: "We are making a concrete proposal to construct a human habitat that will occupy real space . . . in cities conceived ad hoc, based on prior feelings of coexistence and another differentiated *modus vivendi*."[4]

3. Ibid., 12.

4. Ibid., 11.

5. Diyi Laañ participated in all of the group exhibitions held by Madí in the 1940s with her radical paintings, which consisted of polygonal frames painted with geometric motifs and empty space at the center. Her stories and poems were published in the eight issues of the group's journal, *Madí Universal*.

6. See *Diyi Laañ: Selección de poemas* (Buenos Aires: Ediciones La Guillotina, 1997), particularly: "Un ente y su lugar" (1946), dedicated to Gyula Kosice (pp. 7–8); "Poema pedestal" (1978, p. 47); "Numerales" (undated, pp. 59 and 61).

7. Kosice, "Manifiesto," 13.

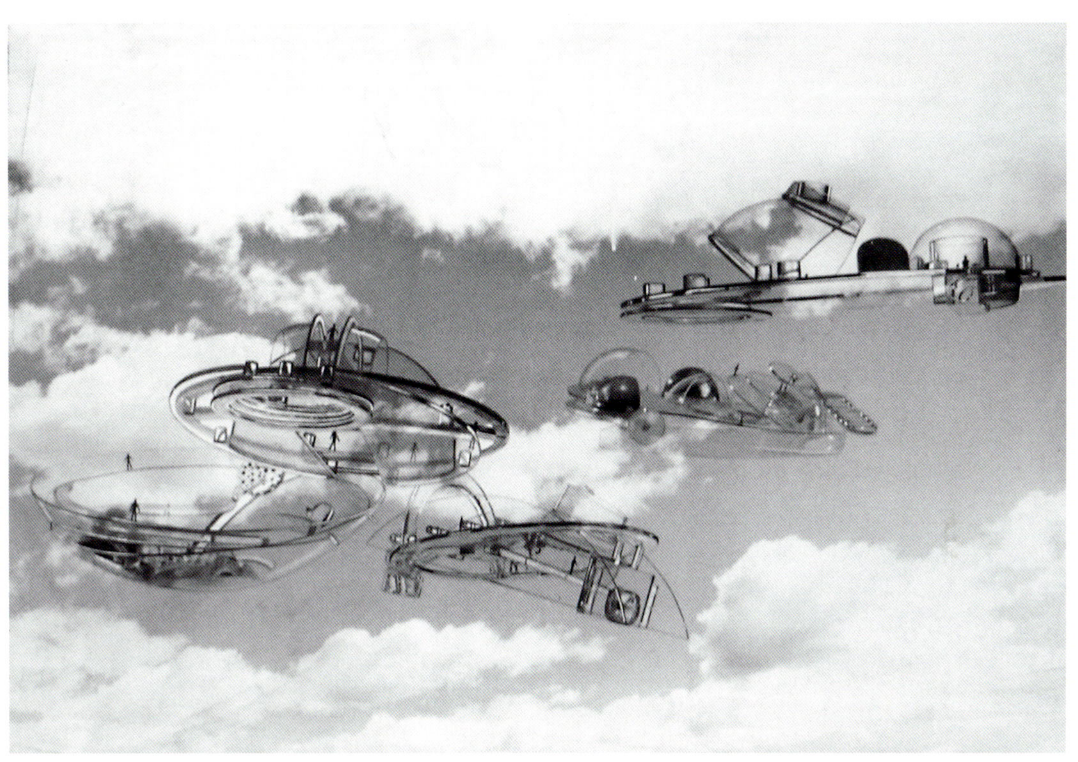

The key idea that opens this (never closed) project entails the radical stance of the Madí generation, of Arte Concreto, of Invención itself, which functions as a *remover* (from the Torres-García workshop's *Removedor* magazine), or as a thinner, which may be an emulsion, alcohol, turpentine, or even water. Some of the ideas that assisted in the creation of the *Hydrospatial City* can also be traced to the persistent — yet until now unrecognized — influence on Kosice of his lifelong partner, also a founding member of the Madí movement, the poet Diyi Laañ.[5] References in her work to notions of "air," "space," a "vertical" dimension, and "inevitable voids" foreshadow or underscore concerns that Kosice addressed in the *Hydrospatial City*.[6] For the artist, the idea was to *dissolve the art into the habitat*. This is not "utopian idealism," and Kosice preempts that notion by seeking to implement such *habitáculos*: to tear down *the cabin*, water down *wars*, as well as disrupt *floods*. These are the three elements used by the manifesto in dismissing skeptics; it does so in order to make its radicalism clear: "Therefore, to dissolve art into the dwelling and into life itself is to pronounce in favor of synthesis and integration."[7]

In traditional artworks, the immediate reaction of the viewer as well as the critic's deliberate contemplation become the source of the many (objective and subjective) interpretations, but here Kosice was proposing something unusual. Right from the start of his project, the artist developed a "descriptive report" almost by way of a specification for each model. In other words, he set forth his own reading of the various spatial *habitáculos*; in his opinion, these *habitáculos* were *places — but not spaces — for the imagination.*

In the *Hydrospatial City*, it is true that we are confronted by a plural "sculptural" work (about twenty suspended models) made of acrylic. The transparency of this material, barely used in 1940s art, had the effect of neutralizing the work in the gallery space, where the rapidly changing effects of light complete the piece. However, it is also true that the proposed *habitáculos* are interior spaces of an *established* poetic language. At first sight, they appear to be spaceships in flight, but in fact they are merely stimuli, what James Joyce would deem "verbivocovisual":[8] words, meaningful sounds and their images, are united into one construct that illustrates the literary concept of "science fiction." The artist's way of doing this is not merely three-dimensional, but refers to time-space: the fourth dimension. Kosice weds a methodical knowledge of the experimental space-science vocabulary of the mid-twentieth century to the fictitious nature of poetic language. Just as nuclear fusion takes place at the point where vision, dreams, invention, and utopia merge into a "scientific fantasy," in this installation, technical mastery, knowledge, industry, theory, and art go beyond science — perhaps to omniscience?

In his hydrosculptural idea, Kosice *neither illustrates nor represents*; what he does is evoke a technological climate and/or suggest a scientific atmosphere through the creative dimension of an art installation that is neither scientific nor technological. In other words, "the plasticity" of his hydrokinetics is a world with a purely mobile, poetic content, and that is just what we infer. In some of his early descriptions of the various *habitáculos*, Kosice takes us to extremes. On the one hand, he objectively describes "an ovoid platform in suspension, moving in the air," using "hydronuclear energy" (model A). On the other, at the same time, he places us in "contact with hydro-urban traffic," in which "a rear-view mirror showing the past" makes us see "a sensitive water mattress that leads us to identify the illusion" (model B). What is unquestionable is this: such specifications of several *habitáculos* show an intention as clear as acrylic, from which poetry (suspended on a thread), *like water in space*, crystalizes into the work concretely. Liquid thesis, solid antithesis, gaseous synthesis.

8. James Joyce, *Finnegan's Wake* (New York: The Viking Press, 1971), 341.

9. Theodor W. Adorno, *Negative Dialectics* (1966; New York: Continuum, 1971). In his various definitions of the *Hydrospatial City*, Kosice constantly uses negative prefixes (anti,- des-/dis-, un-, in-, meta-), creating a tone that makes his concrete images seem abstract.

Gyula Kosice
All maquetas are from *La ciudad hidroespacial*, 1946–1972, acrylic, paint, metal, and light, variable dimensions.
The Museum of Fine Arts, Houston.
Museum purchase funded by the Caroline Wiess Law Accessions Endowment Fund, 2009.29.1-.26

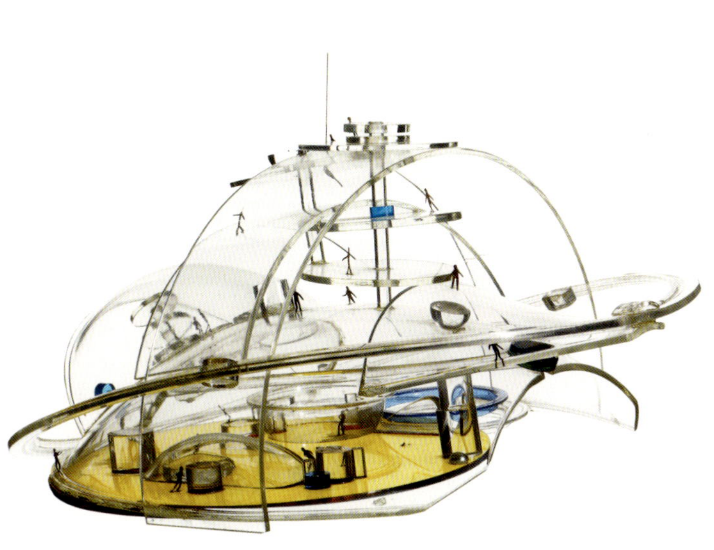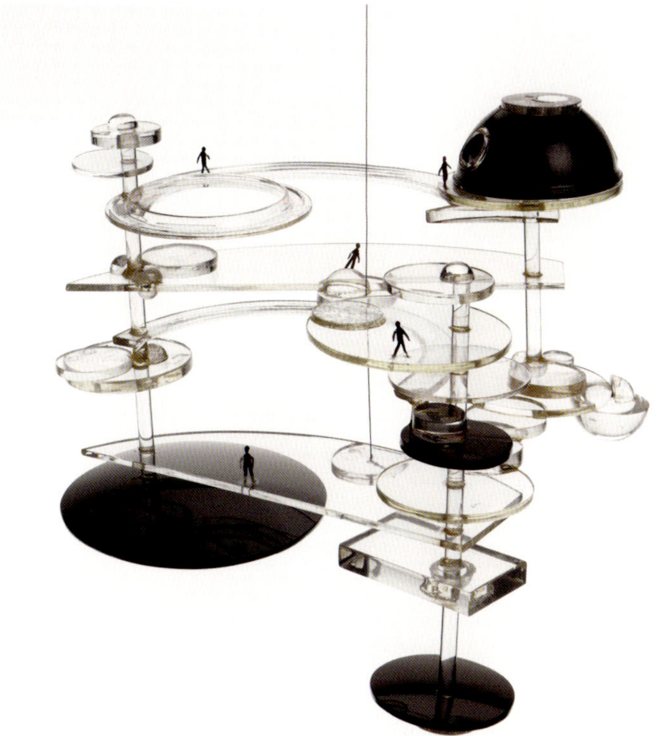

This project has a clearly delineated point of departure: to place human ideas in "outer space" for a single purpose: the concrete awareness that this entire urban utopia is also subjective. Here, Kosice is maneuvering dialectically with the cynicism of a *scientist of poetry*, fully aware that both subjects, the Poet/Scientist constellation, are joined, in principle, in a universe that is just as unreachable and unfathomable as space itself: thought. While theoretical speculation anticipates practice in science, in poetry, pondering includes the purpose of meditation. Thus, both oscillate around an invisible line: moving from the transcendental meaning of abstract art toward the more concrete, something that is beautiful but meaningless. To the viewer whose head is in the clouds, the work (understood as *thinking,* not as an object) suggests fascinating *nonsense* whose dialectic of negativity[9] poetically transmits the latent possibility of other universes, where the thesis of the absurd and the antithesis of reality call each other into question: that is why there is no synthesis. But to the pragmatic (positivist) viewer, the set of objects (acrylic models) suspended in the exhibition room is unconventional "sculptural" work: hydraulic sculpture. That is, the proposal actually entails an environment of water and light that will require the participation of an active viewer, moving among the pieces. That is the main idea of hydrokinetics.

Space is not only unreachable but also rests on poetics; writing rules for poetry is as absurd as explaining a joke. However, in spite of its unlimited scope (which makes it equal to poetry), space is a guide that can be pinned down with guidelines, maxims, and compasses; here, nothing is more apt than Gaston Bachelard's *Poetics of Space*. In the introduction to the chapter titled "House and Universe," there is a line that elicits the Argentine couple. The fragment is from a poem by Paul Éluard, suitable for bringing to the fore the spatial desire of the *yimmos*: "When the summits of our sky come together / my house will have a roof."[10] In Bachelard's view, the idea of "reading the house" or "reading a room" is admissible, since both are psychological diagrams that have oriented world literature in their analysis of intimacy. And, by the way, Kosice proposes his hydrospatial project as a diversity of spaces that make room for inner lives. To begin with, the *Hydrospatial City* is a fathomless *interiorization* that sets forth its cosmic desire: "A place to belong. for one. To read the spectrum of the universe out loud" (GK, 85).[11]

Thus, the *Hydrospatial City* proposes a taut dialectic: the neutral, abstract nature of space and the energy-giving materialization of water. Set forth by Kosice in the only issue (1944) of the journal *Arturo* (named for the largest star in the constellation of Bootes, the Wagoner), his utopia explores in depth the idea that "Man does not have to end up on Earth." Such spatial desires — to transcend earthly gravity and rise to one's best self in a habitat propelled by the essential liquid — evolved over a half century. Kosice continued to re-create these spatial poetics tirelessly, with a thought process that was more philosophical than feasible, and as poetic in its element as it was plastic. His thinking is epitomized in this statement: "To be convinced that the Earth will soon assume a new definition as the Water Planet" (GK, 147).

Bachelard, in turn, introduced his *Poetics of Space* with an emphatic recommendation: that he was offering a phenomenology of the imagination, in which — independent of any doctrine or circuit of knowledge — the poems write their various readings of space. The parallel is undeniable. To Kosice, the *habitáculos* are *places for the imagination* but are not spaces. Since poetry is a spirit that takes a form, the dialectic of this phenomenology always oscillates between the *function of reality* and the *function of unreality*. Given that a poem becomes a new being in our language, says Bachelard, "The reader of poems is asked to consider an image not as an object, or even a substitute for an object, but to seize its specific reality."[12] The data related to the *Hydrospatial City* justify the relevance of this focus; as with Bachelard, the literary background is unquestionable. And one of the constellations on which the French philosopher bases his reading is that of "Big and Small," knowing that, in outer space, "the imagination benefits from the relativity of size."[13] As we will see below, Kosice's dialectic — which operates in the *Hydrospatial City* — establishes the

10. Paul Eluard, *Dignes de vivre* (Paris: Julliard, 1945), 115; Gaston Bachelard, "House and Universe" in *The Poetics of Space (The Classic Look at How We Experience Intimate Spaces),* trans. Maria Jolas (Boston: Beacon Press, 1994), p. 38.

11. Kosice, *La ciudad hidroespacial: 500 lugares para vivir* (2010), 26. The number that appears in parentheses is the one chronologically assigned by the writer, among the 500 concepts; these are given henceforward in the text in parentheses.

12. Bachelard, "Introduction," *Poetics of Space*, xix.

13. Ibid.

14. Kosice, "Manifiesto," 10.

15. Ibid., 11.

16. One of Bachelard's chapters bears this very same title, "Intimate Immensity"; *Poetics of Space*, 183–210.

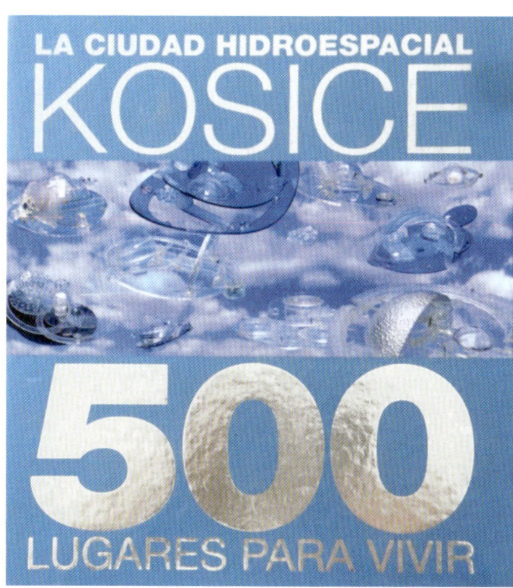

Gyula Kosice, 500 *lugares para vivir: La ciudad hidroespacial*, Buenos Aires: Akian Gráfica, 2010. Courtesy of Museo Kosice, Buenos Aires, Argentina

tension between *big* (space) and *small* (the habitat) under the signs of our miniature daily lives and poetic immensity.

The artist lays out the *Hydrospatial City* within the metaphorical parameters of "500 places to live." That is, he uses 500 phrases to sketch his project, described in the form of a manifesto. Using acrylic models, the writer thinks about constructing his undertaking "*adapted to modules that are in some way derived from modern or 'functional' architecture. . . .*"[14] His proposal for a *Hydrospatial City* is surely an ecological reading with a criticism that is not just original but actually a precursor, and his 1971 "Manifesto" states it well: "To be rooted on Earth or — to be precise — on the Water Planet, even if its atmosphere, food and water are contaminated; to live defenseless, through a persistent geographic and geological depredation; to contemplate how our ecological equilibrium is slowly being destroyed; to verify the constant increase in the population; these are that many more incentives for the drastic changes we are announcing, at this point, as a biological necessity."[15] And that necessity for (biological) space to live in, I repeat, calls for a "verbi-voco-visual" way out: what is poetic, what is metalinguistic, what is castable in art.

These descriptions of the *Hydrospatial City* were written between 1946 and 2010 by Gyula Kosice. They summarize his ideas, over more than a half-century, about his role as an author "beyond any utopia." Through these descriptions we can see how the path he followed was translated into his main approach, or the "Gospel according to GK": the indecisiveness of "poetizing the world." By extrapolating from even the most unreachable of his cosmic yearnings, we may trace (in these *500 places to live*) his evolution as an artist as well as his "changing constellations." My profound identification with his poetic work enables me to track the magnetic orientation of six of these: Water-Light, Art-Oblivion, Existence-Nothingness, Poetry-Cosmos, Dream-Utopia, and Time-Space. The constellational forces displayed in such tensions have a dynamic of such *intimate immensity* that they cannot be communicated through the circuits of knowledge.[16]

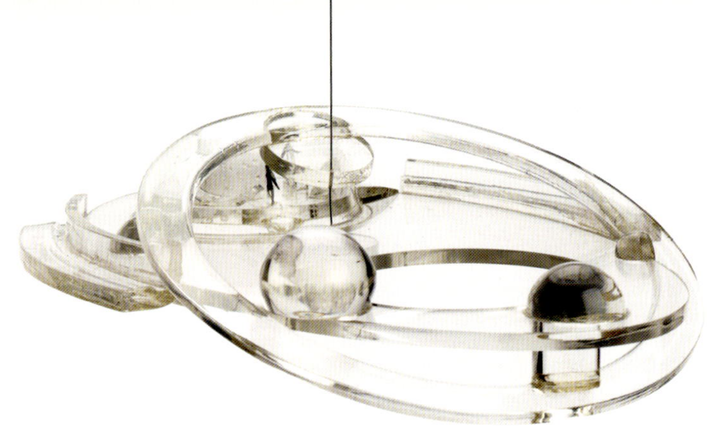

Hábitat hidroespacial, maqueta E, 1969
3 ¼ x 14 ⅝ x 10 ½ in. (8.3 x 37.1 x 26.7 cm),
2009.29.22

The first glimmers of the *Hydrospatial City* project can be detected in the 1946 Madí Manifesto, which had stated that architecture should be "ambient, with forms that can be moved in space." The following steps took years to be consummated, starting (essentially as a poetic endeavor) from a handful of fundamental metaphors. These are a representative few:

WATER-LIGHT

Kosice singles out his model D as a "Place for delving into for taking part in essential hydrokinetic adventures." If space is a desert landscape, GK humanizes it with water. The word *water* becomes the metaphysical argument through which hydrospace and GK's water-thoughts unite. On this planet, the water dimension bears the mark of something unlimited; that is why the poet dreams far away, where water and air are indeed synonyms: the in-another-place-in-another-world, which is also intrauterine. Thus, light metaphors help capture the extension of an idea that is transparent (almost acrylic), clarifying it.

In his view, "*it is not audacious to enter into and investigate the absolute* [space], *through the possible* [water]."[17] The writer condenses his hydrospatial ideas in these few illuminations:
"Potable immensity dwarfed through a drinkable lesson on luminosity." (GK, 82)
"Steps on a stairway of light as an ascent and descent to places we deserve." (GK, 140)
"To live in a habitat of water on water: meta-water." (GK, 100)
"Hydraulicize everything and ciao!" (GK 147–49)
"Avatars of this planet that keeps restarting like ocean waves. Nothing is static."[18] (GK, 136)

Given the radical and experimental artist he was, the key glimmer of Kosice's early project rested on the principle of *dissolving art into habitáculos*: "By going beyond all dependence on intermediaries, art is tacitly integrated into the habitat, dissolves into it and into life; this is how it is presented; it is art's *modus vivendi*." This way of living is simply poetic or, if you prefer, *poiético* (ðïéåóéí), a *making* that is as active as a verb, around which revolves the entire proposal: To say "hydrospatialize" is to say, "There will be places for wanting to do things, for not letting work rule day and night, for stretching out our lives and correcting improvisations, for *forgetting oblivion*."[19]

17. Kosice, "Manifiesto," 10.

18. Kosice lived in France for several years, and some of his phrases have a French literary background. This echoes the well-known lines of the poem by Paul Valéry, *Le cimétière marin* (Sète, 1934): "la mer, la mer toujours récommencée."

19. Kosice, "Manifesto," 12–13; my emphasis.

20. Ibid., 13 and 12, respectively.

The Argentine artist takes a radical step in his model C as an essential point in the space where the unforgettable resides: "Habitat for hydrospatializing the tracks of memory." Nourishing water and diffuse light making *immensity*, with no other backdrop but their own. The writer feels the claustrophobia of Earth but does not fear the agoraphobia of space; that is the most ambiguous tenet of the urban hydrospatial project. In his creation, the reality and unreality of art cooperate, there where imagination, memory, and perception exchange functions, thus neutralizing oblivion. Freed from the power of gravity, the imagination initiates the extraordinary sensation of overcoming offered by high places; the artist is thus playing with the gestation of a sublimating life. "Space raft: a place for sending and receiving waves of playfulness." (GK, 13)

"To live in the Hydrospatial City, from *modus vivendi* to *ars vivendi*." (GK, 181)

"A place for tomorrow's art, which is to forget all the arts." (GK, 112)

"A place for forgetting oblivion. Attachment of free memories." (GK, 118)

"To refrain from having history. Always reemerging." (GK, 94)

In his "poetic space" program, Kosice states, "The human being does not wish to die — period. In the hydrospatial cell, the hydrocitizen in his plurality does not only invent his architecture; he gives names, chooses sites, places to live." Furthermore, the Argentine artist was convinced that existence (without a poetic space to move into) came to nothing; therefore, he imagined degree zero: "art as the 'song of history,' 'currency of the absolute,' 'direct apprehension of reality,' 'ideological superstructure,' or 'individual transcendence.' These definitions would be surpassed by the visionary splendors of a new way of thinking and feeling, of an irreversible cultural dawning."[20]

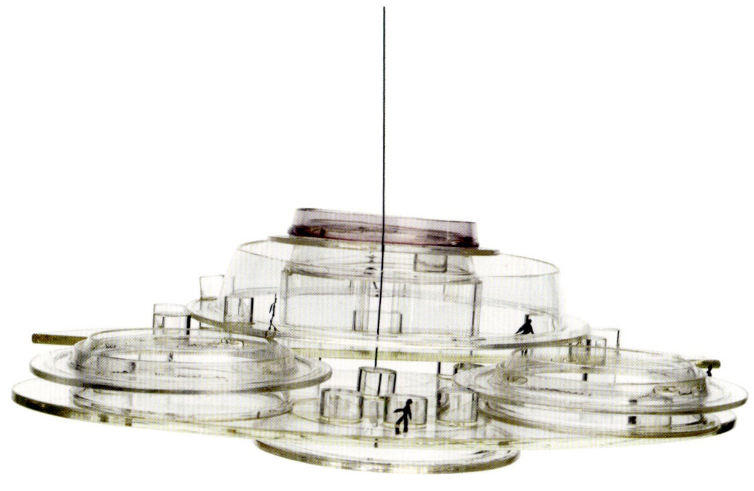

Hábitat hidroespacial, maqueta W, 1971
5 ¼ x 14 ½ x 11 in. (13.3 x 36.8 x 27.9 cm), 2009.29.13

Also in model C, Kosice conceived a specific *habitáculo* "to create antimatter out of nothing, instantaneously" — that is, a site that would distribute the unutterable elements of our human condition. The *Hydrospatial City* mixes a profound existentialism with spatial nothingness, which clarifies that works of *other art* would be a consequence or byproduct of the being who imagines existentially. In tragic struggle against the void, human existence is a pendulum that swings between withdrawing and expanding, reaching toward magnificence and returning to simplicity. The various habitats imagined by GK are as much the nothingness of an urban sort as they are the entire cosmic signal system; that is, they reside in a simple *indefinable house in a definitive sky*. Such an expansion of the being dwells, lives, and is within us all.

"A place for turning lack of definition into architecture." (GK, 411)

"So that the tracks of the absurd leave no traces." (GK, 243)

"A place to desecrate death within the Madí parameters. Ceremonies tempered by passion and smiles that reveal the origin of the being." (GK, 64)

"To unleash simulacra that block out the hustle and bustle of nothingness." (GK, 404)

"So that the cohesion in the immensity of the whole is dissolved into pure conjecture." (GK, 381)

The hydrospatial citizen "will have new languages to communicate not just a message, but the complete form of a spirit; a language enriched only by tensions and new presence immersed in

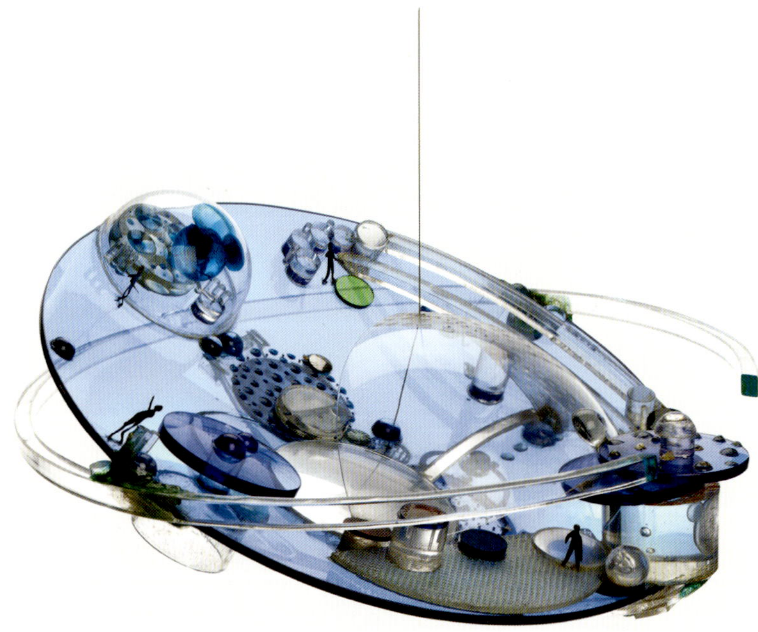

Hábitat hidroespacial, maqueta O, 1969
7 ½ x 18 x 17 ½ in. (19.1 x 45.7 x 44.5 cm), 2009.29.14

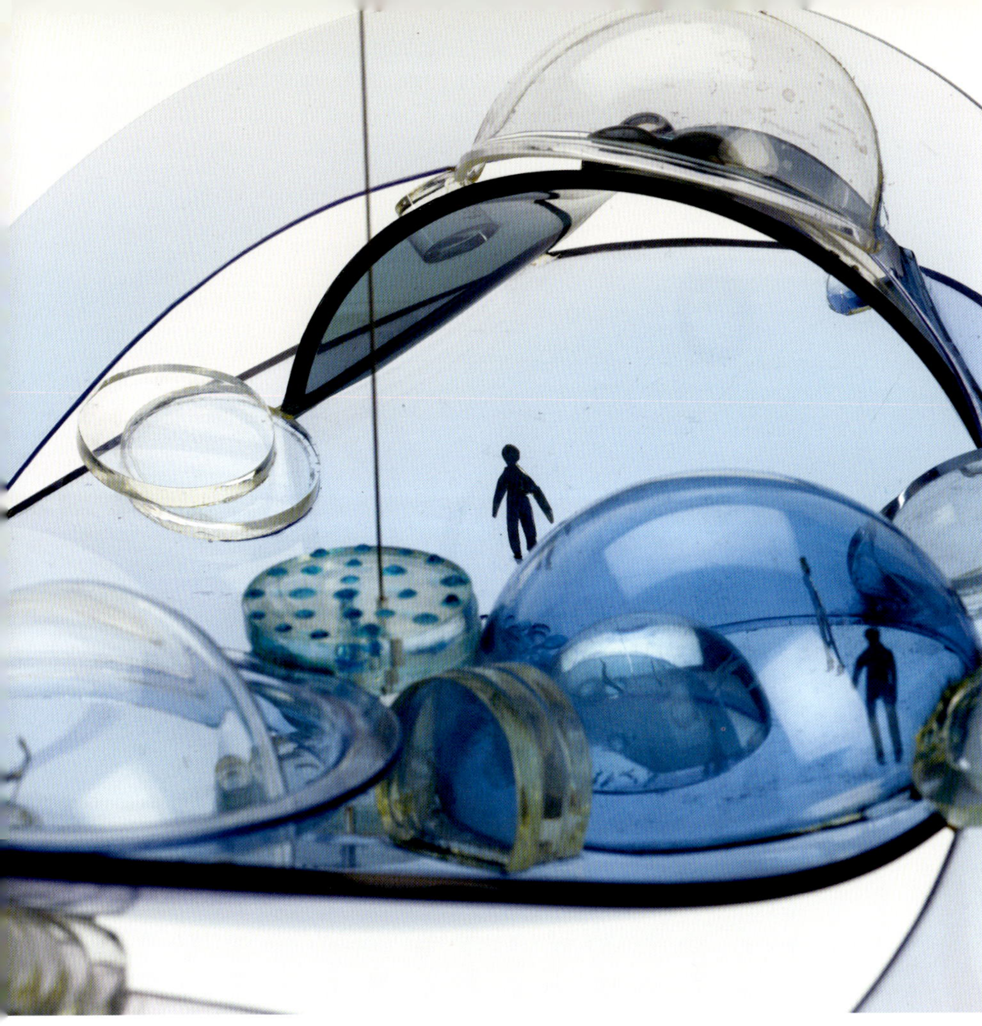

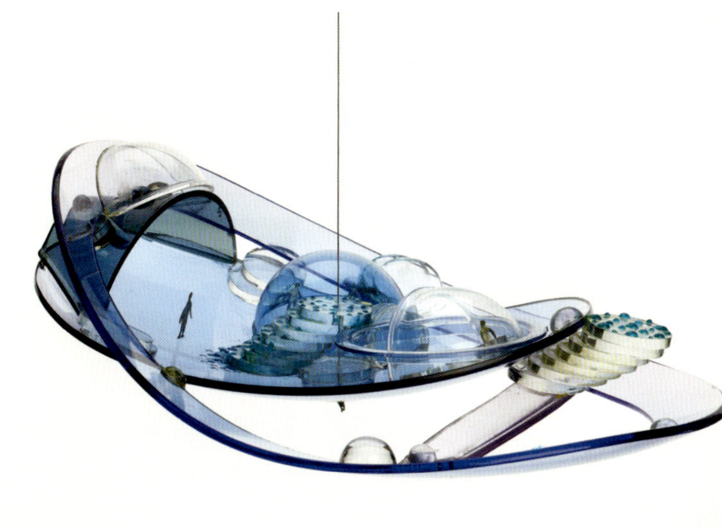

Hábitat hidroespacial, maqueta Q, 1971
5 x 17 ¼ x 13 in. (12.7 x 43.8 x 33 cm), 2009.29.20
(detail at left)

21. Ibid., 13.

22. Bachelard, "House and Universe,"
Poetics of Space, 51.

poetry." That is, a "tendency to transform man, starting from the moment in which body and mind are involved with universal projects in order to participate in a broader universe."[21]

POETRY/COSMOS

In his model B (one of the first), the presence of his wife, Diyi Laañ, seems to be the background for the thought, "Place for housing dreams of a woman and our immediate as well as our abstract desires." Why? Because in his opinion, this would be a "Place for interdisciplinary exercise in order to conjugate new languages of the real, conceptual universe." As a result of scientific reality, we have been expelled from the kingdom of the possible. Bachelard knows this, taking shelter in that possibility: "To give unreality to an image attached to a strong reality is in the spirit of poetry."[22] The paradox is that such an *interior immensity* (poetry) lends true meaning to certain expressions of the visible world (the city, water, space). And every new contact with the cosmos renews our innermost being. Such a dynamic rivalry between "house and universe" prevails over any reference to geometric forms; intimate space loses its clarity while external space leads us astray into its void.

"A continuum designed to absorb poetry by the simple digital impression of light-years." (GK, 16)

"That love may be exempt from testing." (GK, 350)

"To discern the cosmos as it is, miniaturized." (GK, 22)

"Poetry: my manager." (GK, 424)

"To train the cosmos." (GK, 121)

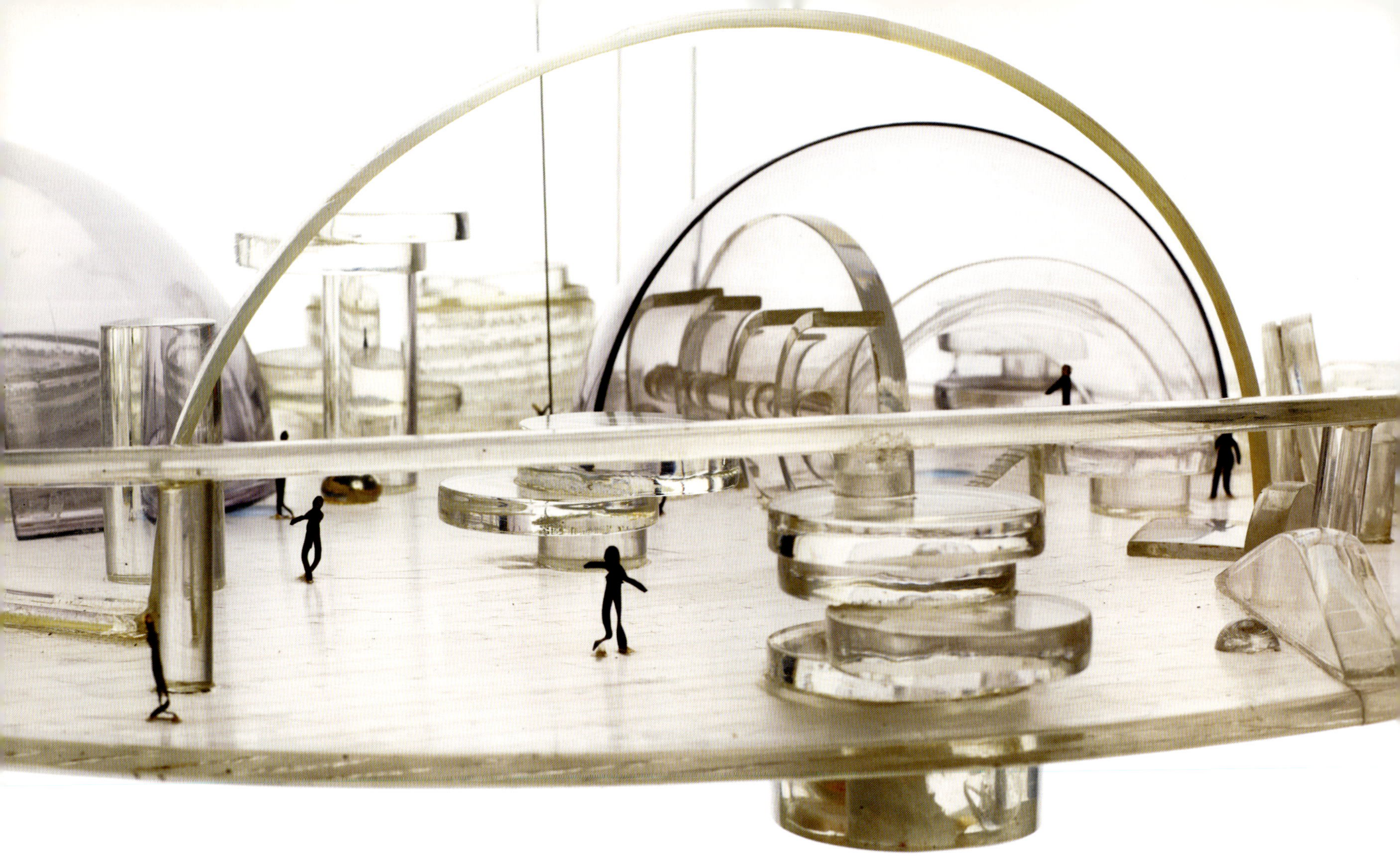

*Hábitat hidroespacial, maqueta
"semiesfera suspendida,"* 1967,
16 x 32 in. dia. (40.6 x81.3 cm),
2009.29.9 (detail above)

Right: *Hábitat hidroespacial,
maqueta B,* 1969,
8 ½ x 21 ¼ in. dia. (21.6 x 54 cm),
2009.29.11

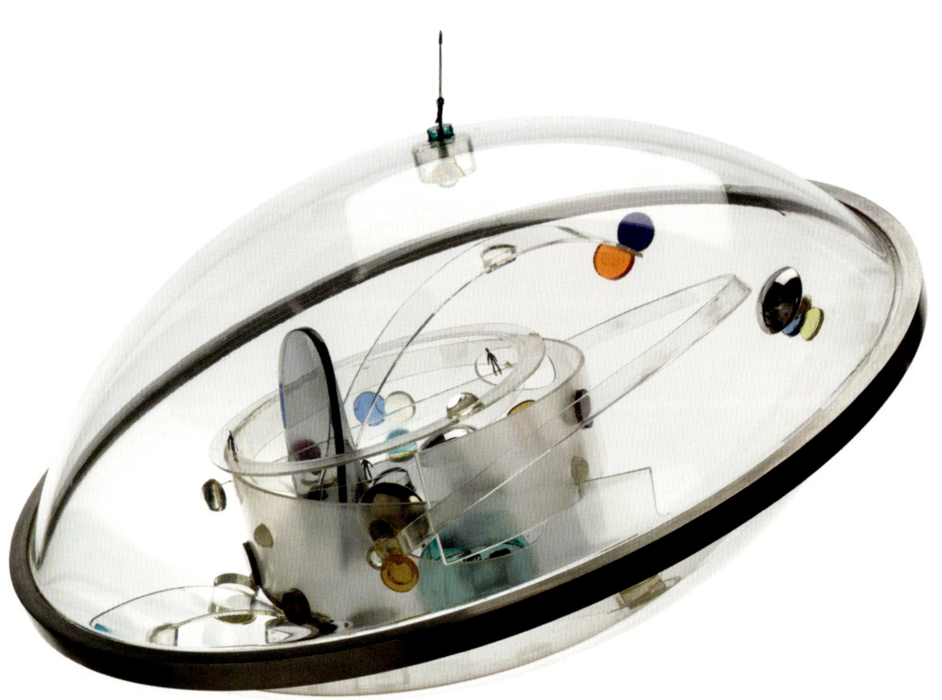

To Kosice, dream and utopia are synonymous; they meet in a place that does not exist but is the imaginary residence of invention, that point of representation in the fantasy of various events that are so yearned for that they may end up being real. That which, like creation, seems to be a simple game. "Probably other conditions will appear, but in the *Hydrospatial City*, we seek to eliminate anxiety and illness while we revalue love, the joy to behold intelligence, humor, playful relaxation, sports, indefinite retirement, and mental options not explored until now; we will seek to abolish the limits set by geography and those placed on thinking. Utopian idealism? Absolutely."[23]

DREAM/UTOPIA

The possibility of a hydrospatial trip induces in the writer a mix of watery dreams and aerial utopia. In model H, Kosice imagines the dissolved sides of a "Place for sleeping beyond the present. Sleep x sleep." Every dream has a utopian horizon. The dialectic between center and horizon is at the core of the *Hydrospatial City*; the various habitats concentrate the internalized idea of the house, and the sensitivity that turns outward toward the confines of the universe complements it. If lack of moderation is utopia, the dream may well be the equivalent of the infinite. In Bachelard's terms, intimacy is the idea of immensity turned inward; in other words, dreaming transports the dreamer outside himself in full daylight, going from the immediate, centered, world, to another utopian world where "one might say that *immensity is* a philosophical category of daydream."[24]

"To entertain a lack of moderation with amenity." (GK, 367)

"Settle in a hammock among the existing Utopias until they no longer seem Utopian; then demand new ones." (GK, 145)

"So that our own breathing may be the domicile of air." (GK, 147)

 "What is dreamable is the point-of departure for reality." (GK, 89)

"An encompassing place where the infinite is reduced." (GK, 31)

Time is a moldable material that sculpts the invisible hands of space: that is the only artwork that Kosice would allow to be shown in the Poetry Room of his *Hydrospatial City*. Why? "Finally, daily life will not only be centered on the supposed conquest of space, but on the conquest of its time, its activation, its yeast."[25]

TIME-SPACE

GK planned his model F, envisioning an essential apology from the human species: "Place to praise life in itinerant light-years." In his *habitáculo*, he sets forth a general thesis on the imagination; the thesis in time and the imagination in space. Every earthly being (and houses

23. Kosice, "Manifesto," 13.

24. Bachelard, "Intimate Immensity," *Poetics of Space,* 183.

25. Kosice, "Manifesto," 13.

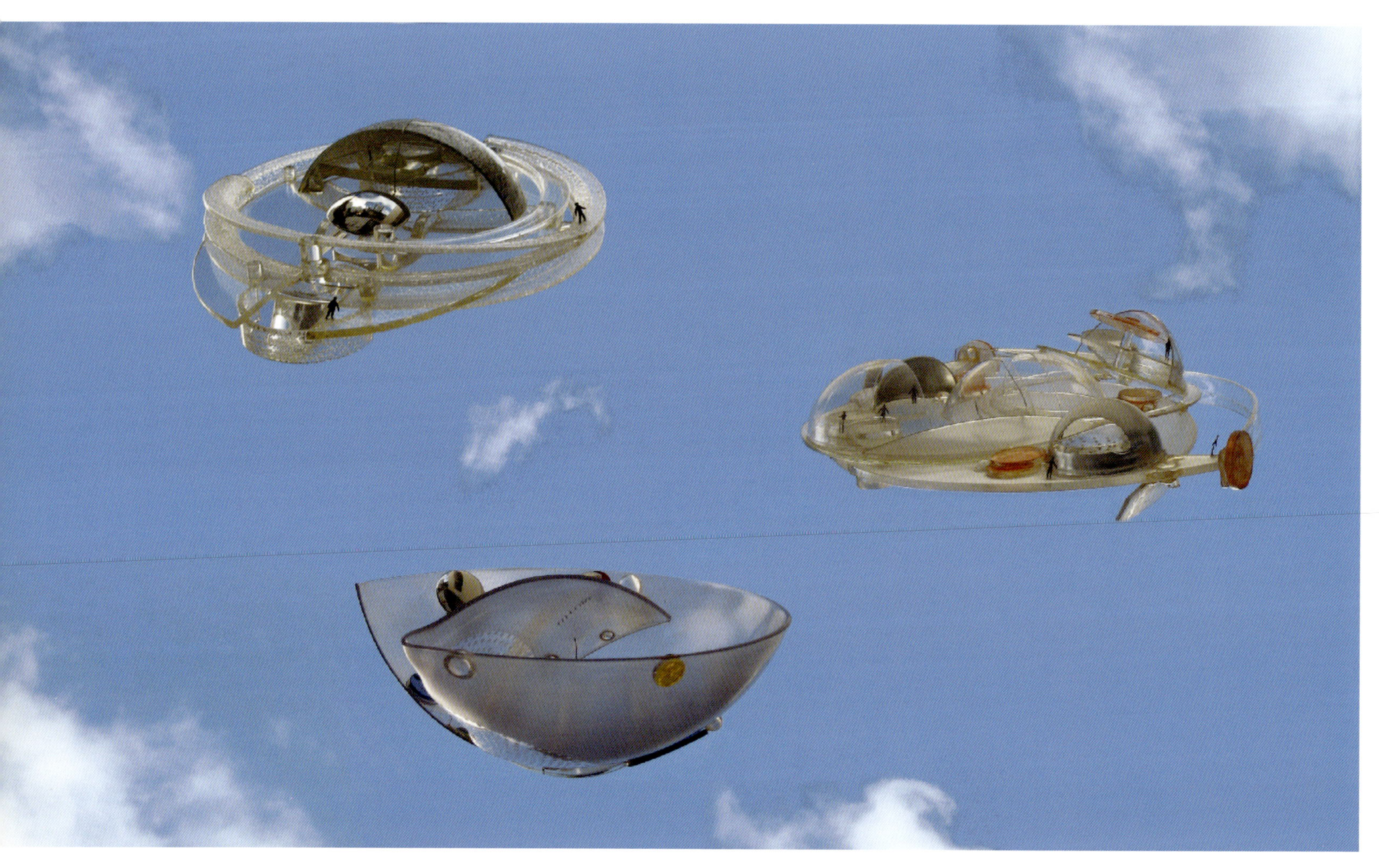

Fotomontaje de la ciudad hidroespacial, 2009.
Courtesy of Museo Kosice, Buenos Aires, Argentina

184

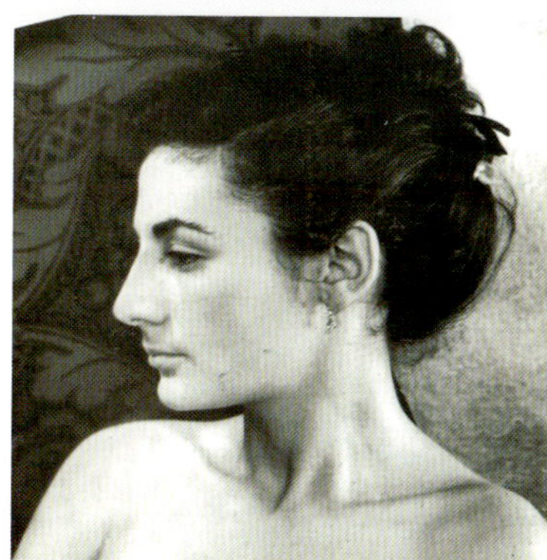

Diyi Laañ, *Diyi Laañ: Selección de poemas*
Buenos Aires: Ediciones La Guillotina, 1997
Courtesy Museo Kosice, Buenos Aires, Argentina

are completely earthly) is subject to the attraction of air, of the celestial. In Bachelard's words: "This house, as I see it, is a sort of airy structure that moves about on the breath of time."[26] Space suggests to the poet that it is the theme of the temporality of two verbs: "begin" and "grow." The space for initiation — an invisible space where man may live through his growth, surrounded by countless presences — is empty. Filling it will require Kosice's city.

"Time, an event we take from space. A gift beyond measure." (GK 138)

"An anti-tower for materializing on matter. A spacecraft with an observatory of parallel, circular time." (GK 5)

"A place where geometric parallels finally meet." (GK 485)

"To be housed in a universe in which fiction crystalizes. Its level of consistency depends on *the truth* that irrigates all languages." (GK, 162)

Both time and space are under the dominion of the image. The in-any-part of the City and the at-any-time of Space have more poetic strength than the *here and now*. Through the house (the hydrospatial *habitáculo*), the warm substance of intimacy takes shape. The amorous duet of space-dreamer and time-in-the-world imagines a city in the immensity of the cosmos, although in dialogue with the most intimate profundity of the being . . . And the thirst of that being cries out: water! Colorless in an unmeasurable world, odorless in terms of any concrete experience where fiction is crystallized as well as insipid revelation facing the enigma. I repeat: *intimate immensity*.

Diyi Laañ confirms this with her own contemplation:

"I want I ask I beg / let it be just that / a gaze."[27]

26. Bachelard, "House and Universe," *Poetics of Space*, 54.

27. Laañ, "Poema Pedestal," *Selección de poemas*, 47–48.

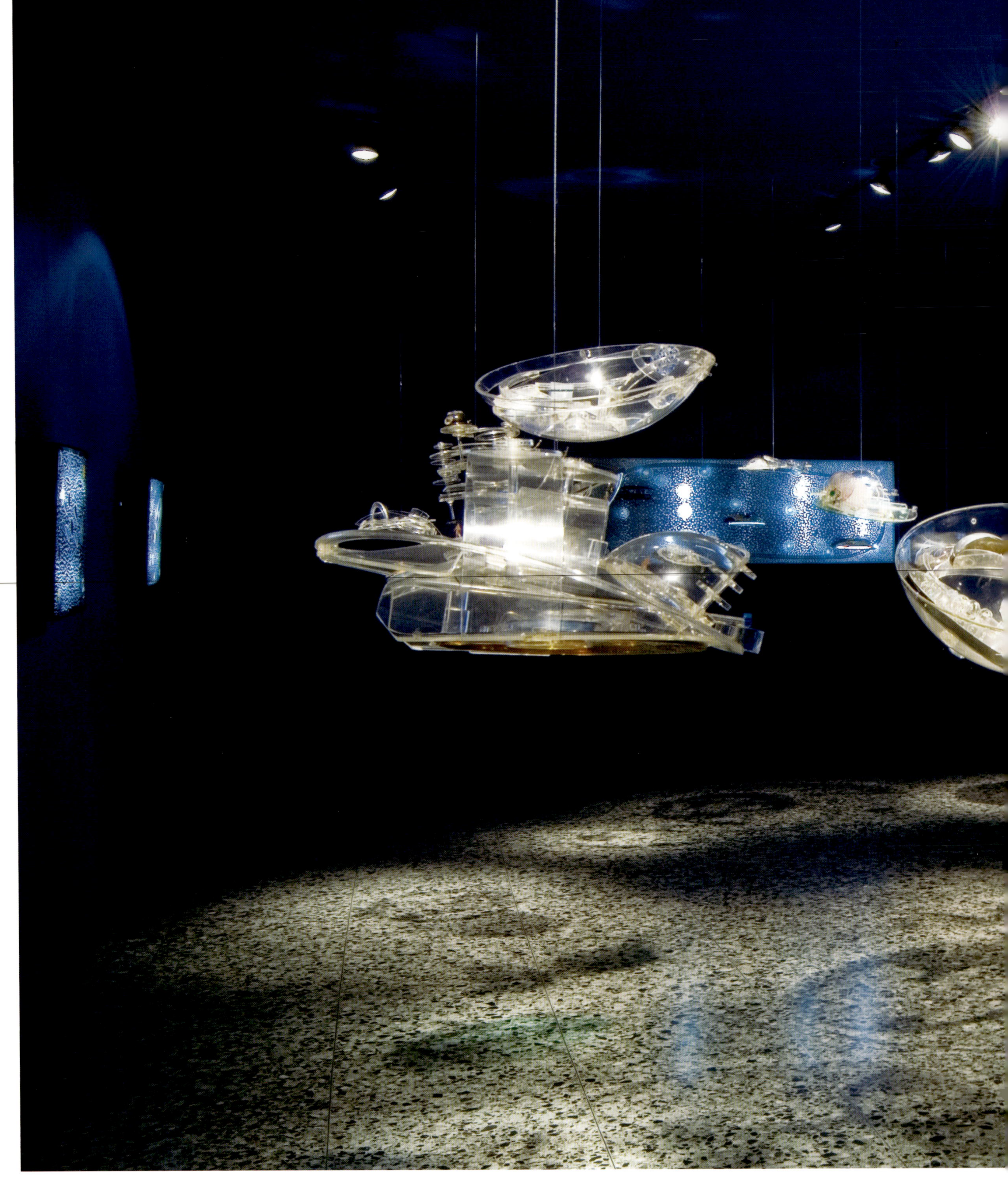

gyula KOSICE

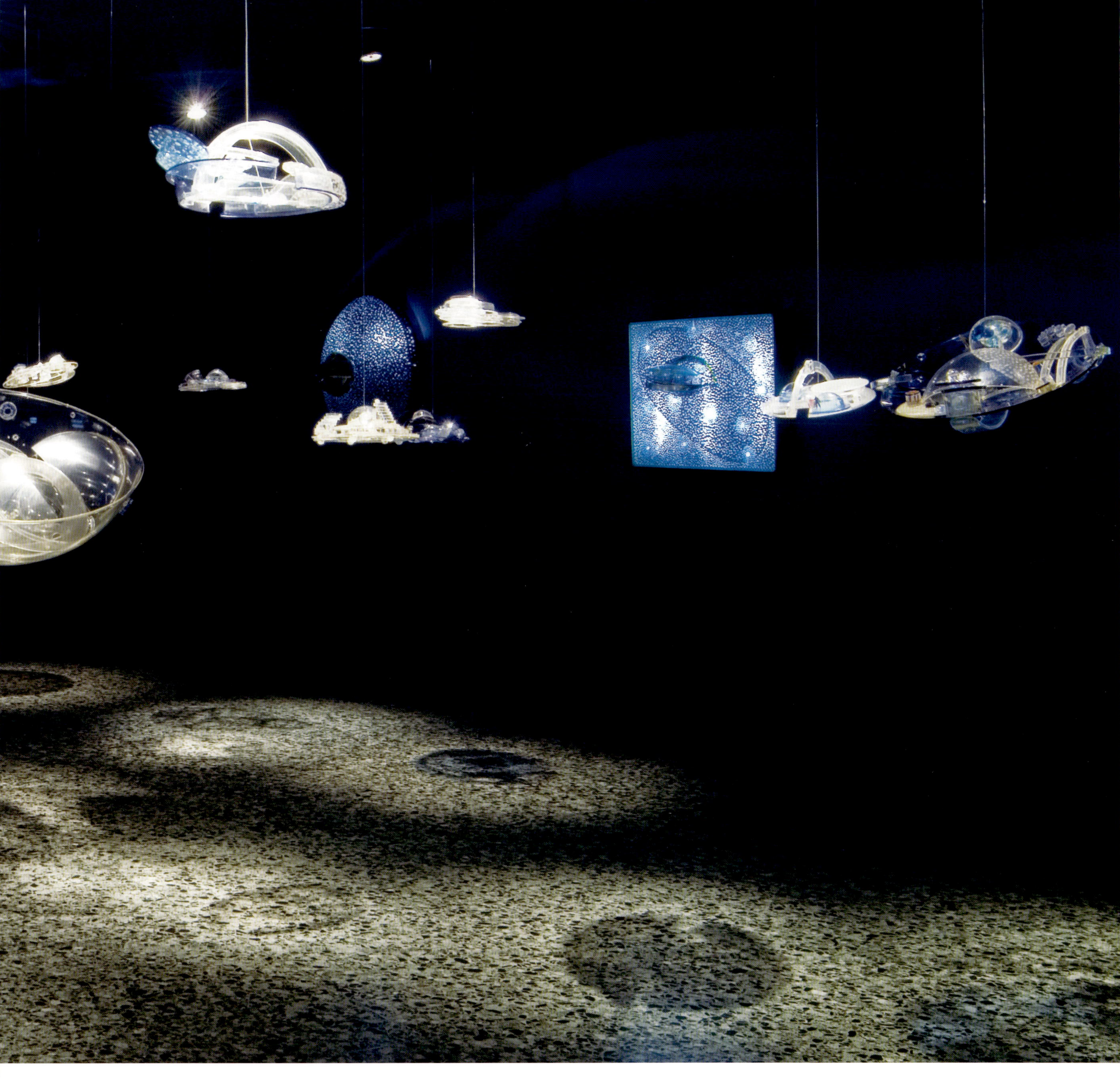

Installation view of the exhibition *Cosmic Dialogues: Selections from the Latin American Art Collection*, Museum of Fine Arts, Houston, May 14–August 23, 2015, featuring
GYULA KOSICE   *La ciudad hidroespacial, 1946–1972*. Acrylic, paint, metal, and light, variable dimensions
The Museum of Fine Arts, Houston. Museum purchase funded by the Caroline Wiess Law Accessions Endowment Fund, 2009.29.1–.26

KINETIC UTOPIAS ON THE ROAD TO THE MAGIC ZONE[1]

Jesús Fuenmayor

THE EXHIBITION *Kinesthesia: Latin American Kinetic Art 1954–1969* frames the history of the region's Kinetic Art by focusing on the 1960s and a few pioneering ventures from the previous decade, thus situating the movement in a period characterized by experimentation and innovation in the arts and a generalized utopian rhetoric. In doing so, the exhibition brought to mind a series of relatively little known but ambitious sculptural projects produced by Venezuelan artist Alejandro Otero in the years 1967–68, sculptures that the Chilean poet Pablo Neruda referred to as "Colossal structures, stairways to heaven, glittering towers." Neruda, one of the most radical and preeminent communist intellectuals from Latin America, described them as "stalactites built with passion, before crowds of people, spreading the faith in the destiny of man through their creative energy."[2] Neruda's comment is clearly a consequence of Otero's conception of this series of sculptures as symbols of modernization for the country, and as infused with the typical utopian grandiloquence that characterized the era's speech.[3] This was also a time of extreme excitement in the Venezuelan art scene: Carlos Cruz-Diez, Jesús Rafael Soto, and Gego were simultaneously developing what would come to be known as their most iconic and monumental works. Soto's first *Penetrable* dates from 1967; Cruz-Diez's *Chromosaturation* appeared in 1965; and Gego's *Reticulárea* was first exhibited in 1969.[4] In addition, Carlos Raúl Villanueva, the most visible and internationally recognized Venezuelan architect, designed the country's pavilion for Expo 67 in Montreal. The pavilion included a space for the integration of the arts that featured a mechanized hanging sculpture by Soto, electronic music by Antonio Estévez, and concrete poems by Alfredo Silva Estrada.[5] Finally, these years also mark the apex of an international wave of Kinetic Art, as reflected in the Venice Biennial prizes awarded to Julio Le Parc (in 1966) and Nicolas Schöffer (in 1968).[6] In the midst of these events, Otero presented his sculptures as his contribution to a sculpture park commemorating the four-hundredth anniversary of the founding of Caracas. Working in collaboration with twenty-five other

1. During the time I was devoted to the research and elaboration of this text, my partner, Kaira Cabañas, was in continuous dialogue with me, offering ideas and suggestions that helped in many ways to develop the conclusions of this article. My deep gratitude goes to her for her permanent presence and intellectual stimulation.

2. Pablo Neruda, "Las torres vibratorias" (1969), in *Alejandro Otero ante la crítica*, ed. Douglas Monroy (Caracas: Artesanogroup Editores, 2006), 122. Unless otherwise noted, all translations are my own.

3. Neruda's grandiloquence is hardly exclusive to the Latin American poets and artists of the time. Anton Nieuwenhuys, known as Constant, the Dutch artist and once-prominent member of the Situationist International, is a paradigmatic example. Reflecting on the conditions of his time, Constant said: "The effects of machine-production are leading slowly to a reduction of human labour, and we can state already with certainty, that we will enter a new era, in which production-labour will be automatic. For the first time in history, mankind will be able to establish an affluent society in which nobody will have to waste his forces, and in which everybody will be able to use

his entire energy for the development of his creative capacities." Quoted in Simon Sadler, *The Situationist City* (Cambridge, Mass.: MIT Press, 1999), 136.

4. Cruz-Diez's *Chromosaturation* comprises environments that immerse visitors in completely monochrome surroundings that activate in them the notion of color as a material or physical situation, extending into space without the aid of form or even support. Soto's *Penetrables* are constructed from flexible tubing in saturated colors and hang from a steel framework through which spectators can move. Gego's *Reticulárea* is an installation with hundreds of stainless steel wires woven together to create an intricate weblike setting that requires viewers' participation.

5. See Ricardo de Sola and Paulina Villanueva, *Crónica: Tres Cubos en Montreal* (Caracas: Armitano Editores, 2007), 89–90.

6. Le Parc and Schöffer were two of the most conspicuous representatives of Kinetic Art in Europe.

7. See Rafael Pineda, "Alejandro Otero: La integración de las artes," *Imagen: Quincenario de arte, literatura e información cultural*, no. 8 (September 1–15, 1967): n.p.

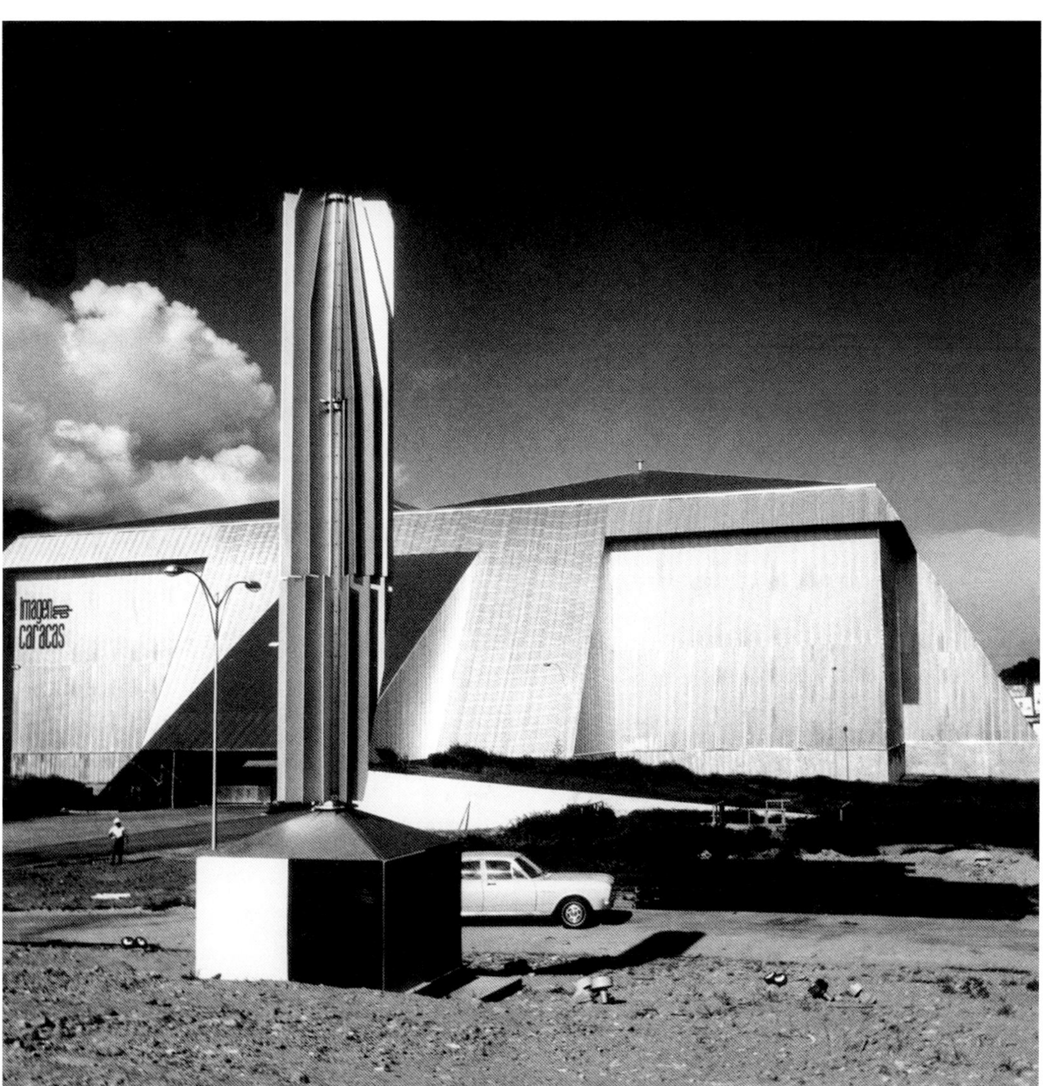

Alejandro Otero, *Rotor*, 1968. View of Zona Feérica, Parque El Conde, Caracas

professionals, including artists, architects, engineers, designers, lighting experts, photographers, and economists, Otero and his team proposed twenty-six projects, including at least fourteen sculptures by Otero himself.[7] Seven of the sculptures were ultimately built and shown, grouped under the title "Zona Feérica" (Magic Zone), in a park surrounding the headquarters for Imagen de Caracas (IDC), another event organized to celebrate the capital city's anniversary.[8]

Investigations of Kinetic Art in North America have generally focused on a few individual achievements in the field of optical art, thereby consigning to oblivion many of the most interesting and substantial accomplishments of this postwar movement. The reigning oversimplified history of Kinetic Art is in part due to the difficult task of assimilating its diversity, a diversity that contradicts the more general and readily grasped idea that it was almost exclusively circumscribed within a formalist debate between virtual and real movement. As Yve-Alain Bois stated fifteen years ago in a review of the exhibition *Force Fields: Phases of the Kinetic*:

> Kinetic art suffered the unhappy fate of a flash in the pan. Drawing crowds and saturating the art market for a brief moment in the mid-'60s (at least in Europe), it faded from sight as rapidly as it had burst on the scene. Behind the quick demise was the confusion with Op art in the mind of the public, fueled by exhibitions such as "The Responsive Eye" (MoMA 1965). Because kinetic art was perceived as an art based almost entirely on easy optical tricks, it would soon be trashed as utter kitsch, on a par with such risible by-products as the Courreges dress and the lava lamp.[9]

8. In addition to the sculptures, the proposal for Zona Feérica also included food kiosks, book and painting exhibitions, a concert, café, restaurant, contests, and shows. Ultimately, only a few of Otero's sculptures were set up, and almost none of the other elements of the plan were implemented. See "Una gigantesca exposición feérica mostrará la Venezuela del futuro," *El Nacional*, August 8, 1967. IDC was a multimedia event organized by Inocente Palacios and Miguel Arroyo, with the participation of many artists under the mandate of Jacobo Borges. For a complete list of IDC staff, see the brochure *Imagen de Caracas* (Caracas: Municipalidad del Distrito Federal, 1968), 5. The city municipality funded both events happening in the same location but organized by independent organizations.

9. Yve-Alain Bois, "*Force Fields: Phases of the Kinetic*, Museu d'Art Contemporani de Barcelona," *Artforum*, November 1, 2000. *Force Fields*, considered one of most important exhibition surveys of Kinetic Art, was curated by Guy Brett.

10. Rosalind Krauss, in one of the inaugural critical reviews of this movement in the United States, asserted: "Op Art in all the multiplicity of its visual guises really operates from behind a single basic concept: the *trompe l'oeil*"; "Afterthoughts on 'Op,'" *Art International* 9, no. 6 (June 1965): 75–76. Clearly, Bois had Krauss in mind when he wrote about the reception of Kinetic Art in North America.

11. Lee, in particular, recognizes the diversity of intention in the works of kinetic artists Jean Tinguely and Paul Bury. According to her, the diametrically opposed intentions in their works are expressed in the critical ways in which Tinguely embraces the ideals of technocratic modernization while Bury draws attention to the uncertainty of those ideals. See Pamela M. Lee, *Chronophobia: On Time in the Art of the 1960s* (Cambridge, Mass.: MIT Press, 2004), 125.

12. The kinetic frenzy went so far as to qualify the buildings of the City University in Caracas as "kinetic architecture," a term used by architecture historian Sibyl Moholy-Nagy to describe the "kaleidoscopic" nature of Villanueva's dramatic juxtapositions of art and architecture. See Maciá Pintó, *Villanueva: La síntesis*, vol. 2, *Síntesis de las artes y abstracción constructiva* (Caracas: Fundación Villanueva,

COPRED [Universidad Central de Venezuela], and Fundación Telefónica, 2013), 20.

13. One exception is Marguerite Katherine Mayhall, "The Dissolution of Utopia: Art, Politics, and the City of Caracas in the 1960s" (PhD diss., University of Texas at Austin, 2001). However, Mayhall's focus is on IDC, and she does not place Zona Feérica in the international context.

14. Michel Ragon wrote an extended article about Nouveau realisme, including Otero's work, in *Jardins des arts*, no. 100 (March 1963): 56–69. French architectural historian Paul Damaz included Otero in his book *Art in Latin American Architecture* (New York: Reinhold Publishing, 1963). André Bloc registered Otero's work in a special issue of *L'architecture d'aujourd'hui*, nos. 67–68 (October 1956) that was devoted to Venezuelan architecture. Letters exchanged between Kepes and Otero in the early 1970s (now collected in the MIT archives) indicate that Otero must have spent a good part of the first half of 1972 working in a studio at CAVS.

15. Otero moved to Paris in 1945 and came back to Caracas in 1952. He then moved again from Caracas to Paris in 1960, remaining until 1964. See "Chronología," in *Alejandro Otero*, exhibition catalogue (Caracas: Museo de Arte Contemporáneo de Caracas, 1985), 13, 27.

16. Larry Busbea, *Topologics: The Urban Utopia in France, 1960–1970* (Cambridge, Mass.: MIT Press, 2007), 3.

Bois's description encapsulates the widespread and common idea of Kinetic Art's status as kitsch, which was incorporated into its reception in the North American context.[10] More recently, however, scholars such as Pamela Lee and Larry Busbea have returned to this history with increased critical nuance.[11] My purpose here is to draw attention to another history — Kinetic Art in South America — and to understand the profound differences in the region's reception of Kinetic Art, particularly in Venezuela, a country once immersed in kineticism across its artistic, social, and political spaces, as the work of Otero attests.[12]

To date, few scholarly studies have addressed the sculptural park known as Zona Feérica. Most of the extant accounts are from the contemporary press or locally published monographs about Otero.[13] As with other Venezuelan kinetic artists, Otero has been treated as a national hero in local narratives, while little has been said about his historical inscription in a broader international context. In the early 1950s and 1960s his work was discussed in several publications and included in exhibitions related to the synthesis of the arts and urban transformations, and in the early 1970s he participated in György Kepes's Center for Advanced Visual Studies (CAVS) at MIT.[14] Otero was also acquainted with many of the figures connected to the Spatial Urbanism movement in France in the 1960s, a movement spearheaded by the Groupe International de Architecture Prospective (GIAP), which included among its members Yona Friedman, Mathias Goeritz, Paul Maymont, Michel Ragon, Ionel Schein, and Nicolas Schöffer. Otero maintained close contact with Schöffer and Victor Vasarely, and critics such as André Bloc (also an artist), Ragon, and Pierre Restany were familiar with his work when he was living in Paris.[15] According to Busbea, Spatial Urbanism was "intensely engaged in speculating on the effects of technology on everyday life." The Spatial Urbanists proposed an architectural program with "rectilinear and polyhedral structures and towers [that] would support biomorphic living cells, and the streets and the buildings themselves would constitute a gigantic work of art. Color, light, and sound would all be synthesized in this urban space into a unified, constantly changing spectacle."[16] Although no historical record connects Otero's urban sculptures with the Spatial Urbanists' ideas, such preoccupations, I argue, also extend to his work.

Otero, a key decision-maker in the Venezuelan art scene from the early 1950s and for the rest of his life, put a lot of effort into exploring these relationships between art and the urban (or built) environment.[17] This interest can be traced to his participation in the "Síntesis de las Artes" project (Synthesis of the Arts) at the University City of Caracas (CU) designed by Villanueva. Considered by many international critics of the time to be one of the most refined examples of the synthesis, the CU campus was an experimental site for international and local artists in the early 1950s, including Jean Arp, Alexander Calder, Fernand Léger, Antoine Pevsner, Bloc, and Vasarely. At the CU, Otero made several stained-glass windows, glass mosaics, and tile murals for the schools of engineering, pharmacy, and architecture.[18] In the postwar years, Le Corbusier's mandate for a synthesis of the arts had spread widely, as evinced by the various resolutions issued by the Congrès Internationaux d'Architecture Moderne (CIAM) during the mid- to late 1940s and early 1950s.[19] For French architecture historian Paul Damaz, the approbation with which the call to synthesize the arts was received was best conveyed by the celebratory words of the Milan Triennial, which declared that the synthesis of the arts was "a collaboration that will bring about new trends in civilization."[20] Bloc, director and founder of the renowned journal *L'architecture d'aujourd'hui* and the Groupe Espace, maintained close ties with Villanueva and also produced a mural for CU. Bloc wrote in similarly radical, utopian terms about the synthesis of the arts, "without which no civilization can assert its existence."[21]

The collaboration between Vasarely — who exerted an influence in Venezuela from the early 1950s through the rest of his life — and Villanueva is also crucial to understanding the evolution of Kinetic Art and Otero's participation. At a certain point Vasarely helped Villanueva contact some of the Parisian artists who ultimately participated in his CU project. Furthermore, Villanueva's conceptualization of the murals for the Plaza Cubierta (Covered Plaza) of the university complex, which he designated *movimientos* (movements), may have influenced Vasarely in his subsequent organization of the first Kinetic Art exhibition at Galerie Denise René in Paris in 1955. That exhibition, titled *Le Mouvement*, thus evoking Villanueva's designation for his murals, became a key historical reference in the history of kineticism and contemporary art.[22] By the time of *Le Mouvement*, the CU campus had become an architectural tour de force for the international intelligentsia, including the likes of Buckminster Fuller and Frei Otto, celebrated architects who came to Caracas at Villanueva's invitation in the early 1960s.[23]

17. See Roberto Guevara, "Conversación con Alejandro Otero," *Imagen: Quincenario de arte, literatura e información cultural*, no. 8 (September 1–15, 1967): n.p.

18. John Rothenstein, director of the Tate Gallery, London, congratulated Venezuela's different governments for placing "such vast resources in the unfettered hands of the country's greatest architect. Their faith has been justified by the building of a university of outstanding architectural quality, in which the visual arts are related on the largest scale with an imagination and authority unsurpassed in the present century." Sir John Rothenstein, "A City of All the Arts in Venezuela," *Signals* 1, no. 2 (September 1964): 5; originally published in *El National*, April 25, 1961. According to urban-planning historian Marco Negrón, at this time Venezuela's investment in modern infrastructure was unparalleled in Latin America; see "Las transformaciones en el ordenamiento territorial venezolano entre 1926 y 1952," in *Alfredo Boulton y sus contemporáneos: Diálogos críticos en el arte venezolano: 1912–1974* (New York: Museum of Modern Art; Fundación Cisneros, 2010), 54.

19. An appeal for a synthesis of the major arts had been made by Le Corbusier in 1944 in the journal *Volonté*. See Paul Damaz, *Art in European Architecture / Synthèse des arts* (New York: Reinhold Publishing, 1956), 73.

20. Milan Triennial program, cited in ibid., 77. The cited phrase reads in its entirety: "the relation of unity between architecture, painting and sculpture, and the collaboration of the art world with the world of industrial production — a collaboration that will bring about new trends in civilization."

21. Ibid.

22. Damaz reproduced in his book *Art in Latin American Architecture* a floor plan originally designed by Sibyl Moholy-Nagy to describe the different *movimientos* created by Villanueva in the Plaza Cubierta (Covered Plaza). See Paul F. Damaz, *Art in Latin American Architecture* (New York: Reinhold Publishing, 1963), 148–49. I am indebted to Professor Rafael Pereira for this key reference. The exhibition *Le Mouvement* was organized by Pontus Hultén, René, and Vasarely. Villanueva acquired several pieces from this exhibition for his personal collection. In a document in the archives of the Fundación Villanueva in Caracas, Vasarely refers to the three works that Villanueva commissioned from him for the CU as "movimientos." See Pintó, *Villanueva*, 216–17.

23. Fuller and Otto were already internationally known for their mega-structure experiments. An illustration Fuller made of Villanueva's face inscribed in the shape of a geodesic dome was published on the cover of *Time* magazine. See de Sola and Villanueva, *Crónica*, 25–26.

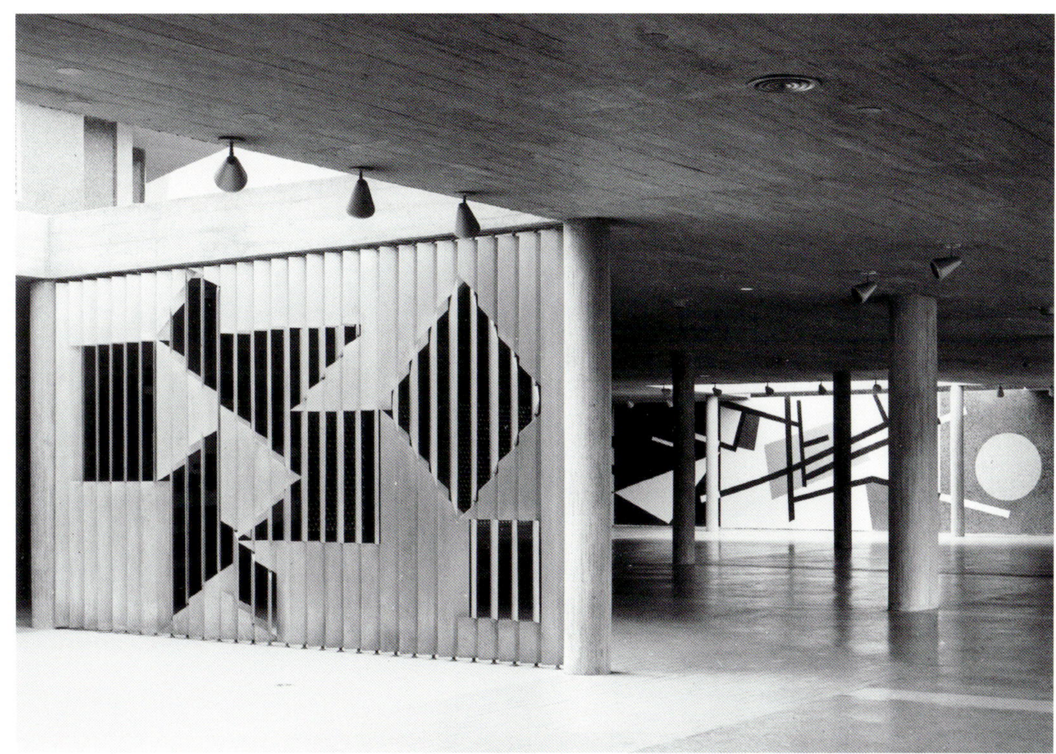

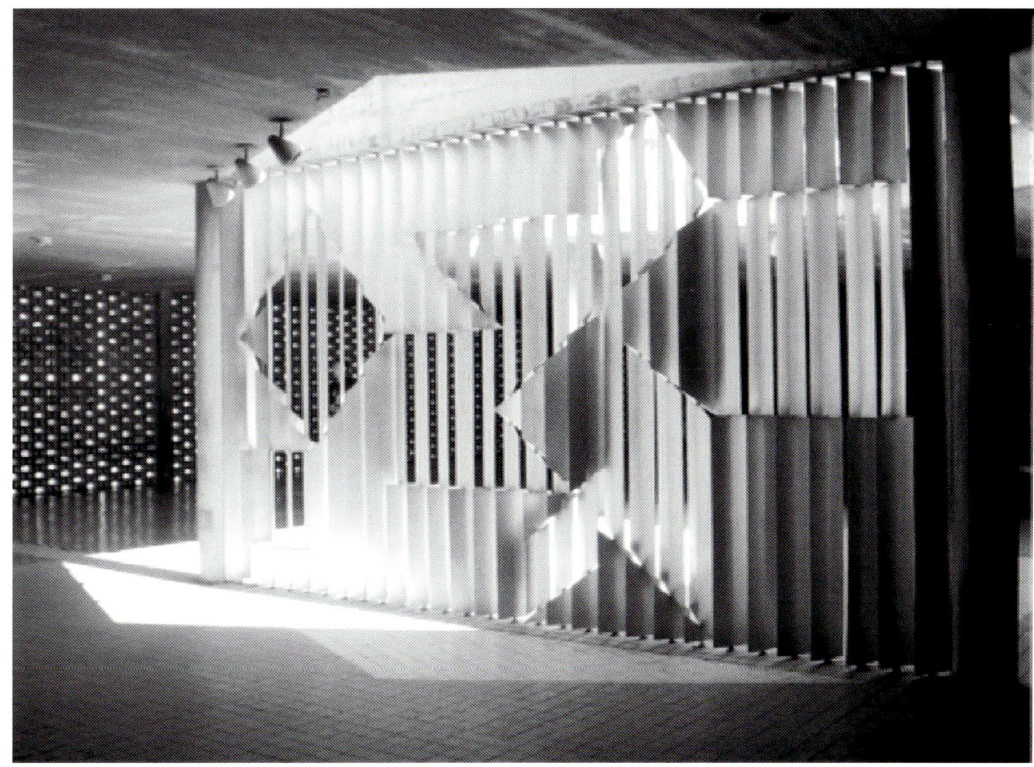

Victor Vasarely, *Positivo Negativo*, 1954. University City, Caracas

In this milieu, Otero developed his mature work, including his Mondrianesque murals and *Coloritmos* during the 1950s, and his urban, kinetic sculptures of the late 1960s, which visibly reference the work of Calder, a figure whose presence in Venezuela had endured on account of his *Nubes* (Clouds) for CU's main auditorium. Otero's *Coloritmos* maintain a structural relationship with his urban sculptures, given that they expressed his interest in space and movement.[24] This series of approximately seventy-five works made between 1955 and 1971, emblematic of the triumph of geometric abstraction in Venezuela, are the product of the artist's fascination with the work of Picasso, Cézanne, and, particularly, Mondrian. They were painted with Duco, an industrial lacquer used in the automotive industry, which Otero would apply with a spray gun or roller onto wood or Plexiglas. Each work, about 240 centimeters in height by 50 in width, comes out of the wall 3 or 4 centimeters — its edge also painted with lacquer — freeing it from the frame and giving it an anthropometric scale. Evenly spaced black or gray lines structure the surface, while polygonal color forms seem to float between the white background and the dark stripes, creating a dynamic spatiality.

Yet the incorporation of real movement into Otero's work would not be achieved prior to his sculptures for Zona Feérica, as part of an ambitious program in search of the modernist ideal of a new individual and society (free, self-determined, and egalitarian), to be materialized through a transformation of the relationship of built structures to the landscape. Also key to this development and to his initial turn to technology was the short-lived but celebrated Signals Gallery in London, which organized the retrospective *A Quarter of a Century of the Beautiful Work of Alejandro Otero* in 1966.[25] At Signals, Otero was part of a generation of kinetic artists gathered around Guy Brett, Paul Keeler, and David Medalla. The *Signals* newsletter brought together science, technology, and art in a mix that included quantum physics, "underground"

24. In a telling recounting, in which he explains the intimate relationship in his *Colortimos* between architecture and painting, Otero recalls: "[at the beginning of the 1950s] . . . some of us stopped painting pictures altogether, convinced that painting had found its definitive realization in space, and that this space was nothing but the street, the city, the new buildings. The conviction did not last long. The architects took it on themselves to disillude [*sic*] us. The university complex was nearly completed, and elsewhere the designers felt themselves able to imitate us, so we changed direction. My 'colorhythms' are one of the answers to that situation, even if they are permeated with the sense of construction such an intimate and fervent relationship with architectonic space and rhythm had given me." José Balza, *Alejandro Otero* (Milan: Olivetti, 1977), 56. (This volume also includes texts by Otero.) In an interview from 1971, Otero refers to his sculptures as "*Coloritmos* in space." See Margarita D'Amico, "Alejandro Otero: Gloria y consgración internacionales," in *VEA*, no. 92 (September 1971): 33. Otero's first urban sculpture was *Mástil reflejante* (Reflecting Stele; 1954); it still stands in Caracas in the same gas station at the entrance to a former suburban residential neighborhood, now transformed into a commercial area.

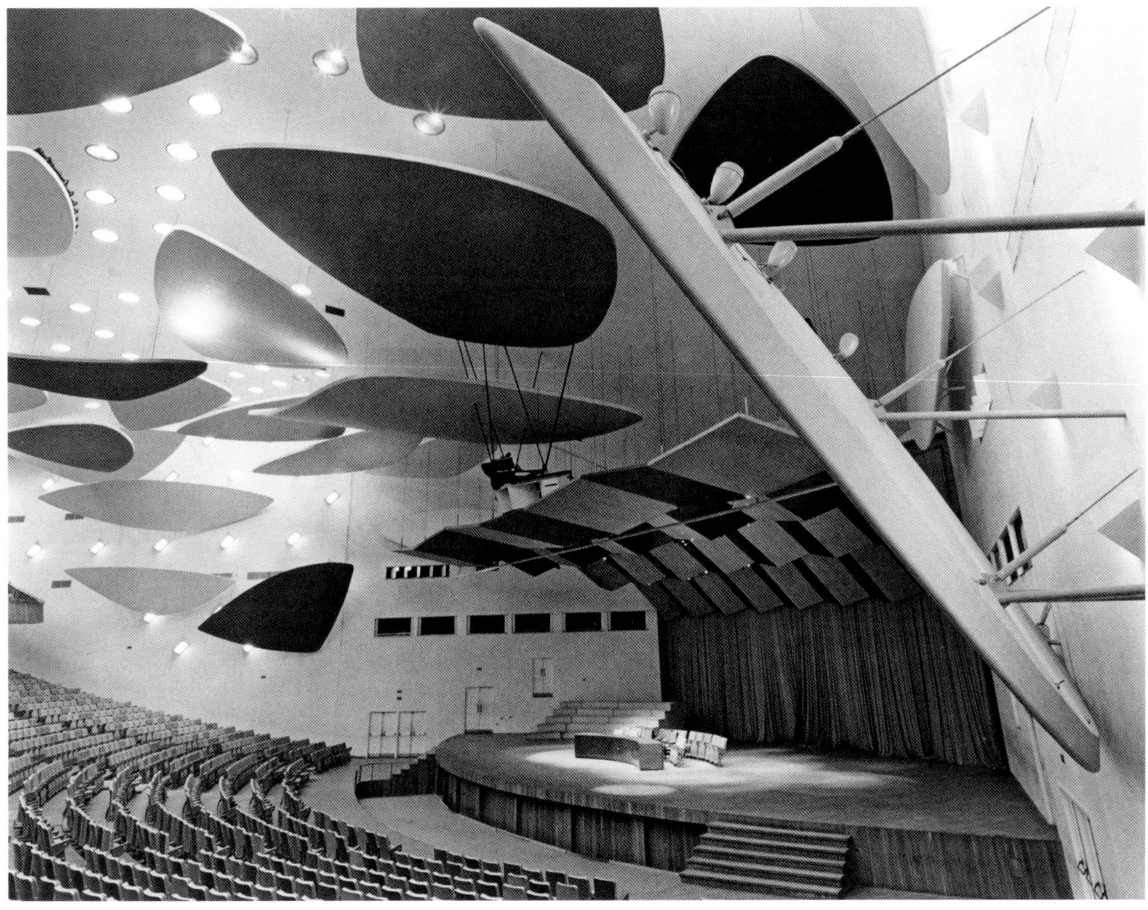

Alexander Calder, *Nubes*, 1954. Aula Magna, University City, Caracas

25. *A Quarter of a Century of the Beautiful Work of Alejandro Otero,* "Stop Press 2," *Signals* 2, no. 2, ed. David Medalla (January-February-March 1966): 24.

26. John Gardiner, "Stop Press," *Signals* 1, no. 6 (February–March 1965): 11–12.

astronomy, bio-architecture, the space race, "robot" art, natural phenomena, and new formal relationships. John Gardiner summarized what the kinetic artists of Signals Gallery were doing as "energy (Chillida, Medalla, Takis); dematerialization and growth (Sérgio de Camargo); vibrations (Carlos Cruz-Diez, J. R. Soto); light-and-color changes (Liliane Lijn, Marcello Salvadori); the animation and total involvement of space (Lygia Clark, Mathias Goeritz, Alejandro Otero)."[26] Upon such fertile ground, Otero was able to begin a new investigation, taking a leap into the void, jumping from the safety of his reputation as Venezuela's most advanced painter into the unpredictable future of the utopias promised by science and technology.

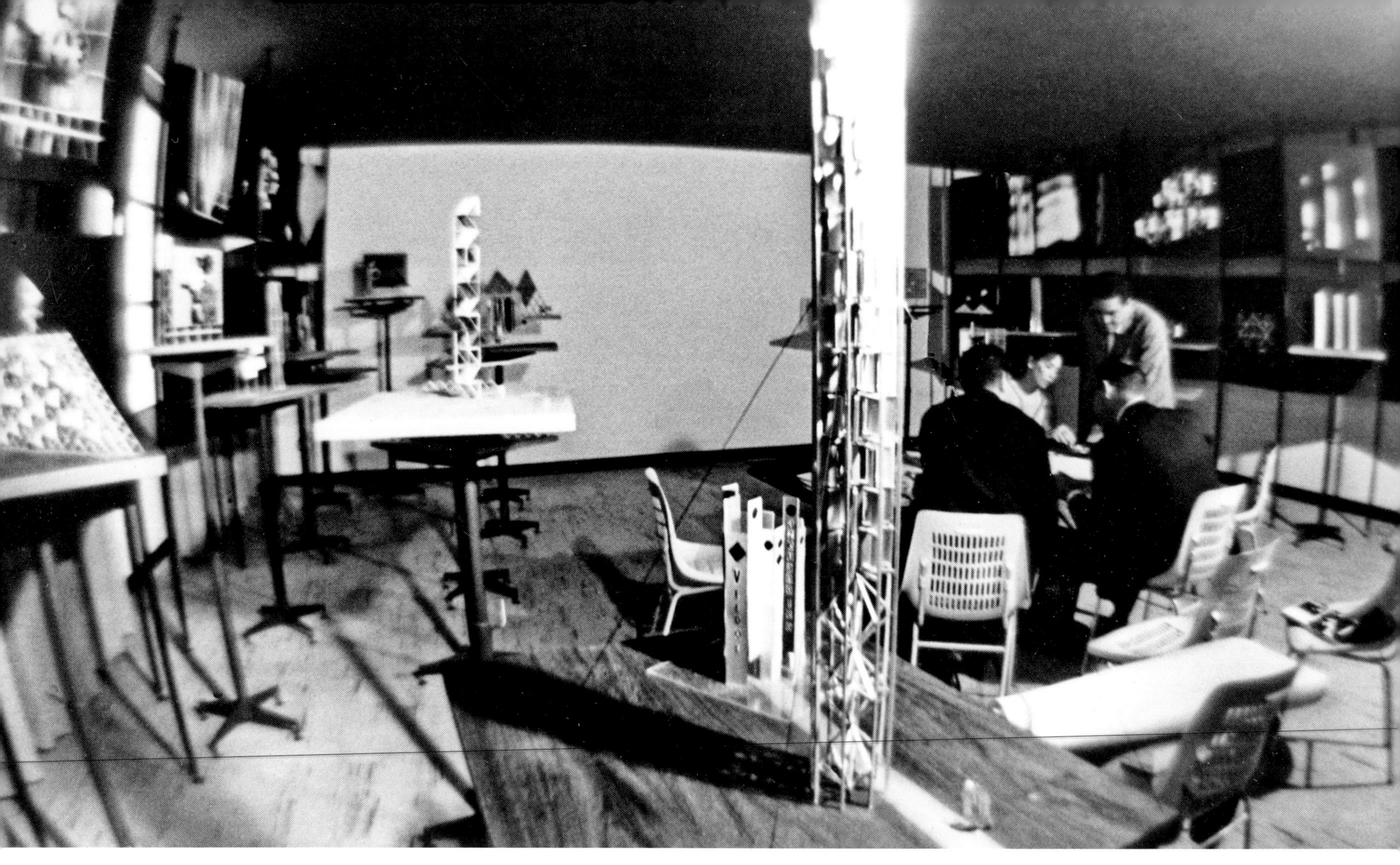

General view of photographs and models of proposals for Zona Feérica. PADSA (Promociones Artísticas y Diseño, S. A.), Caracas, 1967

Zona Feérica was a collaborative process among many professionals working toward a common goal in a collective environment. They were brought together in an office studio called PADSA, or Promociones Artísticas y Diseño, S.A. (Artistic Promotions and Design), and set up in a modernist building designed by General Motors Overseas Operations in 1948 in the vicinity of the CU. In that office, which was open to anyone interested in looking at the projects (Italian architect Gio Ponti was a prominent visitor), Otero and the team of professionals prepared several presentations of their proposals.[27] In many of the photographs shot during what seems to be a press conference at PADSA, exhibition design prepared for the presentation is visible: in a darkened room, black-and-white photographs affixed to panels illustrate the sculptural proposals, including those of Otero and his wife, Mercedes Pardo. Fifteen of the maquettes rest on high-top tables used as pedestals. Another picture shows Otero, flashlight in hand, explaining the project to an attentive audience. The photographs in the panels show lighting and movement simulations that differ according to each sculptural project's need. The ambience conveyed by the pictures is one of professionalism, teamwork, ample resources, and clear, detailed information — more suggestive of an architectural or engineering office than an artist's studio.

27. Some authors attribute the design of this building to Venezuelan architect Pedro Dupouy. It was built by Armando Planchart, a collector and art patron who was a close friend of Otero. See *Catálogo del Patrimonio Cultural Venezolano, 2004-2007* (Instituto del Patrimonio Cultural Caracas, 2007), 59; and Pineda, "Alejandro Otero," n.p.

28. "Una gigantesca exhibición feérica mostrará la Venezuela del future"; and Francia Natera, "Aventura visual alucinante para aprender amar a Caracas," *El Nacional*, September 3, 1967.

29. Mayhall, "Dissolution of Utopia," 225.

30. Venezuelan historian Pino Iturrieta points out that Venezuelan president Raúl Leoní had by 1967 created an amnesty law granting freedom to 250 left-wing rebels. These rebels were subsequently incorporated into the bureaucracy of the country's various cultural institutions at home and abroad. See Elías Pino Iturrieta, "Aproximación a Venezuela contemporánea," in *Alfredo Boulton y sus contemporáneos*, 43.

Zona Feérica was announced with much fanfare by the press. Headlines proclaimed, "A Gigantic Faerie exhibition will show the Venezuela of the Future," and "Amazing adventure to learn to love Caracas."[28] The actual Zona Feérica sculpture park was sited adjacent to a specially designed building constructed for IDC, a multimedia event that was extremely controversial at the time because it was conceived as a spectacular retelling of the city's history by a group of artists who advocated a leftist-Marxist reading of history. Some interpreted the government's "commissioning [of] these revolutionary artists to mount a publicly funded event" as little more than "the government . . . attempting an artistic pacification, equal to that in the political realm."[29] Some of the protagonists of IDC stressed that their intent was to foster a social consciousness about the consequences of technological modernism. Outside IDC, Otero and his sculptures made claims for another way of relating to technology, impregnating it with aesthetic significance. Caracas's four-hundredth-anniversary celebration (which was actually postponed, following a major earthquake in the capital in July 1967) was thus marked with philosophical questioning and political tensions that must be accounted for in any history of Zona Feérica.[30]

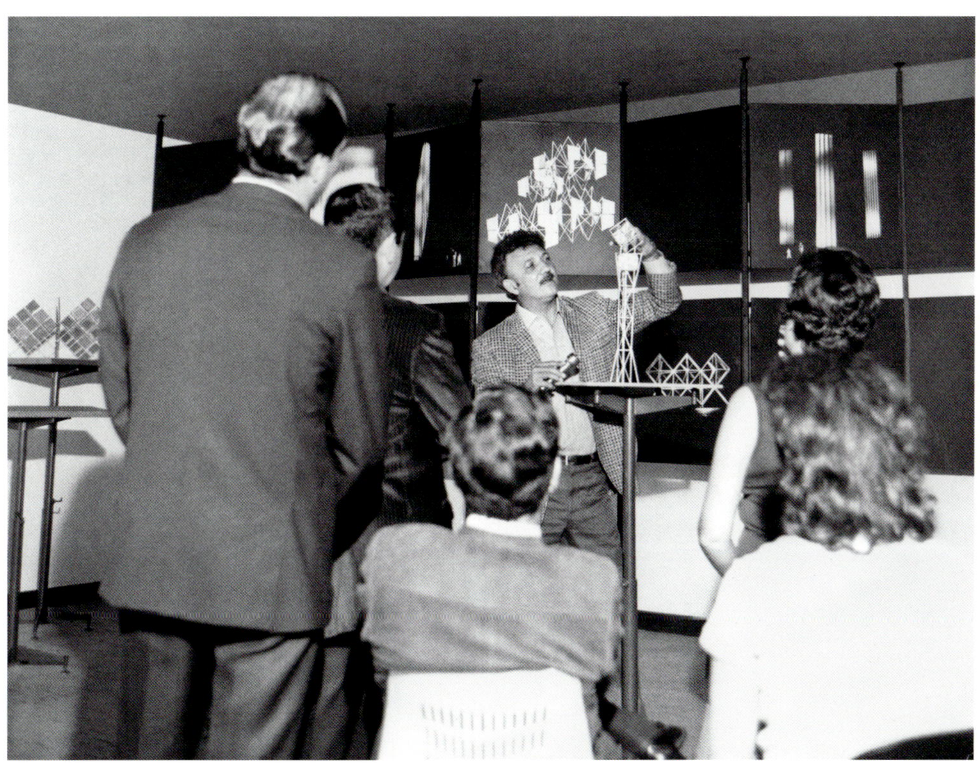

Alejandro Otero showing a model at PADSA (Promociones Artísticas y Diseño, S. A.), Caracas, 1967

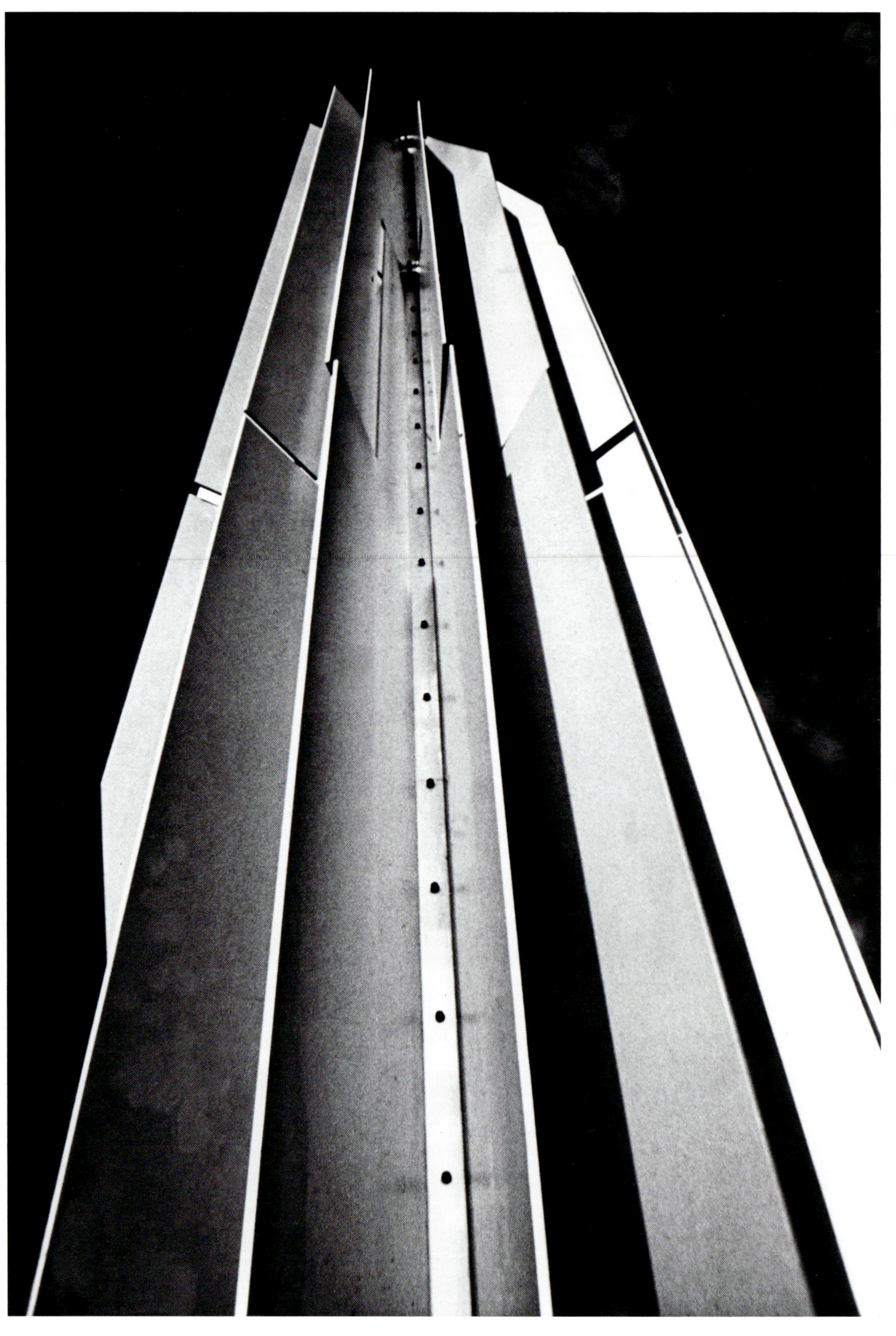

Alejandro Otero, *Rotor*, 1968 (detail). Zona Feérica, Parque El Conde, Caracas

31. In his writings Villanueva explains the integration of the arts in terms of collective reception: "the painter and sculptor just emerged from a personalistic and individualistic tradition, to enter another announcing human intervention as a symbol of social adherence, human and collective sympathy, as a mark of responsibility." Carlos Raúl Villanueva, *Textos escogidos* (Caracas: Facultad de Arquitectura y Urbanismo, Universidad Central de Venezuela, 1980), 70.

32. *Mural espacio cromático* is also known as *Cerritos*. In subsequent years the sculptures were relocated to other sites. Caldera's government was also responsible for tearing down the IDC building.

Otero intended for his sculptures to be read as "diagrams" revealing the natural forces and dynamic relations between technology, the landscape, and human beings. The urban fabric was to become the new institutional frame for the work of art, thereby substituting for the individual dimension of aesthetic reception in the museum environment and fulfilling Villanueva's mandate to uphold individualism in the arts through an integration of the arts.[31]

Otero's immersion in the urban scale — without using architecture as a support for his work — posed many problems and questions for the artist: What kind of viewer should be expected? How would viewers experience art outside of the museum frame? Are the implied sets of modern art values still valid in this context (for example, is art's autonomy a quality that can be transferred from the museum to the streets)? How do color, form, space, structure, and scale change in the urban context?

The seven sculptures built for Zona Feérica were *Rotor, Noria hidroneumática* (an Otero-Pardo collaboration), *Vertical vibrante oro y plata, Integral vibrante, Mural espacio cromático* (an Otero-Pardo collaboration), *Torre acuática*, and *Torre sonovibrátil* (Rotor, Hydropneumatic wheel, Gold and silver vertical vibrant, Vibrant integral, Space chromatic mural, Aquatic tower, and Sound-vibrating tower).[32] They were fabricated in Venezuela with materials produced in the country by the then-surging steel and aluminum industry. The metals in the sculptures reflected both natural and artificial light, and most of them incorporated movement that was either mechanical or produced by natural elements such as water or wind. Trees and grass surrounded the sculptures, and the IDC building and the city served as background. Some of the works, such as *Rotor* and *Torre sonovibrátil*, can be seen in vintage photographs: they stand on top of metal pedestals painted black and white. Others were directly fixed to a concrete base. *Rotor*, now in the collection of the Galería de Arte Nacional (National Gallery of Art, a museum founded by Otero in the 1970s), measuring 5.5 by 1 meters, is a vertical structure made of anodized silver aluminum with a mechanical motor. The piece has two axes that allow it to turn in two directions simultaneously, so it changes form depending on its movement. *Integral vibrante*, relocated to the gardens of Siderúrgica del Orinoco (the state-run steel mega-company in the south of Venezuela), is an impressive latticework 9-by-9-meter cube made of stainless steel

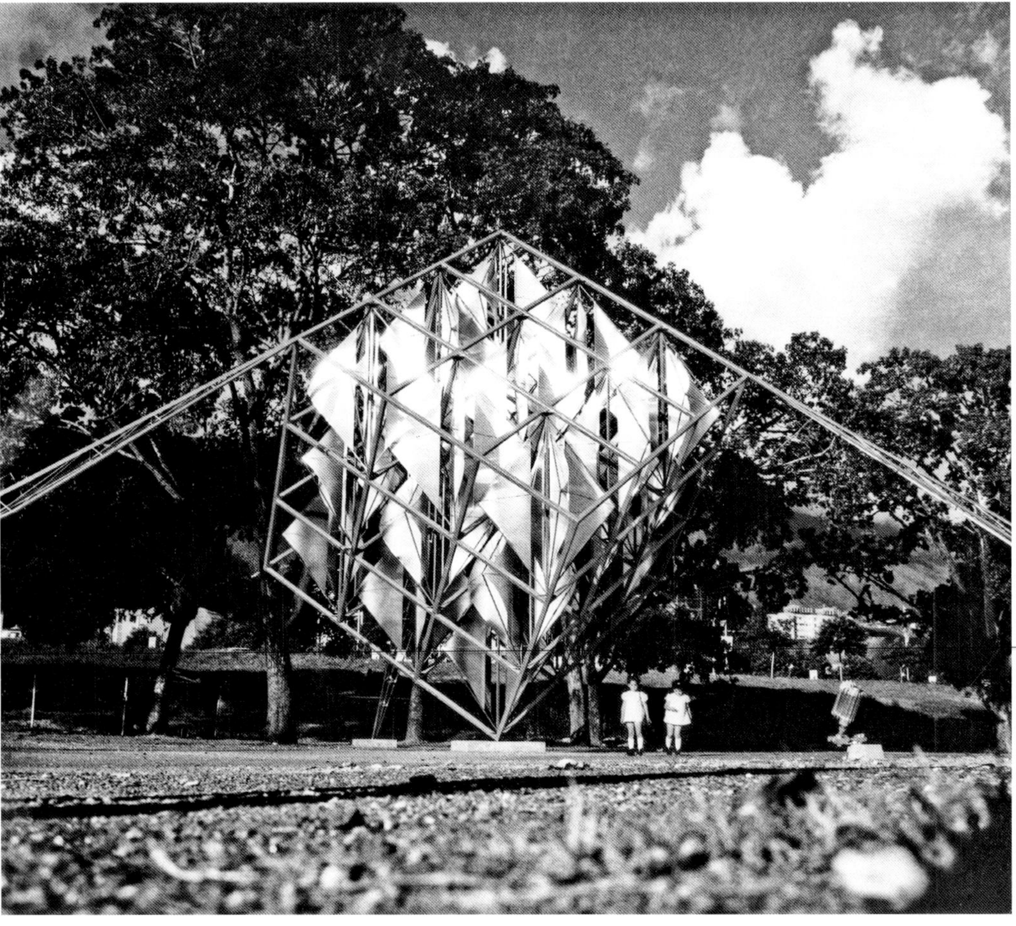

Alejandro Otero, *Vertical vibrante*, 1968. View of Zona Feérica, Parque El Conde, Caracas

with 27 rotating vanes that move with the wind. The vanes change colors according to the angle of the light, and each moves at a different pace. *Noria hidroneumática* is a collaboration between Otero and Pardo. Measuring 9 x 4.5 meters, with its five rotating wheels moved by water (thus suggesting a watermill), the entire work is sited above a mirror of water. Fabricated in anodized aluminum, each vane includes an embedded semi-transparent colored acrylic pane that induces a pictorial spectacle. *Vertical vibrante oro y plata*, now part of the collection of the Museo Nacional de Arquitectura (National Museum of Architecture) in Caracas, has vanes moved by the wind. Made of gold and silver anodized aluminum, the work is 24 meters tall and has 15 vanes or *mariposas* (butterflies) that are in constant movement in response to the wind. *Torre acuática*, a metal tower with a running stream of water inside that amused children, was destroyed. Otero mentioned it as an example of a piece he considered too playful, too ludic. *Torre sonovibrátil*, now in the collection of Compañía Nacional de Telecomunicaciones de Venezuela (National Telecommunications Company of Venezuela), stands 13.5 meters tall and, as its title indicates, is a sound piece: as thin vertical rods crossing the work touch one another, they create metallic sounds.

33. Margarita D'Amico, "Imagen de Caracas: Un sueño de artista altamente tecnificado," *El Nacional*, supplement, October 15, 1967.

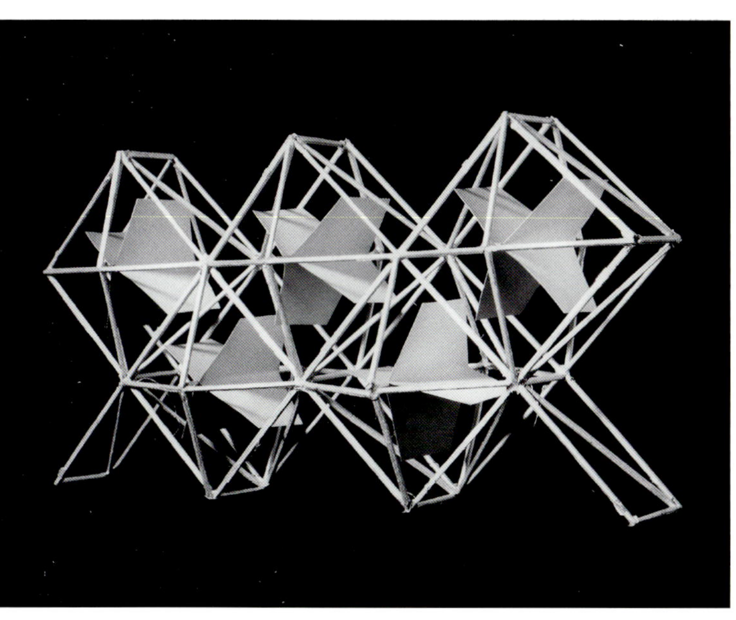

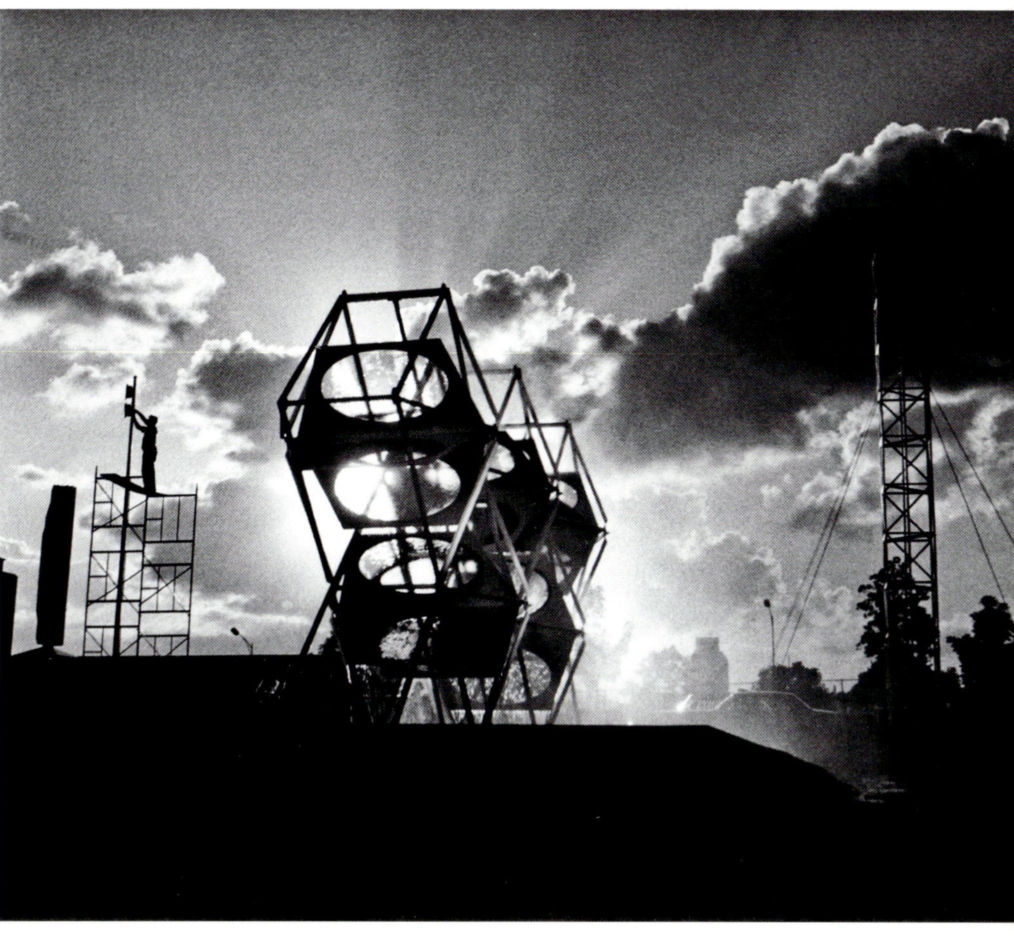

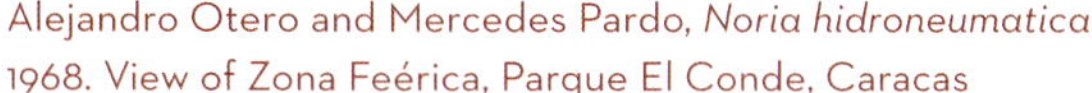

Alejandro Otero and Mercedes Pardo, *Noria hidroneumatica* (model), 1967

Alejandro Otero and Mercedes Pardo, *Noria hidroneumatica*, 1968. View of Zona Feérica, Parque El Conde, Caracas

Descriptions of the sculptures could be read in the newspapers and local magazines that announced the Zona Feérica. One phrase in particular was repeated in several of the reviews: "Imagen de Caracas is the past, and Zona Feérica the future." Several of the periodicals also quoted from an interview in which Otero provided extended explanations of his vision for the sculpture park:

> The aim of this series of works, symbols of Venezuela projected into the future, is to associate ourselves with the world's changes, expressing the vertiginous transformation of the time, its space formed of imponderables that the work is to make visible; the multiplicity of possibilities open to us in all fields and at all roads; the need for new reins to hold on to the otherwise precarious balance in which we live, and a new joy that can only be that of a new poetics of the resources that our time gives us.[33]

Machines of neither production nor reproduction — as Fredric Jameson's division between industrial and postindustrial technologies goes — Otero's sculptures were for him an encounter between technology and nature. In an approach more aesthetic than ideological, Otero turned to his space structures in a conversation with the Venezuelan art critic Roberto Guevara:

> With my space structures I feel I am in a world where everything is possible. Any element, natural or created by man: water, wind, light, metals, energy, machinery, leads me to devise forms and antiforms, space, movement, vibration, or just sensory events that no longer need to be specifically painting or sculpture or combinations of these, to express the nameless new fact — of which we are part — that begins to become itself present reality. These elements, however, do not serve me only as a starting point, but constitute the work's raw material. Vibrations, transparencies, the fluidity of water, for example, are not to suggest a form or a succession of forms but become an alphabet and syntax of themselves. Projected violently on scaffold spaces, a flashing light transmutes pure matter into energy. Energy in this case is synonymous with language.[34]

Otero was highly aware of the questions his work posed about art in the urban space. He was particularly resolute in his opinions about the art institution and the reception of art in public spaces. But "how, in an underdeveloped country," as Hélio Oiticica inquires, "does one explain and justify the appearance of an avant-garde, not as symptom of alienation but as a decisive factor in its collective progress?"[35] That Otero's work, unlike Oiticica's, did not end up becoming a hybrid of favela and concrete art is telling. But like Oiticica, Otero was conscious of the fragility of museums and cultural institutions in a Latin American country. In mid-1968, the government of the conservative leader of the Socialist Christian Party, Rafael Caldera, took down the seven Zona Feérica sculptures because the government was planning to build in that area a mega-complex for public housing that came to be known as *Parque Central* (Central Park). In a matter of weeks, the sculptures went from representing the country's future to temporarily disappearing from sight. According to some oral testimonies, there were political reasons for the demolition of Zona Feérica and Imagen de Caracas's building. Mercedes Otero, the artist's daughter, in conversation with the author, mentioned that Caldera's government had even destroyed the Zona brochures. The closing down of the IDC was violent, as Mayhall explains: "The police closed Imagen de Caracas on 31 August [1968]. Not only did they seize the *Dispositivo* and everything in it, but the *Comisión Especial Homenaje a Caracas* was taken over by the *Contraloría* [comptroller] of the Municipal Council, and the Bello Monte office and archives (which belonged to [Inocente] Palacios) were blocked by the police. Several artists and workers on Imagen's staff were detained[,] that is, they were jailed."[36]

Otero was always at the center of debates about contemporary art in his country, as evinced by his many public polemics against important public figures — from his criticism of Marta Traba's

34. Guevara, "Conversación con Alejandro Otero," n.p.

35. Hélio Oiticica, "Esquema geral da nova objetividade Brasileira," in *Nova objetividade Brasileira*, exhibit catalogue (Rio de Janeiro: MAM-RJ, 1967).

36. Mercedes Otero, in conversation with the author at the Archivo Otero, Caracas, June 2016. *Dispositivo* (Device) was the name given to the IDC building. *Comisión especial homenaje a Caracas* (Special Committee Tribute to Caracas) was in charge of the organization of the IDC event. See Mayhall, "Dissolution of Utopia," 212.

37. "What Marta Traba seems to postulate is not an identification from the roots but a nationalist and continentalist illustration elaborated beforehand that could never have another outcome but the inauthentic." Alejandro Otero, "Mi respuesta a Marta Traba," reproduced in Douglas Monroy, *Memoria crítica: Alejandro Otero*, 2nd ed. (Caracas: Artesanogroup Editores, 2008), 556.

38. Víctor Guedez, "Alejandro Otero: Los fundamentos de sus esculturas de escala cívica," in *Alejandro Otero ante la crítica*, 201.

39. Damaz, *Art in European Architecture*, 35.

40. Quoted in ibid.

41. Ibid., 73.

42. Walter Gropius, once the champion of rationalist architecture, went so far as to declare: "The belief that the sciences are of greater importance than arts has impoverished culture . . . A correction of our educational system is needed which should give arts as much weight as the sciences"; ibid., 75.

43. In a passage bearing similarities to Otero's ideas, Villanueva explains the difference between synthesis of the arts and integration of the arts: "In the case of the synthesis, the arts, preserving their traditional characteristics, particularly painting and sculpture, converge in the architectural space, giving body to a unit of new quality, but old in its features. Based on this space, whose architectural determinants are essential, any other of the arts can be structured, thus accepting the architectural primacy and leading to the best examples of synthesis . . . Quite different is the case of integration. In integration no previous frame exists because it is the conformation and attitude of human labor itself, which will give a unitary significance in a cohesive way to the functional and spatial world of the citizens. At the base of integration is the process of mechanical engineering and a system of social-economic relations." Carlos Raúl Villanueva, "La síntesis de las artes," *Revista Punto*, July 1963, n.p.

44. Olivetti, *Alejandro Otero*, 126.

understanding of Latin American identity to his polemical exchange on the meaning of abstraction with Miguel Otero Silva, editor-owner of the main Venezuelan newspaper in the late 1950s.[37] His art as well as his thought, his critical writings, and even his participation in the creation of the country's cultural apparatus were always center stage. He wanted his Zona Feérica sculptures, detached from architecture, to be "a multitudinous oeuvre," because he thought that art would achieve its potential only in its encounter with people in public space. For him, the idea of art at an urban scale was justified because "art is a necessary product for man's life, as important as the oxygen and the sun."[38] Otero's words resonate with the spirit of art's raison d'être as advanced by many of the most important midcentury architects. As Damaz states, in favor of a synthesis of the arts, "art must be put in touch with the man in the street and placed in our city squares, where disorder and bad taste predominate."[39] Bloc similarly affirms, "to give their human value back to the plastic arts, contact must be re-established with the public, the crowd."[40] According to Damaz, CIAM's preoccupations with problems of standardization, the industrialization of construction, and developments in town planning — in short, rampant rationalism — prompted Le Corbusier to call for a synthesis of the arts, because "our work is addressed to people . . . for whom emotion, art, are as necessary as bread and water."[41] The expectation was that painting and sculpture would bring an emotional dimension to functionalist architecture.[42] The "sister arts," as painting and sculpture were once called, were to be responsible for giving a human face to rationalization. This ideal would continue in Otero's work and in some of the initiatives with which he was associated, although he preferred to understand his own work as an *integration* rather than a synthesis, because he believed art should be capable of being seen from any perspective and as the product of a collaboration among different disciplines.[43] The sculptures Otero produced from the mid 1960s until his death in the early 1990s embody this transition from a *synthesis* of the arts to an *integration* of the arts, wherein the artist attempted to overcome the convention of enclosing art in spaces where it is available only to the elite. Of his sculptures, he asked:

> Where is the notion of sculpture here? In what measure can we call this a machine or impose it as a simple structural combination of components? I don't care, so long as the work contains and communicates this mysterious reality of living space, characteristic of the world we live in; [the work] relating us to it without copying or imitating it and from my point of view, expresses [the world] in what is most surprising and most capable of transformation.[44]

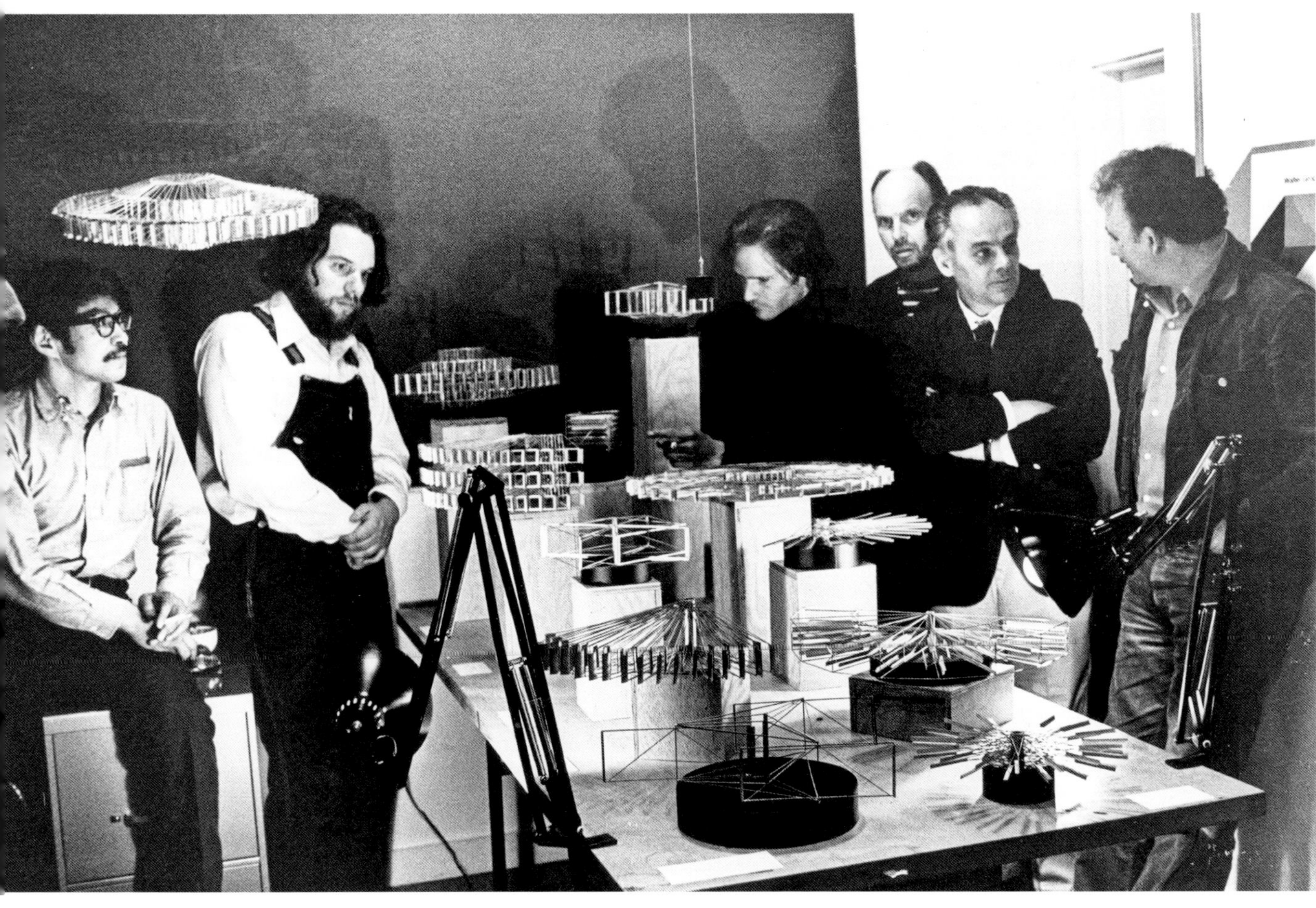

Alejandro Otero and György Kepes at the Center for Advanced Visual Studies, MIT, Cambridge, Massachusetts, 1972

Not long after the Zona Feérica was closed down by the government in 1968, Otero was awarded a Guggenheim Fellowship, which he used to support a residency at the recently founded CAVS in Cambridge, Massachusetts.[45] Kepes had articulated the center's mission as the "recognition of the complementary unity of the two vital aspects of our cultural life, science and art, [which] becomes today a survival necessity," because "the tasks for which the artists are being called upon today are epic tasks, civic and social in character and environmental in dimensions."[46] The traveling CAVS exhibitions Kepes organized were extremely polemical. The first was even canceled. Meant to take place within the purview of the 1968 São Paulo Biennial, it was boycotted by a group of artists opposed to the Brazilian military dictatorship and to the censoring of artists' and intellectuals' work. Another Kepes exhibition was criticized by Lawrence Alloway as a "frivolous and gross fantasy of technology," "an art of mostly trivial effects."[47] This was also at a time when MIT was subject to criticism for its links to research conducted on behalf of the U.S. military, and when Kinetic Art's engagement with technology was still widely seen as a collection of gimmicks.

45. See "Cronología," 33.

46. György Kepes, introduction to *Multiple Interaction Team*, exhibit catalogue (Cambridge, Mass.: Center for Advanced Visual Studies, MIT, 1972), n.p.

47. Lawrence Alloway, "Art," *Nation*, April 20, 1970, p. 477.

During the time Otero spent at MIT, he produced another series of urban sculptures, including one that was supposed to float and navigate Boston's Charles River. Otero aimed to integrate technology and nature with an altruistic purpose, as he stated in the catalogue of the exhibition *Multiple Interaction Team*, organized by Kepes. "I believe in art," Otero said, "which reflects in media, spirit and scope, the technological era in which we are living."[48] Such a predilection for techno-scientific utopianism has been the target of many recent critical inquiries, including Busbea's interpretation of the failure of the Spatial Urbanism movement, owing to its implicit embrace of consumer society at the expense of a Marxist critique of the social role of the artist.[49] In the 1960s, Herbert Marcuse aired such a critique of the dominant relationship of science to art, wherein art takes on the role of affirming science. This was the beginning of the end of many artists' dreams of a collaboration between art and science, and a moment that would come to be known for the emergence of skeptical postmodernist art practices.[50]

Such skepticism was reflected in Venezuela throughout the 1960s in the resistance of artists to Kinetic Art's prevalence and to its supposed lack of connection to the country's social, political, and economic realities.[51] At the precise moment when Zona Feérica was taking place, the government was initiating a process to pacify the guerrillas. The dictatorship had ended less than a decade prior, and the democratic system was being tested on an almost daily basis. But Venezuela's modernization depended on oil wealth — unlike that of other Latin American countries — which lasted for at least another twenty years, undergoing an exponential increase during the oil boom of the early 1970s, and coinciding with the nationalization of the oil industry and the 1973 Yom Kippur War.[52] As a result, utopian dreams of modernization were kept (artificially) alive for a longer period of time, and Otero's large-scale sculptural projects proliferated.[53] Yet the legacy of the experiments and utopian rhetoric associated with the urban, architectural, and artistic practices of the time alternated between a "melancholic fatalism" and an "uncritical techno-optimism," as Felicity Scott argues in relation to the intellectual environment that dominated the transition from modernism to postmodernism.[54]

Otero's sculptural work merits much more investigation and scholarly attention. From a historiographical point of view, it enriches the dominant narrative of modernism by drawing our attention to the otherwise unaccounted for nuances and complex circumstances in the process of modernization in Latin American countries. Brought to the present, Otero's work asks us to consider the fate of the utopian ideals briefly addressed in this essay, ideals that now seem anachronistic given the current late-materialist reading of such ideals as having been wholly assimilated by the culture industry. Contemporary art's refusal to "spread . . . the faith in the destiny of man," the function Neruda once assigned to Otero's work, has not only left us without connections to scientific and technological developments — let alone the ability to articulate such developments — it has also turned the future over to those who do not believe in imagination or the creative mind.

48. "Artist Statement," in *Multiple Interaction Team*, n.p.

49. Busbea, *Topologies*, 180.

50. Herbert Marcuse, "Remarks on a Redefinition of Culture," *Daedalus* 94, no. 1 (Winter 1965): 193.

51. For example, El Techo de la Ballena, a collective opposed to the ideology of progress and modernization implied by Kinetic Art, was associated with the radical left-wing movement in Venezuela.

52. In 1970, the price of oil was $10 (USD) per barrel and by 1975 it was $40 (USD). See U.S. Energy Information Administration, Annual Energy Review 2006 (Washington, DC: U.S. Government Printing Office, 2007); http://www.eia.gov/totalenergy/data/annual/archive/038406.pdf.

53. Otero's utopianism has been addressed by many authors, including Mayhall: "For Otero, for example, works of art had two possibilities: either they created a new reality that formulated a new time/space relation (their formal aspect), or they acted transformatively in the social and cultural plane." Mayhall, "Dissolution of Utopia," 69.

54. Felicity D. Scott, *Architecture or Techno Utopias: Politics after Modernism* (Cambridge, Mass.: MIT Press, 2007), 2.

ALEJANDRO OTERO

Coloritmo 5, 1956
Duco paint on wood, 64 × 18 ¼ × 1 ⅛ in. (162.6 × 46.2 × 2.9 cm)
Collection of The University of Arizona Museum of Art, Tucson
Gift of Edward Joseph Gallagher Jr.

Coloritmo 34, 1957–58
Duco paint on board, 82 ¼ × 22 ½ × 2 ¼ in. (208.9 × 57.2 × 5.7 cm)
OAS AMA | Art Museum of the Americas Collection. Purchase Fund

Coloritmo 41, 1959
Duco paint on wood, 78 ¾ × 23 ¼ × 1 ¼ in. (200 × 59.1 × 3 cm)
The Ella Fontanals-Cisneros Collection, Miami

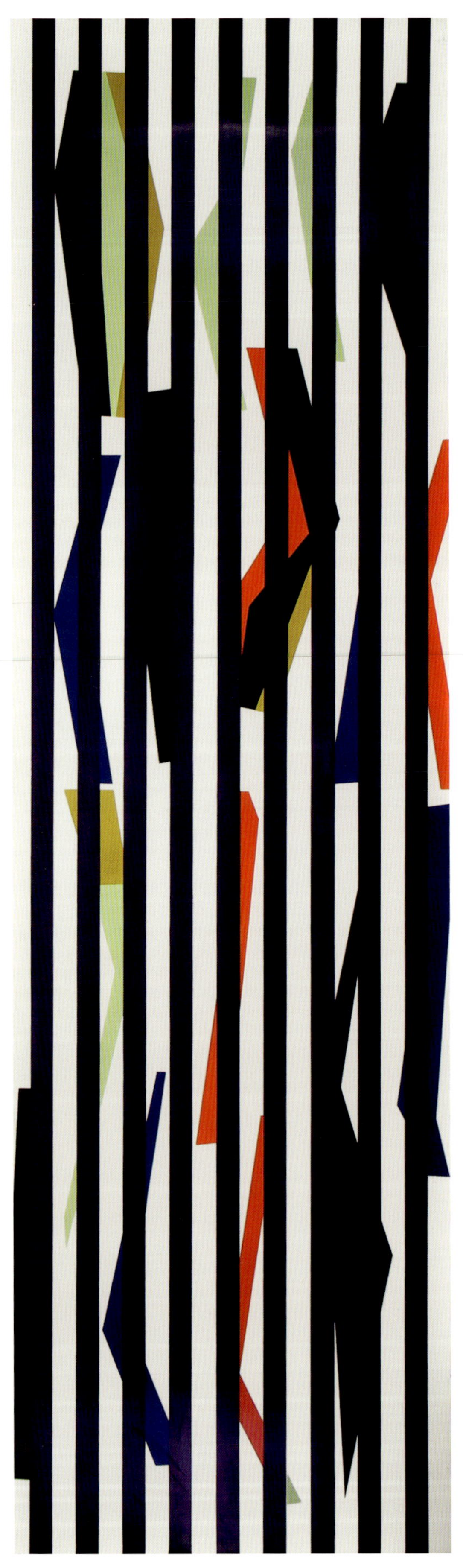

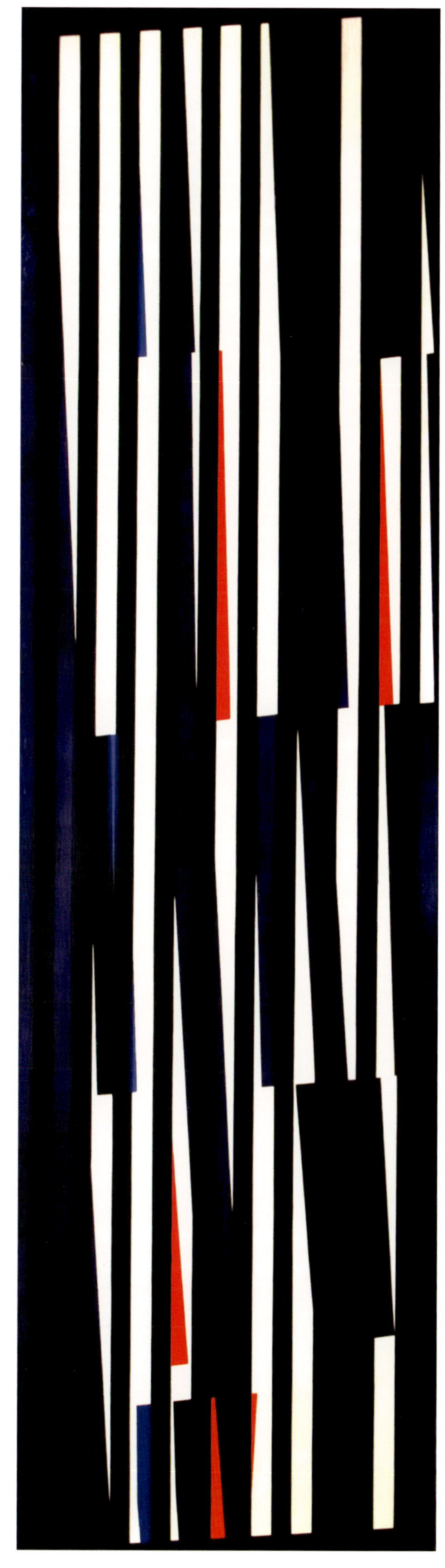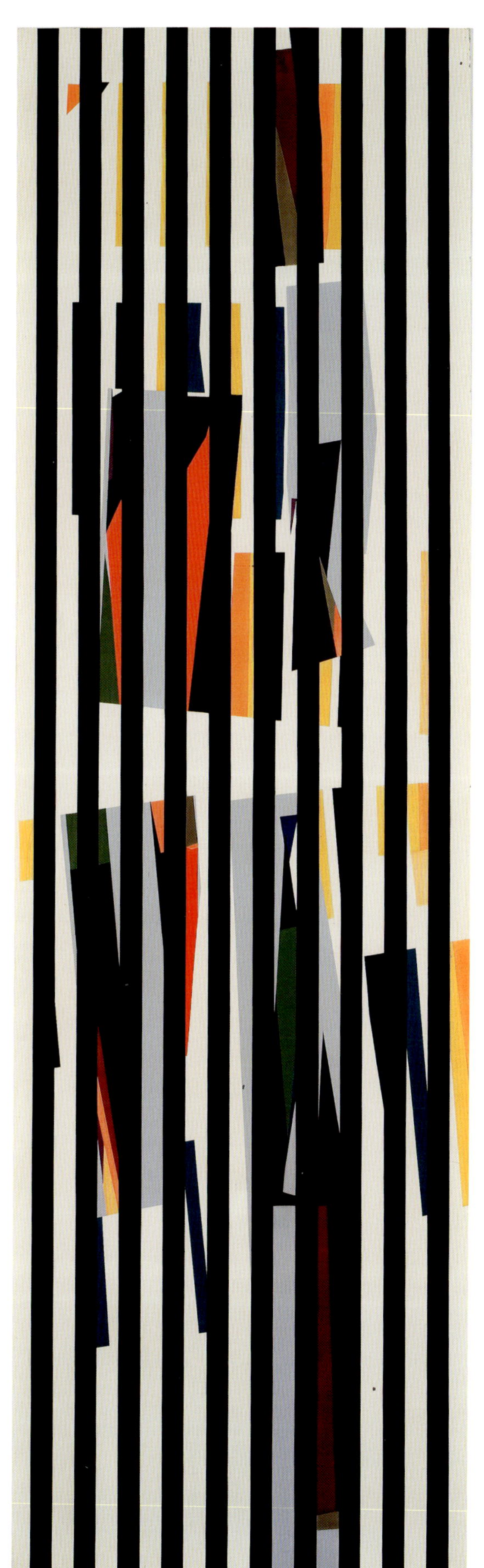

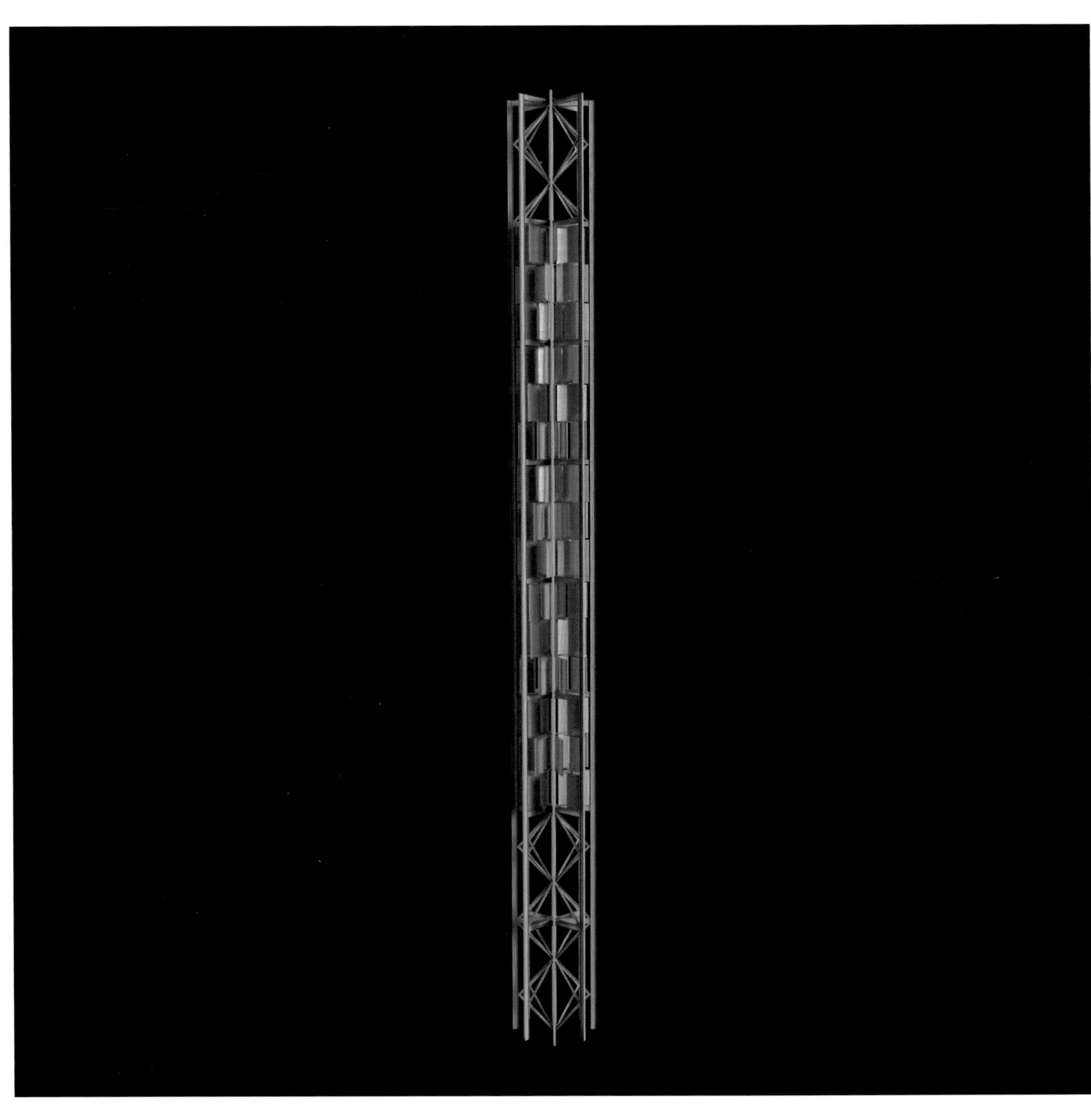

ALEJANDRO OTERO   *Vertical vibrante oro y planta* model, 2017
Exhibition copy of the original model from 1967 developed by Anton Ceballos and rendered by
Jean Giallorenzo and Alexander Gomez, with the assistance of Juan Manuel Lopez
Digital image. Fundación Otero Pardo Collection, Caracas

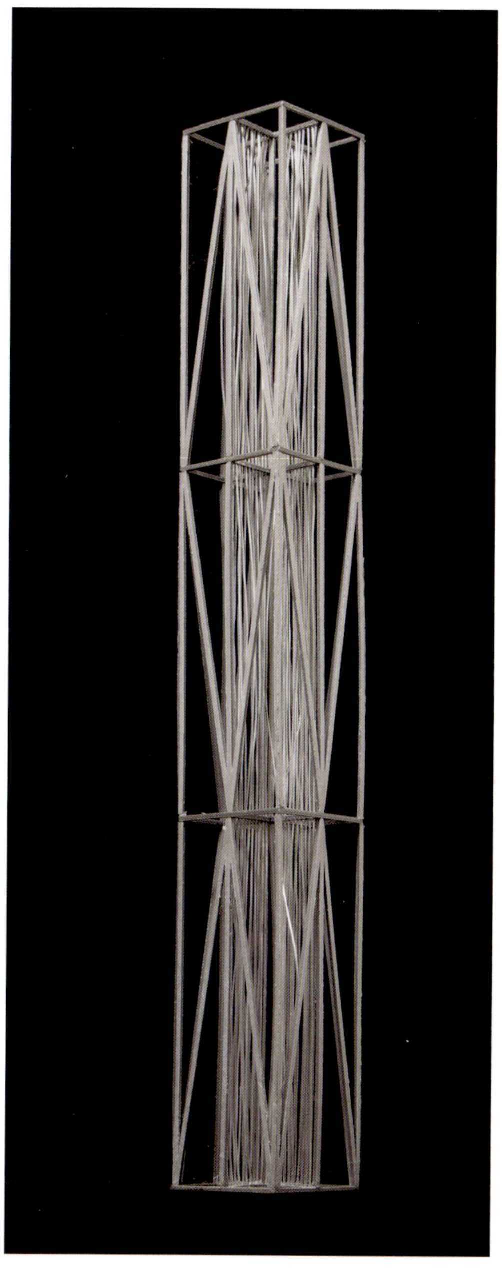 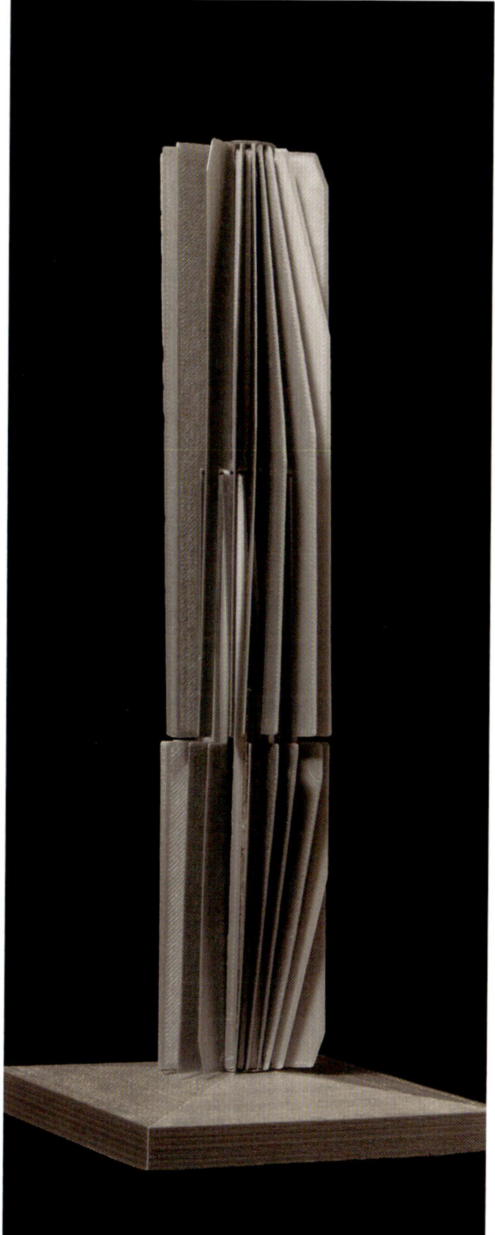 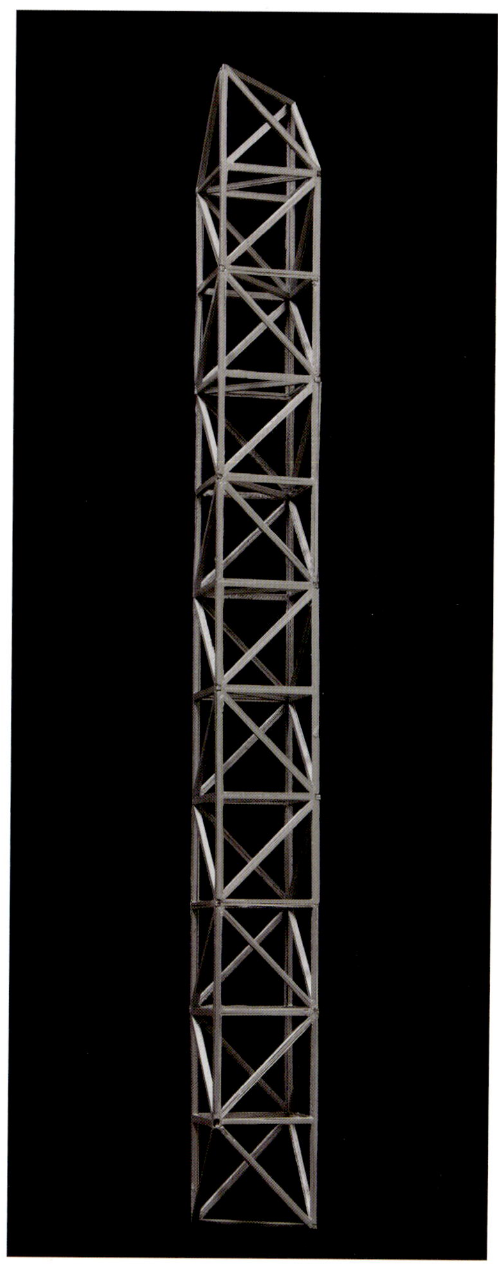

ALEJANDRO OTERO

Torre sonovibrátil model, 2016
Exhibition copy of the original model from 1967 developed by Anton Ceballos
Plastic and wire, scale 1:25, 18 ¼ x 2 ¼ x 2 ¼ in. (46.5 x 5.5 x 5.5 cm)

Rotor model, 2016
Exhibition copy of the original model from 1967 developed by Anton Ceballos
Plastic, scale 1:25, 9 ¼ x 1 ½ x 1 ½ in. (23.6 x 4 x 4 cm)

Torre acuática model, 2016
Exhibition copy of the original model from 1967 developed by Anton Ceballos
Plastic and wire, scale 1:25, 17 ¼ x 1 ½ x 1 ½ in. (44 x 4 x 4 cm)

Fundación Otero Pardo Collection, Caracas

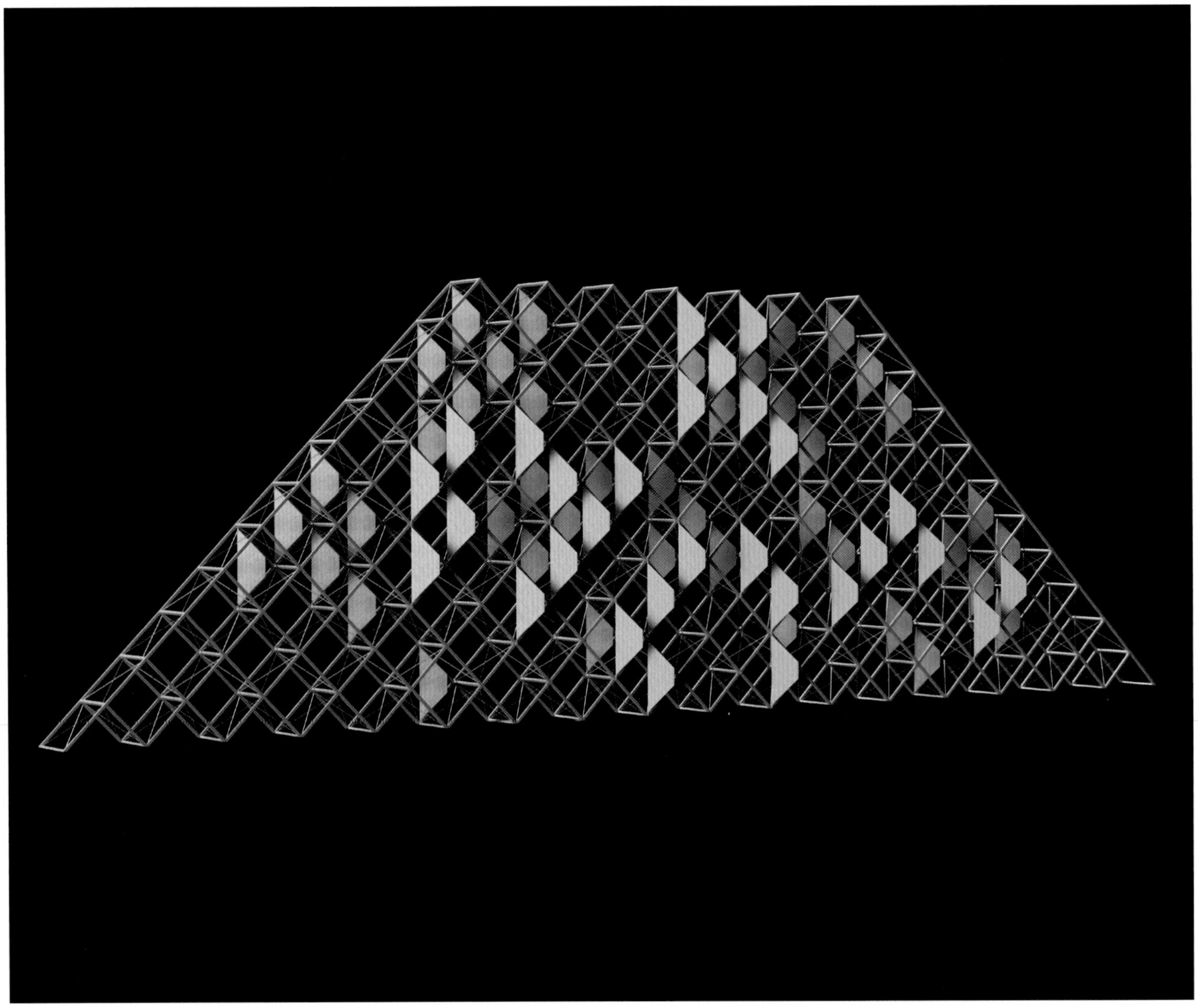

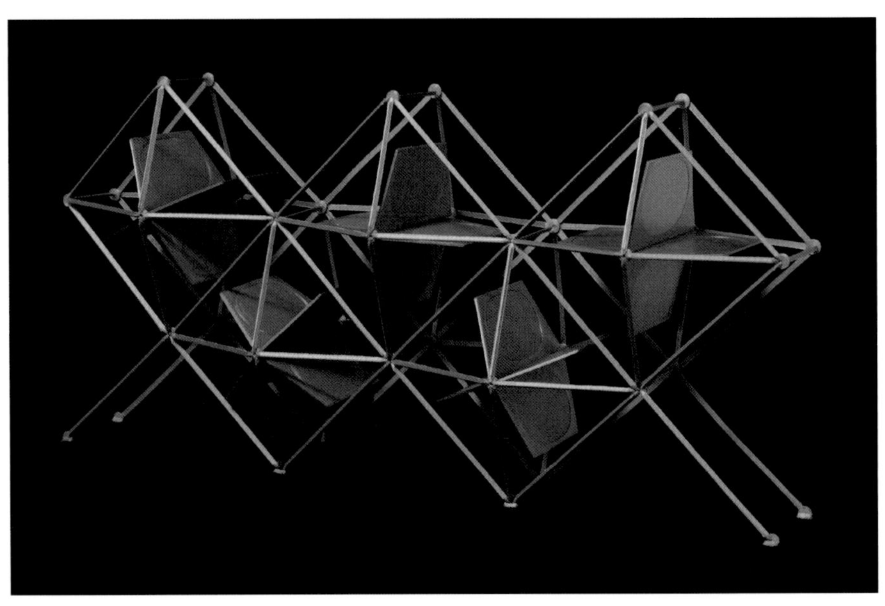

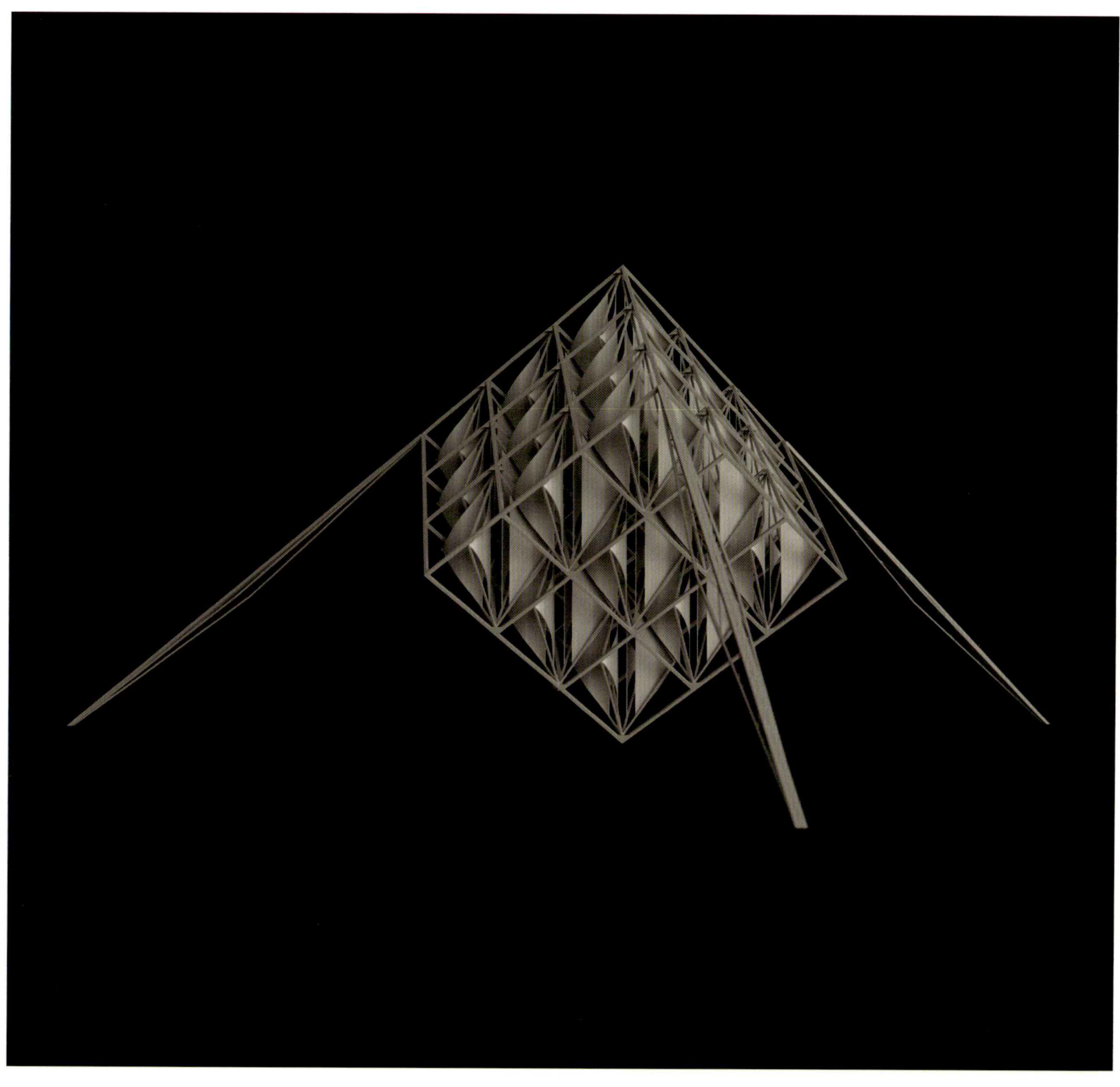

Opposite
ALEJANDRO OTERO AND MERCEDES PARDO

Mural espacio cromático model, 2017
Exhibition copy of the original model from 1967 developed by Anton Ceballos and rendered by
Jean Giallorenzo and Alexander Gomez, with the assistance of Juan Manuel Lopez
Digital image

Noria hidroneumática model, 2016
Exhibition copy of the original model from 1967 developed by Anton Ceballos
Plastic, scale 1:25, 7 x 13 ¾ x 4 ½ in. (17.6 x 35 x 11.3 cm)

Above
ALEJANDRO OTERO
Integral vibrante model, 2017
Exhibition copy of the original model from 1967 developed by Anton Ceballos and rendered by
Jean Giallorenzo and Alexander Gomez, with the assistance of Juan Manuel Lopez
Digital image

Fundación Otero Pardo Collection, Caracas

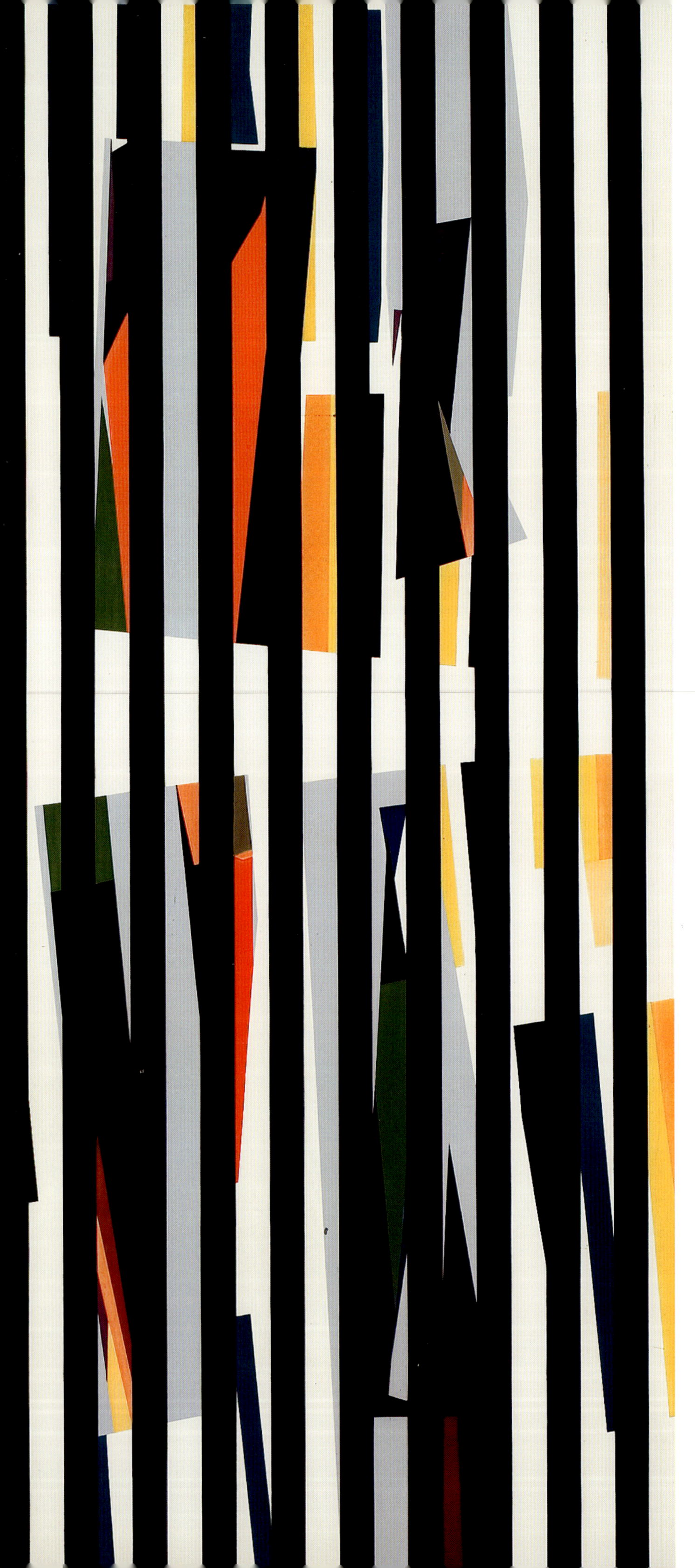

THE ARTISTS

Alejandro Otero, *Coloritmo 41*, 1959 (detail)

MARTHA BOTO (1925–2004) was born in Buenos Aires into an artistic family: her grandfather was an actor and her mother a musician. In the late 1930s and early 1940s, Boto was drawn to the earliest groups of abstract artists in Buenos Aires, and in 1944 she entered the Escuela Superior de Bellas Artes Ernesto de la Cárcova, where she took classes in painting and drawing. In the early 1950s Boto began to build her first mobiles using Plexiglas and colored water, which she showed with some regularity in Buenos Aires galleries. In 1955 she was a founding member of the Asociación Arte Nuevo, and in 1956 co-founded, with Gregorio Vardánega, the group Artistas No Figurativos. Moving to Paris in 1959 with Vardánega, she began her first experiments in Kinetic Art using motorized lights and colored filters, and showed a group of them a year later in the first Paris Biennial. Working with Plexiglas, aluminum, stainless steel, and motors, Boto developed a distinctive vocabulary of simple materials and repetitive movement, and she enjoyed multiple exhibitions at Galerie Denise René.

CARLOS CRUZ-DIEZ (1923–) was born in Caracas, studied art at the Escuela de Artes Plásticas y Aplicadas from 1940 to 1945, where he became interested in the Impressionists' experiments with color. His first visit to Paris in 1955 coincided with final days of the exhibition *Le Mouvement* at Galerie Denise René, where he was particularly inspired by the developments in visual perception represented by Jesús Rafael Soto's work. Returning to Caracas in 1957, Cruz-Diez began to actively study the role of color in Kinetic Art, while teaching at two universities and designing publications for the Ministry of Culture. In 1960 he returned to Paris, where his studio practice has been based ever since, although Cruz-Diez himself now lives mostly in Panama. Focusing his investigation on gradations of color experienced through line, at first Cruz-Diez painstakingly built his series of *Physichromies* by hand, then turned increasingly toward mechanical methods of cutting embedded strips of color that were painted on both sides, and shifted dramatically based on the viewer's movement. Eschewing paint completely, Cruz-Diez relies on *moiré* effects to create the visual impact of his works. His desire to break down color and space to their elemental properties can be experienced in his *Chromosaturation Chambers*, which plunge the viewer into a sequence of radiant spaces, each defined by a singular color.

 was born in Buenos Aires and studied art at the Escuela Nacional de Bellas Artes from 1950 to 1957, alongside Hugo Demarco, Julio Le Parc, and Francisco Sobrino. In 1959 he moved to Paris, where he participated in the first Paris Biennial, and in 1960 was a co-founder of the Groupe de Recherche d'Art Visuel (GRAV), with his compatriots, mentioned above. García-Rossi's earliest "op-kinetic" works, in black, white, and gray, demonstrate the difficulties of trying to achieve the effects of movement on a flat surface in the manner of Victor Vasarely. Embracing instability as a lifelong artistic quest, after GRAV disbanded in 1968 García-Rossi developed kinetic works in which movement and color are brought together in order to interact with a maximum degree of overlap and visual blending.

GYULA KOSICE (1924–2016), a sculptor, theorist, and poet, was born in a Hungarian-speaking part of what is today Slovenia. As a young boy, he came with his parents to Argentina by ship, a voyage that had a profound impact on his imagination. He began making art and writing poetry as a teenager, and was profoundly influenced by the life and works of Leonardo da Vinci. In 1944 he founded the magazine *Arturo* and began regularly publishing his poems and theoretical writings. In 1945 he co-founded the group Arte Concreto-Invención, and created the logo for the influential Madí group. In 1948 he was invited to the Salon des Réalités Nouvelles in Paris, where he met Georges Vantongerloo, whose example led him to center his artistic practice on studying universal laws of the natural world. The same year, Kosice made his first hydrokinetic sculpture, and in 1968 embarked on his lifelong project of articulating the *Hydrospatial City*, which illustrates a future in which mankind is no longer capable of surviving on terra firma, and is confined to cities that float over the oceans. He died in Buenos Aires in May 2016 at the age of ninety-two.

JULIO LE PARC (1928–) was born in Mendoza and as a teenager moved with his family to Buenos Aires. At age fifteen he enrolled in the Academia Nacional de Bellas Artes Prilidiano Pueytrredon, but dropped out before finishing his studies, immersing himself instead in Concrete Art and the spatialism of Lucio Fontana. In 1955 he entered the Escuela Superior de Bellas Artes Ernesto de la Cárcova, where he become involved in the student movement. In 1959 Le Parc was offered a grant to visit Paris, where he has lived and worked ever since. A co-founder of the GRAV collective, Le Parc published the manifesto *Propositions sur le mouvement* in 1961. Shortly afterward he began experimenting with reflections, shadows, movement, and vibrations as his primary materials, which lead the visitor to take a role in actualizing the work. In 1966 Le Parc won the Golden Lion at the Venice Biennial; two years later he was briefly expelled from France as a result of his political activities. Le Parc's first retrospective at a U.S. museum, organized by Estrellita C. Brodsky, took place in November 2016 at the Pérez Art Museum in Miami.

ALEJANDRO OTERO (1921–1990), born in El Manteco in the state of Bolívar, studied at the Escuela de Artes Plásticas y Aplicadas in Caracas. He made his first extended trip to Paris in 1945, where he became deeply interested in abstract art. While in Paris, he painted his series *Las Cafeteras*, first shown in Caracas in 1949 and generally credited with jump-starting the nascent Venezuelan abstract art movement. Back in Venezuela in 1950, Otero started the Los Disidentes group of artists, and from that time forward became a tireless exponent for modernism in Venezuela on both sides of the Atlantic. He collaborated closely with the architect Carlos Raúl Villanueva to develop a program of commissioned, permanent in situ sculptures for the Ciudad Universitaria. Otero's *Coloritmo* series of the late 1950s and early 1960s, inspired by the early kinetic works of Jesús Rafael Soto, were perhaps even more influential than *Las Cafeteras*. At the end of the 1960s Otero presented a project of monumental kinetic sculptures, Zona Feérica, on the outskirts of Caracas. György Kepes then invited him to become a fellow at the Center for Advanced Visual Studies at the Massachusetts Institute of Technology.

 was born in Natal, Rio Grande do Norte, Brazil, and moved at age four with his family to Tel Aviv. He later studied at two institutions, Hertzlia and Montefiori, focusing on engineering at the latter. On his return to Brazil in 1948, Palatnik met the art critic and curator Mario Pedrosa, who introduced him to other artists in Rio de Janeiro interested in abstract, concrete art, including Alvin Mavignier, who in turn introduced Palatnik to the Engenho de Dentro workshop at the D. Pedro Psychiatric Hospital. After his exposure to the work of hospital patients, Palatnik decided to abandon traditional art-making materials and processes. In 1951, following the last-minute cancellation of a delegation of Japanese artists, Palatnik was invited to present a new work in the first São Paulo Biennial, and built his first "kinechromatic" art machine, which was set into an exhibition wall. It took a few more years before Palatnik was able to extend this experiment to the production of several small boxlike machines that compressed reflection, colored light, and movement into a contained space, along with more conventional kinetic works that are closer in spirit to the work of Alexander Calder and Joan Miró.

JESÚS RAFAEL SOTO (1923–2005) was born in Ciudad, Bolívar, an old colonial town on the banks of the Orinoco River, where at age sixteen he had his first artistic employment painting posters for the handful of movie theaters in town. In 1942, on a scholarship, he began formal studies at the Escuela de Artes Plásticas y Artes Aplicadas, where his introduction to modern art came by way of a reproduction of a Cubist work by Georges Braque. In 1949 he had his first exhibition at the Taller Libre de Arte in Caracas, where the Argentine group Arte Concreto-Invención had shown the year before. In 1950, frustrated by the limits of Venezuela's artistic discourse, Soto sailed for Europe, where he settled in Paris and immediately fell in with Carlos Gonzalez Bogen, Narciso Debourg, Alejandro Otero, and other expats, as well as the American painters Ellsworth Kelly and Jack Youngerman. Supporting himself by playing guitar in cafes after his scholarship ran out, Soto made his first works using Plexiglas by 1953, and in 1954 showed his earliest pieces superimposing adjacent planes of Plexiglas painted with oscillating fields of dots at the Salon des Réalités Nouvelles, where they attracted the attention of Denise René and Victor Vasarely. Following the success of *Le Mouvement* at Galerie Denise René in 1955, Soto quickly became recognized as one of the leading artists of his generation, particularly for his monumentally scaled *Penetrables* works, beginning in the late 1960s.

GREGORIO VARDÁNEGA (1923–2007) was born in Possagno, Italy, and moved as a young child with his family to Buenos Aires. In 1939 he entered the Academia Nacional de Bellas Artes, where he continued his studies through 1946, the same year he became a professor of drawing and began participating in the exhibitions of the Arte Concreto-Invención group. In 1948, in the company of Uruguayan artist Carmelo Arden Quin, Vardánega made his first trip to Paris, where he was introduced to a milieu that included Max Bill, Constantin Brancusi, Sonia Delaunay, Nicolas Pevsner, and Georges Vantongerloo, and he showed his own work in the Madí section of the Salon des Réalités Nouvelles. Returning to Argentina the following year, he began combining metallic bands and Plexiglas structures to produce his increasingly kinetic works. Over the next few years he participated in several international biennials from his base in Buenos Aires, but in 1959 he moved, with Martha Boto, to Paris, where he began to experiment with Plexiglas spheres with interiors illuminated by moving projections of colored light.

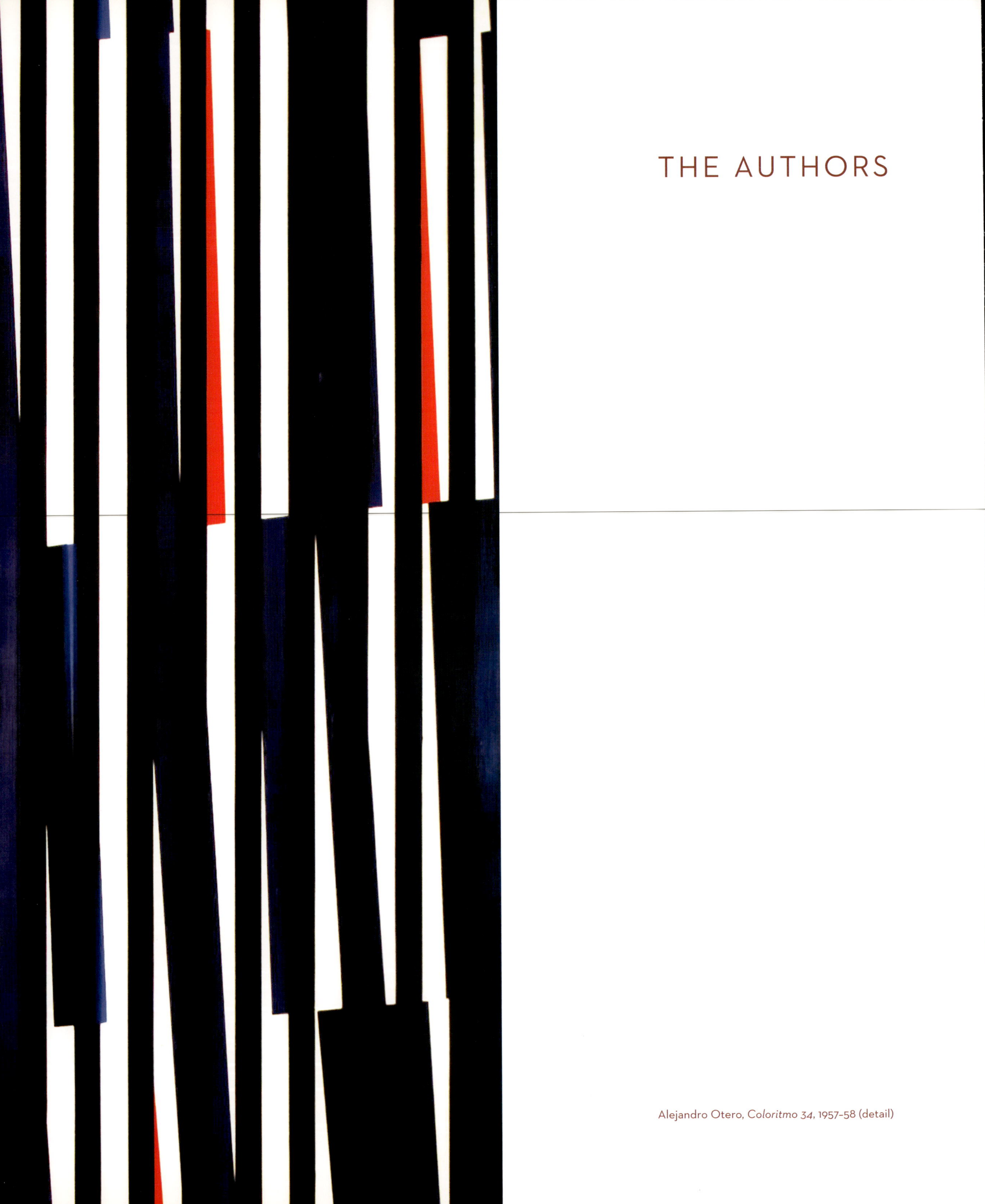

Alejandro Otero, *Coloritmo 34*, 1957–58 (detail)

DAN CAMERON was Chief Curator at Orange County Museum of Art from 2012 to 2015 and Founding Executive Director and Curator of Prospect New Orleans from 2007 to 2011. From 1995 to 2006 he was Senior Curator at New Museum of Contemporary Art, New York, where he organized retrospective exhibitions of Carroll Dunham, William Kentridge, Paul McCarthy, Cildo Meireles, Marcel Odenbach, Pierre et Gilles, Faith Ringgold, Carolee Schneemann, David Wojnarowicz, and Martin Wong, as well as the surveys *East Village USA* (2005) and *Living Inside the Grid* (2003). Along with Prospect New Orleans, Cameron has organized numerous international biennials, including the thirteenth Biennial of Cuenca, Ecuador (2016), the sixth Taipei Biennial (2006), and the eighth Istanbul Biennial (2003), along with the global art survey *Cocido y Crudo* at the Museo Reina Sofía, Madrid (1994).

JESÚS FUENMAYOR was from 2012 to 2015 the Director and Curator of the Cisneros Fontanals Art Foundation in Miami, prior to which he served as Director of the Fundación Periférico in Caracas (2004–11). In 2015 he curated the exhibitions *Eugenio Espinoza: Unruly Supports* at the Pérez Art Museum in Miami, and *Gego: Autobiography of a Line* at the Dominique Lévy Gallery in New York. Fuenmayor has organized curatorial workshops and seminars and published extensively in international art magazines as well as museum catalogues and anthologies of contemporary art. He has been Curatorial Manager for the 2015–16 Faena Art Prize exhibition at the Faena Art Foundation, Buenos Aires (February 2017), and is preparing the first historical anthology of works by the artist Lothar Baumgarten, to be published in 2018.

MARÍA JOSÉ HERRERA was Chief Curator at the Museo Nacional de Bellas Artes in Buenos Aires from 1999 to 2012, where she organized numerous historical surveys of Argentine modern art, including the seminal 2012 exhibition *Real/Virtual: Arte cinético argentino en los años sesenta*, along with retrospective exhibitions of such artists as Ibere Camargo, Ernesto Daira, Jorge Gamarra, Ennio Iommi, David Lamelas, and Maria Martorell. While serving as president of the Asociación Argentina de Criticos de Arte since 2007, she has been Professor of Conservation and Curatorial Practice at Universidad Nacional Tres de Febrero, and is currently Executive Director of Museo de Arte Tigre. She is co-curator of *David Lamelas: A Life of Their Own* at Long Beach Museum of Art, part of Pacific Standard Time: LA/LA. Her most recent book is *Cien años de arte argentino* (2014).

FREDERICO MORAIS is a journalist, historian, and independent curator, and a groundbreaking figure in art criticism in Brazil. After working initially as a film critic, Morais began championing experimental avant-garde art in articles published in a number of print media from Belo Horizonte, the capital of his home state. In 1967, Morais moved to Rio de Janeiro, where, in 1970, he published the widely influential manifesto *Do corpo à terra* (From Body to Earth) in conjunction with an event of the same name, both part of what was called the Semana de Vanguarda. Morais was General Curator of the first Mercosur Biennial (1997), and has published definitive critical texts on such artists as Cildo Meireles and Abraham Palatnik.

HÉCTOR OLEA is a Mexican architect, art critic, writer, and translator. He has written on several key figures of the Latin American avant-garde, including Antonio Berni, León Ferrari, Waldemar Cordeiro, Carlos Cruz-Diez, Luis Felipe Noé, Abraham Palatnik, Xul Solar, and Jesús Rafael Soto. As an independent curator, he conceived with Mari Carmen Ramírez the exhibition *Inverted Utopias: Avant-Garde Art in Latin America* (Museum of Fine Arts, Houston [MFAH], 2004). In tandem with Ramírez, Olea also edited the exhibition catalogues *Building on a Construct: The Adolpho Leirner Collection of Brazilian Constructive Art* (MFAH, 2009) and *Carlos Cruz-Diez: Color in Space and Time* (MFAH, 2010). Olea is in charge of MFAH publications and translations within the framework of the International Center for the Arts of the Americas, one of whose pivotal projects is the series "Critical Documents of 20th Century Latin American and Latino Art." The first volume of the series, *Resisting Categories: Latin and/or Latino Art?,* organized in tandem with Mari Carmen Ramírez and Tomás Ybarra-Frausto, was published in 2012.

ISABEL PLANTE was awarded the PhD in Art History in the Faculty of Arts and Letters at the University of Buenos Aires, and has developed her research in collaboration with the Consejo Nacional de Investigaciones Científicas y Técnicas en el Instituto de Altos Estudios Sociales de la Universidad Nacional San Martín. Since 2015 she has worked as part of the board of the Centro Argentino de Investigadores de Arte. In 2011 she received funding from the Fondo Metropolitano de la Cultura, las Artes, y las Ciencias to publish the book *Argentinos de París: Arte y viajes culturales en los años sesenta* (2013). She has participated in numerous international and national meetings and publication projects, and is currently an instructor at the University of Buenos Aires and the Instituto de Investigación sobre el Patrimonio Cultural de la Universidad Nacional San Martín. As part of the latter, Plante has been active since 2015 in the group responsible for the biannual project "El invencionismo argentino entre la tradición y la innovación material y formal," financed by the J. Paul Getty Foundation.

CRISTINA ROSSI is Professor of Latin American Art at the Universidad de Buenos Aires, where she received her doctorate in art history and theory, and at Universidad Nacional de Tres de Febrero. She coordinated the research for *Modernity, Avant-Garde, and Neo-Avant-Gardes in the Americas: Journals and Archives at Espigas Foundation* (1920s–1950s) for Fundación Espigas–Universidad Nacional San Martín, and she is the author of *Avatares de la forma: Anselmo Piccoli, de la figuración a la abstracción* (2016); *Raúl Mazzoni, Experiencias bi-espaciales* (2015); *Jóvenes y modernos de los años 50* (2012; co-authored with Manuel Aguiar); *Memoria y vigencia* (2015); *Luis Gowland Moreno: Una constante búsqueda de lo expresivo* (2014); and *La abstracción en la Argentina siglos XX y XXI* (2011). She was also author and editor of *Víctor Magariños D. Presencias reales* (2011), and of *Antonio Berni: Lecturas en tiempo presente* (2010).

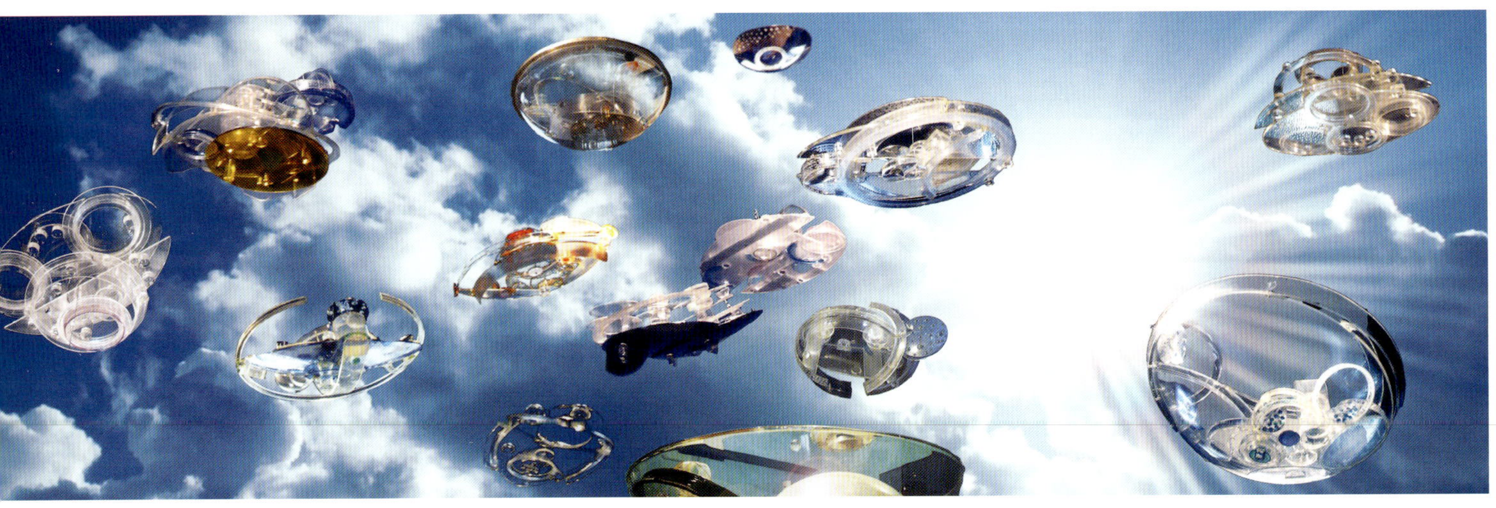

Gyula Kosice, *Fotomontaje de la ciudad hidroespacial*, 2010
Courtesy of Museo Kosice, Buenos Aires, Argentina

Alberro, Alexander. "Julio Le Parc, the Groupe de Recherche d'Art Visuel, and Instability in the 1960s." In *Julio Le Parc*. Rio de Janeiro: Casa Daros and Buenos Aires: Museo de Arte Latinoamericano de Buenos Aires (MALBA), 2014.

Ameline, Jean-Paul, and Ariel Jiménez. *Soto, Collection du Centre Pompidou – Musée national d'art moderne*. Paris: Éditions du Centre Pompidou, 2013.

Balza, José. *Alejandro Otero*. Caracas: Ernesto Armitano, 1982.

Barr, Alfred H., Jr., *Latin American Art, 1931– 1966*. New York: Museum of Modern Art, 1966.

Brett, Guy. *Kinetic Art: The Language of Movement*. London: Studio Vista, 1968.

Brett, Guy, Teresa Grandas, and Mark Nash. *Force Field: Phases of the Kinetic*. Barcelona: Museu d'Art Contemporani, 2000.

Brodsky, Estrellita B. *Soto: Paris and Beyond 1950–1970*. New York: Grey Art Gallery, New York University, 2012.

Carvajal, Rina. *Resonant Space: The Colorhythms of Alejandro Otero*. São Paulo: Instituto de Arte Contemporânea, 2014.

Cassou, Jean, Guy Habasque, and Jacques Ménétrier. *Nicolas Schöffer*. Neuchâtel, Switzerland: Éditions du Griffon, 1963.

Castillo, Ramon. "El teorema visual de Matilde Pérez: Pensamiento, métrica y percepción." In *Matilde x Matilde: Espacio movil*. Santiago: Fundación Telefónica, 2013.

Espinosa, Ana. *Manuel Espinosa: Obra pictórica*. Buenos Aires: Ciudad Autónoma de Buenos Aires, 2012.

Exposition l'art Latino-Americain à Paris: 2 Août – 4 Octobre 1962. Paris: Musée d'Art Moderne de la Ville de Paris, 1962.

Fajardo-Hill, Cecilia, and Jesús Fuenmayor. *Pulses of Abstraction in Latin-America: The Ella Fontanals-Cisneros Collection*. Miami: Cisneros Fontanals Art Foundation, 2012.

Fox, Claire. *Making Art Panamerican: Cultural Policy and the Cold War*. Minneapolis: University of Minnesota Press, 2013.

Garza, Usabiaga. *Cinetismo: Movimiento y transformación en el arte de los 60 y 70*. Mexico City: Museo de Arte Moderno, 2012.

Giunta, Andrea. *Avant-Garde, Internationalism, and Politics: Argentine Art in the Sixties*. Durham, N.C.: Duke University Press, 2007.

Goodman, Shelley. *Carmelo Arden Quin: When Art Jumped Out of Its Cage*. Dallas, Tex.: Madí, 2004.

Guignon, Emmanuel. *L'oeil moteur: Art optique et cinétique 1950–1975*. Strasbourg: Musée d'Art Contemporain, 2005.

Herrera, Maria José. *Cien años de arte argentino.* Buenos Aires: Editorial Biblos-Fundación, 2014.

________. *Real-Virtual: Arte cinético argentino en los años sesenta.* Buenos Aires: Museo Nacional de Bellas Artes, 2012.

Homenaje a Alfredo Boulton: Una vision integral del arte venezolano. Caracas: Museo de Arte Contemporaneo de Caracas, 1987.

Horacio García-Rossi. Paris: Galerie Leila Mordoch, 2010.

Jiménez, Ariel, ed. *Alfredo Boulton and His Contemporaries: Critical Dialogues in Venezuelan Art 1912–1974.* New York: Museum of Modern Art, 2008.

________. *In Conversation with/En conversación con Carlos Cruz-Diez.* New York: Fundación Cisneros, 2010.

________. *In Conversation with/En conversación con Jesús Soto.* New York: Fundación Cisneros, 2011.

Kosice, Gyula. *Arte hidrocinético: Movimiento luz aqua.* Buenos Aires: Mundo Moderno/Paidos, 1968.

Le Mouvement. Paris: Galerie Denise René, 1955.

Ledezma, Juan. *The Sites of Latin American Abstraction: Cisneros Fontanals Art Foundation.* Milano: Edizioni Charta, 2007.

Lo[s] Cinético[s]. Madrid: Museo Nacional Centro de Arte Reina Sofía, 2007.

Maggi, Annamaria. *Horacio García-Rossi: Opere 1955–2000.* Bergamo, Italy: Edizioni Stefano Fumagelli/Maredarte, 2001.

Martins, Sergio B. *Constructing an Avant-Garde: Art in Brazil 1949–1979.* Cambridge, Mass.: MIT Press, 2013.

Matilde Pérez. Santiago: BTG Pactual Chile, 2015.

Messer, Thomas H. *The Emergent Decade: Latin American Painters and Painting in the 1960s.* Ithaca, N.Y.: Cornell University Press, 1966.

Morais, Frederico. "Abraham Palatnik: A Pioneer of Technological Art." Association Leonardo/OLATS, 1997.

Morineau, Camille. *Gyula Kosice.* Paris: Centre Pompidou, 2013.

Oliveras, Elena. *Arte cinético y neocinetismo.* Buenos Aires: Emecé Editores, 2010.

Pantin, Yolanda. *A La altura del tiempo: Cafeteras de Alejandro Otero.* Caracas: Fundación Banco Mercantil, 2002.

Pedrosa, Mario, Rubem Braga, Michael Asbury, Abraham Palatnik, et al. *Abraham Palatnik: A reinvencao da pintura.* São Paulo: Centro Cultural Banco do Brasil, 2012.

Perazzo, Nelly. *El arte concreto en la Argentina.* Buenos Aires: Ediciones de Arte Gaglianone, 1983.

Pérez-Barreiro, Gabriel, and Andrea Giunta. *In Conversation with/En conversación con Gyula Kosice.* New York: Fundación Cisneros, 2012.

Pierre, Arnauld. "Contact: The Cyber-Cosmos of Boto and Vardánega." In *Boto, Vardánega.* Houston: Sicardi Gallery, 2006.

Pierre, Arnauld, Hans Ulrich Obrist, and Jean-Louis Pradel. *Julio Le Parc.* Paris: Palais de Tokyo, 2013.

Plante, Isabel. *Argentinos de Paris: Arte y viajes culturales durante los años sesenta.* Buenos Aires: Edhasa, 2013.

Poirier, Matthieu. "A Penetrating Gaze." In *Soto.* Paris: Galerie Perrotin, 2014.

————. *Dynamo.* Paris: Grand Palais, 2014.

————. "Perceptual Space Invaders." In *Hugo Demarco, Horacio García-Rossi, Francisco Sobrino.* Houston: Sicardi Gallery, 2007.

Popper, Frank. *Kinetics.* London: Hayward Gallery, 1970.

————. *Origins and Development of Kinetic Art.* Greenwich, Conn.: New York Graphic Society, 1968.

Renard, Claude-Louis. "Excerpts from an Interview with Soto." In *Soto: A Retrospective Exhibition.* New York: Guggenheim Museum, 1974.

Rossi, Cristina, Florencia Battiti, Ana Maria Battistozzi, and Rodrigo Alonso. *Eduardo Rodriguez/Perla Benveniste: Dos artistas cinéticos argentinos.* Buenos Aires: Schlifka/Molina, 2013.

Ruiz, Alma. *Suprasensorial: Experiments in Light, Color, and Space.* Los Angeles: Museum of Contemporary Art, 2010.

Seitz, William C. *The Responsive Eye.* New York: Museum of Modern Art, 1966.

Selz, Peter, and George Rickey. *Directions in Kinetic Sculpture.* Berkeley, Calif.: University Art Museum, 1966.

Squirru, Rafael. *Eduardo Mac Entyre.* Buenos Aires: Ediciones de Arte Gaglianone, 1981.

Vega, Elsa. "El Infinito no marca el limite." In *Sandu Darié.* Havana, Cuba: Museo Nacional de Bellas Artes, 2009.

Wechsler, Diana, and Cristina Rossi. *Antonio Asís: Un universo vibrante.* Buenos Aires: Universidad Tres de Febrero, 2012.

PHOTOGRAPHY

Front cover, pp. 17, 53, 54, 82, 112, 113, 151, 167, 172, 175, 178, 179, 180, 181, 182, 186, 187 The Museum of Fine Arts, Houston
Pp. 7, 19, 23 Logan Sebastian Beck
Pp. 11, 39, 63, 118, 119, Atelier Le Parc archive
Pp. 15, 21, 22, 110, 111, 145, 148, 149, 155 Frank White
P. 16 Vieri Tomaselli
Pp. 27, 138, 142 Galerie Denise René archive
P. 29 George Cserna Digital Image © The Museum of Modern Art / Licensed by SCALA / Art Resource, NY
P. 33 © Tate, London 2016
P. 35 Michèle Vasarely
Pp. 36, 45, 171, 172, 173, 177, 184, 185, 222 Museo Kosice, Buenos Aires, Argentina
P. 42, back cover Abraham Palatnik
P. 48 Yale University Art Gallery
Pp. 55, 59, 81, 83, 84, Sicardi Gallery, Houston
Pp. 57, 87 Peter Molick
Pp. 60, 61 The Museum of Fine Arts, Houston. Mary and Tom Lile, Houston EX.2011.CD.039
P. 62 Arturo Sanchez
P. 85, 206, 212 *Coloritmo 41*: Oriol Tarridas
P. 86 David Almeida
Pp. 88, 89 David Blank
Pp. 91, 96, 131, 132, 134, 142 Museo Nacional de Bellas Artes, Buenos Aires, Biblioteca
Pp. 93, 98, 103 Gustavo Cantoni
Pp. 95, 99, 103, 105 Pablo Garber, Área de Documentación MNBA

Pp. 96, 97, 99, 101, 103, 105, 137 Museo Nacional de Bellas Artes
P. 97 Mac Entyre: Gustavo Lowry
P. 101 Brizzi: Ernesto Regales
Pp. 117, 122, 123, 124, 125, 126, 127 Zicarelli
P. 121, overleaf Adrian Fritschi
P. 141 Di Tella Archive, Torcuato Di Tella University, Argentina
Pp. 146, 147 Deedee de Gelia
P. 153 Bruce Talbot
Pp. 164, 165 Romulo Fialdini
Pp. 168, 169 Galeria Nara Roesler, São Paulo
Pp. 189, 193, 195, 196, 197, 198, 200, 201, 204 Archivo Otero-Pardo, Caracas, Venezula
P. 206 The University of Arizona Museum of Art, Tucson
P. 207 *Coloritmo 34*: OAS AMA | Art Museum of the Americas
Pp. 208, 211 rendered by Jean Giallorenzo and Alexander Gomez, with the assistance of Juan Manuel Lopez
P. 209 Rodrigo Benavides
Back cover, Vicente de Mello

INDEX

Pacific Standard Time: LA/LA, is a far-reaching and ambitious exploration of Latin American and Latino art in dialogue with Los Angeles. Supported by grants from the Getty Foundation, Pacific Standard Time: LA/LA takes place from September 2017 through January 2018 at more than 70 cultural institutions across Southern California, from Los Angeles to Palm Springs, and from San Diego to Santa Barbara. Pacific Standard Time is an initiative of the Getty. The presenting sponsor is Bank of America.

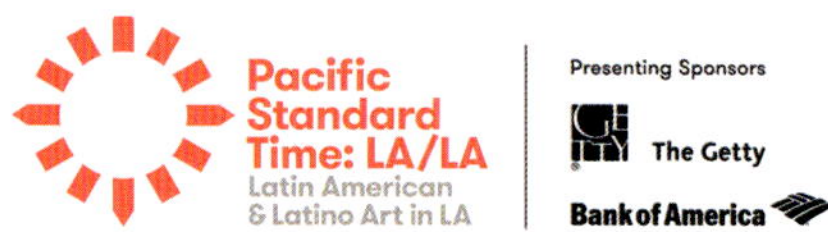

Additional funding for *Kinesthesia: Latin American Kinetic Art 1954–1969* is provided by The Andy Warhol Foundation for the Visual Arts; Palm Springs Art Museum Contemporary Art Council; Erik E. and Edith H. Bergstrom Foundation; Yvonne and Steven Maloney; and Patty and Arthur Newman/ Newman's Own Foundation.

For Palm Springs Art Museum
Guest Curator: Dan Cameron
Publication Manager: Katherine Plake Hough
Graphic Designer: Lilli Colton
Copy Editor: Susan Green
Rights and Reproductions: Alison Leard and Elizabeth Upton, Pacific Coast Conservation
Indexer: Jean Patterson
Translator: Eriksen Translations Inc.
Special Assistance: Frank Lopez and Victoria Taormina

Front cover: Abraham Palatnik, *Aparelho cinecromático*, 1962, wooden box with plastic cover, electric motor, colored light bulbs linked to a programmed electric circuit and cardboard paddles, 38 ⅛ × 28 ¾ × 7 ½ in. (96.8 × 73 × 19.1 cm). The Museum of Fine Arts, Houston. The Adolpho Leirner Collection of Brazilian Constructive Art, museum purchase funded by the Caroline Wiess Law Accessions Endowment Fund, 2007.21
End sheets: Carlos Cruz-Diez, *Physichromie 228*, 1966 (detail)
Back cover: Abraham Palatnik, *Back of a Kinechromatic Device*, ca. 1960. Collection of the artist
Title page: Jesús Rafael Soto, *Cuatro modulaciones*, 1969 (detail)
Last page: Julio Le Parc, *Continuel-lumière avec formes en contorsion*, 1966/2012 (detail)

Printed and bound in China

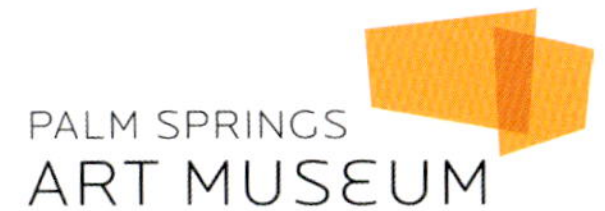

Published in conjunction with the exhibition
Kinesthesia: Latin American Kinetic Art 1954–1969
August 26, 2017 – January 15, 2018

Organized by Palm Springs Art Museum
101 Museum Drive
Palm Springs, California 92262
760.322.4800 www.psmuseum.org

ISBN 978-3-7913-5673-0

Library of Congress Cataloging-in-Publication Data

Names: Cameron, Dan. Electric shadows. | Palm Springs Art Museum, organizer,
  host institution.
Title: Kinesthesia : Latin American kinetic art, 1954-1969 / Dan Cameron ;
  with essays by Jesus Fuenmayor, Maria Jose Herrera, Frederico Morais,
  Hector Olea, Cristina Rossi, and Isabel Plante.
Description: Palm Springs : Palm Springs Art Museum and DelMonico Books/
  Prestel, 2017. | Includes bibliographical references and index.
Identifiers: LCCN 2017005054 | ISBN 9783791356730
Subjects: LCSH: Kinetic art--Latin America—Exhibitions.
Classification: LCC N6502.57.K56 K56 2017 | DDC 709.04/07—dc23
LC record available at https://lccn.loc.gov/2017005054

A CIP catalogue record for this book is available from the British Library.

Published in 2017 by Palm Springs Art Museum
and DelMonico Books • Prestel

DelMonico Books, an imprint of Prestel,
a member of Verlagsgruppe Random House GmbH

Prestel Verlag
Neumarkter Strasse 28
81673 Munich

Prestel Publishing Ltd.
14-17 Wells Street
London W1T 3PD

Prestel Publishing
900 Broadway, Suite 603
New York, NY 10003

www.prestel.com

For DelMonico Books • Prestel
Production Coordinator: Luke Chase

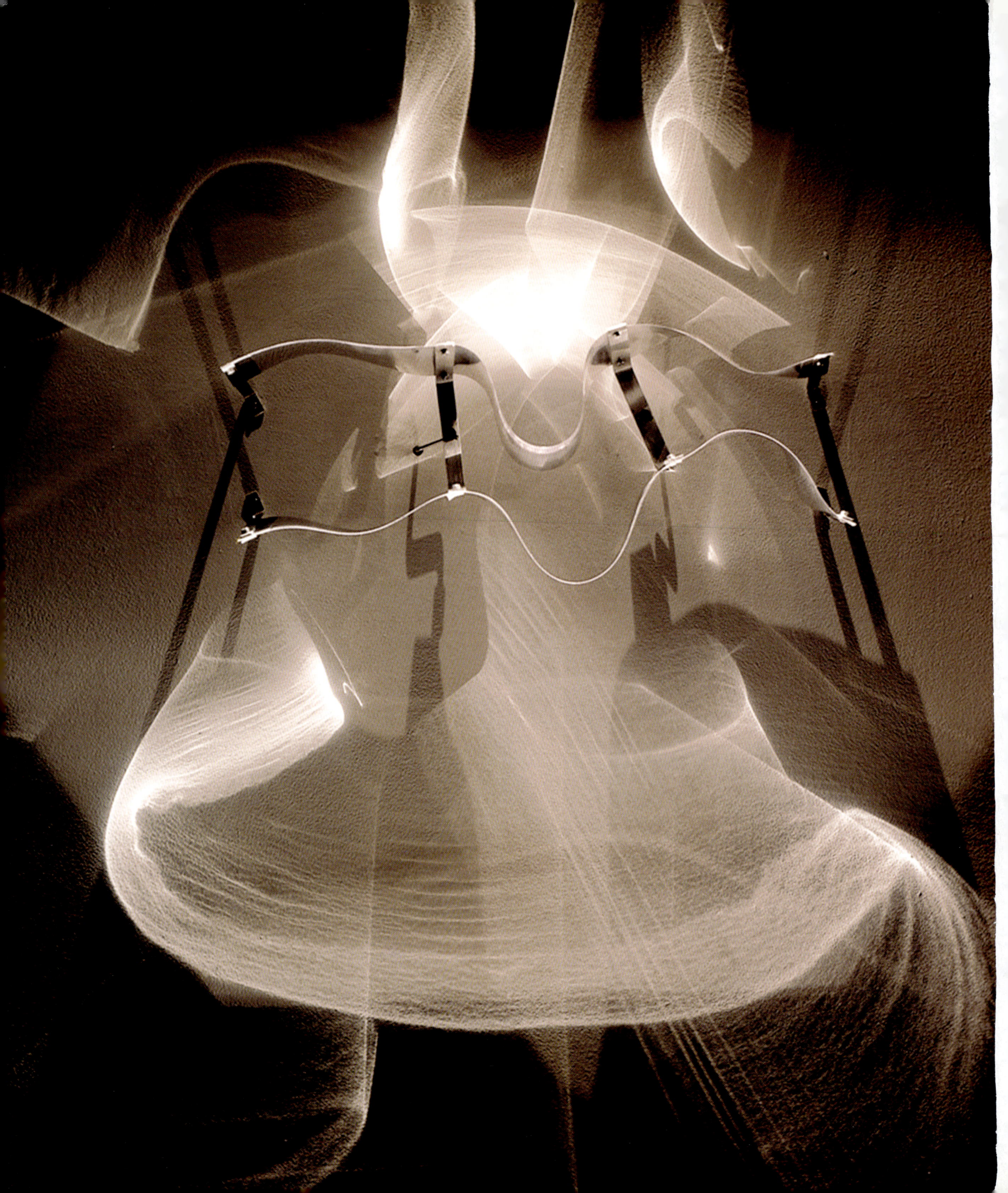